MICROSOFT®
OFFICE 2010
QuickSteps®

CAROLE MATTHEWS

MARTY MATTHEWS

JOHN CRONAN

New York Chicago San Francisco
Lisbon London Madrid Mexico City
Milan New Delhi San Juan
Seoul Singapore Sydney Toronto

The _McGraw-Hill_ Companies

Cataloging-in-Publication Data is on file with the Library of Congress

MICROSOFT® OFFICE 2010 QUICKSTEPS®

1234567890   WDQ WDQ   109876543210

ISBN   978-0-07-174160-6
MHID   0-07-174160-7

SPONSORING EDITOR / Roger Stewart

EDITORIAL SUPERVISOR / Janet Walden

PROJECT MANAGER / Vasundhara Sawhney, Glyph International

ACQUISITIONS COORDINATOR / Joya Anthony

TECHNICAL EDITOR / Jennifer Ackerman Kettell

COPY EDITOR / Lisa McCoy

PROOFREADER / Madhu Prasher

INDEXER / Valerie Perry

PRODUCTION SUPERVISOR / George Anderson

COMPOSITION / Glyph International

ILLUSTRATION / Glyph International

ART DIRECTOR, COVER / Jeff Weeks

COVER DESIGNER / Pattie Lee

SERIES CREATORS / Marty and Carole Matthews

SERIES DESIGN / Bailey Cunningham

Contents

Chapter 3   **Formatting a Document** 49

To Susan Sherman and Dan Paulson, wonderful
friends who have made our lives more
interesting and fun!

About the Authors

Carole and Marty Matthews have been programmers,
systems analysts, managers, executives, and entrepreneurs
in the software business for many years. They have been
on both sides of using computers, both designing software
and using it. For the last 25 years they have authored,
coauthored, or managed the writing and production of more
than 90 books. They live on an island in Puget Sound in
Washington State.

John Cronan has over 30 years of computer experience and
has been writing and editing computer-related books for
more than 18 years. His recent books include *eBay QuickSteps
Second Edition*, *Microsoft Office Excel 2010 QuickSteps*, *Microsoft
Office Access 2010 QuickSteps*, and *Dynamic Web Programming:
A Beginner's Guide*. John and his wife Faye (and cat Little
Buddy) reside in Everett, Washington.

About the Technical Editor

Jennifer Ackerman Kettell has written and contributed to
dozens of books about software applications, web design,
and digital photography. She has worked for Microsoft and
other top companies in addition to doing freelance web
design and online community management. Jenn has lived
all over the United States, but currently calls upstate New
York home.

Acknowledgments

We are, as always, indebted to the editing, layout,
proofreading, indexing, and project management expertise of
a number of people, only some of whom we know. We thank
all of them, and in particular acknowledge:

- **Roger Stewart**, editorial director and sponsoring editor
  of this book and the QuickSteps® series
- **Janet Walden**, editorial supervisor
- **George Anderson**, production supervisor
- **Vasundhara Sawhney**, project manager at Glyph
  International
- **Joya Anthony**, acquisitions coordinator
- **Lisa McCoy**, copy editor
- **Madhu Prasher**, proofreader
- **Valerie Perry**, indexer
- **Glyph International**, layout and production

Introduction

QuickSteps® books are recipe books for computer users. They answer the question "How do I…" by providing a quick set of steps to accomplish the most common tasks with a particular operating system or application.

The sets of steps are the central focus of the book. QuickSteps sidebars show how to quickly perform many small functions or tasks that support the primary functions. QuickFacts sidebars supply information that you need to know about a subject. Notes, Tips, and Cautions augment the steps; they are presented in a separate column so as not to interrupt the flow of the steps. The introductions are minimal rather than narrative, and numerous illustrations and figures, many with callouts, support the steps.

Microsoft® Office 2010 QuickSteps® describes in one book the most commonly used features of Microsoft Office Word 2010, Microsoft Office Excel 2010, Microsoft Office PowerPoint 2010, and Microsoft Office Outlook 2010. Should you find that there is some advanced feature of one of these applications that you need more information about, please see one of these other McGraw-Hill QuickSteps® books:

- *Microsoft® Office Word® 2010 QuickSteps®*
- *Microsoft® Office Excel® 2010 QuickSteps®*
- *Microsoft® Office PowerPoint® 2010 QuickSteps®*
- *Microsoft® Office Outlook® 2010 QuickSteps®*

Conventions Used in This Book

Microsoft® Office 2010 QuickSteps® uses several conventions designed to make the book easier for you to follow:

- A 🔍 or a 🖉 in the table of contents or the How To list in each chapter references a QuickSteps or a QuickFacts sidebar in a chapter.
- **Bold type** is used for words on the screen that you are to do something with, such as click **Save As** or open **File**.
- *Italic type* is used for a word or phrase that is being defined or otherwise deserves special emphasis.
- <u>Underlined type</u> is used for text that you are to type from the keyboard.
- SMALL CAPITAL LETTERS are used for keys on the keyboard such as **ENTER** and **SHIFT**.
- When you are expected to enter a command, you are told to press the key(s). If you are to enter text or numbers, you are told to type them.

How to...

- *Use the Start Menu to Start Office*
- *Start an Office Program in Different Ways*
- *Leaving an Office Program*
- *Understanding the Ribbon*
- *Explore an Office Program Window*
- *Use the Mouse*
- *Using the Mini Toolbar*
- *Use Tabs and Menus*
- *Use Various Views*
- *Work with the Quick Access Toolbar*
- *Show or Hide ScreenTips*
- *Changing the Screen Color*
- *Add Identifying Information*
- *Setting Preferences*
- *Open Help*
- *Using the Help Toolbar*
- *Do Research*
- *Use the Thesaurus*
- *Translate a Document*
- *Accessing Microsoft Resources*
- *Understanding Web Apps*
- *Update Your Office Program*
- *Use SkyDrive*
- *Understanding SkyDrive Folders*

Chapter 1
Stepping into Office

Microsoft Office is the most widely used of all office suite offerings. Most personal computers (PCs) have some version of Office installed, and most people with PCs probably have Office available to them as well as some experience in its use. The upgrade of Office 2003 to Office 2007 was a significant event, resulting in a totally new user interface. Office 2010 continues this event. As you may know, Office is both simple to use and highly sophisticated, offering many features that commonly go unused. Office delivers a high degree of functionality even when only a small percentage of its capabilities are used. The purpose of this book is to acquaint you with how to use the upgrade to Office 2010 within five primary Office programs: Word, Excel, PowerPoint, Outlook, and SharePoint. You will learn not only how to access the newly placed common everyday features, but also about many of those additional features that can enhance your experience with using Office.

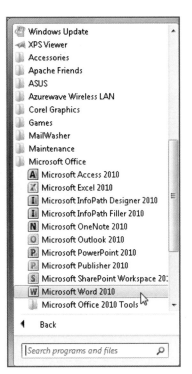

Figure 1-1: The foolproof way to start an Office program, such as Microsoft Word, is via the Start menu.

In this chapter you will familiarize yourself with Office; see how to start and leave programs; use Office's 2010 windows, panes, ribbon, toolbars, and menus; learn how to get help; and find out how to customize the Office program to best meet your needs.

Start and Leave an Office Program

How you start an Office program depends on how it was installed and what has happened to it since its installation. In this section you'll see a surefire way to start Office programs and some alternatives. You'll also see how to leave an Office program.

Use the Start Menu to Start Office

If no other icons for or shortcuts to the Office program you want to start are available on your desktop, you can always start an Office program using the Start menu.

1. Start your computer, if it is not already running, and log on to Windows if necessary.
2. Click **Start**. The Start menu opens.
3. Click **All Programs**, click **Microsoft Office**, and click the Office program name, such as **Microsoft Word 2010**, as shown in Figure 1-1.

Start an Office Program in Different Ways

In addition to using All Programs on the Start menu, a program can be started in several other ways.

USE THE START MENU ITSELF

The icons of the program you use most often are displayed on the left side of the Start menu. If you frequently use Word, for instance, its icon will appear there. To use this technique:

1. Click **Start**. The Start menu opens.
2. Click the Office program, such as the **Microsoft Word** icon on the left of the Start menu.

PIN THE OFFICE PROGRAM TO THE TOP OF THE START MENU

If you think you may use other programs more frequently, you can keep your Office program at the top of the Start menu by "pinning" it there.

1. Click **Start** to open the Start menu.

2. Right-click (click the right mouse button) the Office program icon, such as the **Word** icon, and click **Pin To Start Menu**.

CREATE A DESKTOP SHORTCUT

An easy way to start an Office program is to create a shortcut icon on the desktop and use it to start the program.

1. Click **Start**, click **All Programs**, and click **Microsoft Office**.

2. Right-click the program name, such as **Microsoft Word 2010**, click **Send To**, and click **Desktop (Create Shortcut)**.

USE THE TASKBAR

The taskbar is a bar located on the bottom of the screen next to the Start button. You can put an Office program icon on the taskbar and use it to start your program.

1. Open **Start**, click **All Programs**, click **Microsoft Office**, and drag the Office program, such as **Microsoft Word 2010**, to where you want it on the Quick Launch toolbar on the left of the taskbar. An I-beam icon will help you place it.

   –Or–

   Right-click **Microsoft Word 2010**, and click **Pin To Taskbar** from the menu.

2. Click the icon on the taskbar to start the Office program.

Explore an Office Program

Office 2010 uses a wide assortment of windows, ribbon tabs, some toolbars, menus, and special features to accomplish its functions. Much of this book explores how to find and use all of those items. In this section you'll see and learn to use the most common features of the default window, including the parts of the window, the tabs on the ribbon, and the task pane. (We are using

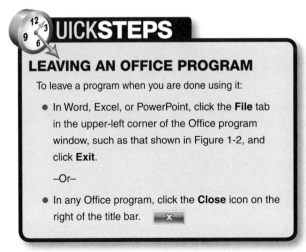

QUICKSTEPS

LEAVING AN OFFICE PROGRAM

To leave a program when you are done using it:

- In Word, Excel, or PowerPoint, click the **File** tab in the upper-left corner of the Office program window, such as that shown in Figure 1-2, and click **Exit**.

  –Or–

- In any Office program, click the **Close** icon on the right of the title bar.

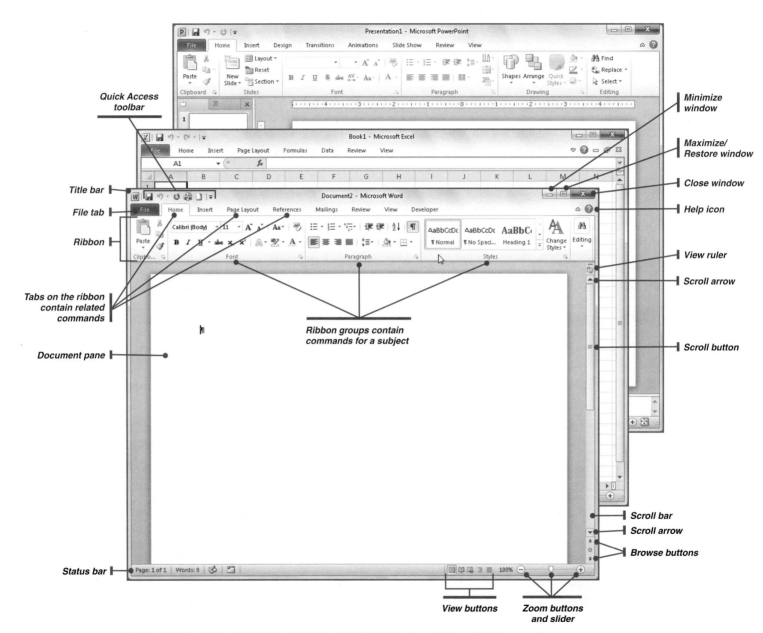

Figure 1-2: *The Office 2010 default windows for Word, Excel, and PowerPoint are used for creating and editing documents, spreadsheets, and slide shows, respectively.*

QUICKFACTS

UNDERSTANDING THE RIBBON

The *ribbon*, the container at the top of most Office program windows, holds the tools and features you are most likely to use (see Figure 1-3, which uses Word as an example). The ribbon collects tools for a given function into *groups*—for example, the Font group provides the tools to work with text. Groups are then organized into tabs for working on likely tasks. For example, the Insert tab contains groups for adding components, such as tables, links, and charts to your slide (or spreadsheet or document). Each Office program has a default set of tabs with additional *contextual* tabs that appear as the context of your work changes. For instance, when you select a picture, a Format tab containing shapes and drawing tools that you can use with the particular object appears beneath the defining tools tab (such as the Picture Tools tab); when the object is unselected, the Format tab disappears. Depending on the tool, you are then presented with additional options in the form of a list of commands, a dialog box or task pane, or galleries of choices that reflect what you'll see in your work. Groups that contain several more tools than can be displayed in the ribbon include a *Dialog Box Launcher* icon that takes you directly to these other choices.

Word for our examples, although most of the Office programs are similar. Specific differences in similar programs will be pointed out in the individual program chapters.)

Explore an Office Program Window

The Office 2010 window has many features to aid you in creating and editing documents. An example view (this one showing Word) is presented to you when you first start a program, and is shown in Figure 1-2. You can see the primary parts of the ribbon in Figure 1-3. Although we are using Word as our example, the principal features of the window, including the various ribbon tabs, are described further in this section and specific differences are explained in other chapters of this book.

Use the Mouse

A *mouse* is any pointing device—including trackballs, pointing sticks, and graphic tablets—with one or more buttons. This book assumes a two-button mouse. Moving the mouse moves the pointer on the screen. You *select* an object on the screen by moving the pointer so that it is on top of the object and then pressing the left button on the mouse.

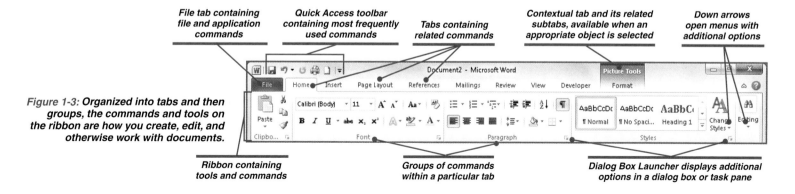

File tab containing file and application commands

Quick Access toolbar containing most frequently used commands

Tabs containing related commands

Contextual tab and its related subtabs, available when an appropriate object is selected

Down arrows open menus with additional options

Figure 1-3: Organized into tabs and then groups, the commands and tools on the ribbon are how you create, edit, and otherwise work with documents.

Ribbon containing tools and commands

Groups of commands within a particular tab

Dialog Box Launcher displays additional options in a dialog box or task pane

TIP

To gain working space in the document pane, you can minimize the size of the ribbon. To do this, double-click the active tab name. Click it again to restore the size of the ribbon. You can also press **CTRL+F1** to toggle the size of the ribbon.

QUICKSTEPS

USING THE MINI TOOLBAR

When you select or highlight text, a mini text toolbar is displayed that allows you to perform a function directly on the text, such as making text bold or centering a paragraph. This toolbar contains a subset of the tools contained in the Fonts and Paragraph groups of the Home tab.

DISPLAY THE TEXT TOOLBAR

1. Select text by clicking it or dragging over the text.
2. Place the pointer over the text, and a vague image of the mini toolbar is displayed. Place your pointer over it to clarify the image.

   –Or–

   You can right-click the selected text and click the mini toolbar to remove the context menu.

USE A TEXT TOOL

Click the button or icon on the mini toolbar that represents the tool.

Continued . . .

You may control the mouse with either your left or right hand; therefore, the buttons may be switched. (See *Windows 7 QuickSteps*, published by McGraw-Hill/Professional, 2009, for how to switch the buttons.) This book assumes the right hand controls the mouse and the left mouse button is *"the* mouse button." The right button is always called the "right mouse button." If you switch the buttons, you must change your interpretation of these phrases.

Five actions can be accomplished with the mouse:

- **Point** at an *object* on the screen (a button, an icon, a menu or one of its options, or a border) to highlight it. To *point* means to move the mouse so that the tip of the pointer is on top of the object.

- **Click an object** on the screen to select it, making that object the item that your next actions will affect. Clicking will also open a menu, select a menu option, or activate a button or "tool" on a toolbar or the ribbon. Click means to point at an object you want to select and quickly press and release the left mouse button.

- **Double-click** an object to open or activate it. Double-click means to point at an object you want to select, then press and release the left mouse button twice in rapid succession.

- **Right-click** an object to open a context menu containing commands used to manipulate that object. Right-click means to point at an object you want to select, then quickly press and release the right mouse button. For example, right-clicking selected text opens the adjacent context menu.

- **Drag** an object to move it on the screen to where you want it moved within the document. Drag means to point at an object you want to move and then press and hold the left mouse button while moving the mouse. The object is dragged as you move the mouse. When the object is where you want it, release the mouse button.

Use Tabs and Menus

Tabs are displayed at the top of the ribbon or a dialog box.
Menus are displayed when you click a down arrow on a button on the ribbon, a dialog box, or a toolbar. Here are some of the ways to use tabs and menus:

- To open a tab or menu with the mouse, click the tab or menu.

USING THE MINI TOOLBAR *(Continued)*

HIDE THE MINI TOOLBAR

You can hide the mini toolbar by changing the default setting.

1. Click the **File** tab, and click **Options**.

2. Click the **General** option.

3. Click **Show Mini Toolbar On Selection** to remove the check mark.

4. Click **OK** to finalize the choice.

TIP

The mini toolbar becomes clearer when you place the pointer directly over it.

Word Document Views group

- To open a tab or menu with the keyboard, press **ALT+** the underlined letter in the tab or menu name. For example, press **ALT+F** to open the File menu. (The identifying keys are displayed when you press **ALT** by itself.)

- To select a tab or menu command, click the tab or menu to open it, and then click the option.

- A number of menu options have a right-pointing arrow on their right to indicate that a submenu is associated with that option. To open the submenu, move the mouse pointer to the menu option with a submenu (it will have a right-pointing arrow). The submenu will open. Move the mouse pointer to the submenu, and click the desired option.

Use Various Views

Each of the Office programs presents documents in several views, allowing you to choose which view facilitates the task you are doing. To access a view, click the **View** tab and then click a Views group button. Here are the various views for Word, Excel, and PowerPoint (Outlook handles its views differently and is explained in Chapters 11 through 13):

- **Word** displays five possible views:

  - **Print Layout** displays the text as it looks on a printed page.

  - **Full Screen Reading** replaces the ribbon with a full-screen toolbar. Click **View Options** to select options for displaying and using this screen view, such as whether to allow typing, tracking changes, displaying one or two pages, enlarged text, showing comments, and so on. Click **Close** to return to the Normal view.

  - **Web Layout** shows how the text will look as a webpage.

- **Outline** displays the text in outline form with a contextual Outlining tab on the ribbon. You can use this view to promote and demote levels of text and rearrange levels, as shown in the Outline Tools group. With the Show Document button, you can toggle commands to extend your ability to create, insert, link, merge, split, and lock the document. Click **Close Outline View** to return to Normal view.

- **Draft** displays the text of the document in draft status for quick and easy editing. Headings and footings may not be visible.

- **Excel** displays five possible views:

  - **Normal** displays the normal spreadsheet view with numbered rows and lettered columns.

  - **Page Layout** displays the spreadsheet as it will be printed.

  - **Page Break Preview** displays where the spreadsheet has page breaks and will allow you to change them.

  - **Custom Views** allows you to select a custom view or add the current view to the list of custom views.

  - **Full Screen** eliminates the menus and status bar to display only the spreadsheet.

- **PowerPoint** contains four possible views:

  - **Normal** displays the larger slide pane with the Slides and Outline panes on the left.

  - **Slide Sorter** view displays thumbnails of slides in the Slides pane.

  - **Notes Page** displays a "split" page showing the slide and any notes that have been entered for that slide.

  - **Reading View** displays a slide show that fits within the window, as opposed to the full screen you see when you start the slide show.

Excel Workbook Views group

PowerPoint Presentation Views group

Personalize and Customize Office 2010 Programs

You can personalize your Office program, or make it your own, by changing the personal defaults it sets on such options as the tools available on the Quick Access toolbar or your user name and initials. You can customize your Office program by customizing the general defaults on editing, proofing, display, and other options. Many of these options will be discussed in the appropriate

chapters. Here we will look at the Quick Access toolbar, display, and other popular options.

Work with the Quick Access Toolbar

The Quick Access toolbar that is normally at the upper-left corner of the Word, Excel, Outlook, and PowerPoint windows can become a "best friend" if you modify it so that it fits your own way of working.

ADD TO THE QUICK ACCESS TOOLBAR

The Quick Access toolbar contains the commands most commonly used. The default tools are Save, Undo, and Redo. You can add commands to it that you use on a regular basis.

1. Click the **File** tab, and click **Options**.

2. Click the **Quick Access Toolbar** option and, if in Word, you will see the dialog box shown in Figure 1-4.

3. Open the **Choose Commands From** drop-down list box on the left, and select the type of command you want from the listed options.

4. In the list box on the left, find and click the command you want to add to the toolbar, and then click **Add** to move its name to the list box on the right. Repeat this for all the commands you want in the toolbar.

5. Click **OK** when you are finished.

MOVE THE QUICK ACCESS TOOLBAR

To move the Quick Access toolbar beneath the ribbon, right-click the **Quick Access toolbar**, and click **Show Quick Access Toolbar Below The Ribbon**.

Show or Hide Screen Tips

When you hold your pointer over a command or tool, a screen tip is displayed. The tip may be just the name

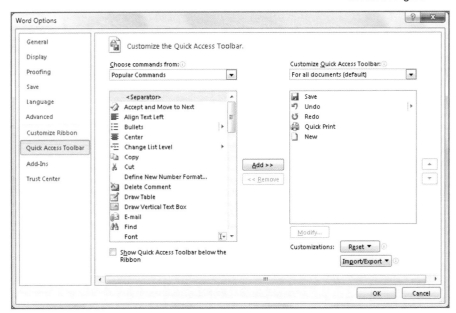

Figure 1-4: You can customize the Quick Access toolbar by adding and removing commands for easy and quick access using the options, such as these for Word.

2 3 4 5 6 7 8 9 10

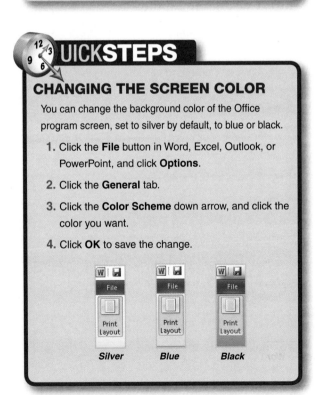

QUICKSTEPS

CHANGING THE SCREEN COLOR

You can change the background color of the Office program screen, set to silver by default, to blue or black.

1. Click the **File** button in Word, Excel, Outlook, or PowerPoint, and click **Options**.
2. Click the **General** tab.
3. Click the **Color Scheme** down arrow, and click the color you want.
4. Click **OK** to save the change.

Silver   Blue   Black

---

of the tool or command, or it may be enhanced with a small feature description. You can hide the tips or cause them to be enhanced or not.

1. Click the **File** tab in Word, Excel, Outlook, or PowerPoint, and click **Options**.
2. Click the **General** option.
3. Click the **ScreenTip Style** drop-down list, and choose the option you want.
4. Click **OK** to finalize the choice.

Add Identifying Information

You can add identifying information to a document to make it easier to organize your information and to find it during searches, especially in a shared environment. In Word, Excel, and PowerPoint (Outlook doesn't have this capability):

1. Click the **File** tab, click **Info**, click **Properties** in the right pane, and then click **Show Document Panel**. A Document Properties panel containing standard identifiers displays under the ribbon, as shown for Word in Figure 1-5.
2. Type identifying information, such as title, subject, and keywords (words or phrases that are associated with the document).
3. To view more information about the document, click the **Document Properties** down arrow in the panel's title bar, and click **Advanced Properties**. Review each tab in the Properties dialog box to see the information available, and make any changes or additions. Close the Properties dialog box when finished by clicking **Close** (the "X" at the rightmost end of the panel's title bar).

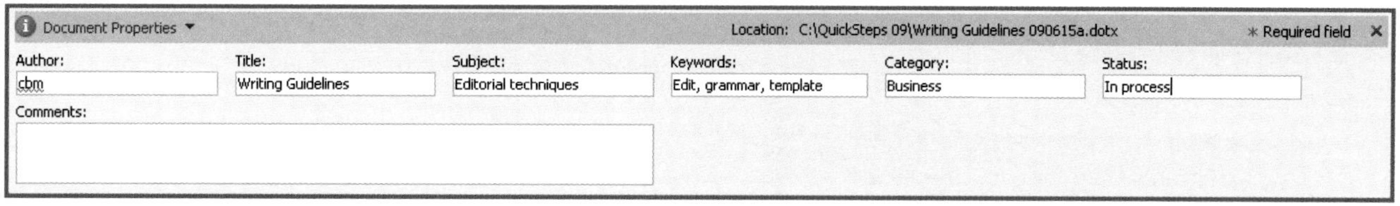

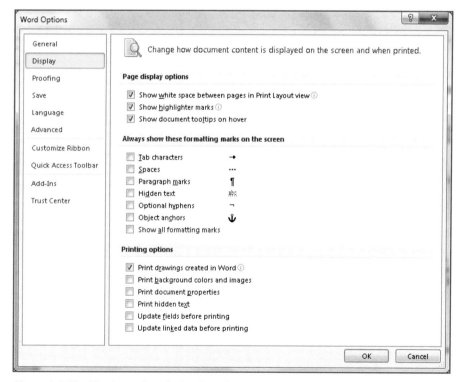

Figure 1-5: *A Document Properties panel beneath the ribbon allows you to more easily locate a document using search tools if you add identifying data.*

QUICKSTEPS

SETTING PREFERENCES

Setting preferences allows you to adapt your Office program to your needs and inclinations. The Word, Excel, Outlook, or PowerPoint Options dialog box provides access to these settings.

Click the **File** tab, and then click **Options**.

SELECT DISPLAY ELEMENTS TO SHOW (WORD ONLY)

Once you have chosen which formatting marks to display, you can toggle them off and on using the Show/Hide command on the Home tab Paragraph group.

To choose which formatting marks to display, click the **Display** option, as shown in Figure 1-6.

- Click the **Page Display Options** that you want to display.
- Click the formatting marks you want to see—**Show All Formatting Marks** is a good choice.
- Click the **Printing Options** you want.

Continued . . .

Figure 1-6: *The Display options in the Word Options view provide page display, formatting, and printing preferences.*

QUICKSTEPS

SETTING PREFERENCES *(Continued)*

SET GENERAL OPTIONS

1. Click the **General** options (see Figure 1-7 for Word's general options. The detail options will differ from program to program).

   - Review and select the options that are correct for your situation by clicking to put a check mark in the box. Earlier in this chapter, you saw how to disable the mini toolbar, show and hide screen tips, and change the color scheme of the Word window. If you are unsure about other options, keep the default and see how well those settings work for you.

   - Type the **user name** you want displayed in documents revised using Track Changes.

   - Type the **initials** associated with the user name that will be displayed in comments you insert into a document.

   - Click the **Start Up Options** to open any e-mail attachments automatically in Full Screen Reading view.

2. When you have set the general and display options you want, click each of the other options, reviewing the settings and making the changes you want. These are discussed further in the applicable chapters.

3. When you have finished selecting your preferences, click **OK** to close the Office program Options dialog box.

NOTE

If you are not connected to the Internet, a limited Help is also available offline.

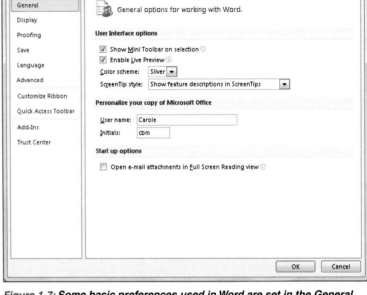

Figure 1-7: Some basic preferences used in Word are set in the General Options view.

Get Help

Help can be accessed from online Microsoft servers. A different kind of help, which provides the Thesaurus and Research features, is also available.

Open Help

The Office Help system is maintained online at Microsoft. It is easily accessed.

Click the **Help** icon 🔘 and the Word Help window will open, shown in Figure 1-8.

- Find the topic you want, and click it.

  –Or–

- Type words in the Search text box, and click **Search**.

Figure 1-8: *When you click the Help icon, you will see the Office program Help dialog box, where you can click the topic you want or search for more specific words.*

Using the Help Toolbar

On the toolbar at the top of the Office program Help window are several options for navigating through the topics and printing one out, as seen in Figure 1-9.

Do Research

You can do research on the Internet using Office's Research command. This displays a Research task pane that allows you to enter your search criteria and specify references to search.

1. Click the **Review** tab, and in the Proofing group, click **Research**. You may be asked for the language you are using. Click it, and the Research task pane will appear on the right of the document pane, as shown in the example in Figure 1-10.

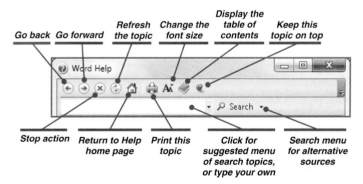

Go back Go forward **Refresh the topic** **Change the font size** **Display the table of contents** **Keep this topic on top**

Stop action **Return to Help home page** **Print this topic** **Click for suggested menu of search topics, or type your own** **Search menu for alternative sources**

Figure 1-9: *The Help toolbar helps you navigate through the topics and then print them out.*

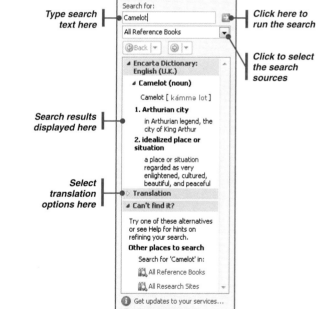

Type search text here

Click here to run the search

Click to select the search sources

Search results displayed here

Select translation options here

Figure 1-10: *In the Research pane, you can search a dictionary, a thesaurus, an encyclopedia, and several other sources.*

2. Type your search criteria in the Search For text box.

3. To change the default reference (All Reference Books), click the reference down arrow to open the drop-down list, and click a reference to be searched.

4. Click the green arrow to the right of the search box to start the search. The results will be displayed in the task pane.

5. Click **Close** to close the task pane.

Use the Thesaurus

You can find synonyms for words with the Thesaurus feature.

1. To use the Thesaurus, first select the text you want to use for the search.

2. Click the **Review** tab, and in the Proofing group, click **Thesaurus**. The Research task pane will appear with the most likely synonyms listed.

- Click a listed word to search for its synonyms.

- Click the word's down arrow to insert, copy, or look up the word.

3. Click **Close** to remove the task pane.

Translate a Document

To translate a whole document from one language to another:

1. Click the **Review** tab, and in the Language group, click the **Translate** down arrow.

2. Click **Translate Document** to translate the current document, or click **Translate Selected Text** if you have selected text, or click **Mini Translator [(French (France)]** to translate a word or selected phrase into French, for example. The Search task pane will appear with the translation as its source reference.

3. Click the **From** and **To** down arrows, and click the appropriate languages.

4. Click the green arrow to begin the translation. A Translate Whole Document message will appear that informs you that your document will be sent over the Internet to a special service, WorldLingo, to be translated.

5. Click **Yes** to start the translation. Your translated document will appear in a browser window; an example is shown in Figure 1-11.

ACCESSING MICROSOFT RESOURCES

Microsoft maintains a resource center online that you can easily access. This resource window allows you to communicate with Microsoft about Office and specific program subjects. In Word, Excel, Outlook, and PowerPoint:

1. Click the **File** tab, and click **Help**. Here are your choices, as shown in Figure 1-12:

   - Click **Microsoft Office Help** to display the Office Help dialog box. It contains a menu of options for which you might be looking.

   - Click **Getting Started** to open an online introduction to getting started with the Office program, with links to new features and overview training on the basics.

   - Click **Contact Us** to send a message to Microsoft experts. You may be seeking advice for a problem or making suggestions for improvements to the product.

   - Click **Options** to open the Office program Options dialog box with choices for changing important program features, such as the ribbon, Quick Access toolbar, and the language being used.

   - Click **Check For Updates** to find out if updates are available for Microsoft Office and then to initiate an update action. (See "Update Your Office Program.")

   - Click **Activate Microsoft Office** if you cannot access all features within the Office program. If you have already activated Office, a "Product Activated" message will be displayed.

   - Click **About Microsoft** *Program* links to access additional version and copyright information, Microsoft customer services and support, and Microsoft license terms.

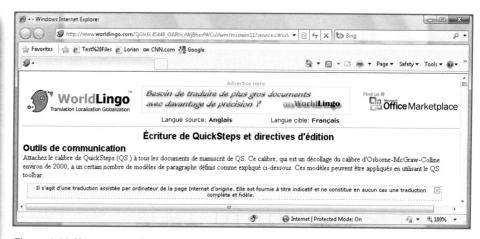

Figure 1-11: *You can translate a document using WorldLingo as the translator.*

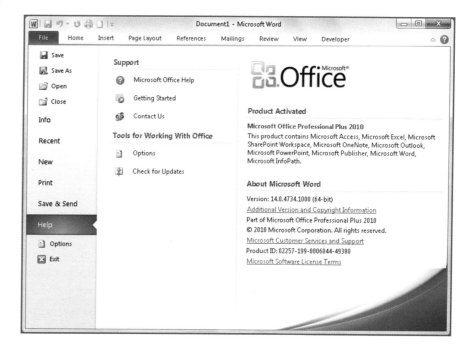

Figure 1-12: *The Help page in the Office program Options view facilitates communication with Microsoft.*

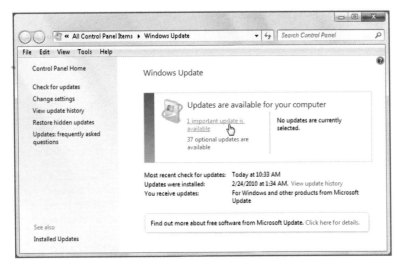

Figure 1-13: *One of the primary reasons to check for and download Office and Windows updates is to get needed security patches.*

Update Your Office Program

Microsoft periodically releases updates for Office programs (these are almost always problem fixes and not enhancements). You can check on available updates, download them, and install them from your Office program. In Word, Excel, and PowerPoint:

1. Click the **File** tab, and click **Help**. Then click **Check For Updates**. Your Internet browser opens and connects to the Microsoft Online website, as shown in Figure 1-13.

2. You will see on the first page whether your Office program needs updating. If so, click the link, ***Number* Important Update Is Available**. If not, click **Check For Updates** in the navigation pane on the left. Your system will be checked for any necessary updates, and you will be given the opportunity to download and install them.

3. When you have downloaded the updates you want, close your Web browser.

NOTE

In Windows 7, you can also check for updates by clicking the **Start** menu, clicking **All Programs**, and clicking **Windows Updates**.

QUICK FACTS

UNDERSTANDING WEB APPS

Microsoft Office Web Applications, called "Web Apps" for short, are a browser-based set of applications for viewing and performing lightweight editing in a familiar layout of your existing Word, Excel, and PowerPoint files over the Internet or an intranet whereever there is a PC or Mac attached.

Continued ...

Use Web Apps for Office Programs

With the appearance of *cloud computing,* or working with computer files and applications hosted on a remote server and viewable in a browser rather than your own PC and Office applications, Microsoft is moving Office to the Internet. This means that your files and programs are stored on an Internet server rather than on your stand-alone PC computer, and that Office programs are accessed through a browser working on the Internet rather than from programs stored on your computer. This is a new world! Why this is even remotely a good idea really revolves around expanded ways of working with data files and other people and making them available any place, any time. The approach is much more about accessing and sharing data and collaboration than it is about

This book introduces you to Web Apps on the Internet using Microsoft SkyDrive, which can also host your data files. When you want to view or edit a Word file, for instance, you bring up a browser, sign into http://skydrive .live.com, and scroll through your folders, just as you would with your own computer folders. When you find the document you want to open, you click it, click **View** or **Edit**, and the Microsoft Word Web App opens to do that.

A second approach, not covered in this book, is where you are working within an organization with its own servers hosting your data files and Office Web Apps. Accessing folders and applications works similarly to using SkyDrive; however, the protocol for signing in and accessing the files will be based on your organization's security. If your organization also is running SharePoint, you may be able to go directly from a file in a SharePoint library to viewing or editing the file in an Office Web App, again from any computer on your intranet, and possibly on the Internet.

NOTE

To set up your SkyDrive credentials and upload a file, you must first establish a Windows Live ID and account. To do this in an Office desktop application, click **File**, click **Save & Send**, and click **Save To Web**. The Save & Send view opens, as seen in Figure 1-14. Click **Sign Up For Windows Live**, and follow the directions to establish a Windows Live ID and SkyDrive account. If it is your first time on Windows Live, you'll be asked to accept the privacy policy. You can also access SkyDrive directly from your browser (http:// www.skydrive.live.com). Once you have a Windows Live ID, you can simply log in and get access to SkyDrive.

an isolated person working alone. When you store data and have programs available from an Internet server:

- You don't have to worry about whether you have the latest program updates.
- You don't have to worry about whether you have access to your home computer, for instance, when you are traveling.
- You don't have to worry about someone else being able to read your documents when they don't own the program or the same version of the program.

Use SkyDrive

SkyDrive (http://skydrive.live.com), the Microsoft server hosting one platform for its Web Apps, is where you can save your Office documents, thus enabling viewers without Office applications or the latest version of them to view the document and do lightweight editing with a browser. If you have created a document on your own computer, saving your files to SkyDrive preserves the links, color schemes, and other design elements created with your local Office application. The file and all the supporting objects are saved to a Web folder that you create on SkyDrive or to a public folder.

ADD A FOLDER TO SKYDRIVE

SkyDrive, shown in Figure 1-15, contains a number of folders to hold your presentations and other documents. Some of these are standard and are in the account at the beginning. Others, such as the Business Presentations in Figure 1-15, are your personal folders that you create. (See the "Understanding SkyDrive Folders" QuickFacts.)

To log on to SkyDrive and create a new folder to hold your documents:

1. Click **Save**, click **Save & Send**, and click **Save To Web**. Then click either **Windows Live** or **Sign Up** to see the SkyDrive window shown in Figure 1-15.
2. Click **Create Folder** to add a new folder to the account. The Create A Folder view will appear.
3. Type the name for the folder.

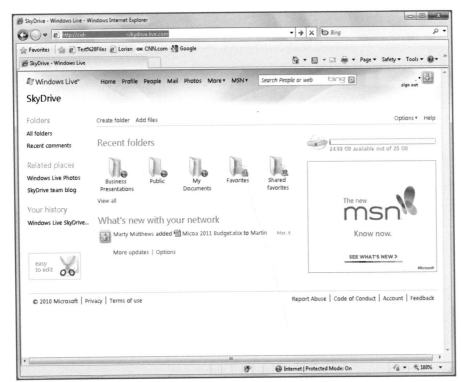

Figure 1-14: *To use Web Apps with SkyDrive, you must first sign up for a Windows Live ID and SkyDrive account.*

Figure 1-15: *You can save your presentations to SkyDrive, where viewers can access them with a browser.*

4. Click **Share With** to choose those permitted to see the contents of the folder. Choose **Everyone (Public)**, **My Network**, **Just Me**, or **Select People**.

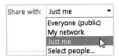

- Click **Select People** to be able to enter the e-mail addresses of those allowed in the Individuals text box.
- Click **Select From Your Contact List** to choose the permitted viewers from your e-mail contact list.

5. Click **Next**. The Add Files to *foldername* window opens. Follow steps in "Add Files to SkyDrive" next.

ADD FILES TO SKYDRIVE

You can upload files to SkyDrive by dragging them from your computer to a designated folder.

1. Click **Add Files** on the SkyDrive home page. (If you have added a folder, you will see the Add Files To *foldername* window when you click **Next**.) You will see a list of folders.

2. Click the folder you want to use. The Add Files To *foldername* window opens, as shown in Figure 1-16.

3. You can upload files in two ways:
   - If you have Windows Explorer open, click your file and drag it to the Add Files To *Foldername* window.
   - Click **Select Files From Your Computer**, find your file, and click **Open** to place it into the SkyDrive window.

TIP

To delete a folder in SkyDrive, sign in and click the folder you want to delete. That folder's page will appear. Click **More** and click **Delete**. Verify that you want to delete the folder. Be warned that any files and photos the folder contains will be deleted as well.

UNDERSTANDING SKYDRIVE FOLDERS

By default, your initial SkyDrive account will contain four folders: My Documents, Public, Favorites, and Shared Favorites. You can tell by the icons whether the folder is shared, private, or public.

- Indicates a public folder that is shared by the public or by people you select
- Indicates a private folder, not shared with anyone else
- Indicates a folder shared with your network of contacts

When you add folders, you choose who will be able to view its contents.

Figure 1-16: *Adding files to SkyDrive is as easy as dragging the files from your Windows Explorer or using the browse function, Select Files From Your Computer.*

4. When all the files you want to upload are displayed in the SkyDrive Add Files window, click **Upload**. You'll see a message informing you that the upload has been successful, along with icons of your other uploaded files.

Chapter 2
Working with Documents

Microsoft Office Word 2010 allows you to create and edit *documents*, such as letters, reports, invoices, plays, and books. The book you are reading now was written in Word. Documents are printed on one or more pages and are probably bound by anything from a paper clip to stitch binding. In the computer, a document is a called a *file*, an object that has been given a name and is stored on a disk drive. For example, the name given to the file for this chapter is Chap02.docx (prior to Word 2007, .doc was the extension). "Chap02" is the file name, and ".docx" is the file extension. By default, documents saved in Word 2010 are saved with the .docx extension.

In this chapter you'll see how to create new documents and edit existing ones. This includes ways to enter, change, and delete text, as well as ways to find, select, copy, and move text.

Create a New Document

In the days before computers, creating a new document was termed "starting with a clean sheet of paper." Today, it is "starting with a blank screen"—actually, a blank area within a window on the screen, as shown in Figure 2-1. Your ribbon options may vary, depending on the size of your window: Windows that are less than maximized size, display abbreviated options, such as Editing in Figure 2-1.

You can create a new document in two ways: using the default, or "normal," document or using a unique template on which to base the document.

Start a New Document

Simply starting Word opens up a blank document pane into which you can start typing a new document immediately. The blinking bar in the upper-left corner

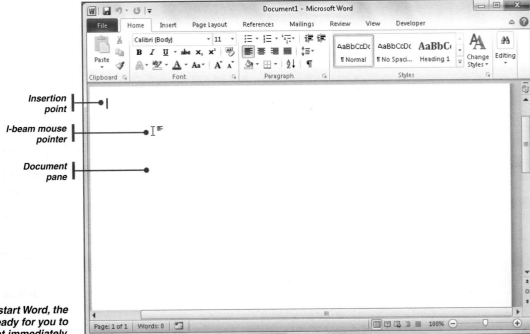

Insertion point

I-beam mouse pointer

Document pane

Figure 2-1: When you first start Word, the blank document pane is ready for you to create a document immediately.

of the document pane, called the *insertion point*, indicates where the text you type will appear.

To start Word, use one of the ways described at the beginning of Chapter 1.

Use a Unique Template

A template is a special kind of document that is used as the basis for other documents you create. The template is said to be "attached" to the document, and every Word document must have a template attached to it. The template acts as the framework around which you create your document. The document that is opened automatically when you start Word 2010 uses a default template called Normal.dotm (prior to Word 2007, Normal.dot was the template file). This is referred to as "the Normal template" and contains standard formatting settings. Other templates can contain boilerplate text, formatting for the types of document they create, and even automating procedures. Word is installed on your computer with a number of templates that you can use, and you can access other templates through Office Online.

USE A TEMPLATE ON YOUR COMPUTER

With Word open on your computer:

1. Click the **File** tab, and then click **New**. The New Document view will open, as shown in Figure 2-2.

2. In the Available Templates pane, you have these options:
   - **Blank:** A new blank template
   - **Blog Post:** A document to be posted to a website blog
   - **Recent Templates:** Templates you have used recently

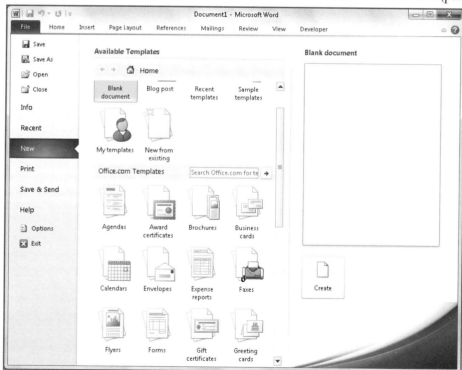

Figure 2-2: *The New Document dialog box gives you choices for how to start a document.*

- **Sample Templates:** Templates available with your Word 2010 installation
- **My Templates:** Custom templates you have created
- **New From Existing:** Templates you can copy from existing documents
- **Office.com Templates:** Template categories that can be obtained from Microsoft's online resources

3. Click **Sample Templates**. Click the template you want, and then beneath the preview of the selected template, click **Document** as shown in Figure 2-3.

4. Click **Create** and a document with the selected template opens.

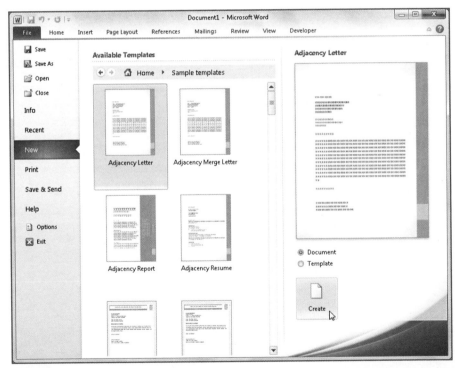

Figure 2-3: Word installs a number of templates on your computer automatically.

USE AN OFFICE ONLINE TEMPLATE

When you download an online template, it will be stored on your computer, ready for your next use without needing to be downloaded again. With Word open on your computer:

1. Click the **File** tab, and then click **New**. The New Document dialog box will appear.

2. In the Templates pane beneath Office.com Templates is a list of categories of templates. Click the category you want to see, and you'll see the possibilities for that category, as seen in Figure 2-4.

3. Find the template you want, and click **Download** in the right pane. A new document is opened with the template in Word.

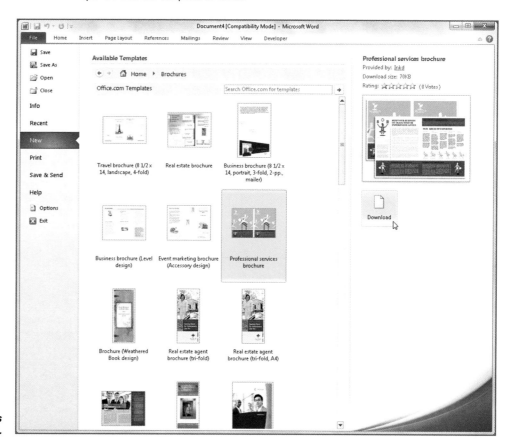

Figure 2-4: Microsoft offers many templates online for Word and its other products.

Open an Existing Document

After creating and saving a document, you may want to come back and work on it later. You may also want to open and work on a Word document (or another kind of document) created by someone else. To do this, you must first locate the document and then open it in Word. You can locate the document either directly from Word or search for it in either Word or Windows.

Locate an Existing Document

If the document has not been used for a while, you find and open it using a typical file-open dialog box. With Word open on your screen:

1. Click the **File** tab, and click **Open**. The Open dialog box appears.

2. Double-click the folder or sequence of folders you need to open in order to find the document.

3. When you have found the document you want to open (see Figure 2-5), double-click it. It will appear in Word, ready for you to begin your work.

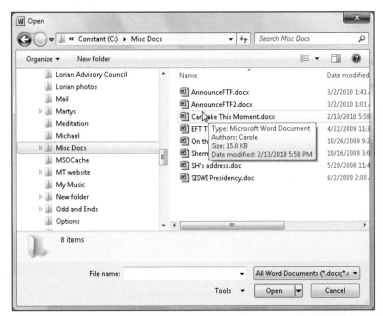

Figure 2-5: When you hold the mouse pointer over a document name, you see additional information about the document.

Open a Recent Document

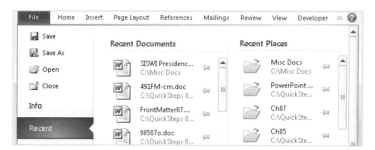

To find a document that you have recently opened or edited, Word 2010 is very efficient.

1. Click the **File** tab. The recently opened files and locations are listed in the right pane. If you have not opened or edited a document, Recent is not displayed, so use the procedure described in "Locate an Existing Document."

2. Click the specific recent file, and it will open; or click the folder containing the file, and then double-click the file.

Search for an Existing Document

If you have a hard time finding a document using the direct approach described previously, you can search for it either in Word or in Windows.

SEARCH FOR A DOCUMENT IN WORD

A document search performed in Word looks for a piece of text that is contained in the document or some property of the document, such as the name of the author, the creation date, or the name of the file. The basic search is for text in the document.

1. Click the **File** tab, and click **Open**. The Open dialog box appears. Display the folder or drive that you want to search.

2. In the Search text field on the top of the dialog box, begin to enter the text you want to search for. As you type, the search will begin. The results will be listed beneath in the right pane of the dialog box, beneath the search text (see Figure 2-6).

3. If you click the search text box instead of typing, you will see a menu. You have these options:

   - You can select a previously used search word or phrase.

   - You can click a filter option to refine the search. For instance, you might see filters for author, type, date modified, or file size. When you select one of these options, it is added to the search text box.

4. When the file you want is displayed, double-click it, or select it and click **Open** to open it in Word.

TIP

Accessing a file search from the Open dialog box is handy when you are trying to open a file and realize you don't know where it is.

TIP

To perform an advanced search, use Windows 7 Explorer.

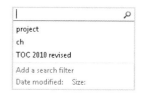

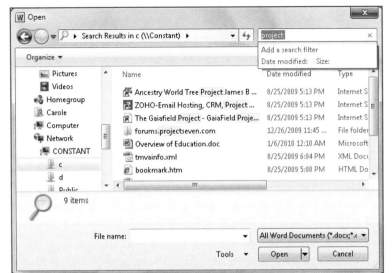

Figure 2-6: *As you type the text you want to search for, the search automatically begins and the results are listed beneath the search text.*

FILE TYPE	EXTENSION
Plain text files	.txt
Rich text format file	.rtf
Webpage files	.htm, .html, .mht, .mhtml
Word 97 to 2003 files	.doc
Word 97 to 2003 template files	.dot
Word 2010 document files (macro-enabled)	.docx (.docm)
Word 2010 template files	.dotx
WordPerfect 5.x and 6.x files	.doc, .wpd
Works 6.0 to 9.0 files	.wps
Word macro-enabled templates	.docm
XML files	.xml
OpenDocument Text	.odt

Table 2-1: *File Types That Word Can Open Directly*

USE SEARCH AND SORT

You can sort the files within the search results using the column headings. The sort allows you to sort files by some special property, such as name, date, folder type, author, or tag.

1. Open the File Open dialog box (see the preceding set of steps), locate the folder containing the file you want, and type your search text. The search results will be listed below as you type.

2. Point to a column heading by which you want to sort the results, and click the down arrow. The content that is displayed will depend on the column header. A Name field, for instance, displays an alphabetic submenu; a Date field, a calendar; a Type field, a menu of file types; and so on.

3. Click the sort option, and the files will be resorted.

Import a Document

If you have a word-processing document created in a program other than Word, you can most likely open it and edit it in Word.

1. Click the File tab, and click Open. The Open dialog box will appear.

2. On the bottom of the dialog box, click the down arrow on the drop-down list box to the right of File Name to display the list of files that you can directly open in Word, as shown next (see Table 2-1 for a complete list).

3. Find the folder or sequence of folders you need to open in order to find the document.

QUICKSTEPS

ENTERING SPECIAL CHARACTERS

Entering a character that is on the keyboard takes only a keystroke, but many other characters and symbols exist beyond those that appear on the keyboard—for example: ©, £, Ã, Ω, Љ, and •. You can enter these characters using either the Symbol dialog box or a sequence of keys.

SELECT SPECIAL CHARACTERS FROM THE SYMBOL DIALOG BOX

1. Move the insertion point to where you want to insert the special character(s).

2. Click the **Insert** tab, and then click **Symbol** in the Symbols group. A Symbol menu will open containing the symbols you most commonly use. If the symbol you want is on the list, click it and the symbol is inserted in the document.

3. If the symbol you want is not on the menu, click **More Symbols**. The Symbol dialog box appears.

   • Click the **Symbols** tab for characters within font styles.

   • Click the **Special Characters** tab for common standard characters, as shown in Figure 2-7.

4. Click the character you want, click **Insert**, and then click **Close**. You should see the special character or symbol where the insertion point was.

Continued . . .

4. Click the file type you want to open. The Open dialog box will list only files of that type.

5. Double-click the file you want to open. Depending on the file, you may see one of several messages.

Write a Document

Whether you create a new document or open an existing one, you will likely want to enter and edit text. Editing, in this case, includes adding and deleting text as well as selecting, moving, and copying it.

Enter Text

To enter text in a document that you have newly created or opened, simply start typing. The characters you type will appear in the document pane at the insertion point and in the order that you type them.

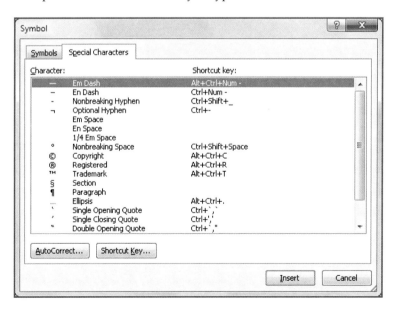

Figure 2-7: **The Symbol dialog box contains special characters as well as several complete alphabets and symbol sets.**

QUICKSTEPS

ENTERING SPECIAL CHARACTERS

(Continued)

ENTER SPECIAL CHARACTERS FROM THE KEYBOARD

You can use keyboard shortcut keys to enter symbols and special characters. The numeric part of the shortcut must be entered on the numeric keypad.

1. Move the insertion point to where you want to insert the special characters.

2. Press **NUM LOCK** to put the numeric keypad into numeric mode.

3. Press and hold **ALT** while pressing all four digits (including the leading zero) on the numeric keypad, not the regular numeric keys above the keypad.

4. Release **ALT**. The special character will appear where the insertion point was.

The shortcut keys for some of the more common special characters are shown in Table 2-2.

CHARACTER	NAME	SHORTCUT KEYS
•	Bullet	ALT+0149
©	Copyright	ALT+CTRL+C
™	Trademark	ALT+CTRL+T
®	Registered	ALT+CTRL+R
¢	Cent	CTRL+/ , C
£	Pound	ALT+0163
€	Euro	ALT+CTRL+E
–	En dash	CTRL+NUM-
—	Em dash	ALT+CTRL+NUM-

Table 2-2: Shortcut Keys for Common Characters

Determine Where Text Will Appear

The *insertion point*, the blinking vertical bar shown earlier in Figure 2-1, determines where text that you type will appear. It tells you where you are right now in a document. In a new document, the insertion point is obviously in the upper-left corner of the document pane. It is also placed there by default when you open an existing document. Until there is some text, your insertion point cannot be moved. However, you can move the insertion point within or to the end of existing text using either the keyboard or the mouse.

MOVE THE INSERTION POINT WITH THE KEYBOARD

When Word is open and active, the insertion point moves every time you press a character or directional key on the keyboard (unless a menu or dialog box is open or the task pane is active). The directional keys include TAB, BACKSPACE, and ENTER as well as the four arrow keys, and HOME, END, PAGE UP, and PAGE DOWN.

MOVE THE INSERTION POINT WITH THE MOUSE

When the mouse pointer is in the document pane, it appears as an I-beam, as you saw in Figure 2-1. The reason for the I-beam is that it fits between characters on the screen. You can move the insertion point by moving the I-beam mouse pointer to where you want the insertion point and clicking.

Insertion|point

Insert Text or Type Over It

When you press a letter or a number key with Word in its default mode (as it is when you first start it), the insertion point and any existing text to the right of the insertion point is pushed to the right and down on a page. This is also true when you press the **TAB** or **ENTER** key. This is called *insert* mode: new text pushes existing text to the right.

NOTE

In Table 2-2, the comma (",") means to release the previous keys and then press the following key(s). For example, for a ¢, press and hold **CTRL** while pressing **/**, then release **CTRL** and the **/**, and press **C**. In addition, "NUM" means to press the following key on the numeric keypad. So, "NUM-" means to press hyphen ("-") in the top-right corner of the numeric keypad.

NOTE

Section breaks are used to define columns within a page and to define different types of pages, as you might have with differently formatted left and right pages. The use of section breaks, columns, and different types of pages are described in Chapter 4.

In previous versions of Word, if you press the **INSERT** (or **INS**) key, Word is switched to *overtype* mode, and the OVR indicator is enabled in the status bar. In Word 2010, this capability is turned off by default and the **INSERT** (or **INS**) key does nothing. The reason is that more often than not the **INSERT** (or **INS**) key gets pressed by mistake and you find out about this after you have typed over a lot of text you didn't want to type over. You can turn on this capability by clicking the **File** tab, then clicking **Options**, clicking **Advanced**, and under Editing Options, clicking **Use The Insert Key To Control Overtype Mode**.

In overtype mode, any character key you press types over (replaces) the existing character to the right of the insertion point. Overtype mode does not affect the **ENTER** key, which continues to push existing characters to the right of the insertion point and down. The **TAB** key does replace characters to the right, *unless* it is pressed at the beginning of the line, in which case it is treated as an indent and pushes the rest of the line to the right.

Insert Line or Page Breaks

In Word, as in all word-processing programs, simply keep typing and the text will automatically wrap around to the next line. Only when you want to break a line before it would otherwise end must you manually intervene. There are four instances where manual line breaks are required:

- At the **end of a paragraph:** To start a new paragraph, press **ENTER**.
- At the **end of a short line** within a paragraph: To start a new line, press **SHIFT+ENTER**. This new line is considered part of the previous paragraph and retains its formatting. When you create a new line in the normal way, by pressing **ENTER**, the new paragraph can be formatted differently.
- At the **end of a page:** To force the start of a new page anywhere on the page, press **CTRL+ENTER**. You may want this, for instance, at the end of a major part of the document when it occurs before the natural end of the page.
- At the **end of a section:** To start a new section, press **CTRL+SHIFT+ENTER**.

You can also enter a page break using the mouse.

TIP

The AutoCorrect As You Type feature, which is discussed in Chapter 4, also provides a quick way of entering commonly used special characters, such as copyright, trademark, and registered symbols, and en and em dashes.

NOTE

When you click a common symbol or special character in the Symbol dialog box, you'll see the shortcut keys for the character.

£ ¥ ® ™ ±

Character code: 00AE

Shortcut key: Alt+0174

TIP

You can insert multiple special characters in sequence by selecting one after the other in the Symbol dialog box.

CAUTION

In Word 2010 there is no "OVR" in the status bar to indicate that you are in overtype mode, which replaces existing text with what you are typing.

NOTE

In both insert and overtype modes, the directional keys move the insertion point without regard to which mode is enabled.

With the insertion point where you want the break, click the **Insert** tab, and click **Page Break** in the Pages group. A page break will be inserted in the text.

Select Text

In order to copy, move, or delete text, you first need to select it. *Selecting text* means to identify it as a separate block from the remaining text in a document. You can select any amount of text, from a single character up to an entire document. As text is selected, it is highlighted with a colored background, as you can see in Figure 2-8. You can select text with both the mouse and the keyboard.

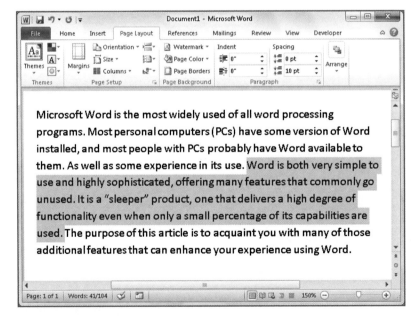

Figure 2-8: **You will always know what you are moving, copying, or deleting because it is highlighted on the screen.**

SELECT TEXT WITH THE MOUSE

You can select varying amounts of text with the mouse.

- **Select a single word** by double-clicking that word.
- **Select a single line** by clicking the far left of the line when the I-beam mouse pointer becomes an arrow (this area on the left where the mouse pointer becomes an arrow is called the *selection bar*).

- **Select a single sentence** by pressing and holding **CTRL** while clicking in the sentence.
- **Select a single paragraph** by double-clicking in the selection bar opposite the paragraph.
- **Select an entire document** by pressing and holding **CTRL+SHIFT** while clicking in the selection bar anywhere in the document. (The selection bar is on the far left edge of the document.) In the Home tab, you can also click **Select** in the Editing group, and then click **Select All**.
- **Select one or more characters** in a word, or select two or more words, by clicking.
  1. Click to place the insertion point to the left of the first character.
  2. Press and hold **SHIFT** while clicking to the right of the last character. The selected range of text will be highlighted.
- **Select one or more characters** in a word, or to select two or more words by dragging:
  1. Move the mouse pointer to the left of the first character.
  2. Press and hold the mouse button while dragging the mouse pointer to the right or left. The selected text will be highlighted.

SELECT TEXT WITH THE KEYBOARD

Use the arrow keys to move the insertion point to the left of the first character you want to select.

- Press and hold **SHIFT** while using the arrow keys to move the insertion point to the right or left.
- To select a line, place the pointer at the beginning of a line by pressing **HOME**. Press and hold **SHIFT** and press **END**.
- To select the entire document using the keyboard, press **CTRL+A**.

TIP

After selecting one area using the keyboard, the mouse, or the two together, you can select further independent areas by pressing and holding **CTRL** while using any of the mouse selection techniques.

NOTE

You select a picture by clicking it. Once selected, a picture can be copied, moved, and deleted from a document in the same ways as text, using either the Windows or Office Clipboard.

NOTE

Under certain circumstances, especially while formatting, the Redo option becomes Repeat.

NOTE

You can recover deleted text using Undo in the same way you can reverse a cut or a paste.

QUICKSTEPS

USING THE OFFICE CLIPBOARD

The Office Clipboard is shared by all Office products. You can copy objects and text from any Office application and paste it into another. As mentioned, the Clipboard contains up to 24 items. The 25th item will overwrite the first one.

OPEN THE CLIPBOARD

To display the Office Clipboard, click the **Home** tab, and click then the **Clipboard** Dialog Box Launcher in the Clipboard group. The Clipboard task pane will open.

ADD TO THE CLIPBOARD

When you cut or copy text with the Clipboard task pane open, it is automatically added to the Office Clipboard.

PASTE FROM THE CLIPBOARD

To paste one item:

1. Click to place the insertion point in the document or text box where you want the item on the Office Clipboard inserted.

Continued . . .

Copy and Move Text

Copying and moving text are similar. Think of copying text as moving it and leaving a copy behind. Both copying and moving are done in two steps.

1. Selected text is copied or cut from its current location to the Clipboard.
2. The contents of the Clipboard are pasted to a new location identified by the insertion point.

USE THE CLIPBOARD

The *Clipboard* is a location in the computer's memory that is used to store information temporarily. There are actually two Clipboards that can be used.

- The **Windows Clipboard** can store one object, either text or a picture, and pass that object within or among Windows programs. Once an object is cut or copied to the Windows Clipboard, it stays there until another object is cut or copied to the Clipboard or until the computer is turned off. The Windows Clipboard is used by default.

- The **Office Clipboard** can store up to 24 objects, both text and pictures, and pass those objects within or among Office programs. Once the Office Clipboard is enabled, all objects that are cut or copied are kept on the Office Clipboard until the 25th object is cut or copied, which will replace the first object. All objects on the Office Clipboard are lost from the Clipboard when Office is exited or the computer is turned off.

CUT TEXT

When you *cut* text, you place it on the Clipboard and delete it from its current location. When the Clipboard contents are pasted to the new location, the text has been *moved* and no longer exists in its original location. To cut and place text on the Clipboard, select it and then:

- Press **CTRL+X**.

  –Or–

- Click the **Home** tab, and then click **Cut** in the Clipboard group. ✂

COPY TEXT

When you *copy* text to the Clipboard, you also leave it in its original location. Once the Clipboard contents are pasted to the new location, you have the same

UICKSTEPS

USING THE OFFICE CLIPBOARD

(Continued)

2. Click the item on the Clipboard to be inserted, or click the down arrow on the item, and click **Paste**.

   –Or–

1. With the Clipboard item selected but no insertion point placed, right-click where you want the item.

2. Select **Paste** from the context menu.

To paste all items:

1. Click to place the insertion point in the text box or placeholder where you want the items on the Office Clipboard inserted.

2. Click **Paste All** on the Clipboard. 🖫 Paste All

DELETE ITEMS ON THE CLIPBOARD

- To delete all items, click **Clear All** on the Clipboard task pane. 🗙 Clear All

- To delete a single item, click the down arrow next to the item, and click **Delete**.

SET CLIPBOARD OPTIONS

1. On the Clipboard task pane, click Options on the bottom. A context menu is displayed.

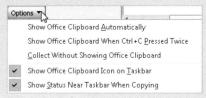

Continued . . .

text in two places in the document. To copy text to the Clipboard, select it and then:

- Press **CTRL+C**.

  –Or–

- Click the **Home** tab, and then click **Copy** in the Clipboard group.

PASTE TEXT

To complete a copy or a move, you must *paste* the text from the Clipboard onto either the same or another document where the insertion point is located. A copy of the text stays on the Clipboard and can be pasted again. To paste the contents of the Clipboard:

- Press **CTRL+V**.

  –Or–

- Click the **Home** tab, and then click **Paste** (located in the upper Clipboard area) in the Clipboard group.

USE THE PASTE OPTIONS SMART TAG

The Paste Options smart tag appears when you paste text. It asks you if you want to keep source formatting (the original formatting of the text), merge formatting (change the formatting to that of the surrounding text), or keep text only (remove all formatting from the text). Set Default Paste displays the Word Options dialog box so that you can set defaults for pasting text during a cut or copy action. The Paste Options smart tag is most valuable when you can see the paste operation has resulted in formatting you don't want.

UNDO A MOVE OR PASTE

You can undo a move or paste by:

- Pressing **CTRL+Z**

  –Or–

- Clicking **Undo** 🔄 in the Quick Access toolbar

USING THE OFFICE CLIPBOARD

(Continued)

2. Click an option to select or deselect it.

- **Show Office Clipboard Automatically** always shows the Office Clipboard when copying.

- **Show Office Clipboard When CTRL+C Pressed Twice** shows the Office Clipboard when you press **CTRL+C** twice to make two copies (in other words, two items on the Clipboard will cause the Clipboard to be displayed).

- **Collect Without Showing Office Clipboard** copies items to the Clipboard without displaying it.

- **Show Office Clipboard Icon On Taskbar** displays the icon on the right of the Windows taskbar when the Clipboard is being used.

- **Show Status Near Taskbar When Copying** displays a message about the items being added to the Clipboard as copies are made.

TIP

You can generally undo the last several operations by repeatedly issuing one of the Undo commands.

REDO AN UNDO

You can redo many undos by:

- Pressing **CTRL+Y**

  –Or–

- Clicking **Redo** in the Quick Access toolbar

Delete Text

Deleting text removes it from its current location *without* putting it in the Clipboard. To delete a selected piece of text:

- Press **DELETE** or **DEL**.

  –Or–

- On the Home tab, click **Cut** in the Clipboard group.

Edit a Document

After entering all the text into a document, most people want to edit it and, possibly, revise it at a later date. You'll want to be able to move around the document, quickly moving from location to location.

Move Around in a Document

Word provides a number of ways to move around a document using the mouse and the keyboard.

MOVE WITH THE MOUSE

You can easily move the insertion point by clicking in your text anywhere on the screen, but how do you move to some place you cannot see? You have to change what you are looking at, and Word provides two sets of tools to use with the mouse to do just that: the scroll bars and the browse buttons, as shown in Figure 2-9.

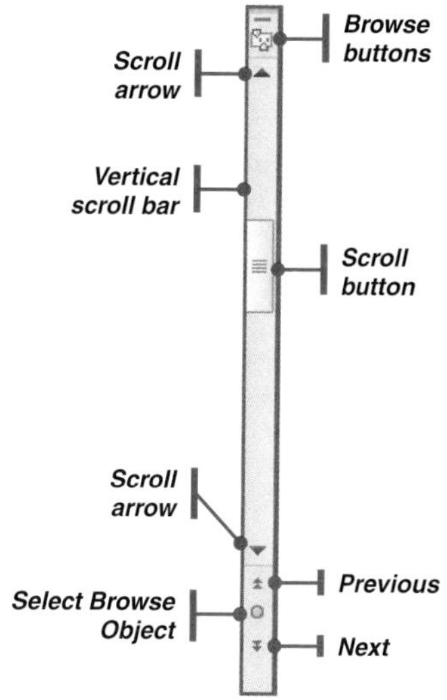

Figure 2-9: *The scroll bars and browse buttons allow you to move easily to different locations within your document.*

NOTE

To close the Office Clipboard and revert to the Windows Clipboard, click the close icon, or click **Close** at the top of the task pane (you may need to click the down arrow to the left of the close icon). The items you placed on the Office Clipboard while it was open will stay there until you shut down Word, but only the last item you cut or copied after closing the Office Clipboard will be displayed.

TIP

Place your pointer over the Clipboard icon in the taskbar to see how many items are currently on it.

USE THE SCROLL BARS

There are two scroll bars: one for moving vertically within the document, and one for moving horizontally. These are only displayed when your text is too wide or too long to be completely displayed on the screen. Each scroll bar contains five controls for getting you where you want to go. Using the vertical scroll bar, you may:

- **Move upward by one line** by clicking the upward-pointing scroll arrow

- **Move upward or downward** by dragging the scroll button in the corresponding direction

- **Move by one screen's height** by clicking in the scroll bar above the scroll button to move towards the beginning of the document, or by clicking below the scroll bar to move towards the end of the document

- **Move downward by one line** by clicking the downward-pointing scroll arrow

- **Move to the previous or next word or phrase** matching the current Find or Go To criteria

The horizontal scroll bar has similar controls (not the previous or next arrows, or Select Browse Object), only these are used for moving in a horizontal plane.

NOTE

Some of the ways used to move around a document move the insertion point as you go, and some only change what you are looking at within the document, moving your view to a new location. In the latter case, if you find that you want the insertion point where you are looking, click there or use one of the arrow keys to move the insertion point. The insertion point will appear.

NOTE

The "view buttons" in the status bar, located in the lower-right corner of the Word window, change the way the document is displayed, not the location in the document.

NOTE

You can also move a number of items relative to your current position by entering a plus (+) or a minus (–) and a number. For example, if Page is selected and you enter -3, you will be moved backwards three pages.

USE THE BROWSE BUTTONS

Clicking **Select Browse Object** opens a menu of objects from which to select. By selecting one of these objects—such as a page, a heading, a comment, or an edit—you can move through the document, going from one chosen object to the next. Often overlooked, this feature can be very handy. Place the pointer over the options to find out what the picture or icon represents.

MOVE WITH THE KEYBOARD

The following keyboard commands, used for moving around your document, also move the insertion point:

- **One character left or right** using the **LEFT** or **RIGHT ARROW**
- **One line up or down** using the **UP** or **DOWN ARROW**
- **One word left or right** using **CTRL+LEFT ARROW** or **CTRL+RIGHT ARROW**
- **One paragraph up or down** using **CTRL+UP ARROW** or **CTRL+DOWN ARROW**
- **To the beginning or end of a line** using **HOME** or **END**
- **To the beginning or end of a document** using **CTRL+HOME** or **CTRL+END**
- **One screen up or down** using **PAGE UP** or **PAGE DOWN**
- **To the previous or next instance of the current browse object** using **CTRL+PAGE UP** or **CTRL+PAGE DOWN**
- **To the top or bottom of the window** using **CTRL+ALT+PAGEUP** or **CTRL+ALT+PAGE DOWN**

GO TO A PARTICULAR LOCATION

The Go To command opens the dialog box, shown in Figure 2-10, that allows you to go immediately to the location of some object, such as a page, a footnote, or a table. You can open the dialog box by:

- Pressing **CTRL+G**
- Clicking the **Home** tab, and clicking **Advanced Find** in the Editing group, and finally clicking the **Go To** tab (if your window is reduced in size, you may have to click **Editing** in the Editing group for a menu with Find and then Advanced Find)
- Clicking **Select Browse Object** beneath the vertical scroll bar, and then clicking **Go To**
- Double-clicking the left end of the status bar in the *Page x of y* area

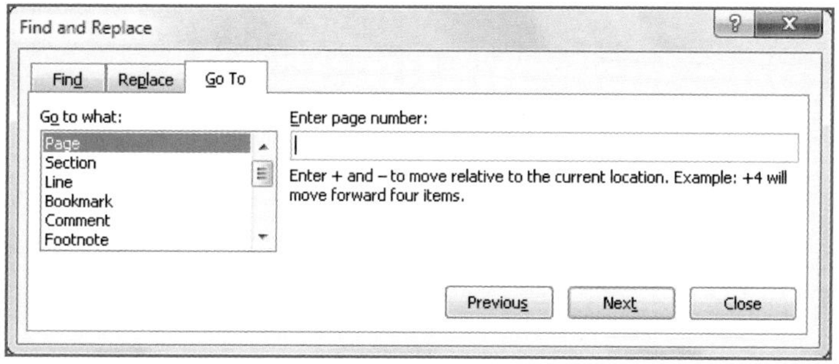

Find and Replace

Find | **Replace** | **Go To**

Go to what:

```
Page
Section
Line
Bookmark
Comment
Footnote
```

Enter page number:

Enter + and – to move relative to the current location. Example: +4 will move forward four items.

Previous | Next | Close

*Figure 2-10: **The Go To command allows you to go to a particular page as well as to other particular items within a document.***

TIP

If you want your search to find just the word "ton" and not words like "Washington" or "tonic," you can either put a space at both the beginning and end of the word (" ton ") or click **More** in the Find And Replace dialog box and then click **Find Whole Words Only**. The latter is the preferred way to do this because putting a space after the word would not find the word followed by a comma or a period. (From the Navigation task pane, you'll need to click the down arrow beside the search text box and click **Options**. Then, in the Find Options dialog box, click **Find Whole Words Only**.)

After opening the dialog box, select the object you want to go to from the list on the left, and then enter the number or name of the object in the text box on the right. For example, select **Page** on the left and enter 5 on the right to go to page 5.

Find and Replace Text

Often, you'll want to find something that you know is in the document, but you are not sure where, or even how many times, that item occurs. This is especially true when you want to locate names or words that are sprinkled throughout a document. For example, if you had repeatedly referred to a table on page 4 and, for some reason or another, the table had moved to page 5, you would need to search for all occurrences of "page 4" and change them to "page 5." In this example, you not only want to *find* "page 4," but you also want to *replace* it with "page 5."

Word allows you to do a simple search for a word or phrase as well as to conduct an advanced search for parts of words, particular capitalization, and words that sound alike.

FIND TEXT—A SIMPLE CASE

In the simple case where you just want to search for a word or phrase:

1. Click the **Home** tab, and click **Find** in the Editing group. (If your window is reduced in size, you may need to click **Editing** in the Editing group and then the **Find** down arrow.) The Navigation task pane will open.

2. In the text box, type the word or phrase for which you want to search. As you type, the results will be posted beneath the text box, as seen in Figure 2-11.

3. Click the result and the document will be repositioned so that you can see the search result in the document.

FIND TEXT—AN ADVANCED CASE

By clicking **More** in the Find And Replace dialog box (or in the task pane, by clicking the search text box down arrow and then **Options**), you will find that Word provides a number of features to make your search more sophisticated

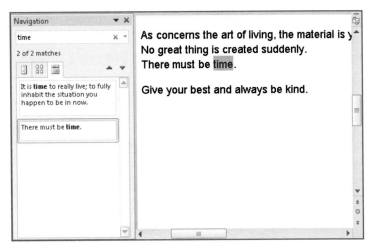

Figure 2-11: When you search for a word or phrase, the Find command can highlight individual occurrences or all occurrences at once.

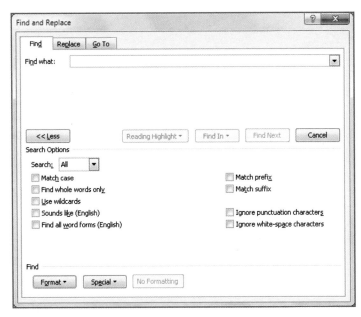

Figure 2-12: Word offers a number of advanced ways to search a document.

If you find that the Find And Replace dialog box is getting in the way after finding the first occurrence of a word or phrase, you can close the dialog box and use **SHIFT+F4** to find the remaining occurrences. Also, once you have used Find, you can close the Find And Replace dialog box and use the Find Next or Previous browse button at the bottom of the vertical scroll bar to browse by Find, or you can press **CTRL+PAGE DOWN** or **CTRL+PAGE UP** to move quickly from one instance of the search term to the next.

(see Figure 2-12). These include specifying the direction of the search as well as what you want to find.

- **Match Case:** Only specific capitalization of a word or phrase
- **Find Whole Words Only:** Only whole words, so when searching for "equip" you don't get "equipment"
- **Use Wildcards:** Words or phrases that contain a set of characters by using wildcards to represent the unknown part of the word or phrase (see the "Using Wildcards" QuickFacts)
- **Sounds Like:** Words that sound alike but are spelled differently (homonyms)
- **Find All Word Forms:** A word in all its forms—noun, adjective, verb, or adverb (for example, ski, skier, and skiing)
- **Match Prefix Or Match Suffix:** Words containing a common prefix or suffix

NOTE

Instead of repeatedly clicking **Find Next** to highlight each occurrence of an item, in the Find And Replace dialog box, you can click **Reading Highlight** and click **Highlight All**. Then click **Find In** and click **Main Document**, and all occurrences will be highlighted and the first occurrence will be displayed. Click **Find Next** to advance to the next occurrence. However, as soon as you click anywhere in the document, the highlights will all go away. If you press **SHIFT+F4**, **CTRL+PAGE UP**, **CTRL+PAGE DOWN**, or one of the browse buttons, you will select the next occurrence, but all occurrences will remain highlighted.

QUICKFACTS

USING WILDCARDS

Wildcards are characters that are used to represent one or more characters in a word or phrase when searching for items with similar or unknown parts. In the More extension to the Find And Replace dialog box, you must select the **Use Wildcards** check box and then type the wildcard characters along with the known characters in the Find What text box. For example, typing **page ?** will find both "page 4" and "page 5." The "?" stands for any single character.

| Find what: | Page ? |
| Options: | Search Down, Use Wildcards |

Word has defined the following characters, as seen in Table 2-3, as wildcard characters when used in the Find command to replace one or more characters.

- **Ignore Punctuation Characters:** Words without regard for any punctuation. This is especially needed when a word might be followed by a comma or period.
- **Ignore White-Space Characters:** Characters such as spaces, tabs, and indents
- **Format:** Specific types of formatting, such as for fonts, paragraphs, etc. (This option is not available from the task pane.)
- **Special:** Specific special characters, such as paragraph marks, em dashes (—), or nonbreaking spaces (can't be the first or last character in a line). (This option is not available from the task pane.)

REPLACE TEXT

Often, when searching for a word or phrase, you want to replace it with something else. Word lets you use all the features of Find and then replace what is found.

1. Click the **Home** tab, and click **Replace** in the Editing group. (You may have to click **Editing** and then **Replace** if your window is reduced in size.) The Find And Replace dialog box will appear with the Replace tab selected.

2. Enter the word or phrase for which you want to search in the Find What text box.

3. Enter the word or phrase you want to replace the found item(s) with in the Replace With text box, as you can see in Figure 2-13.

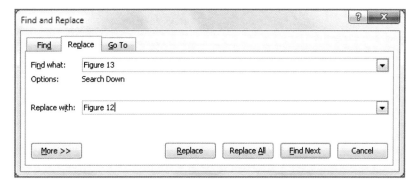

Figure 2-13: **You can replace text either on an individual basis or universally.**

CHARACTER	USED TO REPLACE	EXAMPLE	WILL FIND	WON'T FIND
?	A single character	Page ?	Page 4 or Page 5	Page1
*	Any number of characters	Page *	Page 4 and Page 5	Pages1–5 (no space)
<	The beginning of a word	<(corp)	Corporate	Incorporate
>	The end of a word	(ton)>	Washington	Toner
\	A wildcard character	What\?	What?	What is
[cc]	One of a list of characters	B[io]b	Bib or Bob	Babe
[c-c]	One in a range of characters	[l-t]ook	look or took	Book
[!c-c]	Any character except one in the range	[!k-n]ook	book or took	Look
{n}	n copies of the previous character	Lo{2}	Loo or Look	Lot
{n,}	n or more copies of the previous character	Lo{1,}	Lot or Look	Late
{n,m}	n to m copies of the previous character	150{1,3}	150 to 1500	15
@	Any number of copies of the previous character	150@	15, 150, or 1500	1400

Table 2-3: Wildcard Characters Used in Find

NOTE

When searching with wildcards, both Find Whole Words Only and Match Case are turned on automatically and cannot be turned off; however, the check boxes for these features are cleared but dim.

4. Click **Find Next**. The first occurrence in the document below the current insertion point will be highlighted.

5. You have these options:

   - Click **Replace** if you want to replace this instance with the text you entered. Word replaces this instance and automatically finds the next instance.

   - Click **Find Next** if you don't want to replace the text that was found and find the next occurrence.

   - Click **Replace All** if you want to replace all occurrences of the word you found at one time.

6. When you are done, click **Close**.

Complete and Save a Document

When you have completed a document or feel that you have done enough to warrant saving it and putting it aside for a while, you should go through a completion procedure that includes checking the spelling and grammar, determining where to save the document, and then actually saving it.

Check Spelling and Grammar

By default, Word checks spelling and grammar as you type the document, so it might be that these functions have already been performed. You can tell if Word is checking the spelling and grammar by noticing if Word automatically places a wavy red line under words it thinks are misspelled or a wavy green line beneath words and phrases whose grammar is questioned. You can turn off automatic spelling and grammar checking. You can also have these features run using an array of options. You can ask Word to perform a spelling and/or grammar check whenever you want—most importantly, when you are completing a document.

to its importunings
it's directives.

CONTROL SPELLING AND GRAMMAR CHECKING

Word provides a number of settings that allow you to control how spelling and grammar checking is performed.

1. Click the **File** tab, click **Options**, and click the **Proofing** option on the left. The Word Options dialog box, shown in Figure 2-14, will appear.

2. If you wish to turn off automatic spell checking, deselect **Check Spelling As You Type** under When Correcting Spelling In Microsoft Office Programs.

3. If you wish to turn off the automatic grammar checking, deselect **Mark Grammar Errors As You Type**.

4. Click **Settings**, the button to the left of the Writing Style drop-down list box, to set the rules by which the grammar or grammar and style checking is done.

5. Click **OK** twice to close both the Grammar Settings and the Options dialog boxes.

NOTE

In the Spelling Grammar English dialog box, you may not see Ignore All, Change All, or Autocorrect at first, as seen in Figure 2-15. Instead, you may see Ignore Rule, which allows you to ignore the rule that was seemingly violated by the reported error. You may also see Explain, which allows you to see further explanation of why the word or phrase was flagged as an error. When a rule is not the cause of the flagged error, the Ignore All, Change All, and Autocorrect features will be displayed.

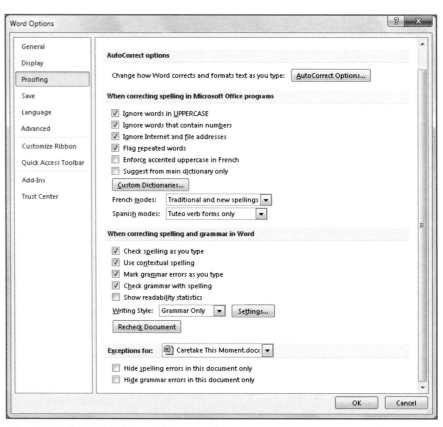

Figure 2-14: *By default, Word checks spelling and grammar as you type, but you can disable those utilities in the Options dialog box.*

INITIATE SPELLING AND GRAMMAR CHECKING

To manually initiate spelling and grammar checking:

1. Click the **Review** tab, and click **Spelling And Grammar** in the Proofing group. The Spelling And Grammar dialog box will appear and begin checking the document. When a word is found that Word believes might not be correct, the dialog box will display both the perceived error and one or more suggestions for its correction (see Figure 2-15).

2. You have these options for flagged spellings:

- If you don't want to correct the perceived error, click **Ignore Once** for this one instance, or click **Ignore All** for all instances. (See the accompanying Note for an explanation of why you may not see Ignore All when the dialog box first appears.)

TIP

AutoRecover is a reserve parachute that you don't want to test unless you must. AutoRecover gives you the impression that you have lost your work. In fact, if you follow the instructions and choose to recover the AutoRecover document, you may not lose anything—at most, you might lose only the very last thing that you did. However, you need to save the file again as soon as you AutoRecover. Also be warned that AutoRecover has a habit of not realizing that you've already recovered the document, so it may prompt you to do so again, which would overwrite any changes you made in your last editing session (after the initial AutoRecover).

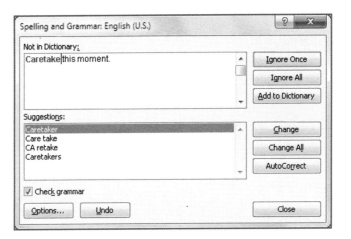

Figure 2-15: The spelling checker is a gift to those of us who are "spelling challenged!"

QUICKSTEPS

SAVING A DOCUMENT

After you have initially saved a document and specified its location, you can quickly save it whenever you wish.

SAVE A DOCUMENT

To save a file:

- Click the **File** tab, and click **Save**.

  –Or–

- Click the **Save** icon in the Quick Access toolbar.

  –Or–

- Press **CTRL+S**.

SAVE A COPY OF YOUR DOCUMENT

When you save a document under a different name, you create a copy of it.

1. Click the **File** tab, and click **Save As**.

Continued ...

- Click **Change** for this one instance, or click **Change All** for all instances if you want to replace the perceived error with the highlighted suggestion. If a suggestion other than the selected one is a better choice, click it before clicking **Change** or **Change All**.

- Click **Add To Dictionary** if you want Word to add your spelling of the word to the custom dictionary to be used for future documents. If you want Word to automatically correct this misspelling with the selected correction every time you type the incorrect word, click **AutoCorrect**. (See Chapter 4 for more on AutoCorrect.)

- Click **Options** to display the Word Options Proofing dialog box, where you can reset many of the spelling and grammar checking rules.

- Click **Undo** to reverse the last action.

3. When Word has completed checking the spelling and grammar, you'll see a message to that effect. Click **OK**.

Save a Document for the First Time

The first time you save a document, you have to specify where you want to save it—that is, the disk drive and the folder or subfolder in which you want

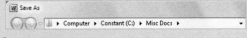

QUICKSTEPS

SAVING A DOCUMENT *(Continued)*

2. In the Save As dialog box, enter the new name in the File Name text box. Then, open the address list box at the top and identify the path to the folder you want.

W Save As
⊙⊙ ▽ ↑ ▶ Computer ▶ Constant (C:) ▶ Misc Docs ▶

3. Click **Save**.

SAVE A DOCUMENT AS A TEMPLATE

To save a newly created document as a template from which to create new documents:

1. Click the **File** tab, and Click **Save As**.

2. In the Save As Type drop-down list box, click **Word Template (*.dotx)**.

3. Enter a name (without an extension) for your template in the File Name text box.

4. Click **Save**.

QUICKSTEPS

EDITING DOCUMENTS IN THE WORD WEB APP

In Chapter 1, we described how, with a Windows Live ID and a SkyDrive account, you can upload files to Microsoft's SkyDrive location in order to keep them in the "cloud" so you, or others with your permission, can access them at any time or place from a browser. Besides simply storing files there, using the integrated Microsoft Word Web App, you can also view, edit, and download documents saved in the Word 2007 and Word 2010 default .docx file format without having Word installed on your device. (You can view documents saved

Continued . . .

it saved. Since this is your first time saving the file, the Save As dialog box will appear so that you can specify the location and enter a file name.

1. Click the **File** tab, and click **Save As**.

2. Click the icon on the left for the major area (for example, Favorite Links or Folders) in which the file is to be saved.

3. If you want to store your new document in a folder that already exists in the major area, double-click that folder to open it.

4. If you want to store your new document in a new folder, click the **New Folder** icon in the toolbar, type the name of the new folder, and press **ENTER**. You'll need to double-click the file name to place it in the Look In text box. (You can create yet another new folder within that folder using the same steps.) New folder

5. When you have the folder identified in which you want to store the document, enter the name of the document, as shown in Figure 2-16, and then click **Save**.

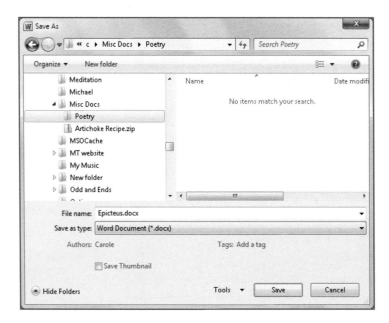

Figure 2-16: When saving a file, you don't have to enter a file extension. The .docx extension will be supplied by Word automatically.

EDITING DOCUMENTS IN THE WORD WEB APP (Continued)

in the earlier .doc file format, but you cannot edit them.) The editing capabilities in the Word Web App are a subset of those in the PC version of Word described here and in Chapters 3 and 4. However, if you are primarily just editing your data and sharing it with others, SkyDrive and the Word Web App provide you a great opportunity to access your information from anywhere with only a browser and Internet connection.

To use a document in the Word Web App:

1. Double-click the SkyDrive folder that contains the document you want to view or edit (see Chapter 1 for information on logging on to SkyDrive).

2. Click the file you want. A document preview screen opens that displays information about the file, shows other files in the folder that you can choose to open, and displays a toolbar of actions that you can do with the file.

3. Click **Edit**. The document opens in a Word window that is similar to the PC Word 2010 user interface (see Figure 2-17), but lacks several features, including the tools located on the missing ribbon tabs and many of the options found on a standard File tab.

4. After performing editing using the tools on the available ribbon tabs, click the File tab and select whether you want to open the file in your device's version of Word, save it under a different file name (you don't need to save the document, as Word Web App does that automatically), or download it to your device as a standard document file or as a snapshot containing only data and formatting (that is, no formulas).

Continued . . .

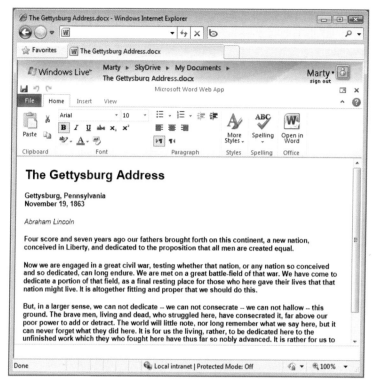

Figure 2-17: Working on a document in Word Web App feels very much like working on it at your desktop.

QUICKSTEPS

EDITING DOCUMENTS IN THE WORD WEB APP *(Continued)*

5. When finished, return to your SkyDrive folders to work with other Office documents in the same manner, navigate to other webpages, or simply close your browser.

TIP

As good as Word's automatic saving is, it is a great idea to manually save your document frequently (like a couple of times an hour). Doing this can save you the frustration of working several hours on a document only to lose it.

NOTE

When you first open Word, the save interval is set to a default of ten minutes.

Save a Document Automatically

It is important to save a document periodically as you work. Having Word save it automatically will reduce the chance of losing data in case of a power failure or other interruption.

1. Click the **File** tab, click **Options**, and click the **Save** option on the left.

2. Beneath Save Documents, click the **Save AutoRecover Info Every** check box.

3. In the Minutes box, use the arrows to select or enter a time for how often Word is to save your document.

Save files in this format:	Word Document (*.docx)	▼
☑ Save AutoRecover information every	10 ▲▼	minutes

4. Click **OK** to close the dialog box.

Chapter 3
Formatting a Document

Plain, unformatted text conveys information, but not nearly as effectively as well-formatted text, as you can see by the two examples in Figure 3-1. Word provides numerous ways to format your text. Most fall under the categories of text formatting, paragraph formatting, and page formatting, which are discussed in the following sections of this chapter. Additional formatting that can be applied at the document level is discussed in Chapter 4.

This chapter discusses the direct, or manual, application of formatting. Much of the character and paragraph formatting discussed in this chapter is commonly applied using styles that combine a number of different individual formatting steps, saving significant time over direct formatting. (Styles are discussed in Chapter 4.) Direct formatting is usually applied only to a small amount of text that needs formatting different from its style.

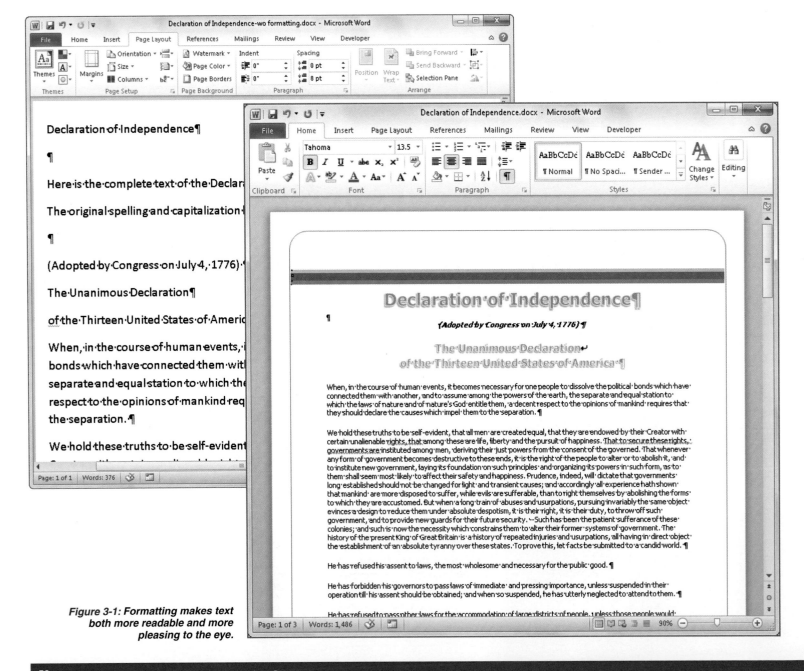

Figure 3-1: Formatting makes text both more readable and more pleasing to the eye.

Figure 3-2: The Font dialog box provides a complete set of character formatting controls.

Format Text

Text formatting covers the formatting that you can apply to individual characters and includes a selection of fonts, font size, color, character spacing, and capitalization.

Apply Character Formatting

Character formatting can be applied using keyboard shortcuts, the Home tab on the ribbon, and a Formatting dialog box. Of these, clicking the **Home** tab and clicking the **Font Dialog Box Launcher** to open the Font dialog box (see Figure 3-2) provides a comprehensive selection of character formatting and spacing alternatives. In the sections that immediately follow, the Font dialog box can be used to accomplish the task being discussed. Keyboard shortcuts and the Font and Paragraph groups on the Home tab (see Figure 3-3) often provide a quicker way to accomplish the same task, and keyboard shortcuts (summarized in Table 3-1) allow you to keep your hands on the keyboard.

APPLY FORMATTING	SHORTCUT KEYS
Align left	CTRL+L
Align right	CTRL+R
All caps	CTRL+SHIFT+A
Bold	CTRL+B
Bulleted list	CTRL+SHIFT+L
Center	CTRL+E
Copy format	CTRL+SHIFT+C
Decrease font size	CTRL+SHIFT+<
Increase font size	CTRL+SHIFT+>

Table 3-1: Formatting Shortcut Keys

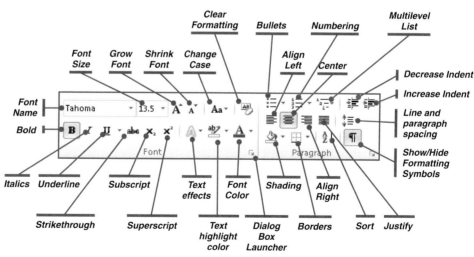

Figure 3-3: The Font and Paragraph groups on the Home tab provide fast formatting with the mouse.

APPLY FORMATTING	SHORTCUT KEYS
Decrease font size one point	CTRL+[
Increase font size one point	CTRL+]
Open font dialog box	CTRL+D
Font name	CTRL+SHIFT+F
Hang paragraph	CTRL+T
Heading level 1	ALT+CTRL+1
Heading level 2	ALT+CTRL+2
Heading level 3	ALT+CTRL+3
Indent paragraph	CTRL+M
Italic	CTRL+I
Justify paragraph	CTRL+J
Line space (single)	CTRL+1
Line space (1.5 lines)	CTRL+5
Line space (double)	CTRL+2
Normal style	CTRL+SHIFT+N
Paste format	CTRL+SHIFT+V
Reset character formatting	CTRL+SPACEBAR
Reset paragraph formatting	CTRL+Q
Small caps	CTRL+SHIFT+K
Subscript	CTRL+=
Superscript	CTRL+SHIFT+=
Symbol font	CTRL+SHIFT+Q
Un-indent paragraph	CTRL+SHIFT+M
Underline continuous	CTRL+U
Underline double	CTRL+SHIFT+D
Underline word	CTRL+SHIFT+W

Table 3-1: Formatting Shortcut Keys (Continued)

NOTE

Prior to applying formatting, you must select the text to be formatted. Chapter 2 contains a description on selecting text.

USE THE MINI-FORMATTING TOOLBAR

In Word 2010, when you right-click text, you see both a context menu and a mini-formatting toolbar. When you select text and place your pointer on the selection, the mini-formatting toolbar also appears. This toolbar has several of the buttons available in the Home tab's Font and Paragraph groups. In the next sections, when we point out that you can use the Home tab Font group to accomplish a function, it is likely that you can perform the same function with the mini-formatting toolbar by selecting text or right-clicking it. However, to reduce repetition, using the mini-formatting toolbar will not be stressed further in this chapter.

SELECT A FONT

A *font* is a set of characters that share a particular design, which is called a *typeface*. When you install Windows, and again when you install Office, a number of fonts are automatically installed on your computer. You can see the fonts on your computer by clicking the down arrow next to the font name in the Home tab Font group and then scrolling through the list (your most recently used fonts are at the top, followed by all fonts listed alphabetically). You can also see the list of fonts in the Font dialog box, where you can select a font in the Font list and see what it looks like in the Preview window at the bottom of the dialog box.

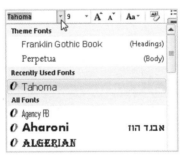

By default, the Calibri font is used for body text in all new documents using the default Normal template. To change this font:

1. Select the text to be formatted (see Chapter 2).

2. Click the **Home** tab, and click the **Font** down arrow in the Font group. Scroll through the list until you see the font you want, and then click that font.

APPLY BOLD OR ITALIC STYLE

Fonts come in four styles: regular (or "roman"), bold, italic, and bold-italic. The default is, of course, regular, yet fonts such as Arial Black and Eras Bold appear bold. To make fonts bold, italic, or bold-italic:

1. Select the text to be formatted (see Chapter 2).
2. Press **CTRL+B** to make it bold, and/or press **CTRL+I** to make it italic.

   –Or–

   Click **Bold** in the Home tab Font group, and/or click **Italic**.

CHANGE FONT SIZE

Font size is measured in *points*, which is the height of a character, not its width. For most fonts, the width varies with the character, the letter "i" taking less room than "w," for example. (The Courier New font is an exception, with all characters having the same width.) There are 72 points in an inch. The default font size is 11 points for body text, with standard headings varying from 11 to 14 points. For smaller print, 8-point type is common, and below 6 point is unreadable. To change the font size of your text:

1. Select the text to be formatted (see Chapter 2).
2. In the Home tab, click the **Font Size** down arrow in the Font group, scroll through the list until you see the font size you want, and then click that font.

   –Or–

   Press **CTRL+SHIFT+<** to decrease the font size, or press **CTRL+SHIFT+>** to increase the font size.

UNDERLINE TEXT

Several forms of underlining can be applied to your text.

1. Select the text to be formatted (see Chapter 2).
2. Click the **Underline** down arrow in the Home tab Font group, and click the type of underline you want.

   –Or–

   Press **CTRL+U** to apply a continuous underline under the entire selection.

TIP

The Underline Style drop-down list in the Font dialog box, as with the Underline button in the ribbon, contains underline choices beyond those the other methods provide—dotted, wavy, and so on.

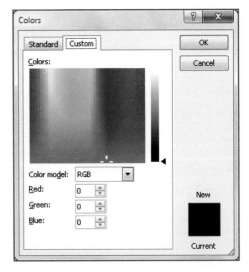

Figure 3-4: You can create any color you want in the Custom tab of the Colors dialog box.

–Or–

Press **CTRL+SHIFT+W** to apply an underline under each word in the selection.

–Or–

Press **CTRL+SHIFT+D** to apply a double underline under the entire selection.

USE FONT COLOR

To change the color of text:

1. Select the text to be formatted (see Chapter 2).

2. Click the **Home** tab, and click **Font Color** in the Font group to apply the current selected color (click the **Font Color** down arrow to select a color from a menu of theme colors).

   –Or–

   Click the **Font Dialog Box Launcher** for the Font dialog box. Click the **Font Color** down arrow, click the color you want, and click **OK**.

3. If, in selecting a color from either the Home tab Font group or the Font dialog box, you do not find the color you want within the 40-color palette, click **More Colors** to open the Colors dialog box. In the Standard tab, you can pick a color from a 145-color palette, or you can use the Custom tab to choose from an almost infinite range of colors by clicking in the color spectrum or by entering the RGB (Red, Green, and Blue) values, as you can see in Figure 3-4, or the HSL (Hue, Saturation, and Luminescent) values.

RESET TEXT

Figure 3-5 shows some of the formatting that has been discussed so far. All of those can be reset to the plain text, or the default formatting. To reset text to default settings:

1. Select the text to be formatted (see Chapter 2).

2. Click **Clear Formatting** 🔄 in the Home tab Font group.

   –Or–

   Press **CTRL+SPACEBAR**. (This will not reset a font size change if it is the only difference with the default.)

3

Word comes with a default set of formatting parameters for body text composed of Calibri, 11-point regular type, and black color. You can change this in the Font dialog box by clicking the **Font Dialog Box Launcher** in the Home tab. In the dialog box, select the font, style, size, and color you want; click **Set As Default**; click **OK** to set these for either this one document or for all documents. Then click **OK** to close the Font dialog box.

QUICKSTEPS

USING THE FONT DIALOG BOX

Although you can apply many effects, such as superscript, emboss, and small caps, using the Fonts group in the Home tab, you have an alternative way to make these changes. Here is how you can use the Font dialog box, shown in Figure 3-6, to change text effects.

1. Select the text you want to change the formatting for.

2. Click the **Home** tab, and click the **Font Dialog Box Launcher** in the Font group to open the Font dialog box. If it isn't already selected, click the **Font** tab.

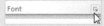

3. In the Effects area, click the options that you think you want to apply (some are mutually exclusive, such as Superscript and Subscript).

4. Check the results in the Preview area. When you are satisfied, click **OK**.

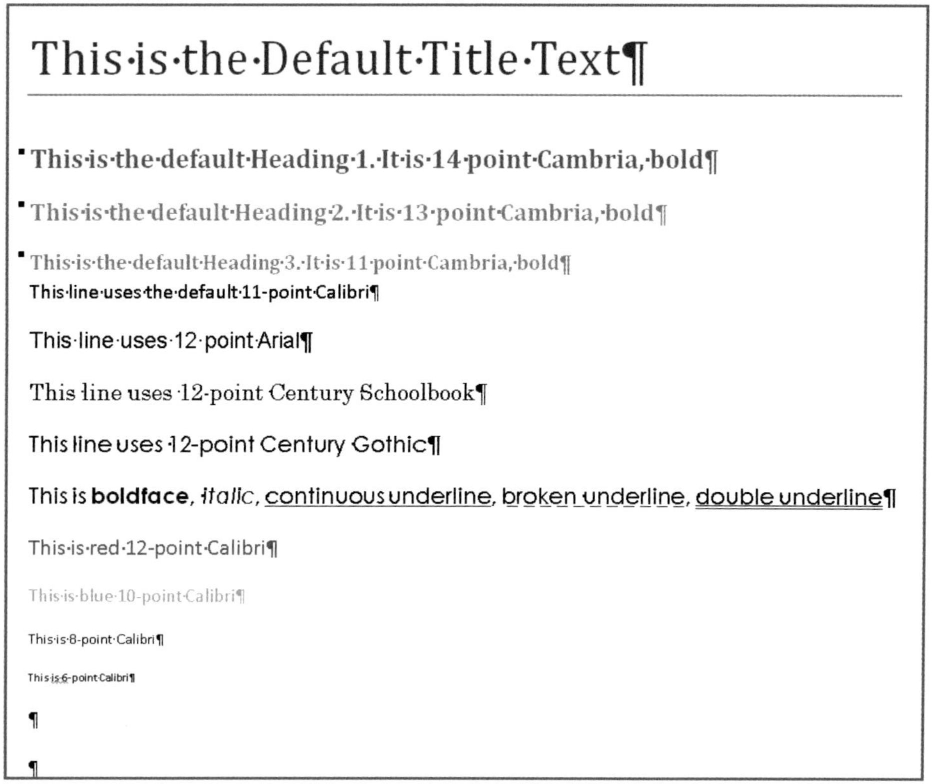

This·is·the·Default·Title·Text¶

This·is·the·default·Heading·1.·It·is·14·point·Cambria,·bold¶

This·is·the·default·Heading·2.·It·is·13·point·Cambria,·bold¶

This·is·the·default·Heading·3.·It·is·11·point·Cambria,·bold¶

This·line·uses·the·default·11-point·Calibri¶

This·line·uses·12·point·Arial¶

This line uses ·12-point Century Schoolbook¶

This line uses ·12-point Century Gothic¶

This is **boldface**, *italic*, <u>continuous underline</u>, <u>broken underline</u>, <u>double underline</u>¶

This·is·red·12-point·Calibri¶

This·is·blue·10-point·Calibri¶

This·is·8-point·Calibri¶

This·is·6-point·Calibri¶

¶

¶

Figure 3-5: Character formatting must be applied judiciously or it will detract from the appearance of a document.

Set Character Spacing

In this context, character spacing is the amount of space between characters on a single line. In the Advanced tab of the Font dialog box, Word gives you the chance to increase and decrease character spacing as well as scale the size of selected text, raise and lower vertically the position of text on the line, and

Figure 3-6: The Font dialog box is an alternative way to add text effects, such as strikethrough, shadow, and small caps.

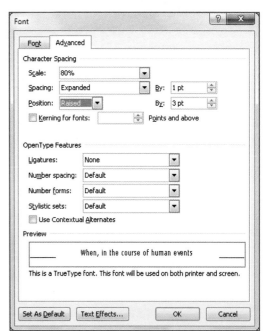

Figure 3-7: The spacing of text can have as much to do with its appearance as the choice of font.

determine when to apply kerning (how much the space for certain characters such as "A" and "V" can overlap). To apply character spacing:

1. Select the text to be formatted.

2. Click the **Home** tab, click the **Font Dialog Box Launcher** to open the Font dialog box, and click the **Advanced** tab. Under Character Spacing you have these options:

   - **Scale:** Select the percentage scale factor you want to apply. (This is not recommended. It is better to change the font size so as not to distort the font.)

   - **Spacing:** Select the change in spacing (Expanded or Condensed) that you want and the amount of that change.

   - **Position:** Select the change in position (Raised or Lowered) that you want and the amount of that change.

   - **Kerning For Fonts:** Determine if you want to apply kerning rules and the point size at which you want to do that.

3. Check the results in the Preview area, an example of which is shown in Figure 3-7. When you are satisfied, click **OK**.

NOTE

Character spacing, especially kerning, is predominantly used when you are creating something like a brochure, flyer, or newspaper ad in which you want to achieve a typeset look.

Change Capitalization

You can, of course, capitalize a character you are typing by pressing and holding SHIFT while you type. You can also press CAPS LOCK to have every letter that you type be capitalized, and then press CAPS LOCK again to turn off capitalization. You can also change the capitalization of existing text.

1. Select the text whose capitalization you want to change.

2. In the Home tab Font group, click **Change Case** Aa▾. Select one of these options:

   - Click **Sentence Case** to capitalize the first character of every selected sentence.
   - Click **Lowercase** to display all selected words in lowercase.
   - Click **UPPERCASE** to display all selected words in all caps. All characters of every selected word will be capitalized.
   - Click **Capitalize Each Word** to put a leading cap on each selected word.
   - Click **tOGGLE cASE** to change all lowercase words into uppercase and uppercase words into lowercase.

Create a Drop Cap

A *drop cap* is an enlarged capital letter at the beginning of a paragraph that extends down over two or more lines of text. To create a drop cap:

1. Select the character or word that you want to be formatted as a drop cap.

2. Click the **Insert** tab, and click **Drop Cap** in the Text group. A context menu will open. As you point to the various options, you'll see a preview of what the result will be if you choose that option. You have these choices:

   - Click **Dropped** to have the first letter dropped within the paragraph text.
   - Click **In Margin** to set the capital letter off in the margin.
   - Click **Drop Cap Options** to see further options. You can change the font, specify how many lines will be dropped (3 is the default), and specify how far from the text the dropped cap will be placed. Click **OK** to close the Drop Cap dialog box.

NOTE

To remove a drop cap, select the character or word, click **Drop Cap** in the Insert tab Text group, and click **None** from the context menu.

The paragraph will be reformatted around the enlarged capital letter. Here are the two options of putting the dropped cap in the paragraph or in the margin:

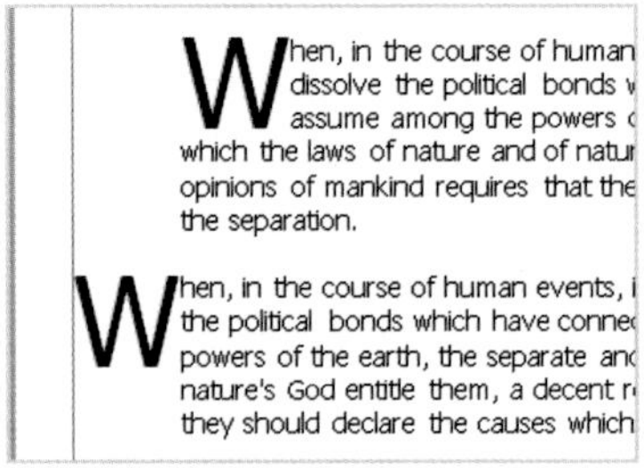

> **W**hen, in the course of human dissolve the political bonds v assume among the powers c which the laws of nature and of natu opinions of mankind requires that the the separation.
>
> **W**hen, in the course of human events, i the political bonds which have connec powers of the earth, the separate and nature's God entitle them, a decent r they should declare the causes which

Format a Paragraph

Paragraph formatting, which you can apply to any paragraph, is used to manage alignment, indentation, line spacing, bullets or numbering, and borders. In Word, a paragraph consists of a paragraph mark (created by pressing **ENTER**) and any text or objects that appear between that paragraph mark and the previous paragraph mark. A paragraph can be empty, or it can contain anything from a single character to as many characters as you care to enter.

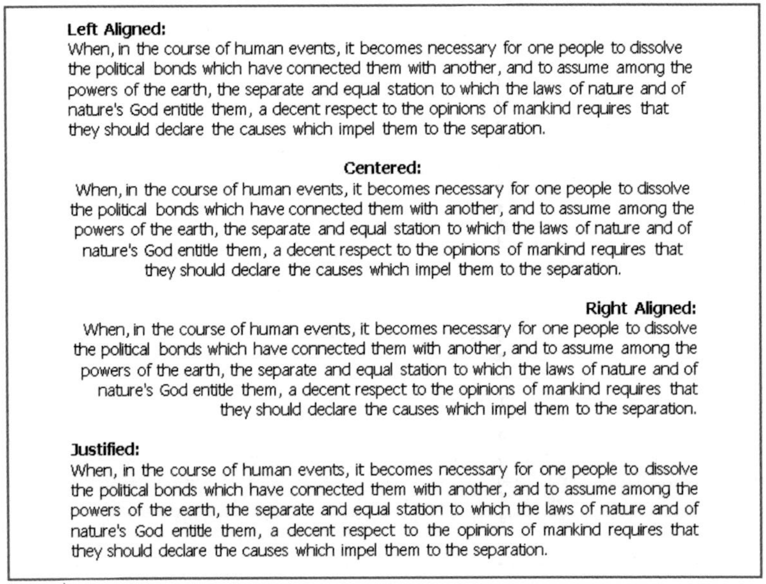

Set Paragraph Alignment

Four types of paragraph alignment are available in Word (see Figure 3-8): left-aligned, centered, right-aligned, and justified. Left-aligned, right-aligned, and centered are self-explanatory. Justified means that the text in a paragraph is spread out between the left and right page margins. Word does this by adding space between words, except for the last line of a paragraph. To apply paragraph alignment:

1. Click in the paragraph you want to align. (You don't need to select the entire paragraph.)

2. For left alignment, press **CTRL+L**; for right alignment, press **CTRL+R**; for centered, press **CTRL+E**; and for justified, press **CTRL+J**.

Left Aligned:
When, in the course of human events, it becomes necessary for one people to dissolve the political bonds which have connected them with another, and to assume among the powers of the earth, the separate and equal station to which the laws of nature and of nature's God entitle them, a decent respect to the opinions of mankind requires that they should declare the causes which impel them to the separation.

Centered:
When, in the course of human events, it becomes necessary for one people to dissolve the political bonds which have connected them with another, and to assume among the powers of the earth, the separate and equal station to which the laws of nature and of nature's God entitle them, a decent respect to the opinions of mankind requires that they should declare the causes which impel them to the separation.

Right Aligned:
When, in the course of human events, it becomes necessary for one people to dissolve the political bonds which have connected them with another, and to assume among the powers of the earth, the separate and equal station to which the laws of nature and of nature's God entitle them, a decent respect to the opinions of mankind requires that they should declare the causes which impel them to the separation.

Justified:
When, in the course of human events, it becomes necessary for one people to dissolve the political bonds which have connected them with another, and to assume among the powers of the earth, the separate and equal station to which the laws of nature and of nature's God entitle them, a decent respect to the opinions of mankind requires that they should declare the causes which impel them to the separation.

Figure 3-8: Paragraph alignment provides both visual appeal and separation of text.

TIP

You can also open the Paragraph dialog box by right-clicking the paragraph you want to format and clicking **Paragraph**.

QUICKFACTS

USING INDENTATION

A good question might be "why use indentation?" There are at least four good reasons:

● To organize and group pieces of text so they can be viewed as elements within a given topic. Bulleted and numbered lists fall into this category.

● To separate and call attention to a piece of text. An ordinary indented paragraph, either just on the left or on both the left and right, is done for this reason.

● To provide a hierarchical structure. An outline uses this form of indentation.

● To indicate the start of a new paragraph by indenting the first line of the paragraph.

Indentation is a powerful formatting tool when used correctly. Like other formatting, it can also be overused and make text hard to read or to understand. Ask yourself two questions about indentation:

● Do I have a good reason for it?

–And–

● Does it improve the readability and/or understanding of what is being said?

–Or–

In the Home tab Paragraph group, click **Align Left**, **Center**, **Align Right**, or **Justify**, respectively, depending on what you want to do.

–Or–

In the Home tab Paragraph group, click the **Paragraph Dialog Box Launcher** to open the Paragraph dialog box. In the Indents And Spacing tab, click the **Alignment** down arrow, click the type of alignment you want, and click **OK**.

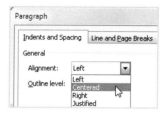

Indent a Paragraph

Indenting a paragraph in Word (see Figure 3-9) means to:

● Move either the left or right edge (or both) of the paragraph inward towards the center

● Move the left side of the first line of a paragraph inward toward the center

● Move the left side of the first line of a paragraph leftward, away from the center, for a *hanging indent*

> This normal paragraph uses the full width provided by the margins.
> When, in the course of human events, it becomes necessary for one people to dissolve the political bonds which have connected them with another, and to assume among the powers of the earth, the separate and equal station to which the laws of nature and of nature's God entitle them, a decent respect to the opinions of mankind requires that they should declare the causes which impel them to the separation.
>
> > This normal paragraph has been indented ½ inch on the left and right.
> > When, in the course of human events, it becomes necessary for one people to dissolve the political bonds which have connected them with another, and to assume among the powers of the earth, the separate and equal station to which the laws of nature and of nature's God entitle them, a decent respect to the opinions of mankind requires that they should declare the causes which impel them to the separation.
>
> This normal paragraph's first line is indented ½ inch on the left.
> When, in the course of human events, it becomes necessary for one people to dissolve the political bonds which have connected them with another, and to assume among the powers of the earth, the separate and equal station to which the laws of nature and of nature's God entitle them, a decent respect to the opinions of mankind requires that they should declare the causes which impel them to the separation.
>
> This normal paragraph is a hanging paragraph, outdented ½ inch on the left.
> When, in the course of human events, it becomes necessary for one people to dissolve the political bonds which have connected them with another, and to assume among the powers of the earth, the separate and equal station to which the laws of nature and of nature's God entitle them, a decent respect to the opinions of mankind requires that they should declare the causes which impel them to the separation.

Figure 3-9: Indenting allows you to separate a block of text visually.

CHANGE THE LEFT INDENT

To move the left edge of an entire paragraph to the right:

1. Click in the paragraph to select it.

2. In the Home tab Paragraph group, click **Increase Indent** [icon] one or more times to indent the left edge a half-inch each time.

   –Or–

   Press **CTRL+M** one or more times to indent the left edge a half-inch each time.

   –Or–

   In the Page Layout tab Paragraph group, click the **Left Indent** spinner.

   –Or–

   Open the Paragraph dialog box. In the Home tab Paragraph group, click the **Paragraph Dialog Box Launcher**. In the Indents And Spacing tab, under Indentation and opposite Left, click the spinner's increase arrow (up) until you get the amount of indentation you want, and then click **OK**.

Indentation	
Left:	0.1"
Right:	0"

REMOVE A LEFT INDENT

To move the left edge of an entire paragraph back to the left:

1. Click in the paragraph to select it.

2. In the Home tab, click **Decrease Indent** [icon] in the Paragraph group one or more times to un-indent the left edge a half-inch each time.

   –Or–

   Press **CTRL+SHIFT+M** one or more times to un-indent the left edge a half-inch each time.

   –Or–

   In the Home tab Paragraph group, click the **Paragraph Dialog Box Launcher** to open the Paragraph dialog box. In the Indents And Spacing tab, under Indentation and opposite Left, click the decrease arrow (down) until you get the amount of indentation you want, and then click **OK**.

CHANGE THE RIGHT INDENT

To move the right edge of an entire paragraph to the left:

1. Click in the paragraph to select it.

2. In the Page Layout tab Paragraph group, click the **Right Indent** spinner.

–Or–

Open the Paragraph dialog box. In the Home tab Paragraph group, click the **Paragraph Dialog Box Launcher**. In the Indents And Spacing tab, under Indentation and opposite Right, click the increase arrow (up) until you get the amount of indentation you want, and then click **OK**.

INDENT THE FIRST LINE

To move the right edge of an entire paragraph to the left:

1. Click in the paragraph to select it.

2. Open the Paragraph dialog box. In the Home tab Paragraph group, click the **Paragraph Dialog Box Launcher**. In the Indents And Spacing tab, under Indentation, click the **Special** down arrow, and click **First Line**. Click the **By** spinner to set the amount of indentation you want, and then click **OK**.

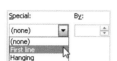

MAKE A HANGING INDENT

To indent all of a paragraph except the first line:

1. Click in the paragraph to select it.

2. Press **CTRL+T** one or more times to indent the left edge of all but the first line a half-inch each time.

   –Or–

   Open the Paragraph dialog box. In the Home tab Paragraph group, click the **Paragraph Dialog Box Launcher**. In the Indents And Spacing tab, under Indentation, click the **Special** down arrow, and select **Hanging**. Enter the amount of the indent, and click **OK**.

REMOVE A HANGING INDENT

To un-indent all but the first line of a paragraph:

1. Click in the paragraph to select it.

2. Press **CTRL+SHIFT+T** one or more times to un-indent the left edge of all but the first line a half-inch each time.

   –Or–

   Open the Paragraph dialog box. In the Home tab Paragraph group, click the **Paragraph Dialog Box Launcher**. In the Indents And Spacing tab, under Indentation, click the **Special** down arrow, and select **None**. Click **OK**.

TIP

You can reset all paragraph formatting, including indents and hanging indents, to their defaults by pressing **CTRL+Q**.

Determine Line and Paragraph Spacing

The vertical spacing of text is determined by the amount of space between lines, the amount of space added before and after a paragraph, and where you break lines and pages.

SET LINE SPACING

The amount of space between lines is most often set in terms of the line height, with *single-spacing* being one times the current line height, *double-spacing* being twice the current line height, and so on. You can also specify line spacing in points, as you do the size of type. Single-spacing is just under 14 points for 12-point type. To set line spacing for an entire paragraph:

1. Click in the paragraph you want to set the line spacing for.

2. In the Home tab Paragraph group, click the **Line And Paragraph Spacing** down arrow, and then click the line spacing, in terms of lines, that you want to use.

   –Or–

   Press **CTRL+1** for single-spacing, press **CTRL+5** for one and one-half line spacing, and press **CTRL+2** for double-spacing.

   –Or–

   In the Home tab Paragraph group, click the **Paragraph Dialog Box Launcher** to open the Paragraph dialog box. In the Indents And Spacing tab, under Spacing, click the **Line Spacing** down arrow, and select the line spacing you want to use, as shown in Figure 3-10. Click **OK**.

ADD SPACE BETWEEN PARAGRAPHS

In addition to specifying space between lines, you can add extra space at the beginning and end of paragraphs. Many people simply add an extra blank line between paragraphs, but it does not always look that good. If you are using single spacing, leaving a blank line will leave an extra 14 points (with 12-point type) between paragraphs. Common paragraph spacing is to leave 3 points before the paragraph and 6 points afterward, so if you have two of these paragraphs, one after the other, you would have a total of 9 points,

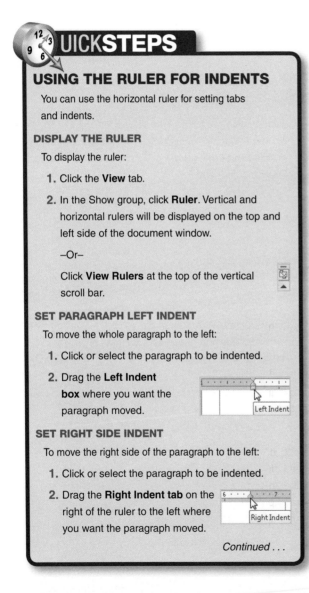

QUICKSTEPS

USING THE RULER FOR INDENTS

You can use the horizontal ruler for setting tabs and indents.

DISPLAY THE RULER

To display the ruler:

1. Click the **View** tab.

2. In the Show group, click **Ruler**. Vertical and horizontal rulers will be displayed on the top and left side of the document window.

   –Or–

   Click **View Rulers** at the top of the vertical scroll bar.

SET PARAGRAPH LEFT INDENT

To move the whole paragraph to the left:

1. Click or select the paragraph to be indented.

2. Drag the **Left Indent box** where you want the paragraph moved.

SET RIGHT SIDE INDENT

To move the right side of the paragraph to the left:

1. Click or select the paragraph to be indented.

2. Drag the **Right Indent tab** on the right of the ruler to the left where you want the paragraph moved.

Continued . . .

USING THE RULER FOR INDENTS

(Continued)

SET FIRST LINE INDENT OR HANGING INDENT

To set the first line to be either indented to the right or left of the rest of the paragraph, or to create a hanging indent:

Click or select the paragraph to be indented.

- To indent the first line, drag the top marker, the first line indent on the left of the ruler, to the right or left of where you want the first line moved.

Hanging indent ⊢◇⊣ **First line indent**

- To create a hanging indent, drag the lower marker, the hanging indent on the left of the ruler, to the right where you want the paragraph, except for the first line, to be moved.

To specify a specific amount of space between lines other than a number of lines, in the Paragraph dialog box, select **Exactly** from the Line Spacing menu and then enter or select the number of points to use between lines. With 12-point type, single spacing is about 14 points, one and one-half-line spacing (1.5) is about 21 points, and so on. With 11-point type, single spacing is about 12 points.

If you reduce the line spacing below the size of the type (below 12 points for 12 point type, for example), the lines will begin to overlap and become hard to read.

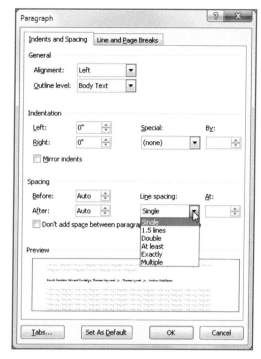

Figure 3-10: Line spacing is another way you can improve the readability of a document.

in comparison to the 14 points from an extra blank line. To add extra space between paragraphs:

1. Click in the paragraph you want to add space to.

2. In the Page Layout tab Paragraph group, click the **Spacing** spinners to set the spacing for before and after paragraphs.

   –Or–

   In the Home tab Paragraph group, click the **Paragraph Dialog Box Launcher** to open the Paragraph dialog box. In the Indents And Spacing tab, under Spacing, click the **Before** spinner or enter a number in points ("pt") for the space you want to add before the paragraph. If desired, do the same thing for the space after the paragraph. When you are ready, click **OK**.

TIP

If you format a paragraph the way you want a group of paragraphs to look, you can often just press **ENTER** to begin a new paragraph with the same formatting. See the discussion of styles in Chapter 4.

SET LINE AND PAGE BREAKS

The vertical spacing of a document is also affected by how lines and pages are broken and how much of a paragraph you force to stay together or be with text either before or after it.

You can break a line and start a new one in two ways, depending on whether you want to create a new paragraph:

- **Create a new paragraph** by moving the insertion point to where you want to break the line and pressing **ENTER**.
- **Stay in the same paragraph** by moving the insertion point to where you want to break the line and pressing **SHIFT+ENTER**. This retains the same formatting as the original paragraph. If you want to change formatting, you must create a new paragraph.
- **Break a page** and start a new one by pressing **CTRL+ENTER**.

  –Or–

  Click the **Insert** tab, and click **Page Break** in the Pages group.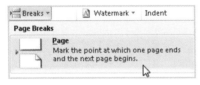

  –Or–

  Click the **Page Layout** tab, and click **Breaks** in the Page Setup group. Click **Page** from the menu.

HANDLE SPLIT PAGES

When a paragraph is split over two pages, you have several ways to control how much of the paragraph is placed on which page.

1. Click in the paragraph you want to change.
2. Click the **Home** tab, click the **Paragraph Dialog Box Launcher**, and click the **Line And Page Breaks** tab.
3. Click the following options that are correct for your situation, and then click **OK**:

   - **Widow/Orphan Control:** Adjusts the pagination to keep at least two lines on one or both pages. For example, if you have three lines, without Widow/Orphan Control, one line is on the first page and two on the second. When you turn on this control, all three lines will be placed on the second page. Widow/Orphan Control is on by default.
   - **Keep With Next:** Forces the entire paragraph to stay on the same page with the next paragraph. Keep With Next is used with paragraph headings that you want to keep with the paragraph.

● **Keep Lines Together:** Forces all lines of a paragraph to be on the same page. Keep Lines Together can be used for a paragraph title where you want all of it on one page.

● **Page Break Before:** Forces a page break before the start of the paragraph. Page Break Before is used with major section headings or titles that you want to start on a new page.

Use Numbered, Bulleted, and Multilevel Lists

Word provides the means to automatically number, add bullets, or create multilevel lists to paragraphs, formatting the paragraphs as hanging indents so the numbers or bullets stick out to the left (see Figure 3-11) or successive indenting for various levels of multilevel lists.

CREATE A NUMBERED LIST USING AUTOCORRECT

You can create a numbered list as you type. Word will automatically format it according to your text. Word's numbered lists are particularly handy because you can add or delete paragraphs in the middle of the list and have the list automatically renumber itself. To start a numbered list:

1. Press **ENTER** to start a new paragraph.

2. Type 1, either press the **SPACEBAR** twice or press **TAB**, and then type the rest of what you want in the first item of the numbered list.

3. Press **ENTER**. The number "2" automatically appears, and both the first and the new line are formatted as hanging indents. Also, the AutoCorrect lightning icon appears as you type the first line.

4. After typing the second item in your list, press **ENTER** once again. The number "3" automatically appears. Type the item and press **ENTER** to keep numbering the list.

5. When you are done, press **ENTER** twice. The numbering will stop, and the hanging indent will be removed.

If you click the AutoCorrect icon, you may choose to undo the automatic numbering that has already been applied, stop the automatic creation of numbered lists, and control the use of AutoCorrect (see Chapter 4 for more on AutoCorrect).

This is an example of a numbered list—in this case, numbered steps:

1. Select the text to be numbered.
2. Click the Home tab.
3. On the Paragraph group, click the Numbering button.

This is an example of a bulleted list which is used often to display:

● Items not related sequentially
● Alternative ways to do or perceive things
● Items or ideas grouped in some way

This is an example of a multilevel list, often used for organizing information:

1. Develop a plan for the party site
   a. Location
      i. Available parking
      ii. Cost for facility
      iii. Capacity for a large party
      iv. Available on the date needed
   b. Decorations
      i. Layout for the theme
      ii. Cost of both decorations and hired decorators
2. Plan for Food
   a. Type of food desired
   b. Caterers and costs

Figure 3-11: Numbered, bulleted, and multilevel lists help organize thoughts.

Figure 3-12: Clicking the Bullets, Numbering, or Multilevel List down arrows displays a list of formatting choices.

CREATE A NUMBERED, BULLETED, OR MULTILEVEL LIST BEFORE YOU TYPE TEXT

You can also create a numbered or bulleted list before you start typing the text they will contain.

Multilevel list

Bullets   Numbering

1. Press ENTER to start a new paragraph.

2. In the Home tab Paragraph group, click **Numbering** to begin a numbered list, click **Bullets** to start a bulleted list, or click **Multilevel List** to create a multilevel list.

3. Type the first item, and press ENTER to start the second numbered or bulleted item with the same style as the first item. When you are done with the list, press ENTER twice to stop the automatic list. With a multilevel list, click **Increase Indent** or **Decrease Indent** to start a new level.

   –Or–

   Click **Numbering**, **Bullets**, or **Multilevel List** in the Home tab Paragraph group to toggle off the list.

CUSTOMIZE BULLETED, NUMBERED, AND MULTILEVEL LISTS

You saw in Figure 3-12 that Word offers seven different types of bullets. Similarly, Word offers eight different styles for numbering paragraphs and creating multilevel lists. For those to whom these choices are not enough, there is a Define New option for bullets, numbering, and multilevel lists that allows you to create new possibilities. In the case of bullets, this includes the ability to select from hundreds of pictures and import others to use as bullets. To create custom bullets or numbering or multilevel lists:

1. In the Home tab Paragraph group, click the **Bullets** or **Numbering** down arrow to open the Bullets or the Numbering context menu.

2. For either bullets or numbering, you have these choices:

   - For bullets, click **Define New Bullet**, and the Define New Bullet dialog box appears (see Figure 3-13). Click **Font** and then select the font and other attributes in the dialog box for the character that you want to use; alternatively, click **Symbol** to select a symbol, or click **Picture** to choose from a number of picture bullets that are included in Office's clip art collection (see Figure 3-14). To use your own picture, click **Import** and select that picture. Click **OK** to close the Picture dialog box, select both the bullet and text position, click **OK** again, and use the new bullet.

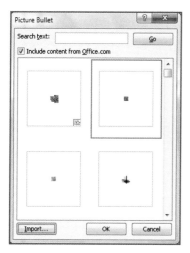

Figure 3-13: You can select any character in any font to use as a bullet.

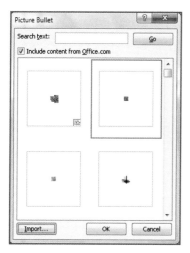

Figure 3-14: Word provides a number of pictures that can be used as bullets.

- For numbering, click **Define New Number Format**, and the dialog box appears (see Figure 3-15). Click the **Number Style** down arrow to choose the style (numbers, capital letters, lowercase letter, roman numerals, and so on), click **Font** to choose the numbers formatted with a particular font, and click **OK** to close the Font dialog box. Press TAB to select the number in the Number Format text box, and type a sample of the number you want (delete the period for a number without the period). Click the **Alignment** down arrow to choose between Right Alignment, Left, or Centered. Click **OK** to apply the customized numbering.

- For multilevel lists, click **Define New Multilevel List**, and a dialog box appears, as shown in Figure 3-16. Select a level to modify, and then change the Number Format, Number Style, or Position areas as needed. Click **More** to see more options, such as applying the changes to the whole list, this point forward, selected text, or to the whole document. You can select a level to show in gallery from the drop-down list. Click **OK** to apply your changes and close the dialog box.

Figure 3-15: Numbered paragraphs can use numbers, letters, or even uppercase or lowercase roman numerals.

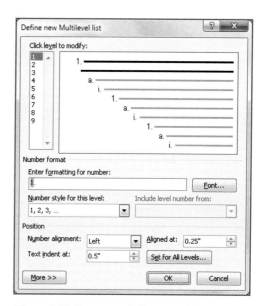

Figure 3-16: You can redefine any of the individual levels for multilevel lists, changing number formats, styles, position and alignment, and more.

TIP

You can switch a numbered list to a bulleted one or vice versa by selecting the list and clicking the other icon in the Home tab Paragraph group.

REMOVE NUMBERING AND BULLETING

To remove the numbering or bulleting formatting (both the numbers or bullets and the hanging indent):

1. Select the paragraphs from which you want to remove the numbering or bulleting.

2. In the Home tab Paragraph group, click **Numbering** or **Bullets**, as appropriate, to toggle the feature off.

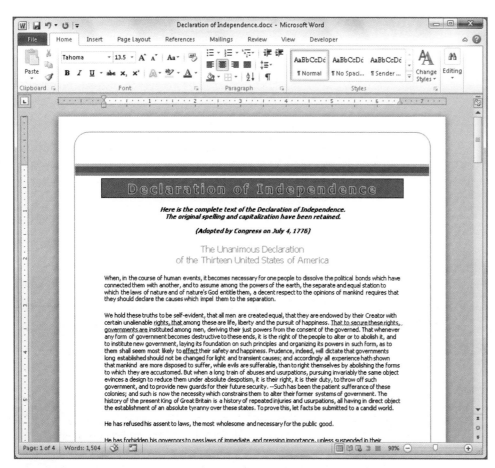

Figure 3-17: *Borders and shading can be applied to text, blank paragraphs, phrases, characters, and words.*

Add Borders and Shading

Borders and shading allow you to separate and call attention to text. You can place a border on any or all of the four sides of selected text, paragraphs, and pages; and you can add many varieties of shading to the space occupied by selected text, paragraphs, and pages—with or without a border around them (see Figure 3-17). You can create horizontal lines as you type, and you can add other borders from both the Formatting toolbar and the Borders and Shading dialog box.

CREATE HORIZONTAL LINES AS YOU TYPE

Horizontal lines can be added as their own paragraph as you type.

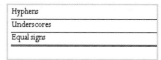

Hyphens
Underscores
Equal signs

1. Press **ENTER** to create a new paragraph.

2. Type - - - (three hyphens) and press **ENTER**. A single, light horizontal line will be created between the left and right margins.

–Or–

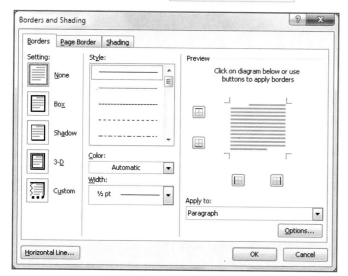

Figure 3-18: *Borders can be created with many different types and widths of lines.*

Type === (three equal signs) and press **ENTER**. A double horizontal line will be created between the left and right margins.

–Or–

Type ___ (three underscores) and press **ENTER**. A single, heavy horizontal line will be created between the left and right margins.

ADD BORDERS AND SHADING TO TEXT

Borders and shading can be added to any amount of text, from a character to pages.

1. Select the text for which you want to have a border or shading.

2. In the Home tab, click the **Borders** down arrow in the Paragraph group, and then select the type of border you want to apply. If you have selected less than a paragraph, you can only select a four-sided box (you actually can select less than this, but you will get a full box).

–Or–

In the Home tab, click **Borders** in the Paragraph group, and click **Borders And Shading** on the context menu. The Borders And Shading dialog box will appear, as shown in Figure 3-18.

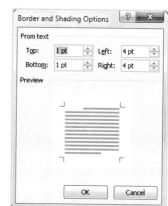

- To add text or paragraph borders, click the **Borders** tab, click the type of box (Custom for fewer than four sides), the line style, color, and width you want. If you want fewer than four sides and are working with paragraphs, click the sides you want in the Preview area. Click **Options** to set the distance the border is away from the text.

- To add page borders, click the **Page Border** tab, click the type of box (Custom for less than four sides), the line style, color, width you want, and any art you want to use for the border. If you want fewer than four sides, click the sides you want in the Preview area. Click **Options** to set the distance the border is away from either the edge of the page or the text. (Figure 3-17 contains a page border.)

- To add shading, click the **Shading tab**, click the color of shading, or fill, you want. If desired, select a pattern (this is independent of the fill), and choose whether to apply it to the entire page, paragraph, or just to the selected text. To add a graphic horizontal line, click **Horizontal Line** on the bottom of the dialog box, click the line you want, and click **OK**.

When you are done with the Borders And Shading dialog box, click **OK**.

1 2 3 4 5 6 7 8 9 10

UICKSTEPS

TURNING ON FORMATTING MARKS

To make formatting and what is causing the spacing in a document easier to see, you can display some of the formatting marks. In the Home tab Paragraph group, click the **Show/Hide Formatting Marks** ¶ to show all of the formatting marks—paragraph marks ¶, line breaks ↵, tabs, and spaces, among other characters—as you can see in Figure 3-19.

You can fine-tune exactly which formatting marks to display by clicking the **File** tab, clicking **Options**, and clicking the **Display** option. Under Always Show These Formatting Marks On The Screen, you can choose which marks to display.

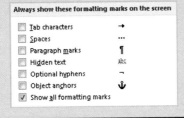

Always show these formatting marks on the screen	
☐ Tab characters	→
☐ Spaces	...
☐ Paragraph marks	¶
☐ Hidden text	ab̶c̶
☐ Optional hyphens	¬
☐ Object anchors	⚓
☑ Show all formatting marks	

Figure 3-19: *Turning on formatting marks helps you see what is making your document look the way it does.*

Format a Page

Page formatting has to do with overall formatting items, such as margins, orientation, size, and vertical alignment of a page. You can set options for page formatting either from the Page Layout tab or in a dialog box.

Set Margins

Margins are the space between the edge of the paper and the text. To set margins:

1. Open the document whose margins you want to set. If you want the margins to apply only to a selected part of a document, select that part now.

2. Click the **Page Layout** tab, and click **Margins** in the Page Setup group. A menu will open, as shown in Figure 3-20. If you have set custom margins previously, they will be displayed in the menu.

3. Click the option you want.

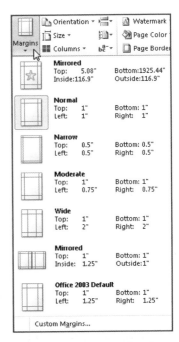

Figure 3-20: *You can select from a group of "canned" margins, according to the needs of your document, or create a custom margin.*

CAUTION

Remember that page formatting changes the margins and other formatting for whole pages. If you select a part of the document to have special formatting, it will separate that section by pages. To change formatting for smaller sections of text, use indenting.

COPYING FORMATTING

Often, you'll want a word, phrase, or paragraph formatted like an existing word, phrase, or paragraph. Word allows you to copy just the formatting.

USE THE FORMAT PAINTER

1. Drag across the word, phrase, or paragraph whose formatting you want to copy. In the case of a paragraph, make sure you have included the paragraph mark (see the "Turning On Formatting Marks" QuickSteps).

2. In the Home tab Clipboard group, click the **Format Painter** ✨.

3. With the special pointer (brush and I-beam) ▲I , drag across the word, phrase, or paragraph (including the paragraph mark) you want formatted.

COPY FORMATTING WITH THE KEYBOARD

1. Select the word, phrase, or paragraph whose formatting you want to copy.

2. Press **CTRL+SHIFT+C** to copy the formatting.

3. Select the word, phrase, or paragraph (including the paragraph mark) you want formatted.

4. Press **CTRL+SHIFT+V** to paste the format.

COPY FORMATTING TO SEVERAL PLACES

If you want to copy formatting to several separate pieces of text or paragraphs:

1. Drag across the text with formatting to be copied.

2. In the Home tab Clipboard group, double-click the **Format Painter**.

3. Drag across each piece of text or paragraph that you want to format.

4. When you are done, click the **Format Painter** again, or press **ESC**.

Use a Dialog Box to Format a Page

You can do much of the page formatting using the Page Layout dialog box.

1. In the Page Layout tab, click the **Page Setup Dialog Box Launcher**. The Page Setup dialog box appears, as shown in Figure 3-21.

2. Click the **Margins** tab. You have these options:

   - Under Margins, click the spinners or manually enter the desired distance in inches between the particular edge of the paper and the start or end of text.

   - Under Orientation, click either **Portrait** (tall page) or **Landscape** (wide page), depending on which you want. (See the upcoming section "Determine Page Orientation.")

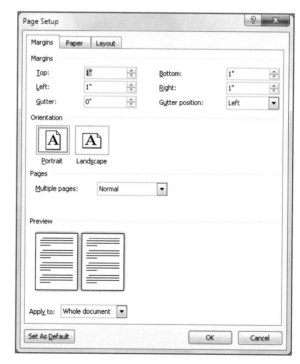

Figure 3-21: Many page formatting tasks can be done on the Page Setup dialog box.

- Under Pages, click the **Multiple Page** down arrow, and select an option: Click **Mirror Margins** when the inside gutter is larger to handle binding, **2 Pages Per Sheet** when a normal sheet of paper is divided into two pages, and **Book Fold** when you are putting together a section of a book ("a signature") with four, eight, or more pages in the signature.

- If you want these changes to apply only to the selected part of a document, under Preview Apply To, click **This Point Forward**.

3. When you are done setting margins, click **OK**.

Use Mirror Margins

Mirror margins allow you to have a larger "inside" margin, which would be the right margin on the left page and the left margin on the right page, or any other combination of margins that are mirrored between the left and right pages. To create mirror margins:

1. Open the document whose margins you want mirrored.

2. Click the **Page Layout** tab, and click **Margins** in the Page Setup group.

3. You'll notice that there are two "Mirrored" choices—one for a single page and another for multiple pages. Next to the double-page thumbnail, click **Mirrored**. When you do that, the left and right margins change to inside and outside.

Determine Page Orientation

Page orientation specifies whether a page is taller than it is wide, called "portrait," or wider than it is tall, called "landscape." For 8½-inch ×11-inch letter size paper, if the 11-inch side is vertical (the left and right edges), which is the standard way of reading a letter, then it is portrait. If the 11-inch side is horizontal (the top and bottom edges), then it is landscape. Portrait is the default orientation in Word. To change it:

1. Open the document whose orientation you want to set. If you want the orientation to apply only to a selected part of a document, select that part now.

2. In the Page Layout tab, click **Orientation** in the Page Setup group.

3. On the menu, click the option you want.

TRACKING INCONSISTENT FORMATTING

When you turned on the formatting marks (see the "Turning On Formatting Marks" QuickSteps earlier in this chapter), you might have felt a bit disappointed that they didn't tell you more. You can direct Word to track inconsistencies in your formatting as you type.

1. Click the **File** tab, and click **Options**.

2. Click **Advanced** on the left pane.

3. Under Editing Options, click both **Keep Track Of Formatting** and **Mark Formatting Inconsistencies**.

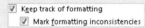

Specify Paper Size

Specifying the paper size gives you the starting perimeter of the area within which you can set margins and enter text or pictures.

1. In the Page Layout tab, click the **Size** down arrow in the Page Setup group. A menu will open, shown in Figure 3-22.

2. Click the size of paper you want.

Set Vertical Alignment

Just as you can right-align, center, left-align, and justify text between margins, as described in "Set Paragraph Alignment," you can also specify vertical alignment so text is aligned at the top, bottom, or center of the page, or justified between the top and bottom.

1. In the Page Layout tab, click the **Page Setup Dialog Box Launcher**. The Page Setup dialog box appears.

2. In the Layout tab, under Page, click the **Vertical Alignment** down arrow, and click the vertical alignment that you want to use.

3. Click **OK** when you are done.

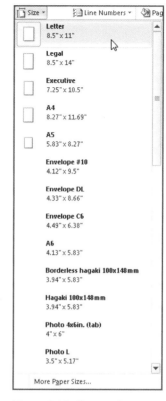

Figure 3-22: Choose the paper size from a selection of popular sizes in the Page Layout tab.

Chapter 4
Customizing a Document

Microsoft Word 2010 provides a number of tools that combine text creation, layout, and formatting features that you can use to customize your documents. Two of the most common tools used at a broad level are styles and templates. Word also provides several other features, such as AutoFormat and AutoText, which help make document creation and formatting easier.

This chapter discusses creating documents through the use of styles and templates; formatting your documents using tabs, headers and footers, and outlines; and inserting front and end matter, such as tables of contents and indexes. The chapter also discusses Word's writing aids, such as AutoText, hyphenation, an equation builder, and the thesaurus.

Use Styles

Word 2010 provides a gallery of Quick Styles that gives you with sets of canned formatting choices, such as font, boldface, and color, that you can apply to headings, titles, text, and lists. You use Quick Styles by identifying what kind of formatting a selected segment of text needs, such as for a header or title. Then you select the style of formatting you want to apply to the document. You can easily apply Quick Styles, change them, and create new ones.

Work with Styles

Styles are applied to segments of text, such as headers or lists. Word comes with preset styles which you can apply to your document. You can modify these styles and save them as custom styles to be used again in similar documents.

IDENTIFY TEXT WITH A STYLE

To identify a segment of text within your document with a consistent style, such as for a heading, you apply a Quick Style from the gallery.

1. Select the text to be formatted, for example, a title or heading.

2. Click the **Home** tab, and click the **Styles More** down arrow in the Styles group. The Quick Styles gallery is displayed, as shown in Figure 4-1.

3. Point at the thumbnails to see the effects of each style on your text, and then click the thumbnail of the style you want to apply.

APPLY STYLE SETS TO A DOCUMENT

Before you begin entering text, or after you have identified the components in your document, you can apply a consistent set of colors, styles, and fonts to your document using the Change Styles function. (See the "Understanding

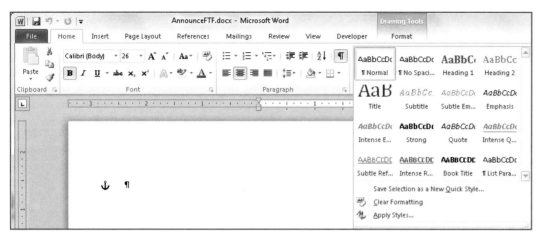

Figure 4-1: *The Quick Styles gallery shows you canned options for formatting headings, text, and paragraphs.*

Themes, Styles, and Templates" QuickFacts to see how styles differ from themes.)

1. Open the document that you want to contain a style set. It can be either a blank document or one that has already had the components identified, such as title, headings, and lists.

2. Click the **Home** tab, click **Change Styles** in the Styles group, and click **Style Set**. A menu is displayed.

3. Point to the various styles until you find one you want. As you point, the document will display the style. Then click the style you want. The document will be changed. However, if you have components that you do not identify with a particular Quick Style—if you miss a heading, for instance—it will not receive the specific formatting for that component.

SAVE A NEW QUICK STYLE

To create a new Quick Style option that will appear in the Quick Styles gallery:

1. Format the text you want to use for setting the style using the mini-formatting toolbar or the commands in the Home tab Font group.

2. Right-click the selected text, click **Styles**, and click **Save Selection As A New Quick Style**. The Create New Style From Formatting dialog box appears.

3. Type the name you want for the style, and click **OK**. It will appear in the Quick Styles gallery.

TIP

If you do not find the style you want in the Quick Styles gallery for a segment of text, either click **Apply Styles** from the Quick Styles More menu or press **CTRL+SHIFT+S** to display the Apply Styles dialog box. Click the **Style Name** down arrow to find the style you want.

QUICKSTEPS

DELETING A STYLE

You might choose to delete a style that you created for a one-time-use document and don't ever plan to use again. You can delete a style from the gallery or from the document being used.

DELETE/RESTORE A STYLE FROM THE GALLERY

To delete a style just from the gallery:

1. In the Home tab Styles group, click **Quick Styles** or the **Styles More** down arrow to display the Quick Styles gallery.

2. Right-click the style you want to delete, and click **Remove From Quick Style Gallery**.

The style will be removed from the Quick Styles gallery. However, this does not mean that the style is gone; it is still in the list of styles.

To restore the style to the gallery:

1. In the Home tab Styles group, click the **Styles Dialog Box Launcher**. The Styles task pane is displayed.

2. Right-click the style that you want to restore, and click **Add To Quick Style Gallery**.

Continued . . .

MODIFY A STYLE

1. In the Home tab Styles group, click either **Quick Styles** or the **Styles More** down arrow. (If the window is narrow enough, the gallery of style thumbnails becomes a Quick Styles button, and you click the button in place of the More down arrow.) The Quick Styles gallery is displayed.

2. Right-click the style to be changed, and click **Modify** on the context menu. The Modify Style dialog box appears, as shown in Figure 4-2.

–Or–

Following the instructions in the earlier "Apply Style Sets to a Document" section, display the Apply Styles dialog box. Click the **Style Name** down arrow, and click the name of the style you wish to change. Click Modify, and the Modify Style dialog box appears.

Figure 4-2: You can change a style by modifying it in the Modify Style dialog box.

3. Change any formatting options you want.

4. To display more options, click **Format** in the lower-left area, and then click the attribute—for example, **Font** or **Numbering**—that you want to modify. Click **OK**.

5. Repeat step 4 for any additional attributes you want to change, clicking **OK** each time you are finished.

6. Type a new name for the style, if desired, unless you want to change existing formatted text.

7. Click **OK** to close the Modify Styles dialog box.

Use Themes

One way that you can make a document look professional is by using themes. Themes combine coordinated colors, fonts (for body text and headings), and design effects (such as special effect uses for lines and fill effects) to produce a unique look. You can use the same themes with PowerPoint and Excel as well, thereby standardizing a look. All documents have themes; one is assigned to a new document by default.

ASSIGN A THEME TO YOUR DOCUMENT

To apply a theme to a document:

1. Click the **Page Layout** tab. Click **Themes** in the Themes group to display a gallery of themes, as seen in Figure 4-3.

2. Click the theme you want, and it will be applied to the current document.

CHANGE A THEME

Themes can be changed to fit your own document requirements. You can change a theme by altering the fonts, color, and design effects. You must have the components of a document, such as a heading or list text, defined with a style before you'll see the effects.

CHANGE THE COLOR OF A THEME

Each theme consists of a set of four colors for text and background, six colors for accents, and two colors for hyperlinks. You can change any single color element

Figure 4-3: Use themes to standardize your documents with other Office products, such as PowerPoint and Excel.

or all of them. When you change the colors, the font styles and design elements remain the same.

1. With your document open, click the **Page Layout** tab.

2. Click **Theme Colors**. The menu of color combinations will be displayed, as seen in Figure 4-4. Any revised or custom themes that you have created are listed at the top.

3. Point at the rows of color combinations to see which ones appeal to you. You'll see the color change reflected in your open document.

4. When you find the color combination you want, click it.

CHANGE THEME FONTS

Each theme includes two fonts: the *body* font is used for general text entry, and a *heading* font is used for headings. The default fonts used in Word for a new, plain document are Calibri for body text and Cambria for headings. After you have assigned a theme to a document, the fonts may be different, and they can be changed.

In the Page Layout tab Themes group, click **Theme Fonts**. The drop-down list displays various theme fonts. The current theme font combination is highlighted in its place in the list.

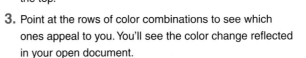

Figure 4-4: The menu of color combinations offers alternatives for your theme colors.

Point to each font combination to see how the fonts will appear in your document.

Click the font name combination you decide upon. When you click a font name combination, the fonts will replace both the body and heading fonts in your document on one or selected pages.

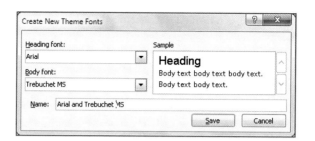

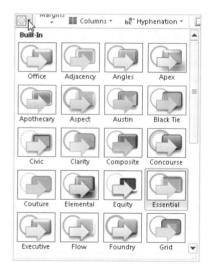

Figure 4-5: You can choose a heading or body font from the fonts available in your Office program.

CREATE A NEW THEME FONT SET

You may also decide that you want a unique set of fonts for your document. You can create a custom font set that is available in the list of fonts for your current and future documents.

1. In the Page Layout tab Themes group, click **Theme Fonts**.

2. Click Create **New Theme Fonts** at the bottom of the drop-down list.

3. In the Create New Theme Fonts dialog box (see Figure 4-5), click either or both the **Heading Font** and **Body Font** down arrows to select a new font combination. View the new combination in the Sample area.

4. Type a new name for the font combination you've selected, and click **Save**. Custom fonts are available for selection at the top of the Theme Fonts drop-down list.

CHANGE THEMED GRAPHIC EFFECTS

Shapes, illustrations, and SmartArt include graphic effects that are controlled by themes. Themed graphics are modulated in terms of their lines (borders), fills, and effects (such as shadowed, raised, and shaded). For example, some themes simply change an inserted rectangle's fill color, while other themes affect the color, the weight of the border, and whether it has a 3-D appearance.

1. In the Page Layout tab Themes group, click **Theme Effects**. The drop-down list displays a gallery of effects combinations. The current effects combination is highlighted.

2. Point to each combination to see how the effects will appear in your document, assuming you have a shape or SmartArt graphic inserted on the document page.

3. Click the effects combination you want.

CREATE A CUSTOM THEME

You can create a new theme, save it, and use it in your documents. For a document, you change colors, fonts, and styles, and then give them a new theme name.

1. To change theme colors, in the Page Layout tab Themes group, click **Theme Colors**.

2. At the bottom of the menu of colors, click the **Create New Theme Colors** link. The Create New Theme Colors dialog box appears, as shown in Figure 4-6.

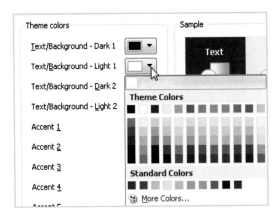

3. To select a color for one of the color groups, click the text/background/accent/hyperlink group, and click the color you want to test. It will be displayed in the Sample area.

4. Go through each set of colors that you want to change.

5. When you find a group of colors that you like, type a name in the Name text box, and click **Save**.

6. In the Page Layout tab Themes group, click **Theme Fonts** and select the font combination you want. Save them.

7. In the Page Layout tab Themes group, click **Theme Effects** and select the effects you want for any SmartArt or shapes you have.

8. When your theme is as you want it, in the Page Layout tab Themes group, click **Save Current Theme**.

9. Give it a unique name, and click **Save**. It will appear in the Themes menu under Custom.

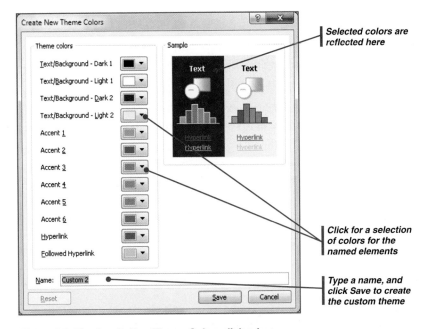

Selected colors are reflected here

Click for a selection of colors for the named elements

Type a name, and click Save to create the custom theme

Figure 4-6: The Create New Theme Colors dialog box allows you to create a new theme to use with multiple documents.

Use Templates

A *template* is a collection of styles, associated formatting and design features, and colors used to determine the overall appearance of a document, A Word 2010 template file has an extension of .docx. Templates are always attached to documents, as you saw in Chapter 2.

Create and Change Templates

Word 2010 comes with several templates that you can use to create letters, faxes, memos, and more. In addition, as you saw earlier, the Microsoft Office website has online templates that you can make use of. You can also create your own templates.

CHANGE THE DEFAULT NORMAL TEMPLATE

The *Normal* template is the default template used by Word unless you tell it otherwise. It, like all templates, includes

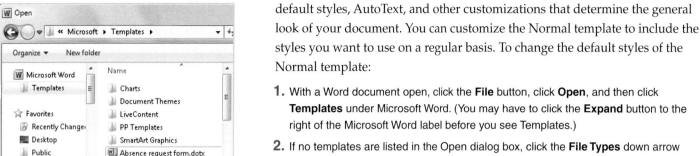

default styles, AutoText, and other customizations that determine the general look of your document. You can customize the Normal template to include the styles you want to use on a regular basis. To change the default styles of the Normal template:

1. With a Word document open, click the **File** button, click **Open**, and then click **Templates** under Microsoft Word. (You may have to click the **Expand** button to the right of the Microsoft Word label before you see Templates.)

2. If no templates are listed in the Open dialog box, click the **File Types** down arrow (immediately above the Open/Cancel buttons), and click **All Files (*.*)**. If you still do not see Normal.dotm (indicating a macro-enabled template), click in the **Search** text box in the upper-right area of the window, type <u>normal.dotm</u> in the Search field, and press **ENTER**. The search will begin as you type.

3. Double-click **Normal.dotm** to open it. Ensure that you're working in the template by verifying that "Normal.dotm" appears in the Word title bar.

4. Change the template by changing the styles using the steps described in "Modify a Style" earlier in this chapter.

5. When you are finished making the changes that you want, click the **File** button, and click **Save** to resave Normal.dotm.

CREATE A TEMPLATE

1. With Word open, click the **File** button, and click **New**. The New Document dialog box appears, as shown in Figure 4-7.

2. Under Available Templates, click **Blank Document** to display a blank document template.

3. Click **Create**. A new document opens.

4. Save the document with a unique name and the .dotm template file type.

APPLY A TEMPLATE TO A NEW DOCUMENT

1. Click the **File** button, and click **New** to open the New Document task pane.

2. Under Available Templates and Office.com Templates, review the list of templates that are installed on your computer and available online.

3. Click the template you want to use, and click **Create**.

4. Save the document with a unique name, using the Word Document (.docx) file type.

TIP

To restore the original colors in the Sample area in the Create New Theme Colors dialog box and start over, click **Reset**.

NOTE

You may find that you want to change something in a custom theme after you've been using it for a while. To edit a custom theme, click the **Theme Colors** button in the Page Layout tab Themes group, and right-click the custom theme you want to edit. From the context menu, click **Edit**. The Edit Theme Colors dialog box, similar to that shown in Figure 4-6, will appear.

CAUTION

Keep in mind that any changes you make to the Normal template will be applied to any future documents you create, unless you specifically apply a different template.

NOTE

If the Normal.dotm template is renamed, damaged, or moved, Word automatically creates a new version (with the original default settings) the next time you start it. The new version will not include any changes or modifications you made to the version that you renamed or moved.

NOTE

You can also create a new template based on a previously created document by saving it as a .dotm template file. Any content will be included in the template along with the theme, styles, headers or footers, etc.

TIP

If you want to create a template based on a different type of document—for example, a webpage or an e-mail message—select the relevant template instead of the Blank Document template in the Available Templates or Office.com lists.

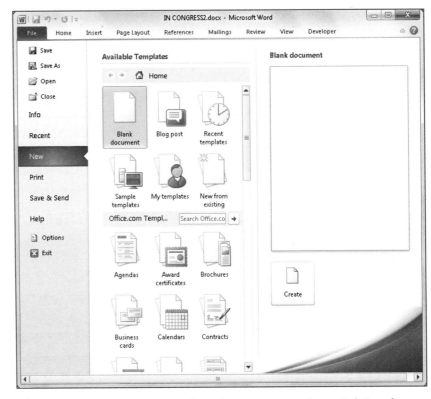

Figure 4-7: *Word comes with several templates you can use to create letters, faxes, and more.*

APPLY A TEMPLATE TO AN EXISTING DOCUMENT

1. If the Developer tab is not showing, click the **File** tab and click **Options** to open the Word Options dialog box. Click **Customize Ribbon**, and then under Customize The Ribbon, in the Main Tabs selection, click the **Developer** check mark to select it. Click **OK**. The Developer tab should now be showing.

2. Click the **Developer** tab, and in the Templates group, click **Document Template**. The Templates And Add-ins dialog box will appear.

3. Click **Attach** to open the Attach Template dialog box.

4. Browse for the template you want, either in the default Microsoft Word Template folder or in one of your own. When you find it, click it to select it, click **Open** to close the Attach Template dialog box, and click **OK** to close the Templates And Add-ins dialog box.

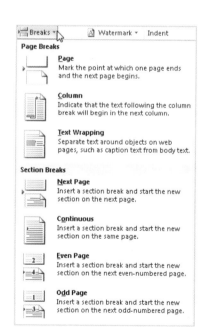

Work with Documents

In addition to using styles and templates to format your documents, you can use section breaks, columns, tabs, headers and footers, tables of contents, and indexes to further refine your documents.

Create Section Breaks

A *section break* indicates the end of a section in a document. You can use section breaks to vary the layout of a document within a page or between pages. For example, you might choose to format the introduction of a magazine article in a single column and format the body of the article in two columns. You must separately format each section, but the section break allows them to be different. Section breaks allow you to change the number of columns, page headers and footers, page numbering, page borders, page margins, and other characteristics and formatting within a section.

INSERT A SECTION BREAK

1. Open the document and click where you want to insert a section break.
2. Click the **Page Layout** tab, and click **Breaks** in the Page Setup group. The Breaks context menu appears.
3. To create a new section, in the Section Breaks area, select what comes after the break. You have the following options:
   - Click **Next Page** to begin a new section on the next page.
   - Click **Continuous** to begin a new section on the same page.
   - Click **Even Page** to start the new section on the next even-numbered page.
   - Click **Odd Page** to start the new section on the next odd-numbered page.
4. When you click the option you want, the section break is inserted. If the Show/Hide Formatting feature is turned on (in the Home tab Paragraph group), you'll be able to see the section breaks in the text.

¶ ·· Section Break (Continuous) ··

DELETE A SECTION BREAK

When a section break is inserted on a page, you will see a note to that effect if the Show/Hide Formatting feature is turned on. You can delete the break by selecting that note.

1. Click the section break that you want to delete.

2. Press **DELETE**.

Create and Use Columns

You can format your documents in a single column or in two or more columns, like text found in newspapers or magazines. You must first create either a continuous or a page break, not a column break, before you create the columns in order to prevent columns from forming in the previous section. To create columns in a document:

1. Place the insertion point at the place where you want the columns to begin. On the Page Layout tab, click **Breaks** in the Page Setup group, and click **Continuous**.

2. Click the **Page Layout** tab, and click **Columns** in the Page Setup group to display a context menu.

3. Click the thumbnail option that corresponds to the number or type of columns you want.

   –Or–

   If you do not see what you want, click **More Columns** to display the Columns dialog box (see Figure 4-8).

   ● Click an icon in the Presets area, or type a number in the Number Of Columns box to set the number of columns you want.

   ● Use the options in the Width And Spacing area to manually determine the dimensions of your columns and the amount of space between columns. To do this, you will have to clear the **Equal Column Width** check box. (You may have to click a thumbnail option to make it available first.)

   ● Click the **Line Between** check box if you want Word to insert a vertical line between columns.

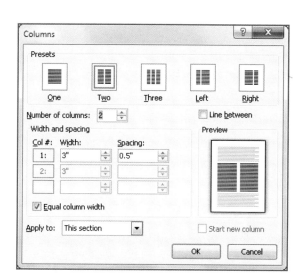

Figure 4-8: Use the Columns dialog box to create and format columns in your documents.

TIP

To see tabs, the ruler needs to appear on the screen. If you do not see the ruler, click the **View** tab, and click **Ruler** in the Show/Hide group.

- Use the **Apply To** list box to select the part of the document to which you want your selections to apply: Whole Document, This Section, or This Point Forward. Click **This Point Forward**, and then click the **Start New Column** check box if you want to insert a column break at an insertion point.

4. Click **OK** when finished.

Use Tabs

A *tab* is a type of formatting used to align text and create simple tables. By default, Word 2010 has *tab stops* (the horizontal positioning of the insertion point when you press **TAB**) every half-inch. Tabs are better than space characters in such instances because tabs are set to specific measurements, while spaces may not always align the way you intend due to the size and spacing of individual characters in a given font. Word 2010 supports seven kinds of tabs:

- **Left tab** left-aligns text at the tab stop.
- **Center tab** centers text at the tab stop.
- **Right tab** right-aligns text at the tab stop.
- **Decimal tab** aligns the decimal point of tabbed numbers at the tab stop.
- **Bar tab** left-aligns text with a vertical line that is displayed at the tab stop.
- **First line indent** aligns text so that the first line only is indented.
- **Hanging indent** aligns text so that only the first line "hangs" out to the left of the rest of the paragraph.

To align text with a tab, press the **TAB** key before the text you want aligned.

SET TABS USING THE RULER

To set tabs using the ruler at the top of a page, you first must select the tab and then select the location.

1. Select the text, from one line to an entire document, in which you want to set one or more tab stops.

2. Click the **Left Tab** icon ⌊, located at the far left of the horizontal ruler, until it changes to the type of tab you want: Left Tab, Center Tab ⊥, Right Tab ⌋, Decimal Tab ⊥, Bar Tab ⌶, First Line Indent ▽, or Hanging Indent ⌂.

3. Click the horizontal ruler where you want to set a tab stop.

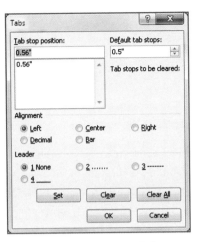

Figure 4-9: *From the Tabs dialog box, you can format specific tab measurements and set tab leaders.*

4. Once you have the tabs set:
   - Drag a tab off the ruler to get rid of it.
   - Drag a tab (the icon) to another spot on the ruler to change its position.

SET TABS USING MEASUREMENTS

To set tabs according to specific measurements:

1. Double-click a tab, and the Tabs dialog box will appear, as shown in Figure 4-9.
2. Enter the measurements you want in the Tab Stop Position text box. Click **Set**.
3. Click the tab alignment option you want.
4. Repeat steps 2 and 3 for as many tabs as you want to set. Click **OK** to close the dialog box.

SET TABS WITH LEADERS

You can also set tabs with *tab leaders*—characters that fill the space otherwise left by a tab—for example, a solid, dotted, or dashed line.

1. Double-click any tab, and the Tabs dialog box appears, as shown in Figure 4-9.
2. In the Tab Stop Position text box, type the position for a new tab or select an existing tab stop to which you want to add a tab leader.
3. In the Alignment area, select the alignment for text typed at the tab stop.
4. In the Leader area, select the leader option you want, and then click **Set**.
5. Repeat steps 2–4 for additional tabs. When you are done, click **OK** to close the dialog box.

Add Headers and Footers

Headers and footers are parts of a document that contain information such as page numbers, revision dates, the document title, and so on. The header appears at the top of every page, and the footer appears at the bottom of every page.

CREATE A HEADER OR FOOTER

When you open the header or footer area, a special context menu appears. Figure 4-10 shows the buttons available on the Header & Footer Tools Design tab.

1. Open the document to which you want to add a header or footer (see Chapter 2).
2. Click the **Insert** tab, and click **Header** or **Footer** in the Header & Footer group. A menu of styles will be displayed. Select a style if you want. The header or footer area will be displayed along with the special contextual Header & Footer Design tab.

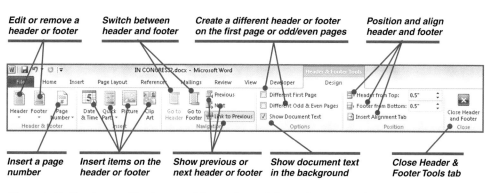

Edit or remove a header or footer

Switch between header and footer

Create a different header or footer on the first page or odd/even pages

Position and align header and footer

Insert a page number

Insert items on the header or footer

Show previous or next header or footer

Show document text in the background

Close Header & Footer Tools tab

Figure 4-10: *Headers and footers provide consistent information across the tops and bottoms of your document pages. These areas can also have unique tabs and other formatting.*

–Or–

Double-click in the top area of the document where a header would be, if it is visible. Or, first double-click the page break line, and then double-click the header or footer area. (If the page break and header area are hidden, you can't use the double-click method.)

3. Type the text you want displayed in the header.

- To switch between typing text in the header and typing it in the footer, click the **Go To Header** or **Go To Footer** button in the Navigation group, and type the text you want.

- Click **Date And Time** in the Insert group to insert a date or time.

- To insert a page number, click **Page Number** in the Header & Footer group, click a location in the drop-down menu, scroll down, choose a format, and then click **OK**. (If you find your page number is wiping out the content of the header, make sure the style of the header or footer includes a placeholder for a page number.)

- To enter a date that is left-aligned, a title that is centered, and a page number that is right-aligned, you can click **Blank (Three Columns)** from the Header menu. Click in the first placeholder, and type the date or click **Date & Time** in the Insert group and select the format you want. Click in the second placeholder and type the title. Click in the third place holder and click **Page Number** in the Header & Footer group. Finally, click **Current Position**, and click the style you want.

When you edit a header or footer, Word automatically changes the same header or footer throughout the document, unless the document contains different headers or footers in different sections. When you delete a header or footer, Word automatically deletes the same header or footer throughout the entire document. To delete a header or footer for part of a document, you must first divide the document into sections, and then create a different header or footer for part of a document. (See "Create Section Breaks," earlier in this chapter, for more information.)

TIP

There are styles available in the Header & Footer style menus for odd and even pages. These simplify the steps to create different odd/even page headers or footers. You simply click a style and fill in the text.

QUICKSTEPS

USING DIFFERENT LEFT AND RIGHT HEADERS

Different left and right pages use section breaks to allow different margins and tabs. Sometimes, you might want to create a document that has different left and right headers and/or footers. For example, you might have a brochure, pamphlet, or manuscript in which all odd-numbered pages have a title in the header and all even-numbered pages have the author's name or other information.

To create different left and right headers and/or footers:

1. Open the document to which you want to add a different left and right header or footer.

Continued...

- To go to the next or last header or footer to enter a different header or footer, click **Previous** or **Next** in the Navigation group.

4. When finished, double-click in the document area or click the **Close Header And Footer** button.

EDIT A HEADER OR FOOTER

1. Open the document to which you want to add a header or footer.

2. Double-click the header or footer area, if it is visible. Or, first double-click the page break line, and then double-click the header or footer area to display the header and footer along with the Header & Footer Tools Design tab, as shown in Figure 4-10.

3. If necessary, click the **Previous** or **Next** button in the Navigation group to display the header or footer you want to edit.

4. Edit the header or footer. For example, you might revise text, change the font, apply bold formatting, or add a date or time. You can also click **Header** and select a style.

5. When finished, double-click in the document area or click **Close Header And Footer** in the Close group.

DELETE A HEADER OR FOOTER

1. Open the document from which you want to delete a header or footer.

2. Double-click the header or footer area of the document, if it is visible. Or, first double-click the page break line, and then double-click the header or footer area. The header or footer area will be displayed along with the Header & Footer Tools Design tab.

3. If necessary, click **Previous** or **Next** in the Navigation group to move to the header or footer you want to delete.

4. Select the text or graphics you want to delete, and press **DELETE**.

   –Or–

   Click **Header** or **Footer** in the Header & Footer group, and click **Remove Header** or **Remove Footer** from the bottom of the menu.

Add Footnotes and Endnotes

Footnotes and *endnotes* are types of annotations in a document used to provide citation information or to provide additional information for readers. The difference between the two is where they appear in a document. Footnotes appear either after the last line of text on the page or at the bottom of the page

USING DIFFERENT LEFT AND RIGHT HEADERS *(Continued)*

2. Double-click in the header area, if it is visible. Or, first double-click the page break line, and then double-click the header or footer area; or click the **Insert** tab, click **Header**, and click **Edit Header** at the bottom of the menu. The header area will be displayed, along with the special contextual Header & Footer Design tab.

3. In the Options group, click the **Different First Page** check box to enter a separate title or no title for the first page. Create a different first page in the First Page Header area, create the normal header in the Header area of the second page, and so on.

4. Click the **Different Odd & Even Pages** check box to have a different heading on the odd- and even-numbered pages. For instance, perhaps your page number is on the left for even-numbered pages and on the right for odd-numbered pages. Create the header or footer for odd-numbered pages in the Odd Page Header or Odd Page Footer area, and create the header or footer for even-numbered pages in the Even Page Header or Even Page Footer area.

5. When finished, double-click in the document area or click the **Close Header And Footer** button in the Close group.

---

on which the annotated text appears. Endnotes appear either at the end of the section in which the annotated text appears or at the end of the document.

INSERT A FOOTNOTE OR ENDNOTE

1. To display the Print Layout view, click the **View** tab, and then click **Print Layout** in the Document View group.

2. In the Print Layout view, position the insertion point immediately after the text you want to annotate.

3. Click the **References** tab, and then click **Insert Footnote** or **Insert Endnote** in the Footnotes group. For a footnote, the insertion point will be positioned at the bottom of the page; for an endnote, it will be positioned at the end of the document.

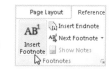

4. Type the text of the endnote or footnote.

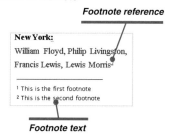

Footnote reference

Footnote text

5. To return to the text where the footnote reference was placed, right-click the footnote and click **Go To Footnote** or **Go To Endnote**.

CHANGE FOOTNOTES OR ENDNOTES

If you want to change the numbers or formatting of footnotes or endnotes, or if you want to add a symbol to the reference, use the Footnote And Endnote dialog box.

1. On the References tab, click the **Footnote & Endnote Dialog Box Launcher** in the Footnotes group. The Footnote And Endnote dialog box appears (see Figure 4-11).

2. You have these options:

- In the Location box, click the **Footnotes** or **Endnotes** option, and click the down arrow to the right to choose where the footnote or endnote will be placed.

- Click the **Number Format** down arrow, and select the type of numbering you want from the drop-down list.

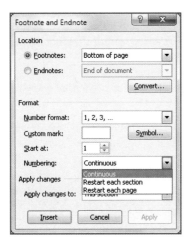

Figure 4-11: Footnotes and endnotes provide supplemental information to the body of your document. Use the dialog box to control location and formatting.

TIP

Sometimes, it is easier to see a footnote or endnote than the text in the document to which it refers. To quickly find the text in the document that a footnote or endnote refers to, right-click the footnote or endnote, and click **Go To Footnote** or **Go To Endnote**. The pointer will be positioned at that location in the text.

NOTE

When deleting an endnote or footnote, make sure to delete the number corresponding to the annotation and not the actual text in the note. If you delete the text but not the number, the placeholder for the annotation will remain.

- To select a custom mark (a character that uniquely identifies a footnote or endnote), click the **Symbol** button, and select and insert the symbol you want. It will be displayed in the Custom Mark text box. You can also just type a character into the text box.
- Click the **Numbering** down arrow, and choose how the numbering is to start.
- Click the **Apply Changes To** down arrow to select the part of the document that will contain the changes.

3. Click **Insert**. Word makes the changes as noted.

4. Type the note text.

5. When finished, return the insertion point to the body of your document, and continue typing.

DELETE A FOOTNOTE OR ENDNOTE

In the document, select the number of the note you want to delete, and then press **DELETE**. Word automatically deletes the footnote or endnote and renumbers the notes.

CONVERT FOOTNOTES TO ENDNOTES OR ENDNOTES TO FOOTNOTES

- Right-click a note and select **Convert To Footnote/Endnote**.

  –Or–

1. Select the reference number or symbol in the body of a document for the footnote or endnote.

2. Click the **References** tab, and click the **Footnotes Dialog Box Launcher**. The Footnote And Endnote dialog box appears.

3. Click **Convert**. The Convert Notes dialog box appears.

4. Select the option you want, and then click **OK**.

5. Click **Close**.

Create an Index

An *index* is an alphabetical list of words or phrases in a document and the corresponding page references. Indexes created using Word can include main entries and subentries as well as cross-references. When creating an index in Word, you first need to tag the index entries and then generate the index. If you

If you want an index entry to use text that you separately enter instead of using existing text in the document, place the insertion point in the document where you want your new index entry to reference.

Figure 4-12: *You need to tag index entries before you can generate an index.*

If you want to create a title for the Index page, you'll need to enter it manually. Also, if you want the index to appear on its own page, insert a page break at the end of the document before generating the index.

find that the index needs to be modified, delete the current one, make changes in the text or dialog boxes, and regenerate the index.

TAG INDEX ENTRIES

1. In the document in which you want to build an index, select the word or phrase that you want to use as an index entry.

2. Click the **References** tab, and click **Mark Entry** in the Index group (you can also press **ALT+SHIFT+X**). The Mark Index Entry dialog box appears (see Figure 4-12).

3. Type or edit the text in the Main Entry box. Customize the entry by creating a subentry or by creating a cross-reference to another entry, if desired.

4. Click the **Bold** or **Italic** check box in the Page Number Format area to determine how the page numbers will appear in the index.

5. Click **Mark**. To mark all occurrences of this text in the document, click **Mark All**.

6. Repeat steps 3–5 to mark additional index entries on the same page.

7. Click **Close** to close the dialog box when finished.

8. Repeat steps 1–7 for the remaining entries in the document.

GENERATE AN INDEX

1. Position the insertion point where you want to insert the finished index (this will normally be at the end of the document).

2. Click the **References** tab, and click **Insert Index** in the Index group. The Index dialog box appears (see Figure 4-13).

3. In the Index tab of the Index dialog box, set the formatting for the index. You have these options:

   - Click the **Type** option to indent subentries beneath the main entries, or click **Run-In** to print subentries in a string immediately following the main entries.
   - Click the **Columns** spinner to set the number of columns in the index page.
   - Click the **Language** down arrow to set the language for the index.
   - Click **Right Align Page Numbers** to right-align the numbers.
   - Click **Tab Leader** to print a leader between the entry and the page number.
   - Click the **Formats** down arrow to use an available design template, such as Classic or Fancy.

4. Click **OK** when finished. Word generates the index.

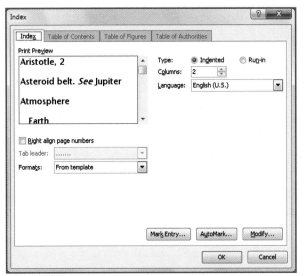

Figure 4-13: Use the options and settings in the Index dialog box to determine how your index will look.

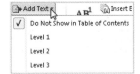

Create a Table of Contents

A *table of contents* is a list of the headings in the order in which they appear in the document. If you have formatted paragraphs with heading styles, you can automatically generate a table of contents based on those headings. If you have not used the heading styles, then, as with indexes, you must first tag table of contents (or TOC) entries and then generate the table of contents. (See "Use Styles," earlier in this chapter.)

TAG ENTRIES FOR THE TABLE OF CONTENTS

Use the Quick Styles gallery to identify a segment of text within your document so that it can contain a consistent style for headings and other text that you want contained in a table of contents.

1. Select the text to be formatted, for example, a title or heading.
2. Click the **Home** tab, and click the **Styles More** down arrow in the Styles group.
3. Point at each thumbnail to determine which style it represents, and then click the thumbnail of the style you want to apply.

PLACE OTHER TEXT IN A TABLE OF CONTENTS

To add text other than identified headings in a table of contents:

1. Highlight the text or phrase to be shown in the table of contents.
2. Click the References tab, and click **Add Text** in the Table Of Contents group. A menu is displayed.
3. Click the option you want. You have these choices:
   - **Do Not Show In Table Of Contents** removes the identification that something should be included in the TOC.
   - **Level 1**, **Level 2**, or **Level 3** assigns selected text to a level similar to Heading 1, Heading 2, or Heading 3.

USE THE OUTLINING TAB FOR THE TABLE OF CONTENTS

The Outlining tab contains an easy way to tag or identify entries for the table of contents.

1. Click the **View** tab, and click **Outline** in the Document Views group. An Outlining tab will become available. Figure 4-14 shows the Outlining tab and explains their functions.
2. Click the right or left arrows to promote or demote the levels, respectively.

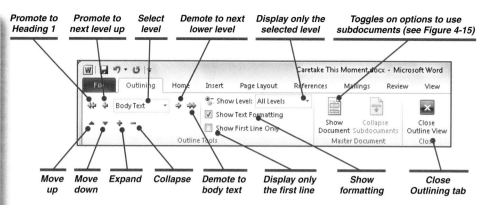

Figure 4-14: Use the Outlining tab to mark entries for a table of contents. The Outlining toolbar provides a number of ways to work with outlines.

WORK WITH SUBDOCUMENTS

Within the Outlining tab, you can insert and manipulate subdocuments.

1. Click the **View** tab, and click **Outline** in the Document Views group. The Outlining tab will become available.

2. In the Master Document group, click **Show Document**. The commands to work with subdocuments will be expanded. Figure 4-15 explains how the commands are used.

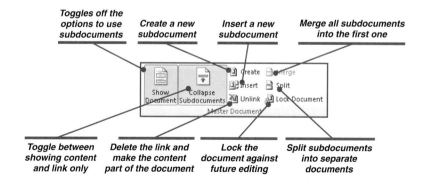

Figure 4-15: The subdocument commands appear when Show Documents on the Outlining tab is clicked. These commands allow subdocuments to be inserted and manipulated.

TIP

It is a good idea to place a table of contents in its own section, where you can have separate formatting, margins, and page numbers. If you want to do this, create the section before creating the TOC. See "Create Section Breaks," earlier in this chapter.

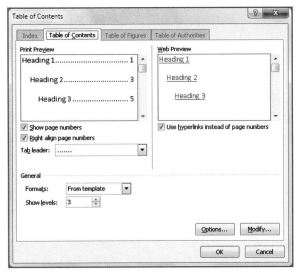

Figure 4-16: Use the options and settings in the Table Of Contents dialog box to determine how your table of contents will look.

GENERATE A TABLE OF CONTENTS

1. Place the insertion point where you want to insert the table of contents (normally at the beginning of the document).

2. Click the **References** tab, and click **Table Of Contents** in the Table Of Contents group. A menu is displayed showing various styles for the table of contents plus commands at the bottom of the menu. If you want a table of contents generated automatically, click a style. The table of contents will be displayed where your pointer is positioned. If you want to control aspects of the table of contents, do not select a style; continue with step 3.

3. On the bottom of the menu, click **Insert Table Of Contents**. The Table Of Contents dialog box, shown in Figure 4-16, appears.

4. The Print Preview and Web Preview features show how the TOC will appear based on the options selected. You have these options:

   - Clear the **Show Page Numbers** check box to suppress the display of page numbers.

   - Clear the **Right Align Page Numbers** check box to allow page numbers to follow the text immediately.

   - Clear the **Use Hyperlinks Instead Of Page Numbers** check box to use page numbers in place of hyperlinks.

   - Click the **Tab Leader** down arrow, and click (**None**) or another option for a leader between the text in the TOC and the page number.

   - Click the **Formats** down arrow to use one of the available designs.

   - Click the **Show Levels** down arrow, and click the highest level of heading you want to display in the TOC.

5. Click **OK** when finished.

Create and Use Outlines

An *outline* is a framework upon which a document is based. It is a hierarchical list of the headings in a document. You might use an outline to help you organize your ideas and thoughts when writing a speech, a term paper, a book, or a research project. The Outline tab in Word makes it easy to build and refine your outlines.

1. Open a new blank document (see Chapter 1). Click the **View** tab, and click **Outline** in the Document Views group. Word switches to the Outlining tab, displayed earlier in Figures 4-14 and 4-15.

USING VIEW BUTTONS

Word 2010 contains five views that you can use to display your document in different ways, as you can see in Figures 4-17 and 4-18.

- **Print Layout** is the default view in Word and shows text as you will see it when the document is printed.

- **Full Screen Reading** displays the document as a "book" with facing pages. You can "flip" through the pages rather than scroll through them. It uses the full screen in order to display as much of the document as possible. On the top is a restricted toolbar with limited options for using the document.

- **Web Layout** displays a document in a larger font size and wraps to fit the window rather than the page margins.

- **Outline** displays the document's framework as it has been laid out with headers identified, etc.

- **Draft** suppresses headings and footers and other design elements in order to display the text in draft form so that you can have an unobstructed view of the contents.

To display any of these views, click the **View** tab, and click the view you want in the Document Views group (Figure 4-17); or click the relevant button on the View toolbar on the right of the status bar (Figure 4-18).

Figure 4-17: Click the View tab, and in the Documents Views group, click the view you want.

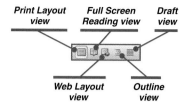

Figure 4-18: You can immediately switch to another view using the Views toolbar on the status bar.

2. Type your heading text, and press **ENTER**. Word formats the headings using the built-in heading style, Heading 1. Continue throughout the document. You have these ways of working with the levels:

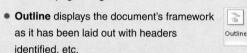

- Assign a heading to a different level by selecting it from the Outline Level drop-down list box.

  –Or–

  Place the insertion point in the heading, and then click the **Promote** or **Demote** button on the Outlining toolbar until the heading is at the level you want.

- To move a heading to a different location, place the insertion point in the heading, and then click the **Move Up** or **Move Down** button ▲ ▼ on the Outlining tab Outline Tools group until the heading is where you want it. (If a heading is collapsed, the subordinate text under the heading moves with it.)

3. When you're satisfied with the organization, click **Close Outline View**, which automatically switches to Print Layout view. (See the QuickSteps "Using View Buttons" for more information.)

Use Word Writing Aids

Word 2010 provides several aids that can assist you in not only creating your document, but also in making sure that it is as professional-looking as possible. These include AutoCorrect, AutoFormat, AutoText, AutoSummarize, an extensive equation-writing capability, character and word counts, highlighting, hyphenation, and a thesaurus.

Figure 4-19: Use the AutoCorrect tab to determine what items Word will automatically correct for you as you type.

Use AutoCorrect and AutoFormat

The AutoCorrect feature automatically corrects common typographical errors when you make them. Although Word 2010 comes preconfigured with hundreds of AutoCorrect entries, you can also manually add entries.

CONFIGURE AUTOCORRECT

1. Click the **File** tab, click **Options**, click **Proofing** in the left column, and click **AutoCorrect Options**. The AutoCorrect: *Language* dialog box appears.

2. Click the **AutoCorrect** tab (if it is not already displayed), and select from the following options, according to your preferences (see Figure 4-19):

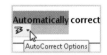

- **Show AutoCorrect Options Buttons** displays a small blue button or bar beneath text that was automatically corrected. Click this button to see a menu, where you can undo the correction or set AutoCorrect options.

- **Correct TWo INitial CApitals** changes the second letter in a pair of capital letters to lowercase.

- **Capitalize First Letter Of Sentences** capitalizes the first letter following the end of a sentence.

- **Capitalize First Letter Of Table Cells** capitalizes the first letter of a word in a table cell.

- **Capitalize Names Of Days** capitalizes the names of the days of the week.

- **Correct Accidental Usage Of cAPS LOCK Key** corrects capitalization errors that occur when you type with the **CAPS LOCK** key depressed and turns off this key.

- **Replace Text As You Type** replaces typographical errors with the correct words as shown in the list beneath it.

- **Automatically Use Suggestions From The Spelling Checker** tells Word to replace spelling errors with words from the dictionary as you type.

3. Click **OK** when finished.

ADD OR DELETE AN AUTOCORRECT ENTRY

1. Click the **File** tab, click **Options**, click **Proofing** in the left column, and click **AutoCorrect Options**. The AutoCorrect: *Language* dialog box appears.

2. Click the **AutoCorrect** tab (if it is not already displayed).

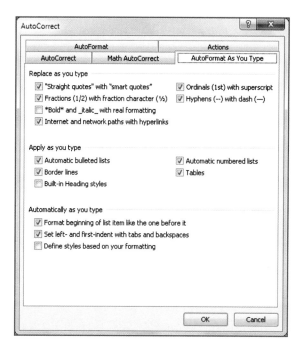

Figure 4-20: Use the AutoFormat As You Type tab to determine what items Word will automatically format for you as you type.

- To add an entry, type the text that you want Word to automatically replace in the Replace box. Type the text that you want to replace it with in the With box. Click **Add**.

- To delete an entry, scroll through the list of AutoCorrect entries, and click the entry you want to delete. Click **Delete**.

3. Click **OK**.

USE AUTOFORMAT

AutoFormat automatically formats a document as you type it by applying the associated styles to text, depending on how it is used in the document. For example, Word will automatically format two dashes (--) into an em dash (—) or will automatically format Internet and e-mail addresses as hyperlinks.

To choose the formatting you want Word to apply as you type:

1. Click the **File** tab, click **Options**, click **Proofing** in the left column, and click **AutoCorrect Options**. The AutoCorrect: *Language* dialog box appears. Click the **AutoFormat As You Type** tab.

2. Select from among the following options, depending on your preferences (see Figure 4-20):

   - **"Straight Quotes" With "Smart Quotes"**   Replaces plain quotation characters with curly quotation characters

   - **Ordinals (1st) With Superscript**   Formats ordinal numbers (numbers designating items in an ordered sequence) with a superscript—for example, 1st becomes 1st

   - **Fractions (1/2) With Fraction Character (½)**   Replaces fractions typed with numbers and slashes with fraction characters

   - **Hyphens (--) With Dash (—)**   Replaces a single hyphen with an en dash (–) and two hyphens with an em dash (—)

   - ***Bold* And _Italic_ With Real Formatting**   Formats text enclosed within asterisks (*) as bold and text enclosed within underscores (_) as italic

   - **Internet And Network Paths With Hyperlinks**   Formats e-mail addresses and URLs (Uniform Resource Locator—the address of a webpage on the Internet or an intranet) as clickable hyperlink fields

   - **Automatic Bulleted Lists**   Applies bulleted list formatting to paragraphs beginning with *, o, or – followed by a space or tab character

   - **Automatic Numbered Lists**   Applies numbered list formatting to paragraphs beginning with a number or letter followed by a space or a tab character

- **Border Lines**   Automatically applies paragraph border styles when you type three or more hyphens, underscores, or equal signs (=)

- **Tables**   Creates a table when you type a series of hyphens with plus signs to indicate column edges

- **Built-In Heading Styles**   Applies heading styles to heading text

- **Format Beginning Of List Item Like The One Before It**   Repeats character formatting that you apply to the beginning of a list item. For example, if you format the first word of a list item in bold, the first word of all subsequent list items are formatted in bold.

- **Set Left- And First-Indent With Tabs And Backspaces**   Sets left indentation on the tab ruler based on the tabs and backspaces you type

- **Define Styles Based On Your Formatting**   Automatically creates or modifies styles based on manual formatting that you apply to your document

3. Click **OK** when finished.

Use Building Blocks

Building blocks are blocks of text and formatting that you can use repeatedly, such as cover pages, a greeting, phrases, headings, or a closing. Word provides a number of these for you, but you can identify and save your own building blocks and then use them in different documents.

CREATE A BUILDING BLOCK

1. Select the text or graphic, along with its formatting, that you want to store as a building block. (Include the paragraph mark in the selection if you want to store paragraph formatting.)

2. Click the **Insert** tab, click **Quick Parts** in the Text group, and then click **Save Selection To Quick Parts Gallery**.

3. The Create New Building Block dialog box appears. Accept the suggested name for the building block, or type a short abbreviation for a new one. For example, I changed this one to "qs" for QuickSteps.

4. In most cases, you will accept the Quick Parts gallery, the General category, and the Building Blocks.dotx file name, since those provide for the easiest retrieval.

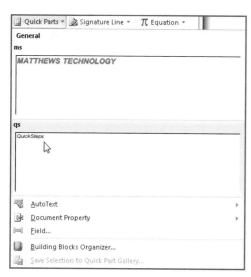

5. Click the **Options** down arrow, and, depending on what you are saving in your building block, click the option that is correct for you. If you want paragraph formatting, you must include the paragraph mark.

6. Click **OK**.

INSERT ONE OF YOUR BUILDING BLOCKS

1. Place the insertion point in the document where you want to insert the building block.

2. Click the **Insert** tab, click **Quick Parts** in the Text group, and then double-click the entry you want, as shown in Figure 4-21.

INSERT ONE OF WORD'S BUILDING BLOCKS

1. Place the insertion point in the document where you want to insert the building block.

2. Click the **Insert** tab, click **Quick Parts** in the Text group, and then click **Building Blocks Organizer**. The Building Blocks Organizer dialog box appears, as shown in Figure 4-22.

Figure 4-21: The Quick Parts feature provides direct access to your building block entries so that you can insert them in documents.

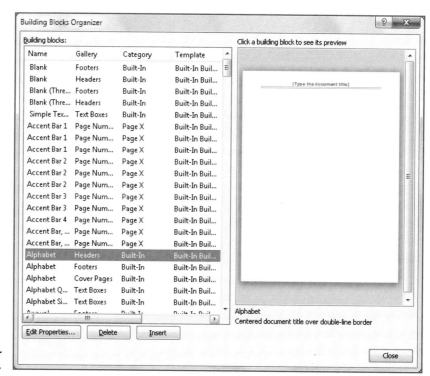

Figure 4-22: Word comes with a large number of building blocks that you can access.

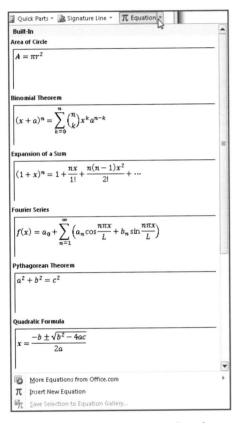

Figure 4-23: Word provides a number of ready-made equations for your use.

3. Scroll through the list of building blocks until you find the one that you want. Click the entry to see it previewed on the right. When you are ready, click **Insert**.

DELETE A BUILDING BLOCK

1. Click the **Insert** tab, click **Quick Parts** in the Text group, and then click **Building Blocks Organizer**. The Building Blocks Organizer dialog box appears.

2. Scroll through the list of building blocks until you find the one that you want. Click the entry to see it previewed on the right. When you are ready, click **Delete**, click **Yes** to confirm the deletion, and click **Close**.

Enter an Equation

If you include mathematical equations in the documents you produce, Word has several helpful tools for producing them. These include ready-made equations, commonly used mathematical structures, a large standard symbol set, and many special mathematical symbols that can be generated with Math AutoCorrect. These tools allow you to create equations by modifying a ready-made equation, using an equation text box with common mathematical structures and symbols, and simply typing an equation as you would ordinary text.

MODIFY A READY-MADE EQUATION

1. Click at the location in the document where you want the equation.

2. Click the **Insert** tab, and click the **Equation** down arrow in the Symbols group. The list of built-in equations appears, as shown in Figure 4-23.

3. Click the equation you want to insert. An equation text box will appear, containing the equation, and the Equation Tools Design tab will display, as shown in Figure 4-24.

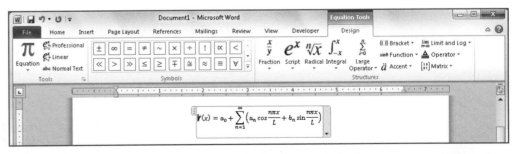

Figure 4-24: The equation text box automatically formats equations, which can be built with the structures and symbols in the Equation Tools Design tab.

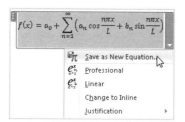

NOTE

Treat an equation in its text box as you would ordinary text and the text box itself as an object in a line of text.

Mathematical theorems express mathematically truths that exist in the universe. Some of these truths are directly observable, such as the Pythagorean Theorem. ¶

The Binomial Theorem, $(x + a)^n = \sum_{k=0}^{n} \binom{n}{k} x^k a^{n-k}$, Wikipedia says, is an important formula giving the expansion of powers of sums. It is often attributed to Blaise Pascal who described them in the 17th century. It was, however, known

NOTE

If you save a document with an equation in any format prior to Word 2010, the equation will be converted to a .tif image and you will not be able to edit it after you reopen it.

4. Click in the equation, and make any needed changes. Use the **RIGHT ARROW** and **LEFT ARROW** keys to move through the text. To save the revised equation, click the down arrow on the text box and click **Save As New Equation**.

5. When you have completed the equation, click outside the text box to close it and leave the equation looking like it is part of ordinary text.

CREATE AN EQUATION IN A TEXT BOX

You can open an equation text box and use the Equation Tools Design tab to create a professional-looking equation.

1. Click at the location in the document where you want to insert the equation.

2. Click the **Insert** tab, and click **Equation** in the Symbols group. An empty equation text box appears.

3. Either begin typing the equation or click one of the structures in the Structures group on the Equation Tools Design tab. If a drop-down menu appears, click the specific format you want.

4. If you use one of the structures, click in the small text boxes, and type the characters or select the appropriate symbols from the Symbols group for the Equation Tools Design tab.

5. Finish the equation using additional structures, symbols, and normal characters, if needed.

6. When you have completed the equation, click outside the text box to close it and leave the equation looking like it is part of ordinary text.

CREATE AN EQUATION FROM SCRATCH

You can also type an equation in a line of text using standard keyboard keys plus special symbols, and then convert it to a professional-looking equation.

1. Click at the location in the document where you want to insert the equation.

2. Begin typing using the keys on your keyboard, and, when needed, enter special characters by either:

- Typing one of the Math AutoCorrect text sequences, like \sqrt to get a square root symbol

    –Or–

- On the Insert tab, click **Symbol** in the Symbols group, and click the symbol you want if you see it; or click **More Symbols**, scroll through the symbols list until you see the one you want, double-click it, and click **Close**

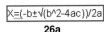
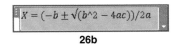
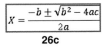

26a **26b** **26c**

Figure 4-26: You can type an equation with normal text (a), place it in an equation box (b), and then convert it to a professional-looking equation (c).

NOTE

To see the Math AutoCorrect text sequences, click the **File** tab, click **Options**, click **Proofing**, and then click **AutoCorrect Options**. Click the **Math AutoCorrect** tab. Scroll through the list to see the text sequences (see Figure 4-25). Click **OK** twice to close both dialog boxes.

3. Finish the equation using the techniques in step 2. When you have completed it (Figure 4-26a shows a quadratic equation created in this manner), select the entire equation, and, in the Insert tab Symbol group, click **Equation**. An equation text box forms around the new equation, shown in Figure 4-26b.

4. Click the equation box down arrow, and click **Professional**. Click outside the text box to close it. The professionally formatted quadratic equation is shown in Figure 4-26c.

Count Characters and Words

Word can tell you the number of characters and words in a document or in just a portion of the document you select.

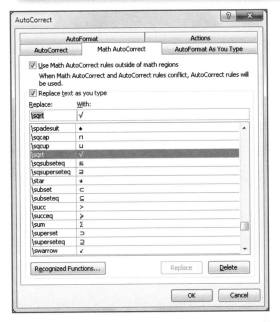

Figure 4-25: Math AutoCorrect allows you to insert math symbols by typing text sequences.

On the Review tab, click **Word Count** in the Proofing group. The Word Count dialog box appears, displaying the following information about your document (see Figure 4-27):

- Number of pages
- Number of words
- Number of characters (not including spaces)
- Number of characters (including spaces)
- Number of paragraphs
- Number of lines

Figure 4-27: The Word Count feature is a quick and easy way to view the specifics of your document.

TIP

To see how to format typed equations, select several of the ready-made equations, and click **Normal Text** in the Equation Tools Design tab Tools group. abc Normal Text

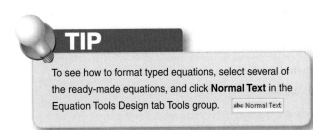

Use Highlighting

The Highlight feature is useful for marking important text in a document or text that you want to call a reader's attention to. Keep in mind, however, that highlighting parts of a document works best when the document is viewed online. When printed, the highlighting marks often appear gray and may even obscure the text you're trying to call attention to.

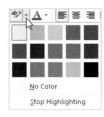

APPLY HIGHLIGHTING

The Highlight button is a toggle that switches color highlighting on and off. First you select a color, and then you apply the highlight to text or a graphic.

1. In the Home tab Font group, click the **Highlight** down arrow, and select a color from the menu. The cursor turns into a paintbrush.

2. Drag the pointer over the text or graphic that you want to highlight. The highlighting is applied to your selection.

3. To turn off highlighting, click **Highlight** again or press **ESC**.

REMOVE HIGHLIGHTING

1. Select the text that you want to remove highlighting from, or press **CTRL+A** to select all of the text in the document.

2. In the Home tab Font group, click **Highlight**. (This requires that the default be "No Color.")

   –Or–

   In the Home tab Font group, click the Highlight drop-down arrow, and then click No Color.

CHANGE HIGHLIGHTING COLOR

In the Home tab Font group, click the **Highlight** drop-down arrow, and then click the color that you want to use.

FIND HIGHLIGHTED TEXT IN A DOCUMENT

1. In the Home tab, click the **Find** down arrow in the Editing group, and click **Advanced Find**. The Find And Replace dialog box will appear.

2. If you don't see the Format button, click the **More** button.

3. Click the **Format** button, and then click **Highlight**.

4. Click **Find Next** and repeat this until you reach the end of the document.

5. Click **OK** when the message box is displayed indicating that Word has finished searching the document, and click **Close** in the Find And Replace dialog box.

Add Hyphenation

The Hyphenation feature automatically hyphenates words at the ends of lines based on standard hyphenation rules. You might use this feature if you want words to fit better on a line, or if you want to avoid uneven margins in right-aligned text or large gaps between words in justified text. (See Chapter 3 for information on text alignment.)

AUTOMATICALLY HYPHENATE A DOCUMENT

To automatically hyphenate a document, you must be in Print Layout format.

1. In the Page Layout tab, click **Hyphenation** in the Page Setup group. A drop-down menu appears.

2. Click **Hyphenation Options** to open the Hyphenation dialog box. Select the option you want (see Figure 4-28).

   - **Automatically Hyphenate Document**   Either enables automatic hyphenation as you type or after the fact for selected text (this option is turned off in Word by default)
   - **Hyphenate Words in CAPS**   Hyphenates words typed in all uppercase letters
   - **Hyphenation Zone**   Sets the distance from the right margin within which you want to hyphenate the document (the lower the value, the more words are hyphenated)
   - **Limit Consecutive Hyphens To**   Sets the maximum number of hyphens that can appear in consecutive lines

3. Click **OK** when finished.

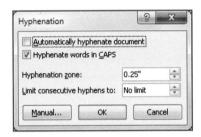

Figure 4-28: You can determine how Word will automatically hyphenate words.

MANUALLY HYPHENATE TEXT

1. In the Page Layout tab, click **Hyphenation** in the Page Setup group. A drop-down menu appears.

2. Click **Manual**.

3. Word searches for possible words to hyphenate. When it finds one, the Manual Hyphenation dialog box appears.

4. Do one of the following:
   - Click **Yes** to hyphenate the word at the suggested blinking hyphen.
   - Click one of the other hyphen choices, and then click **Yes**.
   - Click **No** to continue without hyphenating the word.

You can also hyphenate existing text by selecting the text, clicking **Hyphenation** in the Page Layout tab, and clicking **Automatic** in the Page Setup group.

QUICKSTEPS

EXPLORING THE THESAURUS

A *thesaurus* is a book or list of synonyms (words that have similar meanings), and Word contains a Thesaurus feature that will help you find just the right word to get your message across.

1. Select the word in your current document for which you want a synonym. You can also type a word in step 3.

2. In the Review tab, click **Thesaurus** in the Proofing group. The Research task pane is displayed (see Figure 4-29) and the search results are displayed.

3. If you did not select a word in step 1, type the word you want to find synonyms for in the Search For field, and click the green arrow to start searching.

4. In the list of possible words, point to the word you want to use. Click the arrow that appears, and click **Insert**.

5. Close the Research pane when finished.

TIP

You can also open the Thesaurus by selecting the word you want to look up and pressing **SHIFT+F7**.

5. Word will continue searching for words to hyphenate and display the Manual Hyphenation dialog box until the entire document has been searched. A message box is displayed to that effect. Click **OK**.

Figure 4-29: The Thesaurus feature enables you to find exactly the right word.

Chapter 5

Entering and Editing Data

Data is the heart and soul of Excel, yet before you can calculate data, chart it, analyze it, and otherwise *use* it, you have to place it on a worksheet. Data comes in several forms—such as numbers, text, dates, and times—and Excel handles the entry of each form uniquely. After you enter data into Excel's worksheets, you might want to make changes. Simple actions—such as removing text and numbers, copying and pasting, and moving data—are much more enhanced in Excel than the standard actions most users are familiar with.

In addition, Excel provides several tools to assist you in manipulating your data. You can have Excel intelligently continue a series without having to manually enter the sequential numbers or text. Automatic tools are available to help you verify accuracy and provide pop-ups—small toolbars related to the Excel task you're working on. These, and other ways of entering and editing data, are covered in this chapter.

UNDERSTANDING DATA TYPES

Cells in Excel are characterized by the type of data they contain. *Text* is composed of characters that cannot be used in calculations. For example, "Quarterly revenue is not meeting projection." is text, and so is "1302 Grand Ave." *Numbers* are just that: numerical characters that can be used in calculations. *Dates* and *times* occupy a special category of numbers that can be used in calculations, and are handled in a variety of ways. Excel lets you know what it thinks a cell contains by its default alignment of a cell's contents; that is, text is left-aligned and numbers (including dates and times) are right-aligned by default (of course, you can change these, as described later in the chapter).

Text: left-   Number:
aligned   right-aligned

	A	B	C
	D6		*fx*
1	Supplies	23567	
2			

Enter Data

An Excel worksheet is a matrix, or grid, of lettered *column headings* across the top and numbered *row headings* down the side. The first row of a typical worksheet is used for column *headers*. The column headers represent categories of similar data. The rows beneath a column header contain data that is further categorized either by a row header along the leftmost column or listed below the column header. Figure 5-1 shows examples of two common worksheet arrangements. Worksheets can also be used to set up *tables* of data, where columns are sometimes referred to as *fields* and each row represents a unique *record* of data. Tables are covered in Chapter 14.

Each intersection of a row and column is called a *cell*, and is referenced first by the column location and then by the row location. The combination of a column letter and row number assigns each cell an *address*. For example, the cell at the intersection of column D and row 8 is called D8. A cell is considered *active* when it is clicked or otherwise selected as the place in which to place new data.

Enter Text

In an Excel worksheet, text is used to identify, explain, and emphasize numeric data. It comprises characters that cannot be used in calculations. You enter text by typing, just as you would in a word-processing program.

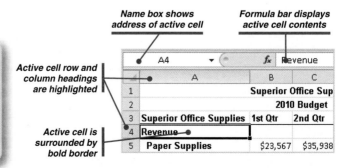

Name box shows
address of active cell

Formula bar displays
active cell contents

Active cell row and
column headings
are highlighted

Active cell is
surrounded by
bold border

	A	B	C
	A4		*fx*	Revenue
1			Superior Office Sup
2			2010 Budget
3	Superior Office Supplies	1st Qtr	2nd Qtr
4	Revenue		
5	Paper Supplies	$23,567	$35,938

TIP

Excel provides several highly visible identifiers for the active cell (see illustration at right): the Name box at the left end of the Formula bar displays the address; the column and row headings are highlighted in color; the Formula bar displays cell contents; and the cell borders are bold.

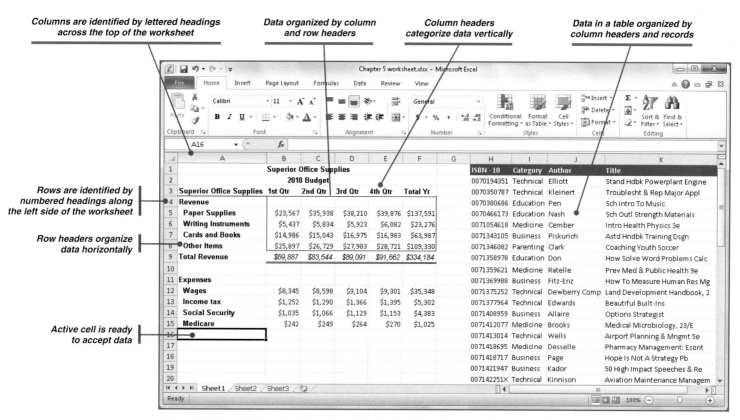

Figure 5-1: *The grid layout of Excel worksheets is defined by several components.*

Columns are identified by lettered headings across the top of the worksheet

Data organized by column and row headers

Column headers categorize data vertically

Data in a table organized by column headers and records

Rows are identified by numbered headings along the left side of the worksheet

Row headers organize data horizontally

Active cell is ready to accept data

ENTER TEXT CONTINUOUSLY

Text (and numbers) longer than one cell width will appear to cover the adjoining cells to the right of the active cell. The covered cells have not been "used"; their contents have just been hidden, as shown in Figure 5-2. To enter text on one line:

1. Click the cell where you want the text to start.

2. Type the text. The text displays in one or more cells (see rows 2 and 4 in Figure 5-2).

3. Complete the entry. (See the "Completing an Entry" QuickSteps later in the chapter for several ways to do that.)

NOTE

See Chapter 6 for ways to increase column width to accommodate the length of text in a cell.

	A	B	C	D	E	F	G
	B4	▾		f_x	Costs of Goods Sold (Seattle property)		
1							
2		Supplies					
3							
4		Costs of Goods Sold (Seattle property)					
5							
6		Costs of Goods Sold (Seattle property)					
7							
8		Costs of Goods Sold (Seattle property)					
9							

Figure 5-2: **Text in a cell can cover several cells or be placed on multiple lines.**

NOTE

The *beginning cell* is in the same column where you first started entering data. For example, if you started entering data in cell A5 and continued through E5, pressing **TAB** between entries A5 through D5 and pressing **ENTER** in E5, the active cell would move to A6 (the first cell in the next row). If you had started entering data in cell C5, after pressing **ENTER** at the end of that row of entries, the active cell would move to C6, the cell below it. This often causes confusion when you go back to edit a cell while you're in the middle of a row and then click in another cell in that row to continue entering data.

WRAP TEXT ON MULTIPLE LINES

You can select a cell and wrap text at the end of its column width, much like how a word-processing program wraps text to the next line when entered text reaches its right margin.

1. Click the cell where you want to enter text.

2. Type all the text you want to appear in a cell. The text will continue to the right, overlapping as many cells as its length dictates (see row 4 in Figure 5-2).

3. Press **ENTER** to complete the entry. (See the "Completing an Entry" QuickSteps.) Click the cell a second time to select it.

4. Click the **Home** tab at the left end of the ribbon. In the Alignment group, click the **Wrap Text** button. The text wraps within the confines of the column width, increasing the row height as necessary (see row 6 in Figure 5-2).

CONSTRAIN TEXT ON MULTIPLE LINES

When you want to constrain the length of text in a cell:

1. Click the cell where you want to enter text.

2. Type the text you want to appear on the first line.

3. Press **ALT+ENTER**. The insertion point moves to the beginning of a new line.

4. Repeat steps 2 and 3 for any additional lines of text. (See row 8 in Figure 5-2.)

5. Complete the entry. (See the "Completing an Entry" QuickSteps.)

Enter Numeric Data

Numbers are numerical data, from the simplest to the most complex. Excel provides several features to help you work more easily with numbers used to represent values in various categories, such as currency, accounting, and mathematics.

ENTER NUMBERS

Enter numbers by simply selecting a cell and typing the numbers.

1. Click the cell where you want the numbers entered.

TIP

You can cause a number to be interpreted by Excel as text by typing an apostrophe (') in front of it and completing the entry. The "number" is left-aligned as text and a green triangle is displayed in the upper-left corner of the cell. When selected, an error icon displays next to the cell, indicating a number is stored as text.

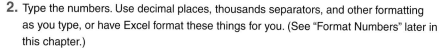

TIP

You can convert a number to scientific notation from the Home tab Number group on the ribbon. Click the **Number Format** down arrow, and click **Scientific** near the bottom of the list. To set the number of decimal places, click the **Increase Decimal** or **Decrease Decimal** button at the bottom of the Number group. Also, note that the Number Format box displays the type of number format in the selected cell.

QUICKSTEPS

COMPLETING AN ENTRY

You can complete an entry using the mouse or the keyboard and control where the active cell goes next.

STAY IN THE ACTIVE CELL

To complete an entry and keep the current cell active, click **ENTER** on the Formula bar.

MOVE THE ACTIVE CELL TO THE RIGHT

To complete the entry and move to the next cell in the same row, press **TAB**.

Continued . . .

2. Type the numbers. Use decimal places, thousands separators, and other formatting as you type, or have Excel format these things for you. (See "Format Numbers" later in this chapter.)

3. Complete the entry. (See the "Completing an Entry" QuickSteps.)

ENTER NUMBERS USING SCIENTIFIC NOTATION

Exponents are used in scientific notation to shorten (or round off) very large or small numbers. The shorthand scientific notation display does not affect how the number is used in calculations; however, rounding provides a less precise result when moving a decimal point several orders of magnitude. (To retain precision, see the associated Tip regarding converting numbers to scientific notation.)

1. Click the cell where you want the data entered.

2. Type the number using three components:

- **Base**: For example: 4, 7.56, -2.5

- **Scientific notation identifier**: Type the letter "e."

- **Exponent**: The number of times 10 is multiplied by itself. Positive exponent numbers increment the base number to the right of the decimal point, negative numbers to the left. For example, scientific notation for the number 123,456,789.0 is written to two decimal places as 1.23×10^8. In Excel, you would type 1.23e8.

3. After completing the entry (see the "Completing an Entry" QuickSteps), it will display as: 1.23E+08

Enter Dates

If you can think of a way to enter a date, Excel can probably recognize it as such. For example, Table 5-1 shows how Excel handles different ways to make the date entry use the date of March 1, 2010 (assuming it is sometime in 2010) in a worksheet.

In cases when a year is omitted, Excel assumes the current year.

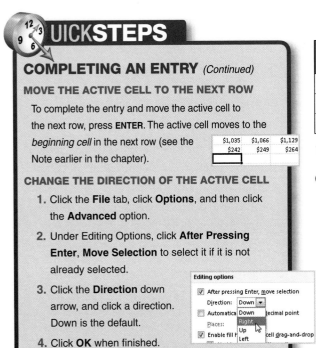

COMPLETING AN ENTRY *(Continued)*

MOVE THE ACTIVE CELL TO THE NEXT ROW

To complete the entry and move the active cell to the next row, press **ENTER**. The active cell moves to the *beginning cell* in the next row (see the Note earlier in the chapter).

$1,035	$1,066	$1,129
$242	$249	$264

CHANGE THE DIRECTION OF THE ACTIVE CELL

1. Click the **File** tab, click **Options**, and then click the **Advanced** option.

2. Under Editing Options, click **After Pressing Enter, Move Selection** to select it if it is not already selected.

3. Click the **Direction** down arrow, and click a direction. Down is the default.

4. Click **OK** when finished.

Editing options

☑ After pressing Enter, move selection
Direction: Down ▾
  Down
☐ Automatica Right   ecimal point
Places: Up
☑ Enable fill Left cell drag-and-drop

MOVE THE ACTIVE CELL TO ANY CELL

To complete the entry and move the active cell to any cell in the worksheet, click the cell you want to become active.

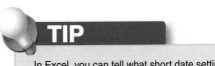

TIP

In Excel, you can tell what short date setting is currently in use by clicking a cell with a date in it and seeing what appears in the Formula bar.

	fx	12/21/2009
	D	E
		21-Dec

TYPING THIS...	DISPLAYS THIS AFTER COMPLETING THE ENTRY
3/1, 3-1, 1-mar, or 1-Mar	1-Mar
3/1/10, 3-1-10, 3/1/2010, 3-1-2010, 3-1/10, or 3-1/2010	3/1/2010
Mar 1, 10, March 1, 2010, 1-mar-10, or 1-Mar-2010	1-Mar-10

Table 5-1: **Examples of Excel Date Formats**

CHANGE THE DEFAULT DISPLAY OF DATES

Two common date formats (long and short) are displayed by default in Excel based on settings in the Windows Region And Language item in Control Panel, shown in Figure 5-3.

1. In Windows 7, click **Start** and click **Control Panel**.

2. In Control Panel Category view, click the **Clock, Language, And Region** category, and then click **Region And Language**.

   –Or–

   In Icons view, click **Regional And Language Options**.

Figure 5-3: **You can change how Excel and other Windows programs display dates.**

TIP

To enter the current date in a cell, click the cell and press **CTRL+;** (press and hold **CTRL** and press **;**). The current date is displayed in the date format applied to the cell, the default of which is the short date.

3. On the Formats tab, click **Additional Settings**.

4. Click the **Date** tab, click the **Short Date Format** down arrow, and select a format. Similarly, change the long date format as necessary.

5. Click **OK** twice and close Control Panel.

FORMAT DATES

You can change how a date is displayed in Excel by choosing a new format.

1. Right-click the cell that contains the date you want to change. (See the "Selecting Cells and Ranges" QuickSteps later in the chapter to see how to apply formats to more than one cell at a time.)

2. Click **Format Cells** on the context menu. The Format Cells dialog box appears. If needed, click the **Number** tab and then the **Date** category, as shown in Figure 5-4.

3. Select a format from the Type list.

   –Or–

   Use custom number codes to create a new format. To learn about number format codes, search Excel Help for the topic "Create or delete a custom number format."

4. You can see how the new date format affects your date in the Sample area. Click **OK** when finished.

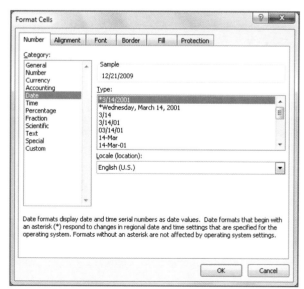

Figure 5-4: You can choose from among several ways to display dates in Excel.

QUICKFACTS

UNDERSTANDING EXCEL DATES AND TIMES

If you select a cell with a date and open the Number Format list in the Number group, you'll notice several of the formats show examples with a number around 40,000. Is this just an arbitrary number Excel has cooked up to demonstrate the example formats? Hardly. Dates and times in Excel are assigned values so that they can be used in calculations (Chapter 7 describes how to use formulas and functions). Dates are assigned a serial value starting with January 1, 1900 (serial value 1). The number you see on the Number Format list is the value of the date in the active cell (you can convert a date to its serial value by changing the format from Date to Number). For example, January 1, 2010, has a serial value of 40,179. Times are converted to the decimal equivalent of a day. For example, 4:15 P.M. is converted to 0.68. Since Excel considers dates and times as numerics, they are right-aligned in a cell. If you see what you think is a date but it is left-aligned, Excel is treating it as text, not a date, and you would receive an error message if you tried to use it in a formula.

TIP

To enter the current time in a cell, click the cell and press **CTRL+SHIFT+:** (press and hold **CTRL** and **SHIFT**, and press **:**). The current time in the form h:mm AM/PM is displayed.

Date and time formats	
Short date:	M/d/yyyy
Long date:	dddd, MMMM dd, yyyy
Short time:	h:mm tt
Long time:	h:mm:ss tt
First day of week:	Sunday

What does the notation mean?

Use Times

Excel's conventions for time are as follows:

- Colons (:) are used as separators between hours, minutes, and seconds.
- AM is assumed unless you specify PM or when you enter a time from 12:00 to 12:59.
- AM and PM do not display in the cell if they are not entered.
- You specify PM by entering a space followed by "p," "P," "pm," or "PM."
- Seconds are not displayed in the cell if not entered.
- AM, PM, and seconds are displayed in the Formula bar of a cell that contains a time.

ENTER TIMES

1. Select the cell in which you want to enter a time.
2. Type the hour followed by a colon.
3. Type the minutes followed by a colon.
4. Type the seconds, if needed.
5. Type a space and PM, if needed.
6. Complete the entry.

CHANGE THE DEFAULT DISPLAY OF TIMES

By default, times are displayed in Excel based on settings configured in the Windows Region And Language feature of Control Panel. To change the default settings:

1. In Windows 7, click **Start** and click **Control Panel**.
2. In Category view, click the **Clock, Language, And Region** category, and then click **Region And Language**.

   –Or–

   In Icons view, click **Region And Language**.
3. On the Formats tab, click the **Short Time** and/or **Long Time** down arrow, and select the formats you want. (If you don't understand the meaning of the shorthand, click **What Does The Notation Mean?** to view an explanation of the time symbology.)
4. Click **OK** and close Control Panel.

FORMAT TIMES

You can change how a time is displayed in Excel by choosing a new format.

1. Select the cell that contains the time you want to change. (See the "Selecting Cells and Ranges" QuickSteps later in the chapter for how to apply formats to more than one cell at a time.)

2. Click the **Dialog Box Launcher** arrow in the Home tab Number group. The Format Cells dialog box appears with the Number tab displaying the Custom category.

3. Under Type, select a format.

    –Or–

    Use custom number codes to create a new format. To learn about number format codes, search Excel Help for the topic "Create or delete a custom number format."

4. You can see how the new time format will affect your time in the Sample area. Click **OK** when finished.

Format Numbers

Numbers in a cell can be formatted in any one of several numeric categories by first selecting the cell containing the number. You can then use the tools available in the Home tab Number group or have the full range of options available to you from the Format Cells dialog box.

DISPLAY THE NUMBER TAB

Click the **Dialog Box Launcher** in the lower-right corner of the Number group. The Format Cells dialog box appears with the Number tab displayed (shown in Figure 5-5).

ADD OR DECREASE DECIMAL PLACES

1. On the Number tab of the Format Cells dialog box, choose the appropriate numeric category (Number, Currency, Accounting, Percentage, or Scientific) from the Category list box.

2. In the Decimal Places text box, enter a number or use the spinner to set the number of decimal places you want. Click **OK**.

    –Or–

Figure 5-5: The Format Cells Number tab provides a complete set of numeric formatting categories and options.

In the ribbon's Home tab Number group, click the **Increase Decimal** or **Decrease Decimal** button.

ADD A THOUSANDS SEPARATOR

- On the Number tab of the Format Cells dialog box, click the Number category, and click Use 1000 Separator (,). Click OK.

    –Or–

- In the ribbon's Home tab Number group, click the **Comma Style** button in the Number group.

ADD A CURRENCY SYMBOL

1. On the Number tab, choose the appropriate numeric category (Currency or Accounting) from the Category list box.

2. Click **OK** to accept the default dollar sign ($), or choose another currency symbol from the Symbol drop-down list, and click **OK**.

    –Or–

    Click the **Accounting Number Format** button $ ⌄ in the Number group. (You can change the currency symbol by clicking the down arrow next to the current symbol and choosing another one.)

CONVERT A DECIMAL TO A FRACTION

1. On the Number tab, click the **Fraction** category.

2. Click the type of fraction you want. View it in the Sample area, and change the type if needed. Click **OK**.

CONVERT A NUMBER TO A PERCENTAGE

1. On the Number tab, click the **Percentage** category.

2. In the Decimal Places text box, enter a number or use the spinner to set the number of decimal places you want. Click **OK**.

    –Or–

    Click the **Percent Style** button % in the Number group.

FORMAT ZIP CODES, PHONE NUMBERS, AND SOCIAL SECURITY NUMBERS

1. On the Number tab, click the **Special** category.

2. Select the type of formatting you want. Click **OK**.

ADDING DATA QUICKLY

Excel provides several features that help you quickly add more data to existing data with a minimum of keystrokes.

USE AUTOCOMPLETE

Excel will complete an entry for you after you type the first few characters of data that appears in a previous entry in the same column. Simply press **ENTER** to accept the completed entry. To turn off this feature if you find it bothersome:

1. Click the **File** tab, click **Options**, and click the **Advanced** option.

2. Under Editing Options, click **Enable AutoComplete For Cell Values** to remove the check mark.

FILL DATA INTO ADJOINING CELLS

1. Select the cell that contains the data you want to copy into adjoining cells.

2. Point to the fill handle in the lower-right corner of the cell. The pointer turns into a cross.

3. Drag the handle in the direction you want to extend the data until you've reached the last cell in the range you want to fill.

4. Open the smart tag 🔡 by clicking it, and select fill options.

   –Or–

   Select the contiguous cells you want to fill in with the data in a cell (see the "Selecting Cells and Ranges" QuickSteps later in the chapter). In the Home tab Editing group, click the **Fill** button 🔽▾, and click the direction of the fill.

   Continued . . .

Edit Data

The data-intensive nature of Excel necessitates easy ways to change, copy, or remove data already entered on a worksheet. In addition, Excel has facilities to help you find and replace data and check the spelling.

Edit Cell Data

You have several choices on how to edit data, depending on whether you want to replace all the contents of a cell or just part of the contents, and whether you want to do it in the cell or in the Formula bar.

EDIT CELL CONTENTS

To edit data entered in a cell:

- Double-click the text in the cell where you want to begin editing. An insertion point is placed in the cell. Type the new data, use the mouse to select characters to be overwritten or deleted, or use keyboard shortcuts. Complete the entry when finished editing. (See the "Completing an Entry" QuickSteps earlier in the chapter.)

–Or–

- Select the cell to edit, and then click the cell's contents in the Formula bar where you want to make changes. Type the new data, use the mouse to select characters to overwrite or delete, or use keyboard shortcuts. Click **Enter** on the Formula bar or press **ENTER** to complete the entry.

–Or–

- Select the cell to edit, and press **F2**. Edit in the cell using the mouse or keyboard shortcuts. Complete the entry.

REPLACE ALL CELL CONTENTS

Click the cell and type new data. The original data is deleted and replaced by your new characters.

QUICKSTEPS

ADDING DATA QUICKLY *(Continued)*

CONTINUE A SERIES OF DATA

Data can be *logically* extended into one or more adjoining cells. For example, 1 and 2 extend to 3, 4...; Tuesday extends to Wednesday, Thursday...; January extends to February, March...; and 2008 and 2009 extend to 2010, 2011....

1. Select the cell or cells that contain a partial series. (See the "Selecting Cells and Ranges" QuickSteps later in the chapter for more information on selecting more than one cell.)

2. Point to the fill handle in the lower-right corner of the last cell. The pointer turns into a cross.

3. Drag the handle in the direction you want until you've reached the last cell in the range to complete the series.

	A	B
1	January	
2	February	
3		
4		April
5		

4. To copy the partial series into the adjoining cells instead of extending the series, drag the fill handle to cover as many occurrences of the copy you want, click the smart tag, and click **Copy Cells** (see Figure 5-6).

REMOVE THE FILL HANDLE

To hide the fill handle and disable AutoFill:

1. Click the **File** tab, under Excel click **Options**, and click the **Advanced** option.

2. Under Editing Options, click **Enable Fill Handle And Cell Drag And Drop** to remove the check mark.

Continued . . .

CANCEL CELL EDITING

Before you complete a cell entry, you can revert back to your original data by pressing **ESC** or clicking **Cancel** on the Formula bar.

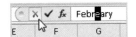

Remove Cell Contents

You can easily delete cell contents, move them to other cells, or clear selective attributes of a cell.

DELETE DATA

Remove all contents (but not formatting) from a cell by selecting the cell and pressing **DELETE**. You can delete the contents of more than one cell by selecting

	A	B	C	D
1	January			
2	February			
3	March			
4	January			
5	February			
6	March			
7	January			
8	February			
9	March			
10	January			
11	February			
12	March			
13				
14	⦿ Copy Cells			
15	○ Fill Series			
16				
17	○ Fill Formatting Only			
18	○ Fill Without Formatting			
19	○ Fill Months			
20				

Figure 5-6: You can copy a series (January, February, and March, in this case) by using the smart tag that appears after dragging the fill handle.

the cells or the cell range and pressing **DELETE**. (See the "Selecting Cells and Ranges" QuickSteps for more information on selecting various configurations.)

MOVE DATA

Cell contents can be removed from one location and placed in another location of equal size. Select the cell or range you want to move. Then:

- Place the pointer on any edge of the selection, except the lower-right corner where the Fill handle resides, until it turns into a cross with arrowhead tips. Drag the cell or range to the new location.

10				
11	**Expenses**			
12	**Wages**	$8,345	$9,104	$9,301	$35,348
13	**Income tax**	$1,252	$1,366	$1,395	$5,302
14	**Social Security**	$1,035	$1,129	$1,153	$4,383
15	**Medicare**	$242	$264	$270	$1,025
16					
17					

–Or–

- On the Home tab Clipboard group, click **Cut**. Select the new location, and click **Paste** in the Clipboard group. (See "Copy and Paste Data" for more information on pasting options.)

REMOVE SELECTED CELL CONTENTS

A cell can contain several components, including:

- **Formats:** Consisting of number formats, conditional formats (formats that display if certain conditions apply), and borders
- **Contents:** Consisting of formulas and data
- **Comments:** Consisting of notes you attach to a cell

TIP

To undo a data-removal action, even if you have performed several actions since removing the data, click **Undo** on the Quick Access toolbar next to the File tab (or press **CTRL+Z**) for the most recent action. For earlier actions, continue clicking **Undo** to work your way back; or click the down arrow next to the button, and choose the action from the drop-down list.

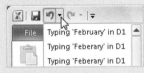

- **Hyperlinks:** Consisting of links to other ranges on the current worksheet, other worksheets in the current workbook, other workbooks or other files, and webpages in websites

1. Choose which cell components you want to clear by selecting the cell or cells.

2. On the Home tab Editing group, click the **Clear** button, and click the applicable item from the menu. (Clicking **Clear Contents** performs the same action as pressing **DELETE**.)

Copy and Paste Data

Data you've already entered on a worksheet (or in other programs) can be copied to the same or other worksheets, or even to other Windows applications. You first *copy* the data to the Windows Clipboard, where it is temporarily stored. After selecting a destination for the data, you *paste* it into the cell or cells. You can copy all the data in a cell or only part of it. You can paste it on your worksheet one time, in one location, or at different locations several times. (The copied data remains on the Clipboard until you replace it with another copy action.) While many computer users are familiar with a basic copy, Excel's paste feature lets you selectively paste attributes of the data and even shows you a preview of how the pasted information will look in its new location.

COPY DATA

1. Select the cells that contain the data you want to copy; or double-click a cell and select the characters you want to copy.

2. In the Home tab Clipboard group, click the **Copy** down arrow, and click **Copy** (to copy data as letters and characters), or click **Copy As Picture** to choose a picture format of the material (see Chapter 14 for more information on working with pictures and graphics).

–Or–

Press **CTRL+C**.

QUICKSTEPS

SELECTING CELLS AND RANGES

The key to many actions in Excel is the ability to select cells in various configurations and use them to perform calculations. You can select a single cell, nonadjacent cells, and adjacent cells (or *ranges*).

SELECT A SINGLE CELL

Select a cell by clicking it, or move to a cell using the arrow keys or by completing an entry in a cell above or to the left.

Continued . . .

SELECTING CELLS AND RANGES

(Continued)

SELECT NONADJACENT CELLS

Select a cell and then press **CTRL** while clicking the other cells you want to select. The selected cells remain highlighted.

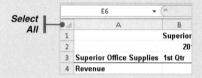

$8,345	$9,104
$1,252	$1,366
$1,035	$1,129
$242	$264

SELECT A RANGE OF ADJACENT CELLS

Select a cell and drag over the additional cells you want to include in the range.

–Or–

Select the first cell in the range, press and hold **SHIFT**, and click the last cell in the range.

SELECT ALL CELLS ON A WORKSHEET

Click the **Select All** button in the upper-left corner of the worksheet, or press **CTRL+A**.

Select All

	E6		
	A	B	
1		Superior	
2		20	
3	Superior Office Supplies	1st Qtr	
4	Revenue		

SELECT A ROW OR COLUMN

Click a row (number) heading or column (letter) heading.

H	I
ISBN	**Category**
0070194351	Technical
0070350787	Technical
0070380686	Education

SELECT ADJACENT ROWS OR COLUMNS

Drag down the row headings or across the column headings.

Continued . . .

In either case, the selected data is copied to the Clipboard and the border around the cells displays a flashing dotted line.

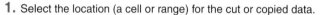

Social Security	$1,035	$1,129	$1,153	$4,383

PASTE DATA

Once data is placed on the Windows Clipboard through a *copy* action, you can selectively include or omit formulas, values, formatting, comments, arithmetic operations, and other cell properties *before* you copy or move data. (See Chapter 7 for information on formulas, values, and arithmetic operations.) You can preview several variations of a paste by choosing from several tools, either on the ribbon or from a dialog box. Even after you perform a paste, you can easily change your mind by selecting and previewing paste options from a smart tag.

1. Select the location (a cell or range) for the cut or copied data.

2. On the Home tab Clipboard group, click the **Paste** down arrow. A menu of several pasting tools appears, each as an icon.

   –Or–

   Right-click the selected cell or range, and on the context menu, view a few tools under Paste Options, or even more tools by pointing to Paste Special.

3. Point to each tool to see a short description of the pasting characteristic(s) it supports. As you point to an icon, the cell or range you

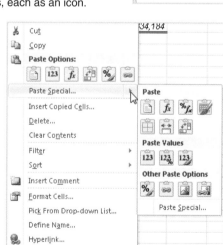

SELECTING CELLS AND RANGES

(Continued)

SELECT NONADJACENT ROWS OR COLUMNS

Select a row or column heading, and then press **CTRL** while clicking other row or column headings you want selected.

RESIZE AN ADJACENT SELECTION

Press **SHIFT** and click the cell you want to be at the end of the selection.

SELECT A COMBINATION OF CELLS

By dragging, combined with clicking while pressing **CTRL** or **SHIFT**, you can include single cells, rows, columns, and ranges all in one selection. Figure 5-7 shows one example.

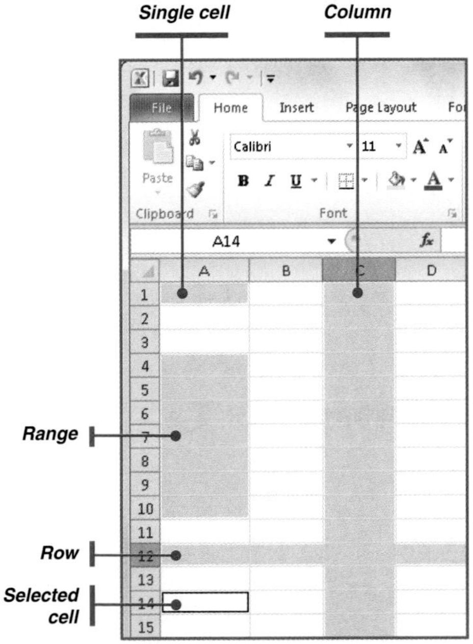

had selected will show how the pasting characteristic affects the data, as shown in Figure 5-8.

4. Click the tool you want to use to perform the paste. If you want a different pasting tool, click the smart tag 📋(Ctrl)▾ that appears next to the pasted cell or range and select another option.

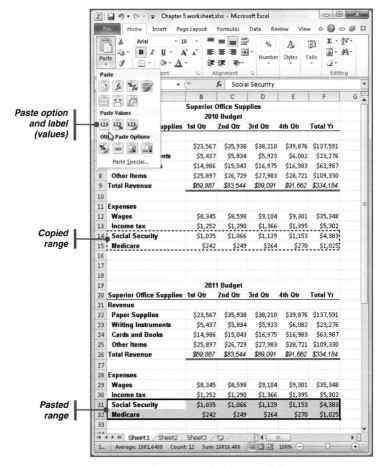

Figure 5-8: *You can preview how each tool will show your pasted data.*

Single cell   **Column**

Range

Row

Selected cell

Figure 5-7: *You can include a single cell, a row, a column, and a range all in one selection.*

TIP

To select larger numbers of adjacent cells, rows, or columns, click the first item in the group, and then press **SHIFT** while clicking the last item in the group.

TIP

Another way to send information to the Clipboard is to *cut* the data. When you cut data ✂ Cut , like a copy action, information is placed on the Clipboard and removes any existing data already there. However, when you cut data, it is removed from its original location (it's essentially moved), unlike copying, where the data is retained at its original location.

CAUTION

If you paste data into a cell that contains existing data, that existing data will be replaced with the pasted data. To avoid losing data, insert blank cells, rows, and columns to accommodate the data you are pasting. See Chapter 6 for more information on inserting cells, rows, and columns.

5. Repeat steps 1 through 4 to paste the copied data to other locations. Press **ESC** when finished to remove the flashing border around the source cells.

6. Alternatively, you can choose options from a list in a dialog box without previewing the effects. After selecting the destination cell or cells to where you want the data copied or moved, in the Clipboard group, click the **Paste** down arrow, and click **Paste Special**; or right-click the destination cells, and click **Paste Special**. The Paste Special dialog box appears, as shown in Figure 5-9.

7. Select the paste options you want in the copied or moved cells, and click **OK**.

Find and Replace Data

In worksheets that might span thousands of rows and columns (more than one million rows and 16,000 columns are possible), you need the ability to locate data quickly, as well as to find instances of the same data so that consistent replacements can be made.

FIND DATA

1. In the Home tab Editing group, click **Find & Select**, and click **Find**; or press **CTRL+F** to open the Find And Replace dialog box with the Find tab displayed.

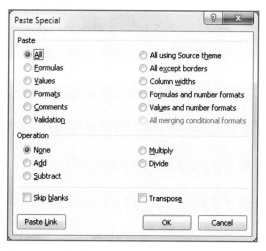

Figure 5-9: *Pasting options are listed in the Paste Special dialog box.*

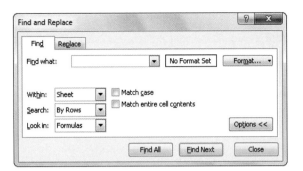

Figure 5-10: *The Find tab lets you refine your search based on several criteria.*

2. Type the text or number you want to find in the Find What text box.

3. Click **Options** to view the following options to refine the search (see Figure 5-10):

- **Format:** Opens the Find Format dialog box, where you select from several categories of number, alignment, font, border, pattern, and protection formats

- **Choose Format From Cell:**(From the Format drop-down list) lets you click a cell that contains the format you want to find

- **Within:** Limits your search to the current worksheet or expands it to all worksheets in the workbook

- **Search:** Lets you search to the right by rows or down by columns. You can search to the left and up by pressing SHIFT and clicking **Find Next**

- **Look In:** Focuses the search to just formulas, values, or comments

- **Match Case:** Lets you choose between uppercase or lowercase text

- **Match Entire Cell Contents:** Searches for an exact match of the characters in the Find What text box

4. Click **Find All** to display a table of all occurrences (shown here), or click **Find Next** to find the next singular occurrence.

REPLACE DATA

The Replace tab of the Find And Replace dialog box looks and behaves similar to the Find tab covered earlier.

1. In the Home tab Editing group, click **Find And Select**, and click **Replace**; or press CTRL+H to open the Find And Replace dialog box with the Replace tab displayed.

2. Enter the text or number to find in the Find What text box; enter the replacement characters in the Replace With text box. If formatting or search criteria are required, click **Options**. See "Find Data" for the options' descriptions.

The Go To option on the Find & Select drop-down menu lets you find cells and ranges by name or address. Using the Go To dialog box in this manner is covered in Chapter 7.

3. Click **Replace All** to replace all occurrences in the worksheet, or click **Replace** to replace occurrences one at a time.

FIND SPECIFIC EXCEL OBJECTS

You can quickly locate key Excel objects, such as formulas and comments, without having to type any keywords. The objects you can directly search for are listed on the Find & Select drop-down menu.

1. In the Home tab Editing group, click **Find & Select**. The drop-down menu lists several categories of objects from which you can choose.

2. Click the item whose instances you want selected. The first instance is surrounded by a light-colored border, and all other instances in the worksheet are selected/highlighted (see Figure 5-11).

–Or–

Click **Go To Special** to open a dialog box of the same name, and select from several additional objects. Click **OK** after making your selection.

3. To remove the selection/highlight from found objects, click **Find & Select** again, and click **Select Objects** to turn off that feature.

B7		ƒ	14986		
	A	B	C	D	E	F
1		Superior Office Supplies				
2		2010 Budget				
3	Superior Office Supplies	1st Qtr	2nd Qtr	3rd Qtr	4th Qtr	Total Yr
4	Revenue					
5	Paper Supplies	$23,567	$35,938	$38,210	$39,876	$137,591
6	Writing Instruments	$5,437	$5,834	$5,923	$6,082	$23,276
7	Cards and Books	$14,986	$15,043	$16,975	$16,983	$63,987
8	Other Items	$25,897	$26,729	$27,983	$28,721	$109,330
9	Total Revenue	$69,887	$83,544	$89,091	$91,662	$334,184

Figure 5-11: Certain Excel objects, such as comments, can be located and identified with just a few clicks.

QUICKSTEPS

EDITING WORKBOOKS IN THE EXCEL WEB APP

As described in Chapter 1, with a Windows Live account you can upload files to Microsoft's SkyDrive location in order to keep them in the "cloud" so you, or others, can access them at any time or place from a browser. Besides simply storing files there, using the integrated Microsoft Excel Web App, you can also view, edit, and download workbooks saved in the Excel 2007 and Excel 2010 default .xlsx file format without necessarily having a version of Excel installed on your device. (You can view workbooks saved in the earlier .xls file format, but you cannot edit them.) The editing capabilities in the Excel Web App are limited to the more basic features of Excel, such as those described in this chapter, as well as minor formatting actions (described in Chapter 6) and working with tables (described in Chapter 14). In fact, if the workbook contains more advanced features such as shapes or a watch window, you cannot edit it (although you can view and download it). However, for those cases where your edits are predominately data-centric, SkyDrive and the Excel Web App provide you a great opportunity to access your information from anywhere with only a browser and Internet connection.

Continued ...

Verify Spelling

You can check the spelling of selected cells—or the entire worksheet—using Excel's main dictionary and a custom dictionary you add words to (both dictionaries are shared with other Office programs).

1. Select the cells to check; to check the entire worksheet, select any cell.

2. In the Review tab Proofing group, click **Spelling** or press **F7**. When the spelling checker doesn't find anything to report, you are told the spelling check is complete. Otherwise, the Spelling dialog box appears, as shown in Figure 5-12.

3. Choose to ignore one or more occurrences of the characters shown in the Not In Dictionary text box, or change the characters by picking from the Suggestions list and clicking one of the Change options.

4. Click **AutoCorrect** if you want to automatically replace words in the future. (See "Modify Automatic Corrections," next, for more information on using AutoCorrect.)

5. Click **Options** to change language or custom dictionaries and set other spelling criteria.

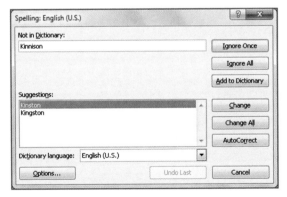

*Figure 5-12: **The Spelling dialog box provides several options to handle misspelled or uncommon words.***

QUICKSTEPS

EDITING WORKBOOKS IN THE EXCEL WEB APP *(Continued)*

To use a workbook in the Excel Web App:

1. Open the SkyDrive folder that contains the workbook you want to view or edit (see Chapter 1 for information on logging on to SkyDrive).

2. Click the file you want. A document preview screen opens, and displays a toolbar of actions that you can do with the file.

3. Click **Edit In Browser**. The workbook opens in a screen that appears similar to the Excel 2010 user interface (see Figure 5-14) but lacks certain features, including the tools located on the missing ribbon tabs and many of the options found on a standard File menu.

4. After performing editing using the tools on the available ribbon tabs, click the **File** tab and select whether you want to open the file in your device's version of Excel, save it under a different file name (you don't need to save the workbook, as Excel Web App does that automatically), share it with others, or download it to your device as a standard workbook file or as a

Continued . . .

Modify Automatic Corrections

Excel automatically corrects common data entry mistakes as you type, replacing characters and words you choose with other choices. You can control how this is done.

1. Click the **File** tab, click **Options**, click the **Proofing** option, and click **AutoCorrect Options**. The AutoCorrect dialog box appears, as shown in Figure 5-13. As appropriate, do one or more of the following:

   - Choose the type of automatic corrections you do or do not want from the options at the top of the dialog box.
   - Click **Exceptions** to set capitalization exceptions.

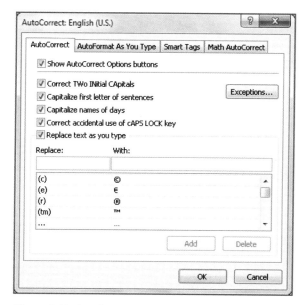

Figure 5-13: AutoCorrect provides several automatic settings and lets you add words and characters that are replaced with alternatives.

UICKSTEPS

EDITING WORKBOOKS IN THE EXCEL WEB APP *(Continued)*

snapshot containing only data and formatting (that is, no formulas).

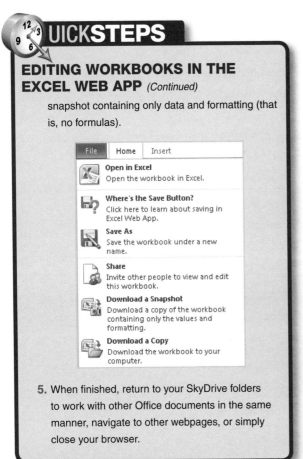

5. When finished, return to your SkyDrive folders to work with other Office documents in the same manner, navigate to other webpages, or simply close your browser.

- Click **Replace Text As You Type** to turn off automatic text replacement (turned on by default).

- Add new words or characters to the Replace and With lists, and click **Add**; or select a current item in the list, edit it, and click **Replace**.

- Delete replacement text by selecting the item in the Replace and With lists and clicking **Delete**.

2. Click **OK** when you are done.

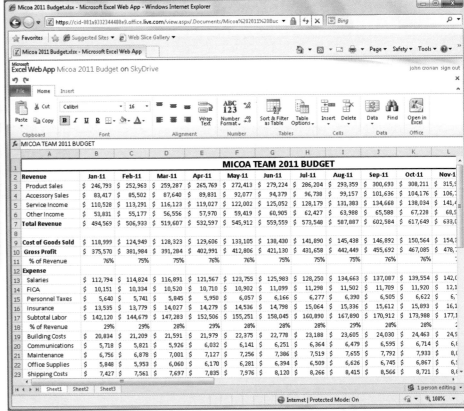

Figure 5-14: Working on a worksheet in Excel Web App feels very much like working on it at your desktop.

Chapter 6
Formatting a Worksheet

Arguably, the primary purpose of a worksheet is to provide a grid to calculate numbers, generally regarded as a rather boring display of numeric data. Excel provides you with the tools to adjust and rearrange the row-and-column grid to meet your needs, but it goes much further to bring emphasis, coordinated colors, and other features that let you add *presentation* to your data.

In this chapter you will learn how to add and delete cells, rows, and columns, and how to change their appearance, both manually and by having Excel do it for you. You will see how to change the appearance of text, how to use themes and styles for a more consistent look, and how to add comments to a cell to better explain important points. Techniques to better display workbooks and change worksheets are also covered.

![UICKSTEPS clock logo]

ADDING AND REMOVING ROWS, COLUMNS, AND CELLS

You can insert or delete rows one at a time or select adjacent and nonadjacent rows to perform these actions on them together. (See Chapter 5 for information on selecting rows, columns, and cells.)

ADD A SINGLE ROW

1. Select the row below where you want the new row.

2. In the Home tab Cells group, click the **Insert** down arrow, and click **Insert Sheet Rows**; or right-click a cell in the selected row, and click **Insert**.

ADD MULTIPLE ADJACENT ROWS

1. Select the number of rows you want immediately below the row where you want the new rows.

2. In the Home tab Cells group, click the **Insert** down arrow, and click **Insert Sheet Rows**; or right-click a cell in the selected rows, and click **Insert**.

ADD ROWS TO MULTIPLE NONADJACENT ROWS

1. Select the number of rows you want immediately below the first row where you want the new rows.

2. Hold down the **CTRL** key while selecting the number of rows you want immediately below any other rows.

3. In the Home tab Cells group, click the **Insert** down arrow, and click **Insert Sheet Rows**; or right-click any selection, and click **Insert**.

ADD A SINGLE COLUMN

1. Select the column to the right of where you want the new column.

2. In the Home tab Cells group, click the **Insert** down arrow, and click **Insert Sheet Columns**; or right-click a cell in the selected column, and click **Insert**.

Continued . . .

Work with Cells, Rows, and Columns

Getting a worksheet to look the way you want will probably involve adding and removing cells, rows, and/or columns to appropriately separate your data and remove unwanted space. You might also want to adjust the size and type of cell border and add comments to provide ancillary information about the contents of a cell. This section covers these features and more.

Adjust Row Height

You can change the height of a row manually or by changing cell contents.

CHANGE THE HEIGHT USING A MOUSE

1. Select one or more rows (they can be adjacent or nonadjacent).

2. Point at the bottom border of a selected row heading until the pointer changes to a cross with up and down arrowheads.

3. Drag the border up or down to the row height you want (as you are dragging, the row height is shown in *points*—there are 72 points to an inch—and in *pixels*).

CHANGE THE HEIGHT BY ENTERING A VALUE

1. Select the rows you want to adjust.

2. In the Home tab Cells group, click **Format**, and under Cell Size, click **Row Height**; or right-click a cell in the selected rows, and click **Row Height**. The Row Height dialog box appears.

3. Type a new height in points, and click **OK**. The cell height changes, but the size of the cell contents stays the same.

QUICKSTEPS

ADDING AND REMOVING ROWS, COLUMNS, AND CELLS (Continued)

ADD MULTIPLE ADJACENT COLUMNS

1. Select the number of columns you want immediately to the right of the column where you want the new columns.

2. In the Home tab Cells group, click the **Insert** down arrow, and click **Insert Sheet Columns**; or right-click a cell in the selected columns, and click **Insert**.

ADD COLUMNS TO MULTIPLE NONADJACENT COLUMNS

1. Select the number of columns you want immediately to the right of the first column where you want the new columns.

2. Hold down the **CTRL** key while selecting the number of columns you want immediately to the right of any other columns.

3. In the Home tab Cells group, click the **Insert** down arrow, and click **Insert Sheet Columns**; or right-click any selection, and click **Insert**.

ADD CELLS

1. Select the cells adjacent to where you want to insert the new cells.

2. In the Home tab Cells group, click the **Insert** down arrow, and click **Insert Cells**; or right-click the cell, and click **Insert**.

3. In the Insert dialog box, choose the direction to shift the existing cells to make room for the new cells. Click **OK**.

Continued . . .

CHANGE ROW HEIGHT BY CHANGING CELL CONTENTS

1. Select one or more cells, rows, or characters that you want to change in height.

2. Change the cell contents. Examples of the various ways to do this include:

- **Changing font size:** In the Home tab Font group, click the **Font Size** down arrow, and click a size from the drop-down list. You can drag up and down the list of font sizes and see the impact of each on the worksheet before selecting one, as shown in Figure 6-1. However, if you have already manually changed the row height, changing the font size of a cell's contents will not automatically change the row height.

- **Placing characters on two or more lines within a cell:** Place the insertion point at the end of a line or where you want the line to break, and press **ALT+ENTER**.

- **Inserting graphics or drawing objects:** See Chapter 14 for information on working with graphics.

When a selected object changes size or a new object is inserted, if its height becomes larger than the original row height, the height of all cells in the row(s) will be increased. The size of the other cell's contents, however, stays the same.

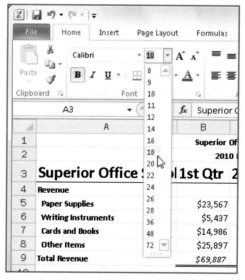

Figure 6-1: **You can preview the effects of changing row heights by increasing or decreasing the font size in selected cells.**

QUICKSTEPS

ADDING AND REMOVING ROWS, COLUMNS, AND CELLS *(Continued)*

REMOVE CELLS, ROWS, AND COLUMNS

1. Select the single or adjacent items (cells, rows, or columns) you wish to remove. If you want to remove nonadjacent items, hold down the **CTRL** key while clicking them.

2. In the Home tab Cells group, click the **Delete** down arrow, and click the command applicable to what you want to remove; or right-click the selection, and click **Delete**.

3. When deleting selected cells, the Delete dialog box appears. Choose from which direction to fill in the removed cells, and click **OK**.

MERGE CELLS

Select the cells you want to combine into one cell; for example, you can create one long cell across your column headers and center a title in it.

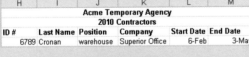

1. In the Home tab Alignment group, click the **Merge & Center** down arrow. (If all you want to do is merge and center, click the button.)

2. Click the applicable tool from the drop-down list.

CHANGE ROW HEIGHT TO FIT THE SIZE OF CELL CONTENTS

Excel automatically adjusts row height to accommodate the largest object or text size added to a row. If you subsequently removed larger objects or text and you need to resize to fit the remaining objects, you can do so using AutoFit.

- Double-click the bottom border of the row heading for a row or selected rows.

  –Or–

- Select the cell or rows you want to size. In the Home tab Cells group, click **Format** and click **AutoFit Row Height**.

The row heights(s) will adjust to fit the highest content.

Adjust Column Width

As with changing row height, you can change the width of a column manually or by changing cell contents.

CHANGE THE WIDTH USING A MOUSE

1. Select one or more columns (columns can be adjacent or nonadjacent).

2. Point at the right border of a selected column heading until the pointer changes to a cross with left and right arrowheads.

3. Drag the border to the left or right to the width you want.

CHANGE THE WIDTH BY ENTERING A VALUE

1. Select the columns you want to adjust.

2. In the Home tab Cells group, click **Format** and click **Column Width**; or right-click the cell, and click **Column Width**. The Column Width dialog box appears.

NOTE

You cannot change the width of a single cell without changing the width of all cells in the column.

TIP

The default column width for a worksheet is determined by the average number of characters in the default font that will fit in the column (not in points, as with row height). For example, the default Calibri 11 pt. font provides a standard column width of 8.43 characters. If you want to change the default column width, in the Home tab Cells group, click **Format** and click **Default Width**. Type a width and click **OK**. Columns at the original standard width will change to reflect the new value.

TIP

If you hide one or more rows or columns beginning with column A or row 1, it does not look like you can drag across the rows or columns on both sides of the hidden rows or columns to unhide them. However, you can by selecting the row or column to the right or below the hidden row or column and dragging the selection into the heading. Then when you click **Unhide** from the context menu or **Unhide Rows** or **Unhide Columns** from the Format menu, the hidden object will appear. If you don't do this, you won't be able to recover the hidden row or column.

3. Type a new width, and click **OK**. The cell width changes, but the size of the cell contents stays the same.

CHANGE COLUMN WIDTH TO FIT THE SIZE OF CELL CONTENTS

- Double-click the right border of the column header for the column or selected columns.

  –Or–

- Select the cell or columns you want to size. In the Home tab Cells group, click **Format** and click **AutoFit Column Width**.

The column width(s) will adjust to fit the longest entry.

Hide and Unhide Rows and Columns

Hidden rows and columns provide a means to temporarily remove rows or columns from view without deleting them or their contents.

HIDE ROWS AND COLUMNS

1. Select the rows or columns to be hidden (see Chapter 5).

2. In the Home tab Cells group, click **Format**, click **Hide & Unhide**, and click **Hide Rows** or **Hide Columns**; or right-click the selection, and click **Hide**.

   –Or–

   Drag the bottom border of the rows to be hidden *up*, or drag the right border of the columns to be hidden to the *left*.

The row numbers or column letters of the hidden cells are omitted, as shown in Figure 6-2. (You can also tell cells are hidden by the slightly darker border in the row or column headers between the hidden rows or columns.)

UNHIDE ROWS OR COLUMNS

1. Drag across the row or column headings on both sides of the hidden rows or columns.

2. In the Home tab Cells group, click **Format**, click **Hide & Unhide**, and click **Unhide Rows** or **Unhide Columns**.

   –Or–

   Right-click the selection and click **Unhide**.

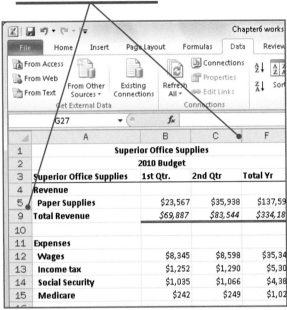

Darker heading border identifies hidden rows and columns

Figure 6-2: *Rows 6, 7, and 8 and columns D and E are hidden in this worksheet.*

Change Cell Borders

Borders provide a quick and effective way to emphasize and segregate data on a worksheet. You can create borders by choosing from samples or by setting them up in a dialog box. Use the method that suits you best.

PICK A BORDER

1. Select the cell, range, row, or column whose border you want to modify.

2. In the Home tab Font group, click the **Border** down arrow, and select the border style you want. (The style you choose remains as the available border style on the button.)

3. To remove a border, select the cell(s), click the **Border** down arrow, and click **No Border**.

PREVIEW BORDERS BEFORE YOU CHANGE THEM

1. Select the cell, range, row, or column that you want modify with a border.

2. In the Home tab Font group, click the **Border** down arrow, and click **More Borders**.

   –Or–

   In the Home tab Font group, click the **Dialog Box Launcher**; or right-click the selection, and click **Format Cells**. Click the **Border** tab in the Format Cells dialog box.

   In either case, the Format Cells dialog box appears with the Border tab displayed, as shown in Figure 6-3.

3. In the Border area in the center of the dialog box, you will see a preview of the selected cells. Use the other tools in the dialog box to set up your borders.

   - **Presets buttons:** Set broad border parameters by selecting to have no border, an outline border, or an inside "grid" border (can also be changed manually in the Border area).

   - **Line area:** Select a border style and color (see "Change Themed Colors" later in the chapter for information on color options).

   - **Border buttons:** Choose where you want a border (click once to add the border; click twice to remove it).

   - **Preview box:** You can add borders directly by clicking in the Preview area where you want the border. The border selected in the Style box is added.

4. Click **OK** to apply the borders.

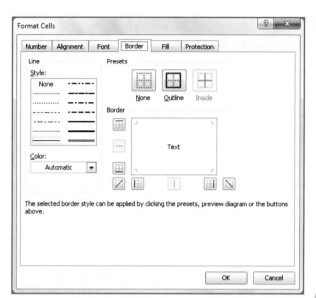

Figure 6-3: **You can build and preview borders for selected cells in the Border tab.**

DRAW BORDERS

1. In the Home tab Font group, click the **Border** down arrow, and under Draw Borders, select the color and style of border you want.

2. From the Border menu, click **Draw Border** to draw an outer border.

   –Or–

   Click **Draw Border Grid** to include interior borders.

3. Use the pencil mouse pointer to drag over the cells you want to have a border.

4. If you want to change a drawn border, click **Erase Border** and drag over a border to remove it.

5. When you are finished, press ESC to turn off the border drawing feature.

Draw Borders
Draw Border
Draw Border Grid
Erase Border
Line Color
Line Style
More Borders...

$8,345	$8,59?	$9,104
$1,252	$1,290	$1,366
$1,035	$1,066	$1,129

Add a Comment

A comment acts as a "notepad" for cells, providing a place on the worksheet for explanatory text that can be hidden until needed.

1. Select the cell where you want the comment.

2. In the Review tab Comments group, click **New Comment**; or right-click the cell, and click **Insert Comment**. In either case, a text box labeled with your user name is attached to the cell.

3. Type your comment and click anywhere on the worksheet to close the comment. An indicator icon (red triangle) in the upper-right corner of the cell shows that a comment is attached.

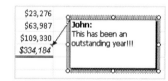

VIEW COMMENTS

You can view an individual comment, view them in sequence, or view all comments on a worksheet.

- To view any comment, point to or select a cell that displays an indicator icon (red triangle) in its upper-right corner. The comment stays displayed as long as your mouse pointer remains in the cell.

TIP

The default behavior for comments is to show the indicator icon (red triangle) and display the comment text when the mouse pointer is hovered over a cell containing a comment. You can also choose to always show the comment text and indicators or to not show the indicators and text. Click the **File** tab, click **Options**, and click the **Advanced** option. In the Display area, under For Cells With Comments, Show, select the behavior you want, and click **OK**.

For cells with comments, show:
- ○ No comments or indicators
- ◉ Indicators only, and comments on hover
- ○ Comments and indicators

TIP

You can also delete comments by selectively clearing them from a cell. In the Home tab Editing group, click **Clear** 🖉▾ and then click **Clear Comments** from the drop-down menu.

NOTE

Moving a comment only moves the editing text box's position in relationship to its parent cell—it does not move the comment to other cells. The new location of moved comments only appears when editing the comment or when you display all comments in the worksheet; otherwise, when either the cell is selected or the mouse hovers over the cell, it appears in its default position.

- • To view comments in sequence, in the Review tab Comments group, click **Next**. The next comment in the worksheet, moving left to right and down the rows, displays until you click another cell or press **ESC**. Click **Previous** in the Comments group to reverse the search direction.

- • To keep the comment displayed while doing other work, select the cell that contains the comment. In the Review tab Comments group, click **Show/Hide Comments**; or right-click the cell, and click **Show/Hide Comments**. (Click either command to hide the comment.)

- • To view all comments in a worksheet and keep the comment displayed while doing other work, in the Review tab Comments group, click **Show All Comments**. (Click the command a second time to hide all comments.)

EDIT A COMMENT

1. Select a cell that displays an indicator icon (red triangle) in its upper-right corner.

2. In the Review tab Comments group, click **Edit Comment**; or right-click the cell, and click **Edit Comment**.

3. Edit the text, including the user name if appropriate. Click anywhere in the worksheet when finished.

DELETE A COMMENT

1. Select the cell or cells that contain the comments you want to delete.

2. In the Review tab Comments group, click **Delete**; or right-click the cell, and click **Delete Comment**.

MOVE AND RESIZE A COMMENT

Display the comment (see "Edit a Comment" for steps to open a comment for editing).

- • To **resize**, point to one of the corner or mid-border sizing handles. When the pointer becomes a double arrow-headed line, drag the handle in the direction you want to increase or decrease the comment's size.

- • To **move**, point at the wide border surrounding the comment. When the pointer becomes a cross with arrowhead tips, drag the comment to where you want it.

FORMATTING COMMENTS

You can apply several formatting techniques to comments, including changing text, borders, and color. These and other attributes are changed using the Format Comment dialog box, available after a comment is opened for editing (see "Edit a Comment").

CHANGE THE APPEARANCE OF COMMENT TEXT

1. To change the formatting of existing text, select the text first. If you do not select existing text, only new text you type will show the changes after you make them.

2. Right-click the interior of the comment, and click **Format Comment**. Make and preview the changes you want in the Font tab, and click **OK**. Alternatively, in the Home tab Font group, click the applicable control to change the font, size, and styling (see "Change Fonts" later in this chapter).

CHANGE A COMMENT'S COLOR AND BORDER

1. Right-click the border of the comment, and click **Format Comment**.

2. In the Format Comment dialog box, click the **Colors And Lines** tab.

3. Click the **Fill Color** down arrow to open the gallery. Click the new color you want (see "Change Themed Colors" for information on color options).

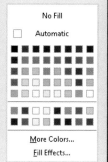

4. In the Line area, change the attributes that control the comment's border. Click **OK** when finished.

COPY A COMMENT

1. Select the cell that contains the comment you want to copy (only the comment will be added to a new cell, not any other cell contents).

2. In the Home tab Clipboard group, click **Copy**; or right-click the cell, and click **Copy**; or press **CTRL+C**. The cell is surrounded by a flashing border.

3. Select the cells to which you want the comment copied. Then, in the Clipboard group, click the **Paste** down arrow, and click **Paste Special**. In the Paste Special dialog box, under Paste, click **Comments**, and then click **OK**.

4. Repeat step 3 to paste the comment into other cells. When finished, press **ESC** to remove the flashing border.

Apply Formatting

Formatting gives life to a worksheet, transforming a rather dull collection of text and numbers into pleasing colors, shades, and variations in size and effects that bring attention to points you are trying to emphasize. You can apply or create *themes* (consistent use of color, fonts, and graphics effects) to give your worksheets a coordinated appearance. If you want more control, you can apply *styles* (consistent formatting parameters applicable to specific worksheet objects) and *direct formatting* (use of ribbon buttons and dialog boxes) to cells and text. (See the "Understanding Excel Formatting" QuickFacts for more information on these formatting types.) In addition, you can transfer formatting attributes from one cell to others.

Apply Themes

Themes are the most hands-off way to add a coordinated look and feel to a worksheet. Built-in themes control the formatting of themed elements, such as the color of table headers and rows and the font used in chart text. In addition, you can change themes and modify themed elements (colors, fonts, and graphic effects).

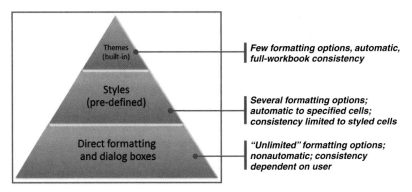

Figure 6-4: *Excel provides three levels of formatting assistance.*

UNDERSTANDING EXCEL FORMATTING

There are a plethora of ways you can change the appearance of text and worksheet elements. Without having a sense of the "method behind the madness," it's easy to become confused and frustrated when attempting to enhance your work. Excel (as well as Microsoft Word and Microsoft PowerPoint) operates on a hierarchy of formatting assistance (see Figure 6-4). The higher a formatting feature is on the stack, the broader and more automatic are its effects; the lower on the stack, the more user intervention is required, although you will have more control over the granularity of any given feature.

- **Themes** are at the top of the formatting heap. Themes provide an efficiently lazy way to apply professionally designed color, font, and graphic elements to a workbook. Each theme (with names like Office, Currency, and Solstice) includes 12 colors (4 text colors, 6 accent colors, and 2 hyperlink colors), along with 6 shades of each primary theme color. Separate collections of theme fonts are available for headings and the body text (the default workbook theme is Office, which is where the Calibri font comes from that you see in new workbooks). When you switch themes, all theme-affected elements are changed. You can modify existing themes and save them, creating your own theme.

Continued . . .

CHANGE THE CURRENT THEME

By default, Excel applies the Office theme to new workbooks. You can easily view the effects from the other built-in themes and change to the one you prefer.

1. In the Page Layout tab Themes group, click **Themes**. A gallery of the available themes (built-in, custom, and a selection from those available from Office Online) is displayed, as shown in Figure 6-5.

2. Point to each theme and see how colors, fonts, and graphics change in themed elements. The best way to view changes is to create a table and associated chart, and with it displayed, point to each theme in the gallery and see how the table and chart look (see Figure 6-5). Chapter 14 provides more information on charts and tables.

3. Click the theme you want, and save your workbook.

CHANGE THEMED COLORS

Each theme comes with 12 primary colors (see the "Understanding Excel Formatting" QuickFacts) affecting text, accents, and hyperlinks. You can choose a theme with different colors or modify each constituent color.

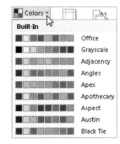

1. In the Page Layout tab Themes group, click **Colors**. The drop-down list displays the built-in and online themes and 8 of the 12 colors associated with each theme.

UNDERSTANDING EXCEL FORMATTING *(Continued)*

- **Styles** occupy the middle tier of Excel formatting. Styles apply consistent formatting to directed Excel components, such as cells, tables, charts, and PivotTables. Styles, similar to themes, can be modified and saved for your own design needs. Both themes and styles are supported by several galleries of their respective formatting options, and provide a live preview when you hover your mouse pointer over each choice. Certain attributes of a style are *themed*, meaning they are consistent with the current theme and change accordingly.

- **Direct formatting** is the feature most of us have used to get the look we want, found in buttons on the ribbon and formatting dialog boxes divided into several tabs of options. Direct formatting provides the greatest control and access to formatting features, but even though Excel now provides live previews for many options, most still require you to accept the change, view the result in the workbook, and then repeat the process several times to get the result you want (and then require you to start all over when moving, for example, from formatting a table to a chart).

So how do you best put this hierarchy to work? Start at the top by applying a theme. If its formatting works for you, you're done! If you need more customization, try simply changing to a different theme. Need more options? Try applying a style to one of the style-affected components. Finally, if you need total control, use a component's formatting dialog box and ribbon buttons to make detailed changes. When you're all done, save all your changes as a new theme that you can apply to new workbooks, and also to your Word documents and PowerPoint presentations.

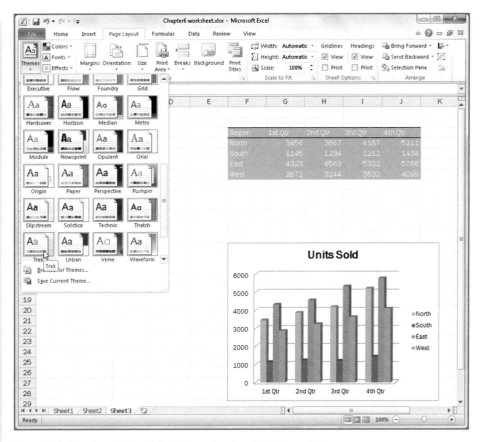

Figure 6-5: ***Excel provides 40 built-in professionally designed themes.***

2. At the bottom of the list, click **Create New Theme Colors**. The Create New Theme Colors dialog box displays each constituent theme color and a sample displaying the current selections (see Figure 6-6).

3. Click the theme color you want to change. A gallery of colors displays and provides the following three options from which you select a new color:

- **Theme Colors** displays a matrix of the 12 primary colors in the current theme and 6 shades associated with each. Click a color and see the change in the Sample area of the Create New Theme Colors dialog box.

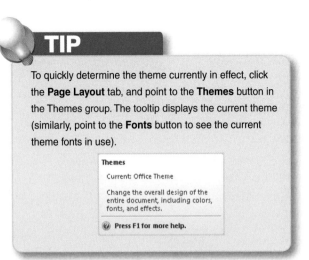

To quickly determine the theme currently in effect, click the **Page Layout** tab, and point to the **Themes** button in the Themes group. The tooltip displays the current theme (similarly, point to the **Fonts** button to see the current theme fonts in use).

> **Themes**
>
> Current: Office Theme
>
> Change the overall design of the entire document, including colors, fonts, and effects.
>
> ⓘ **Press F1 for more help.**

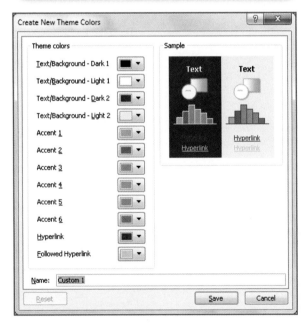

Figure 6-6: *Each theme color can be modified from an essentially infinite number of choices.*

- **Standard Colors** displays the 10 standard colors in the color spectrum (red through violet). Click the color you want.

- **More Colors** opens the Colors dialog box, shown in Figure 6-7, from where you can select a custom color by clicking a color and using a slider to change its shading, or by selecting a color model and entering specific color values. In addition, you can click the **Standard** tab and select from a hexagonal array of Web-friendly colors.

4. Repeat step 3 for any other theme color you want to change. If you get a bit far afield in your color changes, don't panic. Click **Reset** at the bottom of the Create New Theme Colors dialog box to return to the default theme colors.

5. Type a new name for the color combination you've selected, and click **Save**. Custom colors are available for selection at the top of the theme Colors drop-down list.

CHANGE THEMED FONTS

Each theme includes two fonts. The *body* font is used for general text entry (the Calibri font in the default Office theme is the body font). A *heading* font

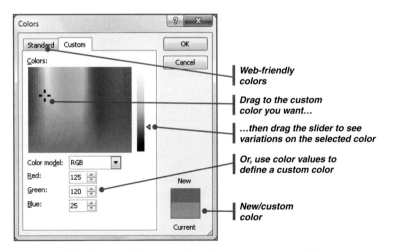

Figure 6-7: *The Colors dialog box offers the greatest control of custom color selection, as well as a collection of standard Web-friendly colors.*

is also included and used in a few cell styles (see "Use Cell Styles" later in this chapter).

1. In the Page Layout tab Themes group, click **Fonts**. The drop-down list, shown in Figure 6-8, displays a list of theme font combinations (heading and body). The current theme font combination is highlighted.

2. Point to each combination to see how the fonts will appear on your worksheet.

3. Click the combination you want, or click **Create New Theme Fonts** at the bottom of the drop-down list (see Figure 6-8).

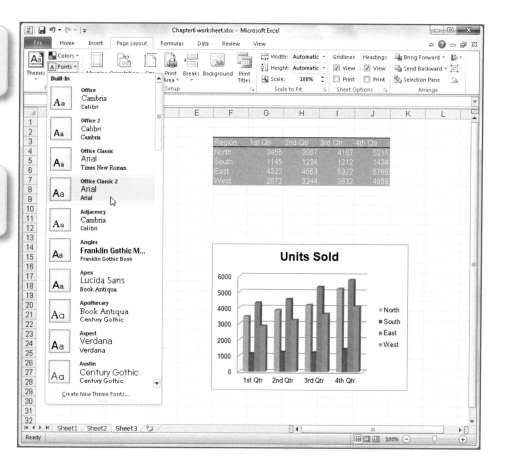

Figure 6-8: **You can see how different theme body and heading font combinations affect your worksheet simply by pointing to them.**

4. In the Create New Theme Fonts dialog box, click either or both the **Heading Font** and **Body Font** down arrows to select new fonts. View the new combination in the Sample area.

5. Type a new name for the font combination you've selected, and click **Save**. Custom fonts are available for selection at the top of the theme Fonts drop-down list.

CHANGE THEMED GRAPHIC EFFECTS

Shapes, illustrations, pictures, and charts include graphic effects that are controlled by themes. Themed graphics are modulated in terms of their lines (borders), fills, and effects (such as shadowed, raised, and shaded). For example, some themes simply change an inserted rectangle's fill color, while other themes affect the color, the weight of its border, and whether it has a 3-D appearance.

1. In the Page Layout tab Themes group, click **Effects**. The drop-down list displays a gallery of effects. The current effect is highlighted.

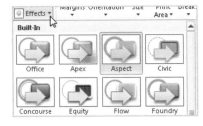

2. Point to each effect to see how it changes your worksheet, assuming you have a theme-based graphic or other element inserted on the worksheet (see Chapter 14 for information on inserting charts and graphics).

3. Click the effect you want.

Create Custom Themes

Changes you make to a built-in theme (or to a previously created custom theme) can be saved as a custom theme and reused in other Office 2010 documents.

1. Make color, font, and effects changes to the current theme (see "Apply Themes" earlier in this chapter).

2. In the Page Layout tab Themes group, click **Themes** and click **Save Current Theme**. The Save Current Theme dialog box appears with the custom Office themes folder displayed, as shown in Figure 6-9.

3. Name the file and click **Save** to store the theme in the Document Themes folder.

–Or–

Name the file and browse to the folder where you want to store it. Click **Save** when finished.

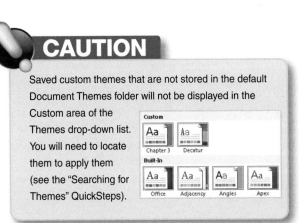

CAUTION

Saved custom themes that are not stored in the default Document Themes folder will not be displayed in the Custom area of the Themes drop-down list. You will need to locate them to apply them (see the "Searching for Themes" QuickSteps).

SEARCHING FOR THEMES

You can quickly find individual theme files and themed documents, and apply them to your workbook. In addition, you can use prebuilt themes that are available from Microsoft Online.

LOCATE AND APPLY THEMES

You can apply themes from other files to your workbooks, either as individual theme files or from other Office 2010 files that have themes applied to them.

1. In the Page Layout tab Themes group, click **Themes** and click **Browse For Themes** at the bottom of the gallery.

2. In the Choose Theme Or Themed Document dialog box, browse to the folder where the themes or themed documents are located. Only those documents will display. (*Themed documents* are Office 2010 files that contain a theme, such as Word files, Excel workbooks, PowerPoint presentations, and their respective templates.)

3. If you are only looking for theme files (.thmx), click **Office Themes And Themed Documents**, and click **Office Themes (.thmx)**.

4. Select the Office document whose theme you want to apply or the theme file you want to apply, and click **Open**.

ACQUIRE THEMES FROM OFFICE ONLINE

In the Page Layout tab Themes group, click **Themes** and below the gallery of Built-In themes, click one of the themes you acquired from Office.com, often from a template you downloaded. Since these are Office themes and are shared across products, you may acquire them from the work you do in other Office products such as Word or PowerPoint.

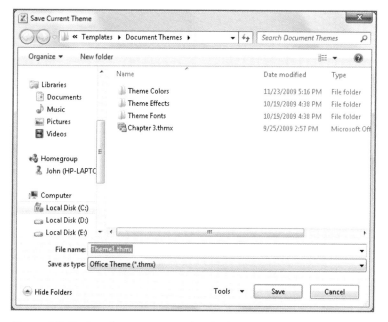

Figure 6-9: **Custom themes are saved as individual files, along with custom theme colors, effects, and fonts.**

Use Cell Styles

Cell styles allow you to apply consistent formatting to specific cells, and let you make changes to styled cells with a few mouse clicks instead of changing each cell individually. Excel provides dozens of predefined styles, categorized by use. One category, themed cell styles, has the additional advantage of being fully integrated with the current theme. Colors associated with a theme change will automatically carry over to themed cell styles, preserving the coordinated appearance of your worksheet. Of course, you can modify any applied style and save the changes to create your own custom style.

APPLY A STYLE

1. Select the cells you want to format with a style.

2. In the Home tab Styles group, click **Cell Styles**. A gallery of cell styles is displayed, as shown in Figure 6-10.

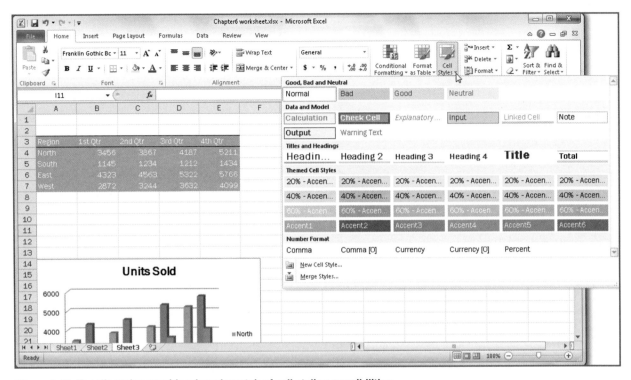

Figure 6-10: *Excel's styles provide a broad swatch of cell styling possibilities.*

TIP

The easiest way to ensure a common look and feel to your Excel 2010 workbooks is to create or apply the theme you want and save the workbook as a *template* (a template being a workbook that contains data or a layout from which you want to create other workbooks). In addition to the theme-controlled aspects of a workbook, the template allows you to consistently re-create formulas, tables, charts, and all else that Excel has to offer. To save a workbook as a template, click **Save As** on the File menu, select **Excel Template (.xltx)** from the Save As Type drop-down list, and click **Save**.

3. Point to several styles in the gallery to see how each style affects your selected cells.

4. Click the style that best suits your needs. The style formatting is applied to your selected cells.

CREATE A CUSTOM STYLE

You can create your own style by starting with a predefined style and making changes, or you can start from scratch and apply all formatting directly, using the formatting tools on the ribbon or in a formatting dialog box. In either case,

NOTE

Styles also can be applied to charts and tables. Using styles with these components is covered in Chapter 14.

NOTE

The default font used in each style is derived from the current theme. When you change themes, the font used in styled cells will change according to the font used in the new theme. Themed cell styles, unlike other cell styles, will change color in accordance with the new theme.

TIP

You can avoid going back and forth between the Page Layout and Home tabs to apply themes and styles by placing the respective galleries on the Quick Access toolbar. Right-click a gallery icon, and click **Add To Quick Access Toolbar**; or right-click anywhere in the open gallery, and click **Add Gallery To Quick Access Toolbar**.

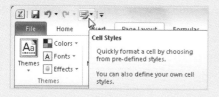

NOTE

Direct formatting using the ribbon and the Format Cells dialog box is discussed in other sections of this chapter.

you can save your changes as a custom style and apply it from the Cell Styles gallery.

1. Use one or more, or a combination, of the following techniques to format at least one cell as you want:

   • Apply a predefined style to the cell(s) you want to customize.

   • Use the formatting tools in the ribbon (Home tab Font, Alignment, and Number groups).

   • Right-click a cell to be styled, click **Format Cells**, and use the six tabs in the Format Cells dialog box to create the styling format you want. Click **OK** when finished.

2. In the Home tab Styles group, click **Cell Styles** and click **New Cell Style** at the bottom of the gallery.

3. In the Style dialog box, type a name for your style, and review the six areas of affected style formatting. If necessary, click **Format** and make formatting adjustments in the Format Cells dialog box. Click **OK** to apply formatting changes.

4. Click **OK** in the Style dialog box to create the style. The new custom style will be displayed in the Custom area at the top of the Cell Styles gallery.

CHANGE A CELL STYLE

1. In the Home tab Styles group, click **Cell Styles**.

2. Right-click a style (custom or predefined) in the gallery, and click **Modify**.

3. In the Style dialog box, click **Format** and make any formatting adjustments in the Format Cells dialog box. Click **OK** to apply the formatting changes.

4. Click **OK** in the Style dialog box to save changes to the style.

REMOVE A CELL STYLE

You can remove a style's formatting applied to selected cells, or you can completely remove the cell style from Excel (and concurrently remove all style formatting from affected cells).

- To remove style formatting from cells, select the cells, click **Cell Styles** in the Styles group, and click the **Normal** style.

- To permanently remove a style, click **Cell Styles** in the Styles group, right-click the cell style you want removed, and click **Delete**.

ADD CELL STYLES FROM OTHER WORKBOOKS

1. Open both the workbook whose styles you want to add and the workbook where you want the styles to be added in the same Excel window.

2. In the View tab Window group, click **Switch Windows** and click the workbook to which you want the styles added, making it the active workbook.

3. In the Home tab Styles group, click **Cell Styles** and below the gallery, click **Merge Styles**.

4. In the Merge Styles dialog box, click the workbook from which you want to add styles. Click **OK**.

Change Fonts

Each *font* is composed of a *typeface*, such as Calibri; a *style*, such as italic; and a size. Other characteristics, such as color and super-/subscripting, further distinguish text. Excel also provides several underlining options that are useful in accounting applications.

1. On a worksheet, select:
   - Cells to apply font changes to all characters
   - Characters to apply font changes to just the selected text and numbers

2. Use one of the following techniques to access font tools and options:
   - On the ribbon, click the **Home** tab, and click the appropriate Font group tools (see Figure 6-11).

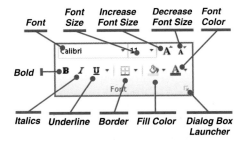

Figure 6-11: **Font group tools apply formatting to text.**

Figure 6-12: Change the appearance of text by changing its font and other characteristics.

- Double-click or right-click a cell or selection, and use the font tools available on the mini toolbar (you might need to move the cursor over the faded toolbar to see it more clearly).

- Click the Font group **Dialog Box Launcher** arrow (located in the lower-right corner of group).

- Right-click a cell or selection, click **Format Cells**, and then click the **Font** tab.

3. In the latter two cases, the Format Cells dialog box appears with the Font tab displayed, as shown in Figure 6-12. Make and preview changes, and click **OK** when finished.

Change Alignment and Orientation

You can modify how characters appear within a cell by changing their alignment, orientation, and "compactness."

1. Select the cells whose contents you want to change.

2. Use one of the following techniques to access font tools and options:

- On the ribbon, click the **Home** tab, and click the appropriate Alignment group tools (see Figure 6-13).

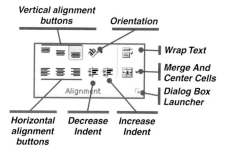

Figure 6-13: Alignment group tools allow you to reposition text.

- Click the Alignment group **Dialog Box Launcher**.

- Right-click a cell or selection, click **Format Cells**, and then click the **Alignment** tab.

3. In the latter two cases, the Format Cells dialog box appears with the Alignment tab displayed, as shown in Figure 6-14. The specific features of the Alignment tab are described in Table 6-1.

4. Click **OK** when you are finished.

FEATURE	OPTION	DESCRIPTION
Text Alignment, Horizontal	General	Right-aligns numbers, left-aligns text, and centers error values; Excel default setting
	Left (Indent)	Left-aligns characters with optional indentation spinner
	Center	Centers characters in the cell
	Right (Indent)	Right-aligns characters with optional indentation spinner
	Fill	Fills cell with recurrences of content
	Justify	Justifies the text in a cell so that, to the degree possible, both the left and right ends are vertically aligned
	Center Across Selection	Centers text across one or more cells; used to center titles across several columns
	Distributed (Indent)	Stretches cell contents across cell width by adding space between words, with optional indentation spinner
Text Alignment Vertical	Top	Places the text at the top of the cell
	Center	Places the text in the center of the cell
	Bottom	Places the text at the bottom of the cell; Excel's default setting
	Justify	Evenly distributes text between the top and bottom of a cell to fill it by adding space between lines
	Distributed	Vertically arranges characters equally within the cell (behaves the same as Justify)
Orientation		Angles text in a cell by dragging the red diamond up or down or by using the Degrees spinner
Text Control	Wrap Text	Moves text that extends beyond the cell's width to the line below
	Shrink To Fit	Reduces character size so that cell contents fit within cell width (cannot be used with Wrap Text)
	Merge Cells	Creates one cell from contiguous cells, "increasing" the width of a cell without changing the width of the column(s)
Right To Left, Text Direction	Context	Text entry flows according to keyboard language in use
	Left To Right	Text entry flows from the left as in Western countries
	Right To Left	Text entry flows from the right as in many Middle Eastern and East Asian countries

Table 6-1: *Text-Alignment Options in Excel*

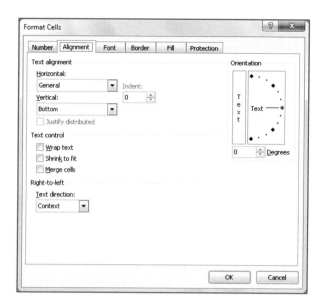

Figure 6-14: *The Alignment tab provides detailed text-alignment options.*

Add a Background

You can add color and shading to selected cells to provide a solid background. You can also add preset patterns, either alone or in conjunction with a solid background, for even more effect.

1. Select the cell, range, row, or column that you want to modify with a background.

2. In the Home tab Alignment group, click its **Dialog Box Launcher**.

   –Or–

   Right-click the selection and click **Format Cells**.

   In either case, the Format Cells dialog box appears.

3. Click the **Fill** tab (see Figure 6-15), and choose colored and/or patterned fills.

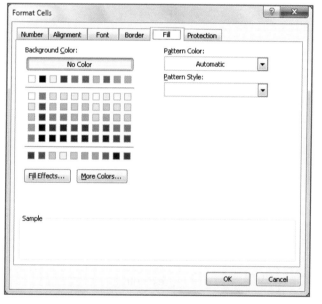

Figure 6-15: *Use the Fill tab to apply colored or patterned backgrounds to cells.*

USE SOLID-COLORED BACKGROUNDS

1. In the Fill tab, click one of the color options in the Background Color area (see "Change Themed Colors" earlier in this chapter for information on the various color options).

   –Or–

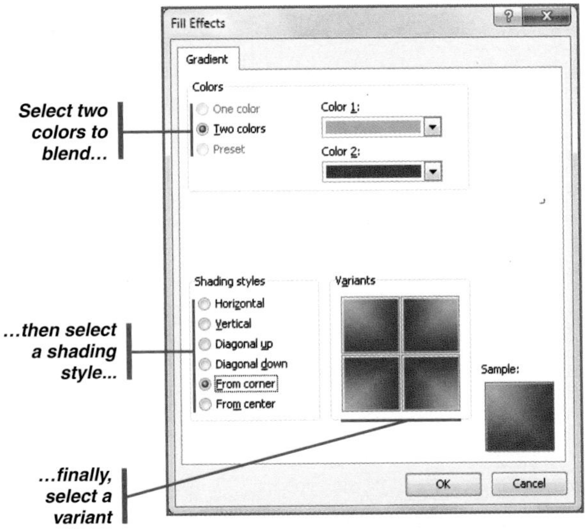

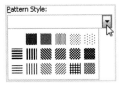

Select two colors to blend...

...then select a shading style...

...finally, select a variant

Figure 6-16: **You can add pizzazz to cell fills using gradient effects.**

Click **Fill Effects** to apply blended fills, as shown in Figure 6-16. Preview your selections in the Sample area, and click **OK**.

2. Preview your selections in the larger Sample area at the bottom of the Fill tab, and click **OK** when finished.

USE PATTERNED BACKGROUNDS

1. In the Fill tab, click the **Pattern Style** down arrow to display a gallery of patterns. Click the design you want, and see it enlarged in the Sample area at the bottom of the Fill tab.

2. If you want to colorize the pattern, click the **Pattern Color** down arrow to display the color gallery (see "Change Themed Colors" earlier in this chapter for information on the various color options), and select one of the color options.

3. Click **OK** when finished to close the Format Cells dialog box.

Copy Formatting

You can manually copy formatting from one cell to other cells using the Format Painter, as well as when you are inserting cells.

USE THE FORMAT PAINTER

1. Select the cell whose formatting you want to copy.

2. In the Home tab Clipboard group, click the **Format Painter**  button once if you only want to apply the formatting one time.

    –Or–

    Double-click the **Format Painter** button to keep it turned on for repeated use.

3. Select the cells where you want the formatting applied.

4. If you single-clicked the Format Painter before applying it to your selection, it will turn off after you apply it to your first selection; if you double-clicked the button, you may select other cells to continue copying the formatting.

5. Double-click the **Format Painter** to turn it off, or press **ESC**.

NOTE

If you choose Automatic for the pattern color in the Format Cells Fill tab, the pattern is applied to the background color, but if you pick both a background color and a pattern color, the colors are merged.

CAUTION

When the Format Painter is turned on by double-clicking it, every time you select an object on the worksheet, formatting will be applied to it. For this reason, be sure to turn off the Format Painter immediately after you are done copying formats.

You can also copy formatting by using Paste Preview, Paste Special, and the Paste Options smart tag (see Chapter 5).

ATTACH FORMATTING TO INSERTED CELLS, ROWS, AND COLUMNS

Click the **Insert Options** smart tag (the paintbrush icon that appears after an insert), and choose from which direction you want the formatting applied, or choose to clear the formatting.

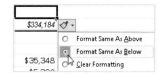

$334,184	○ Format Same As Above
	⊙ Format Same As Below
$35,348	○ Clear Formatting

Arrange and Organize Worksheets

Excel provides several features to help you work with and view worksheets. You can retain headers at the top of the worksheet window as you scroll through hundreds of rows, split a worksheet, and view worksheets from several workbooks. In addition, there are several techniques you can use to add, remove, copy, and organize worksheets.

Lock Rows and Columns

Freezing panes is not the same as freezing data. In an external data range, you can prevent the data from being refreshed, thereby freezing it.

You can lock (or *freeze*) rows and columns in place so that they remain visible as you scroll. Typically, row and column headers are locked in larger worksheets, where you are scrolling through large numbers of rows or columns. You can quickly lock the first row and/or first column in a worksheet, or you can select the rows or columns to freeze.

LOCK ROWS

- In the View tab Window group, click **Freeze Panes** and click **Freeze Top Row**. The top row (typically, your header row) remains in place as you scroll down.

  –Or–

- Select the row below the rows you want to lock, click **Freeze Panes** and click **Freeze Panes** again. A thin border displays on the bottom of the locked row, as shown in Figure 6-17. All rows above the locked row remain in place as you scroll down.

The first two rows are locked in place...

	H	I	J	K
1			Acme Books	
2	ISBN - 10	Category	Author	Title
8	0071343105	Business	Piskurich	Astd Hndbk Training Dsgn
9	0071346082	Parenting	Clark	Coaching Youth Soccer
10	0071358978	Education	Don	How Solve Word Problems Calc
11	0071359621	Medicine	Ratelle	Prev Med & Public Health 9e
12	0071369988	Business	Fitz-Enz	How To Measure Human Res Mg
13	0071375252	Technical	Dewberry Comp	Land Development Handbook, 2
14	0071377964	Technical	Edwards	Beautiful Built-Ins
15	0071408959	Business	Allaire	Options Strategist
16	0071412077	Medicine	Brooks	Medical Microbiology, 23/E
17	0071413014	Technical	Wells	Airport Planning & Mngmt 5e
18	0071418695	Medicine	Desselle	Pharmacy Management: Esent
19	0071418717	Business	Page	Hope Is Not A Strategy Pb

Row: 8

...as you scroll through the rows below them

Figure 6-17: **You can lock rows in place and scroll through only those rows below the frozen rows.**

TIP

You can save the arrangement of Excel windows you set up for future viewing in the workbook. After you have the layout looking as you want, in the View tab Window group, click **Save Workspace**. In the Save Workspace window, type a name for the workspace layout, and click **Save** to save the workspace file (.xlw). To change the arrangement, resave a different layout and/or use the Arrange tool to change how windows are displayed.

LOCK COLUMNS

- In the View tab Window group, click **Freeze Panes** and click **Freeze First Column**. The leftmost column (typically, your header column) remains in place as you scroll to the right.

  –Or–

- Select the column to the right of the columns you want to lock, click **Freeze Panes**, and click **Freeze Panes** again. A thin border displays on the right side of the locked column. All columns to the left of the locked column remain in place as you scroll to the right.

LOCK ROWS AND COLUMNS TOGETHER

1. Select the cell that is below and to the right of the range you want to lock.

2. In the View tab Window group, click **Freeze Panes** and click **Freeze Panes**. A thin border displays below the locked rows and to the right of the locked columns. The range will remain in place as you scroll down or to the right.

⬜	H	I	J	K
1			Acme Books	
2	ISBN - 10	Category	Author	Title
3	0070194351	Technical	Elliott	Stand Hdbk Powerplant Engine
4	0070350787	Technical	Kleinert	Troublesht & Rep Major Appl
5	0070380686	Education	Pen	Sch Intro To Music
6	0070466173	Education	Nash	Sch Outl Strength Materials
7	0071054618	Medicine	Cember	Intro Health Physics 3e
8	0071343105	Business	Piskurich	Astd Hndbk Training Dsgn
9	0071346082	Parenting	Clark	Coaching Youth Soccer
10	0071358978	Education	Don	How Solve Word Problems Calc
11	0071359621	Medicine	Ratelle	Prev Med & Public Health 9e
12	0071369988	Business	Fitz-Enz	How To Measure Human Res Mg
13	0071375252	Technical	Dewberry Comp	Land Development Handbook, 2

Two locked columns

Two locked rows

UNLOCK ROWS AND COLUMNS

In the View tab Window group, click **Freeze Panes** and click **Unfreeze Panes**.

Split a Worksheet

You can divide a worksheet into two independent panes of the same data, as shown in Figure 6-18.

1. To split the worksheet horizontally, drag the row split icon down the worksheet to where you want the split.

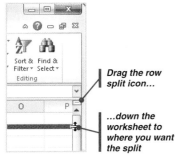

Drag the row split icon...

...down the worksheet to where you want the split

–Or–

To split the worksheet vertically, drag the column split icon (at the right end of the horizontal scroll bar) to the left to where you want the split.

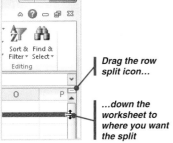

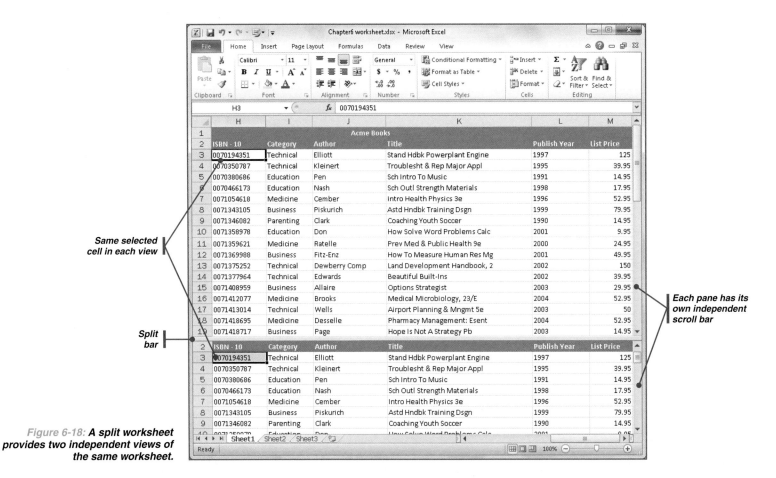

Same selected cell in each view

Split bar

Each pane has its own independent scroll bar

Figure 6-18: **A split worksheet provides two independent views of the same worksheet.**

In either case, a split bar is displayed either across or down the worksheet.

2. Use the scroll bars to view other data within each pane.

3. Remove the split bar by double-clicking it.

WORKING WITH WORKSHEETS

Excel provides several tools you can use to modify the number and identification of worksheets in a workbook.

ADD A WORKSHEET

Right-click the worksheet tab to the right of where you want the new worksheet, click **Insert**, and click **OK**.

–Or–

On the worksheet bar, click **Insert Worksheet**. A new worksheet is added to the right of any current tabs.

DELETE A WORKSHEET

Right-click the worksheet tab of the worksheet you want to delete, and click **Delete**.

MOVE OR COPY A WORKSHEET

You can move or copy worksheets within a workbook or between open workbooks by dragging a worksheet's tab. (See "View Worksheets from Multiple Workbooks" for steps to arrange multiple open workbooks to facilitate dragging objects between them.)

- To move a worksheet, drag the worksheet tab to the position on the worksheet bar where you want it to appear.

- To copy a worksheet, press and hold **CTRL**, and drag the worksheet tab to the position on the worksheet bar where you want it to appear.

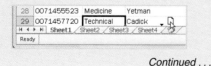

Continued . . .

View Worksheets from Multiple Workbooks

You can divide the Excel worksheet area so that you can view worksheets from multiple workbooks. This arrangement makes it easy to copy data, formulas, and formatting among several worksheets.

1. Open the workbooks that contain the worksheets you want to view.

2. In the View tab Window group, click **Arrange All**. The Arrange Windows dialog box appears.

3. Select an arrangement and click **OK**. (Figure 6-19 shows an example of tiling four workbooks.)

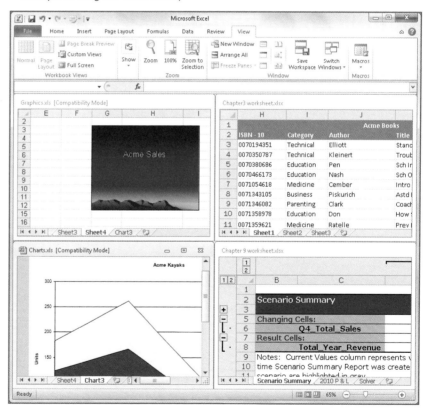

Figure 6-19: **You can look at several workbooks at the same time to compare them or to transfer information among them.**

QUICKSTEPS

WORKING WITH WORKSHEETS

(Continued)

RENAME A WORKSHEET

1. Right-click the worksheet tab of the worksheet you want to rename, and click **Rename**.

   –Or–

   Double-click the worksheet tab.

2. Type a new worksheet name, and press **ENTER**.

COLOR A WORKSHEET TAB

1. Right-click the worksheet tab of the worksheet you want to color, and click **Tab Color**.

2. Select a color from the gallery (see "Change Themed Colors" earlier in this chapter for information on using the color gallery).

CHANGE THE DEFAULT NUMBER OF WORKSHEETS IN A WORKBOOK

1. Click the **File** tab, click **Options**, and click the **General** option.

2. Under When Creating New Workbooks, click the **Include This Many Sheets** spinner to change the number of worksheets you want.

3. Click **OK** when finished.

MOVE THROUGH MULTIPLE WORKSHEETS

Click the navigation buttons on the left end of the worksheet bar.

When clicked, the first left arrow button displays the beginning of the sheet tabs; the second left arrow button cycles the sheet tabs to the left, one per click; the first right arrow button cycles the sheet tabs to the right, one per click; and the second right arrow button displays the end of the sheet tabs.

4. To change the arrangement, simply close the worksheets you do not want to view by selecting a worksheet to close and clicking the ⊠ in its upper-right corner. Return a worksheet to full view in the Excel window by double-clicking its title bar.

Compare Workbooks

Excel provides a few tools that allow easy comparison of two workbooks.

1. Open the workbooks you want to compare.

2. In the View tab Window group, click **View Side By Side** 🔲.

   If you have only two workbooks open, they will appear next to one another. If you have more than two workbooks open, you can select the workbook to view along with the currently active workbook from the Compare Side By Side dialog box.

By default, both workbook windows will scroll at the same rate. To turn off this feature, click **Synchronous Scrolling** 🔳 in the Window group.

Chapter 7

Using Formulas and Functions

Excel lets you easily perform powerful calculations using formulas and functions. Formulas are mathematical statements that follow a set of rules and use a specific syntax. In this chapter you will learn how to reference cells used in formulas, how to give cells names so that they are easily input, how to use conditional formatting to identify cells that satisfy criteria you specify, and how to build formulas. Functions—ready-made formulas that you can use to get quick results for specific applications, such as figuring out loan payments—are also covered. Finally, you will learn about several tools Excel provides to find and correct errors in formulas and functions.

UNDERSTANDING CELL REFERENCING TYPES

There are three basic methods and one extended method for referencing cells used in formulas that adhere to the Excel default "A1" cell reference scheme used in this book.

- **Relative references** in formulas move with cells as cells are copied or moved around a worksheet. This is the most flexible and common way to use cell references, and is the Excel default (for example, the cell in the first row and first column of a sheet is referenced as A1 in the Name box and Formula bar. For example, if you sum a list of revenue items for the first quarter, =SUM(B5:B8), and then copy and paste that summary cell to the summary cells for the other three quarters, Excel will deduce that you want the totals for the other quarters to be =SUM(C5:C8), =SUM(D5:D8), and =SUM(E5:E8). Figure 7-1 shows how this appears on the worksheet.

- **Absolute references** do not change cell addresses when you copy or move formulas. Absolute references are displayed in the worksheet and Formula bar with the dollar sign preceding the reference—for example, A1.

- **Mixed references** include one relative and one absolute cell reference. Such references are displayed in the worksheet and Formula bar with a dollar sign preceding the absolute reference but no dollar sign before the relative reference. For example, $A1 indicates absolute column, relative row; A$1 indicates relative column, absolute row.

- **External (or 3-D) references** are an extended form of relative, absolute, and mixed cell references. They are used when referencing cells from other worksheets or workbooks. Such a reference might look like this in the worksheet and Formula bar: [*workbook name*]*worksheet name*!A1.

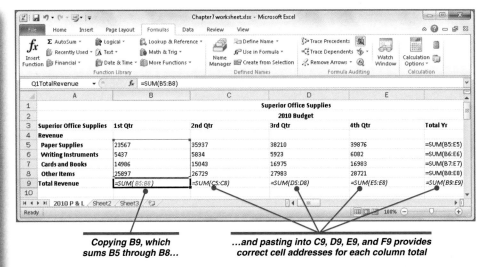

Copying B9, which sums B5 through B8...

...and pasting into C9, D9, E9, and F9 provides correct cell addresses for each column total

Figure 7-1: **Using relative references, Excel logically assumes cell addresses in copied formulas.**

Reference Cells

Formulas typically make use of data already entered in worksheets and need a scheme to locate, or *reference*, that data. Shortcuts are used to help you recall addresses as well as a *syntax*, or set of rules, to communicate to Excel how you want cells used.

Change Cell References

To change cell referencing:

1. Select the cell that contains the formula reference you want to change.

2. In the Formula bar, select the cell address, and press **F4** to switch the cell referencing, starting from a relative reference to the following in this order:

   - Absolute (A1)
   - Mixed (relative column, absolute row) (A$1)

- Mixed (absolute column, relative row) ($A1)
- Relative (A1)

–Or–

Edit the cell address by entering or removing the dollar symbol ($) in front of row and/or column identifiers.

Change to R1C1 References

You can change the A1 cell referencing scheme used by Excel to an older style that identifies both rows and columns numerically, starting in the upper-left corner of the worksheet, rows first, and adds a leading R and C for clarification. For example, cell B4 in R1C1 reference style is R4C2.

1. Click the **File** tab, click **Options**, and click the **Formulas** option.
2. Under Working With Formulas, click the **R1C1 Reference Style** check box.
3. Click **OK** when finished.

Name Cells

You can name a cell (MonthTotal, for example) or a range to refer to physical cell addresses, and then use the names when referencing the cell in formulas and functions. Names are more descriptive, easier to remember, and often quicker to enter than A1-style cell references. You can name a cell directly on the worksheet, use a dialog box and provide amplifying information, or use column or row names.

NAME A CELL OR RANGE DIRECTLY

1. Select the cells you want to reference.
2. Click the **Name** box at the left end of the Formula bar.
3. Type a name (see the accompanying Caution for naming rules), and press **ENTER**. (See "Use the Name Manager" for ways to modify cell names.)

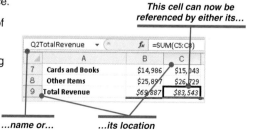

This cell can now be referenced by either its...

...name or...   *...its location*

USING CELL REFERENCE OPERATORS

Cell reference operators (colons, commas, and spaces used in an address, such as E5:E10 E16:E17,E12) provide the syntax for referencing cell ranges, unions, and intersections.

REFERENCE A RANGE

A *range* defines a block of cells.

Type a colon (:) between the upper-leftmost cell and the lower-rightmost cell (for example, B5:C8).

SUM	▾	× ✓ *fx*	=SUM(B5:C8)	
◢	A	B	C	
4	**Revenue**			
5	**Paper Supplies**	$23,567	$35,937	
6	**Writing Instruments**	$5,437	$5,834	
7	**Cards and Books**	$14,986	$15,043	
8	**Other Items**	$25,897	$26,729	

REFERENCE A UNION

A *union* joins multiple cell references.

Type a comma (,) between separate cell references (for example, B5,B7,C6).

●	× ✓ *fx*	=SUM(B5,B7,C6)
	B	C
	$23,567	$35,938
	$5,437	$5,834
	$14,986	$15,043

REFERENCE AN INTERSECTION

An *intersection* is the overlapping, or common, cells in two ranges.

Type a space (press the **SPACEBAR**) between two range-cell references (for example, B5:B8 B7:C8). B7 and B8 are the common cells (and are summed in this example).

●	× ✓ *fx*	=SUM(B5:B8 B7:C8)	
	B	C	D
	$23,567	$35,938	$38
	$5,437	$5,834	$5
	$14,986	$15,043	$16
	$25,897	$26,729	$27

NAME A CELL OR RANGE IN A DIALOG BOX

1. Select the cells you want to reference.

2. In the Formulas tab Defined Names group, click **Define Name**.

   –Or–

   Right-click the selection and click **Define Name**.

   In either case, the New Name dialog box appears, shown in Figure 7-2.

3. Type a name for the cell or range (see the Caution on the previous page for naming rules).

4. Click the **Scope** down arrow, and select whether the name applies to the entire workbook or to one of its worksheets.

5. If desired, type a comment that more fully explains the meaning of the named cells. Comments can be upwards of 1,000 characters and will appear as a tooltip when the name is used in formulas and functions.

6. If you want to modify the cell or cells to be named, click the **Refers To** text box, and type the reference (starting with the equal [=] sign) or reselect the cells from the worksheet.

7. Click **OK** when finished.

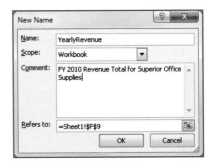

Figure 7-2: **You can easily name cells and add descriptive information.**

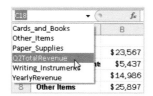

Go to a Named Cell

Named cells are quickly found and selected for you.

Click the **Name** box down arrow to open the drop-down list, and click the named cell or range you want to go to.

–Or–

In the Home tab Editing group, click **Find & Select** and click **Go To**. In the Go To dialog box, double-click the named cell or range you want to go to.

Use the Name Manager

Excel provides several related tools and a Name Manager to help you manage and organize your named cells. To open the Name Manager:

In the Formulas tab Defined Names group, click **Name Manager**. The Name Manager window opens, as shown in Figure 7-3, listing all named cells in the workbook.

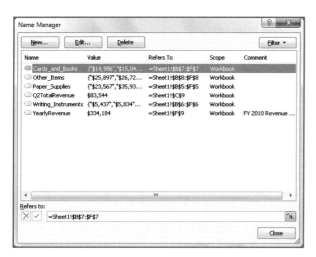

Figure 7-3: The Name Manager provides a central location for organizing, creating, and modifying named cells.

CHANGE CELL NAMES

1. Select the name of the cell reference whose parameters you want to change, and click **Edit**.

2. In the Edit Name dialog box, type a new name, add or change the comment, and/or modify the cell reference (you cannot change the scope—that is, whether the reference applies to a particular worksheet or globally within the workbook). Click **OK** when finished.

DELETE NAMED CELLS

1. Select the name of the cell reference that you want to delete (to select more than one cell name to delete, hold down the **CTRL** key while clicking noncontiguous names in the list; or select the first name in a contiguous range, and hold down **SHIFT** while clicking the last name in the range).

2. Click **Delete** and click **OK** to confirm the deletion.

SORT AND FILTER NAMED CELLS

If you have several named cells in a workbook, you can easily view only the ones you are interested in.

1. To sort named cells, click a column heading to change the sort order from ascending (numerals first 0-9, then A-Z) to descending (Z-A, numerals last 9-0). Click the heading a second time to return to the original order.

   –Or–

   To see only specific categories of named cells, click **Filter** and click the category of named cells you want to see. Only named cells that belong in the category you select will appear in the list of cell names.

2. To return a filtered list to a complete list of named cells, click **Filter** and click **Clear Filter**.

VIEW MORE DATA

The default width of the Name Manager and its columns might not readily display longer cell names, references, or comments.

- To increase a column width, drag the right border of the column heading to the right as far as you need.

- To increase the width of the window, drag either the window's right or left border to the left or right, respectively.

Build Formulas

Formulas are mathematical equations that combine *values* and *cell references* with *operators* to calculate a result. Values are actual numbers or logical values, such as True and False, or the contents of cells that contain numbers or logical values. Cell references point to cells whose values are to be used, for example, E5:E10, E12, and MonthlyTot. Operators, such as + (add), > (greater than), and ^ (use an exponent), tell Excel what type of calculation to perform or logical comparison to apply. Prebuilt formulas, or *functions*, that return a value also can be used in formulas. (Functions are described later in this chapter.)

TIP

To quickly open the Name Manager, press **CTRL+F3** or add the Name Manager icon to the Quick Access toolbar. (Chapter 1 describes how to add tools to the Quick Access toolbar.)

Create a Formula

You create formulas by either entering or referencing values. The character that tells Excel to perform a calculation is the equal sign (=), and it must precede any combination of values, cell references, and operators.

Excel formulas are calculated from left to right according to an ordered hierarchy of operators. For example, exponents precede multiplication and division, which precede addition and subtraction. You can alter the calculation order (and results) by using parentheses; Excel performs the calculation within the innermost parentheses first. For example, =12+48/24 returns 14 (48 is divided by 24, resulting in 2; then 12 is added to 2). Using parentheses, =(12+48)/24 returns 2.5 (12 is added to 48, resulting in 60; then 60 is divided by 24).

ENTER A SIMPLE FORMULA

1. Select a blank cell, and type an equal sign (=).

   –Or–

   Select a blank cell and click in the Formula bar in the blank area directly to the right of the Insert Function f_x icon. The function area expands with the addition of the Cancel $\times$ and Enter $\checkmark$ icons.

   The equal sign displays both in the cell and in the Formula bar, as will the additional characters you type. The insertion point (where Excel expects you to type the next character) is placed to the right of the equal sign in either the cell or Formula bar, depending on where you typed it.

2. Type a value, such as 64.

3. Type an operator, such as +.

4. Type a second value, such as 96.

5. Complete the entry by pressing **ENTER** or clicking **Enter** on the Formula bar; or add additional values and operators, and then complete the entry. The result of your equation displays in the cell. (See Chapter 5 for other methods to complete an entry.)

QUICKSTEPS

QUICKSTEPS

ADDING A SYMBOLIC FORMULA

Another way to add a formula, though it won't work as one, is to use the Equation Editor, an Office-wide tool. This will allow you to display the characters of a complex formula without actually performing the calculation. To install the Equation Editor (it is not part of an Express Office installation):

1. Click **Start**, click **Control Panel**, and then under Programs, click **Uninstall A Program**. Select your version of Office, and click **Change**.

2. In the Change Your Installation Of Microsoft Office dialog box, click **Add Or Remove Features**, and click **Continue**. Click the plus sign (+) next to Office Tools, and click the **Equation Editor** down arrow.

3. Click **Run From My Computer**, and click **Continue**.

4. To use the Equation Editor, restart Excel, select where you want the equation placed, and then in the Insert tab Symbols group, click **Equation**.

USE CELL REFERENCES

The majority of formulas use the values in other cells to produce a result, that is, the cell that contains the formula may have no value of its own—it's derived from other cells whose values are manipulated by arithmetic operators. For example, the cell at the bottom of several values contains a formula that sums the values to produce a total.

1. Select a blank cell, and type an equal sign (=). The equal sign displays in the cell and in the Formula bar.

2. Enter a cell reference in one of the following ways:

   ● Type a cell reference (for example, B4) that contains the value you want.

   ● Click the cell whose value you want. A blinking border surrounds the cell.

   ● Select a named cell. In the Formulas tab Defined Names group, click **Use In Formula**, and click the named cell you want.

   ● Type a named cell.

3. Type an operator.

4. Enter another cell reference or a value.

5. Complete the entry by pressing **ENTER**; or add additional cell references, values, and operators, and then complete the entry. The result of your formula is displayed in the cell, as shown in Figure 7-4.

Edit a Formula

You can easily change a formula after you have entered one.

1. Double-click the cell that contains the formula you want to change. The formula is displayed in the cell and in the Formula bar. Cell references for each cell or range are color-coded.

2. Edit the formula by:

   ● Making changes directly in the cell or on the Formula bar

USING FORMULAS

There are several techniques you can use to get more out of working with formulas.

REPLACE AN ENTIRE FORMULA WITH ITS VALUE

To replace an entire formula with its value:

1. Right-click the cell that contains the formula, and click **Copy**.

2. Right-click the cell a second time, and under Paste Options, click **Values** .

REPLACE A PORTION OF A FORMULA WITH ITS VALUE

1. Double-click the cell that contains the formula.

2. In either the cell or the Formula bar, select the portion of the formula you want to replace with its value.

3. Press **F9** to calculate and insert the value, and press **ENTER** to complete the entry.

CANCEL ENTERING OR EDITING A FORMULA

Press **ESC** or click **Cancel** on the Formula bar.

DELETE A FORMULA

Select the cell that contains the formula, and press **DELETE**.

If you do not see the Cancel, Enter, and Insert Function buttons in the Formula bar when editing or creating a formula, click anywhere in the Formula bar and they will be displayed.

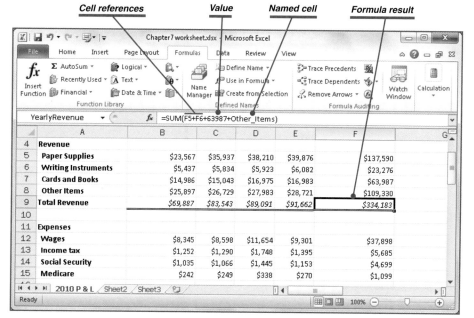

Figure 7-4: *A formula in Excel comprises cell references, values, and named cells.*

- Dragging the border of a colored cell or range reference to move it to a new location

- Dragging a corner sizing-box of a colored cell or range reference to expand the reference

3. Complete the entry by pressing **ENTER**.

Move Formulas

You move formulas by cutting and pasting. When you move formulas, Excel uses absolute referencing—the formula remains exactly the same as it was originally with the same cell references. (See "Change Cell References" earlier in the chapter for more information on cell referencing.)

1. Select the cell whose formula you want to move.

2. In the Home tab Clipboard group, click **Cut** or press **CTRL+X**.

–Or–

Right-click the cell whose formula you want to move, and click **Cut**.

3. Select the cell where you want to move the formula.

4. In the Home tab Clipboard group, click **Paste** or press **CTRL+V**.

   –Or–

   Right-click the cell where you want to move the formula, and under Paste Options, click **Paste**.

Copy Formulas

When you copy formulas, relative referencing is applied. Therefore, cell referencing in a formula will change when you copy the formula, unless you have made a reference absolute. If you do not get the results you expect, click **Undo** on the Quick Access toolbar, and change the cell references before you copy again.

COPY FORMULAS INTO ADJACENT CELLS

1. Select the cell whose formula you want to copy.

2. Point at the fill handle in the lower-right corner of the cell, and drag over the cells where you want the formula copied.

COPY FORMULAS INTO NONADJACENT CELLS

1. Select the cell whose formula you want to copy.

2. In the Home tab Clipboard group, click **Copy** or press **CTRL+C**.

   –Or–

   Right-click the cell you want to copy, and click **Copy**.

3. Copy formatting along with the formula by selecting the destination cell. Then, in the Home tab Clipboard group, click **Paste** and then click the **Paste** icon.

   –Or–

   Copy just the formula by selecting the destination cell. Then, in the Home tab Clipboard group, click the **Paste** down arrow, and click the **Formulas** icon.

	A	B	C
4	Revenue		
5	Paper Supplies	$23,567	$35,937
6	Writing Instruments	$5,437	$5,834
7	Cards and Books	$14,986	$15,043
8	Other Items	$25,897	$26,729
9	Total Revenue	$69,887	

Recalculate Formulas

By default, Excel automatically recalculates formulas affected by changes to a value, to the formula itself, or to a changed named cell. You also can recalculate more frequently using the tips presented in Table 7-1.

To turn off automatic calculation and select other calculation options:

1. In the Formulas tab Calculation group, click **Calculation Options**.

2. In the drop-down menu, click **Manual**. You can also force an immediate calculation by clicking **Calc Now** to recalculate the workbook or clicking **Calc Sheet** to recalculate the active worksheet.

TO CALCULATE...	IN...	PRESS...
Formulas, and formulas dependent on them, that have changed since the last calculation	All open workbooks	F9
Formulas, and formulas dependent on them, that have changed since the last calculation	The active worksheet	SHIFT+F9
All formulas, regardless of any changes since the last calculation	All open workbooks	CTRL+ALT+F9
All formulas, regardless of any changes since the last calculation, after rechecking dependent formulas	All open workbooks	CTRL+SHIFT+ALT+F9

Table 7-1: **Formula Recalculations in Excel**

Use External References in Formulas

You can *link* data using cell references to worksheets and workbooks other than the one you are currently working in. For example, if you are building a departmental budget, you could link to each division's budget workbook and have any changes made to formulas in those workbooks be applied automatically to your total budget workbook. Changes made to the *external* references in the *source* workbooks are automatically updated in the *destination* workbook when the destination workbook is opened or when the source workbooks are changed and the destination workbook is open.

CREATE EXTERNAL REFERENCE LINKS

1. Open both the source and destination workbooks in your computer.

2. Arrange the workbooks so that they are all displayed. For example, in the View tab Window group, click **Arrange**, click **Tiled**, and click **OK**. (See Chapter 5 for more information on arranging workbooks in the Excel window.)

3. In the destination worksheet, create the formula or open an existing formula.

4. Place the insertion point in the formula where you want the external reference.

5. In the source workbook, click the cell whose cell reference you want. The external reference is added to the formula, as shown in Figure 7-5.

6. Press **ENTER** to complete the entry.

TIP

It is a good practice to save and close the source workbook before saving the destination workbook.

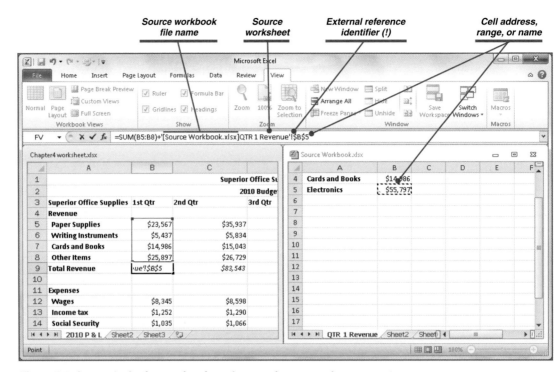

Figure 7-5: *An external reference in a formula comprises several components.*

UPDATE AND MANAGE EXTERNAL REFERENCES

You can control how external references are updated, check on their status, and break or change the link.

1. Open the destination workbook.

2. In the Data tab Connections group, click **Edit Links**. The Edit Links dialog box appears, as shown in Figure 7-6.

3. Select a link and then use the command buttons on the right side of the dialog box to perform the action you want.

4. Click **Close** when finished.

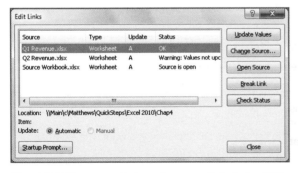

Figure 7-6: *You can update and manage links in the Edit Links dialog box.*

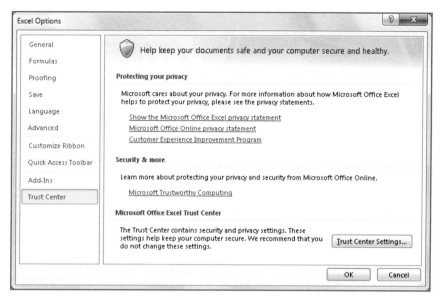

Figure 7-7: *The Trust Center provides a focal point for accessing privacy and security information and settings for Office 2010 programs.*

UPDATE LINKS

When you open a destination workbook with external links to source workbooks, you are potentially introducing a security risk to your computer by allowing data from other sources into your system. By default, automatic updating is disabled and the user opening a destination workbook needs to provide permission to enable the links (unless the source workbooks are open on the same computer as the destination workbook).

1. Open the destination workbook. A message box, shown in Figure 7-8, opens to tell you that updating links will use new data from the source files and warns you about the possibility of sharing confidential information. Click **Update**, assuming you trust the source file; click **Don't Update** if you do not.

TIP

If you are unsure of the origination of the source workbooks when updating links in a destination workbook, open the Edit Links dialog box to view the files involved in the links. See how in the section "Update and Manage External References."

Figure 7-8: **To protect you from erroneous or malicious data, Office asks if you want to update external links.**

2. When you open the source file, which also has a link to an external workbook, unless default settings have been changed, a Security Warning message displays below the ribbon notifying you that automatic link updating is disabled. Click **Enable Content** to allow updates to occur.

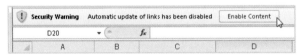

3. For additional protection, if your source workbook is located in a network location (that is, not on the same computer as your destination workbook), a second warning is displayed. Assuming you trust the source data, click **Yes**. The links will be updated.

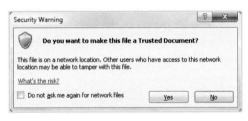

CHANGE AUTOMATIC LINK UPDATING FOR ALL WORKBOOKS

You can change how links are updated in the Trust Center security settings window.

NOTE

Just as there can be a myriad of combinations of links and referencing in your workbooks from source files on your own computer to lose on networks, there are also several permutations of security warnings you may see, depending on your specific circumstance. To try and describe each situation and show its result would take a chapter in of itself and not really provide much value. Suffice it to say that when you see security warnings, read them carefully, and just be cognizant of what you are accepting.

1. Click the **File** tab, click **Options**, and click the **Trust Center** option. In the Trust Center window, click **Trust Center Settings**.

2. In the Trust Center security settings window, click the **External Content** category, shown in Figure 7-9.

3. In the Security Settings For Workbook Links area, select the automatic link updating behavior you want, and click **OK** twice.

Trust Center

Trusted Publishers
Trusted Locations
Trusted Documents
Add-ins
ActiveX Settings
Macro Settings
Message Bar
External Content
File Block Settings
Privacy Options

Security settings for Data Connections

○ Enable all Data Connections (not recommended)
◉ Prompt user about Data Connections
○ Disable all Data Connections

Security settings for Workbook Links

○ Enable automatic update for all Workbook Links (not recommended)
◉ Prompt user on automatic update for Workbook Links
○ Disable automatic update of Workbook Links

OK   Cancel

*Figure 7-9: **The Trust Center allows you to set the degree to which you trust the links among your workbooks.***

4	Revenue	
5	Paper Supplies	$23,567
6	Writing Instruments	$5,437
7	Cards and Books	$14,986
8	Other Items	$25,897
9	Total Revenue	$69,887

CHANGE AUTOMATIC LINK UPDATING FOR INDIVIDUAL WORKBOOKS

You can choose to not display the security alert in a destination workbook prompting users to update links. You can also choose to update links, or not, without user intervention.

1. Open the destination workbook whose security alert behavior you want to change.

2. In the Data tab Connections group, click **Edit Links**, and click **Startup Prompt**.

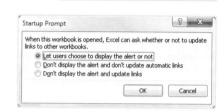

3. In the Startup Prompt dialog box, select the behavior you want, click **OK**, and click **Close**. The next time the workbook is opened, the new behavior will be enabled.

Startup Prompt

When this workbook is opened, Excel can ask whether or not to update links to other workbooks.

◉ Let users choose to display the alert or not
○ Don't display the alert and don't update automatic links
○ Don't display the alert and update links

OK   Cancel

Format Conditionally

Excel 2010 continues to improve the ease and capabilities with which data can be identified in a worksheet based on rules you select. Rules are organized into several types that allow you to easily format cells that compare values against each other; meet specific values, dates, or other criteria; match top and bottom percentile values you choose; match values above or below an average; or identify unique or duplicate values. If no pre-existing rule accommodates your needs, you can use a formula to set up criteria that cells must match.

COMPARE CELLS

You can highlight the comparative values of selected cells by using one of three formatting styles:

- **Data bars** display in each cell colored bars whose length is proportional to their value as compared to the other values in the selection.

- **Color scales** blend two or three colors (such as a green-yellow-red traffic light metaphor) to differentiate among high to low values.

4	Revenue	
5	Paper Supplies	$23,567
6	Writing Instruments	$5,437
7	Cards and Books	$14,986
8	Other Items	$25,897
9	Total Revenue	$69,887

NOTE

If your selected cells don't change as you point to different style options, Live Preview has been turned off. To turn on Live Preview, click the **File** tab, click **Options**, and click the **General** option. Under User Interface Options, select **Enable Live Preview**, and click **OK**.

4	Revenue			
5	Paper Supplies	●	$23,567	$35,938
6	Writing Instruments	○	$5,437	$5,834
7	Cards and Books	◑	$14,986	$15,043
8	Other Items	●	$25,897	$26,729
9	Total Revenue		$69,887	$83,544

- **Icon sets** use from three to five similar icons (such as the red and black circles used in *Consumer Reports*) to differentiate among high to low values.

1. Select the cells that will be compared.

2. In the Home tab Styles group, click **Conditional Formatting** and click the style you want to see for a submenu of options.

3. Point to each option to see a live preview of its effect on your selected data, as shown in Figure 7-10. Click the option you want to use.

4. For more choices of each style, click **More Rules** at the bottom of each of their respective submenus.

5. In the New Formatting Rule dialog box, under Edit The Rule Description, you can change from one style to another and, depending on the style, change colors, change the values attributed to an icon or color, and make other customizations (see Figure 7-11). Click **OK** when finished.

Point to a conditional formatting style and see the effect on selected cells

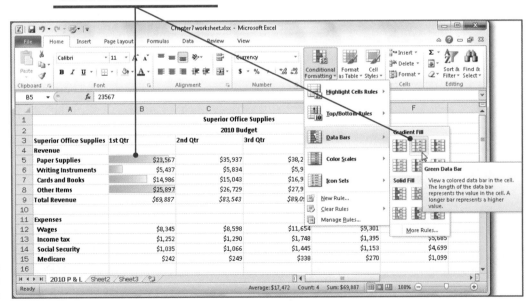

Figure 7-10: **You can see a live preview of each formatting style on your data before selecting one.**

TIP

When changing values in dialog boxes for conditional formatting, as in the New Formatting Rule dialog box (and when setting up functions, described later in this chapter), you can type a value or formula in the associated text box, or you can select a cell that contains the value or formula you want and have it entered for you. When selecting a cell, click the **Collapse Dialog** 📷 button to shrink the dialog box so that you can see more of the worksheet. Click **Expand Dialog** to return to the full-size dialog box.

FORMAT CELLS THAT MATCH VALUES OR CONDITIONS

Excel provides several pre-existing rules that let you easily format cells that meet established criteria.

1. Select the cells that will be formatted if they meet conditions you select.

2. In the Home tab Styles group, click **Conditional Formatting** and click **Highlight Cell Rules** to view a submenu of rules that compare values to conditions.

   –Or–

   Click **Top/Bottom Rules** to view a submenu that lets you select cells based on top/bottom ranking or whether they're above or below the average of the selected cells.

3. For more choices, click **More Rules** at the bottom of each of the respective submenus.

4. In the New Formatting Rule dialog box, under Edit The Rule Description, you can change criteria and the formatting you want applied (see Chapter 6 for more information on using the Format Cells dialog box). Click **OK** when finished.

MANAGE CONDITIONAL FORMATTING RULES

Using the Conditional Formatting Rule Manager, you can view any conditional formatting rules in a workbook, as well as edit, delete, reorder, and create new rules.

1. In the Home tab Styles group, click **Conditional Formatting** and click **Manage Rules**. The Conditional Formatting Rule Manager appears, as shown in Figure 7-12.

2. Click the **Show Formatting Rules For** down arrow to select the scope of where you want to look for rules.

3. Select a rule and perform one or more of the following actions:

   ● Click **Edit Rule** to open the Edit Formatting Rule dialog box and change criteria or conditions. Click **OK** to close the Edit Formatting Rule dialog box.

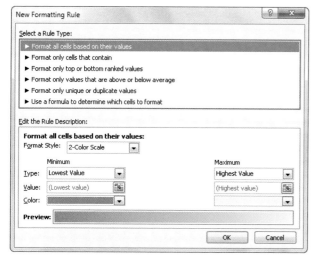

*Figure 7-11: **Each style has a set of customizations (or rules) that apply to how data is visually identified.***

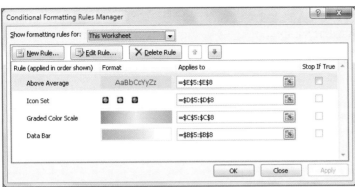

Figure 7-12: *You can view and manage conditional formatting rules set up in a workbook.*

- Click **Delete Rule** to remove it (alternatively, you can click **Clear Rules** on the Conditional Formatting drop-down menu to remove all rules in the selected cells or worksheet).

- Click the up and down arrows to change the order in which rules are applied (rules are applied in order from top to bottom).

- Click the **Stop If True** check box to discontinue further rules from being applied if the selected rule is satisfied as being True.

4. Click **New Rule** to open the New Formatting Rule dialog box and create a new rule. Click **OK** to close the New Formatting Rule dialog box.

5. Click **OK** when finished.

Use Functions

Functions are prewritten formulas that you can use to perform specific tasks. They can be as simple as =PI(), which returns 3.14159265358979, the value of the constant pi; or they can be as complex as =PPMT(rate,per,nper,pv,fv,type), which returns a payment on an investment principal.

A function comprises three components:

- **Formula identifier**, the equal sign (=), is required when a function is at the beginning of the formula.

- **Function name** identifies the function, and typically is a two- to five-character uppercase abbreviation.

- **Arguments** are the values acted upon by functions to derive a result. They can be numbers, cell references, constants, logical (True or False) values, or a formula. Arguments are separated by commas and enclosed in parentheses. A function can have up 255 arguments.

Enter a Function

You can enter functions on a worksheet by typing or by a combination of typing and selecting cell references, as described earlier in this chapter for formulas. In addition, you can search for and choose functions from Excel's library of built-in functions.

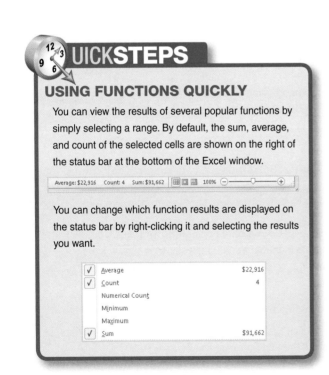

TYPE A FUNCTION

To type a function in a cell on the worksheet:

1. Select a blank cell, and type an equal sign (=). The equal sign displays in the cell and the Formula bar.

2. Start typing the function name, such as <u>AVERAGE</u>, <u>MAX</u>, or <u>PMT</u>. As you start typing, functions with related spellings are displayed. Click any to see a description of the function.

3. Double-click the function you want. The function name and open parenthesis are entered for you. Excel displays a tooltip showing arguments and proper syntax for the function.

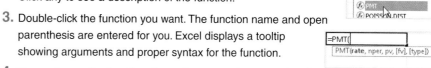

4. Depending on the function, for each argument you need to do none, one, or both of the following:

   - Type the argument.
   - Select a cell reference.

5. Type a comma to separate arguments, and repeat steps 4 and 5 as necessary.

6. Type a closing parenthesis, and press **ENTER** or click **Enter** on the Formula bar to complete the entry. A value will be returned. (If a *#code* is displayed in the cell or a message box displays indicating you made an error, see "Find and Correct Errors" later in this chapter.)

INSERT A FUNCTION

You can find the function you want using the Function Wizard or using the function category buttons on the ribbon.

In either case, the wizard helps you enter arguments for the function you chose.

1. Select a blank cell. In the Formulas tab Function Library group, click the relevant function category button, and scroll to the function you want. Point to a function and wait a second to see a tooltip that describes it. When ready, click the function and skip to step 5 to view its arguments.

   –Or–

   Click **Insert Function** in the Function Library group or its button on the Formula bar f_x, or press **SHIFT+F3**. The Insert Function dialog box appears, as shown in Figure 7-13.

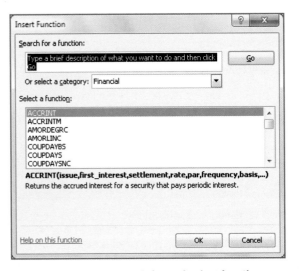

Figure 7-13: *You can search for and select functions from Excel's extensive library in the Insert Function dialog box.*

2. Type a brief description of what you want to do in the Search For A Function text box, and click **Go**. A list of recommended functions is displayed in the Select A Function list box.

   –Or–

   Open the **Select A Category** drop-down list, and select a category.

3. Click the function you want from the Select A Function list box. Its arguments and syntax are shown, as well as a description of what the function returns.

4. If you need more assistance with the function, click **Help On This Function**. A Help topic provides details on the function and an example of how it's used.

5. Click **OK** to open the Function Arguments dialog box, shown in Figure 7-14. The function's arguments are listed in order at the top of the dialog box, and the beginning of the function displays in the cell and in the Formula bar.

6. Enter values for the arguments by typing or clicking cell references. Click the **Collapse Dialog** button to shrink the dialog box so that you can see more of the worksheet. The formula on the worksheet is built as you enter each argument.

7. Click **OK** to complete the entry.

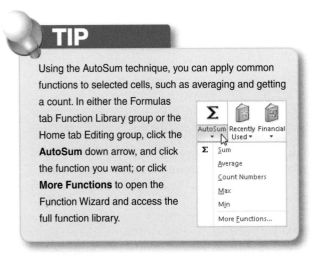

TIP

Using the AutoSum technique, you can apply common functions to selected cells, such as averaging and getting a count. In either the Formulas tab Function Library group or the Home tab Editing group, click the **AutoSum** down arrow, and click the function you want; or click **More Functions** to open the Function Wizard and access the full function library.

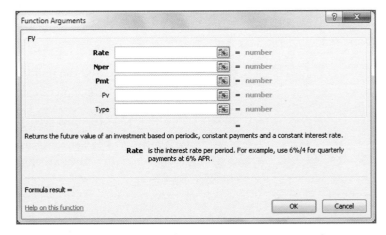

Figure 7-14: *Type or click cell references to enter argument values.*

	A	B	C
11	Expenses		
12	Wages	$8,345	
13	Income tax	$1,252	
14	Social Security	$1,035	
15	Medicare	$242	
16	=SUM(B12:B15)		
17		SUM(**number1**, [number2], ...)	

![NOTE]

You can perform the same actions and access the same dialog boxes from the smart tag that is displayed next to a selected cell containing an error as you can using the Error Checking button in the Formula Auditing group.

$80,609

- Formula Omits Adjacent Cells
- Update Formula to Include Cells
- Help on this error
- Ignore Error
- Edit in Formula Bar
- Error Checking Options...

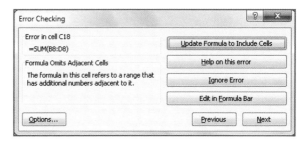

Error Checking

Error in cell C18
  =SUM(B8:D8)

Formula Omits Adjacent Cells

The formula in this cell refers to a range that has additional numbers adjacent to it.

- Update Formula to Include Cells
- Help on this error
- Ignore Error
- Edit in Formula Bar

Options...   Previous   Next

*Figure 7-15: **You can manage how errors are checked and locate cells that contain errors.***

Enter a Sum in Columns or Rows Quickly

AutoSum uses the SUM function to add contiguous numbers quickly.

1. Select a blank cell below a column or to the right of a row of numbers.
2. In the Formulas tab Function Library group, click **AutoSum**. The cells Excel "thinks" you want to sum above or to the left of the blank cell are enclosed in a border, and the formula is displayed in the cell and in the Formula bar.
3. Modify the cells to be included in the sum by dragging a corner sizing-box, editing the formula in the cell or the Formula bar, or by selecting cells.
4. Press **ENTER** or click **Enter** on the Formula bar to complete the entry. The sum of the selected cells is returned.
5. Alternatively, for an even faster sum, select a contiguous column or row of cells, and click **AutoSum**. The sum is entered in the first blank cell at either the bottom of a column of cells or to the right of a row of cells.

Find and Correct Errors

Excel provides several tools that help you see how your formulas and functions are constructed, recognize errors in formulas, and better locate problems.

Check for Errors

Excel can find errors and provide possible solutions.

1. In the Formulas tab Formula Auditing group, click **Error Checking**. If you have an error on the worksheet, the Error Checking dialog box appears, as shown in Figure 7-15.
2. Use the command buttons on the right side of the dialog box to perform the indicated action. Click **Next** or **Previous** to check on other errors.
3. Click **Options** to view the Excel Options Formulas window (see Figure 7-16), where you can customize error checking.
   - **Error Checking**, **Enable Background Error Checking** lets you turn on or off error checking as you enter formulas and determines the color of flagged cells that contain errors. Errors are flagged in green by default.
   - **Error Checking Rules** provides several criteria that cells are checked against for possible errors.

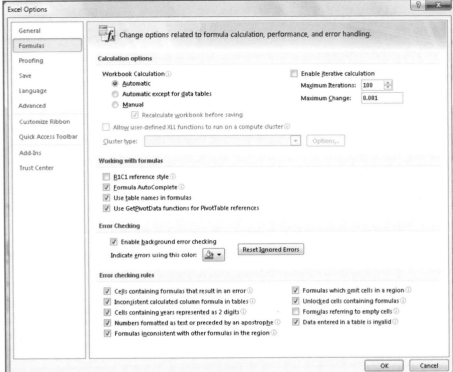

Figure 7-16: *You can customize how Excel performs error checking.*

Trace Precedent and Dependent Cells

Precedent cells are referenced in a formula or function in another cell; that is, they provide a value to a formula or function. *Dependent* cells contain a formula or function that uses the value from another cell; that is, they depend on the value in another cell for their own value.

This interwoven relationship of cells can compound one error into many, making a visual representation of the cell dependencies a vital error-correction tool.

1. Click a cell that uses cell references and/or is itself used as a reference by another cell in its formula or function.

2. In the Formulas tab Formula Auditing group, click **Trace Precedents** to display blue arrows that point to the cell from other cells.

3	Superior Office Supplies	1st Qtr
4	Revenue	
5	Paper Supplies	$23,567
6	Writing Instruments	$5,437
7	Cards and Books	$14,986
8	Other Items	$25,897
9	Total Revenue	$69,887

–Or–

Click **Trace Dependents** to display blue arrows that point to other cells.

3. Click the **Remove Arrows** down arrow, and select whether to remove precedent, dependent, or all arrows.

Watch a Cell

You can follow what changes are made to a cell's value as its precedent cells' values are changed, even if the cells are not currently visible.

1. In the Formulas tab Formula Auditing group, click **Watch Window**. The Watch Window window opens.

TIP

To remove a watch you have placed, in the Formulas tab Formula Auditing group, click **Watch Window**, select the watch you want to remove, and click **Delete Watch**.

2. Click **Add Watch** to open the Add Watch dialog box.

3. Select the cell or cells you want to watch, and click **Add**. Each selected cell will be listed individually in the Watch Window. As changes are made to a precedent cell, the value of the cells "being watched" will be updated according to the recalculation options you have set. (See "Recalculate Formulas" earlier in the chapter.)

4. Close the Watch Window window when you are done.

Evaluate a Formula in Pieces

You can see what value will be returned by individual cell references or expressions in the order they are placed in the formula.

1. Select the cell that contains the formula you want to evaluate.

2. In the Formulas tab Formula Auditing group, click **Evaluate Formula**. The Evaluate Formula dialog box, shown in Figure 7-17, appears.

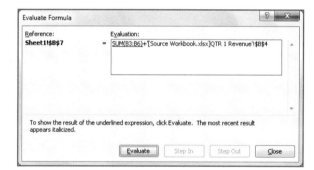

3. Do one or more of the following:

- Click **Evaluate** to return the value of the first cell reference or expression. The cell reference or expression is underlined.

Figure 7-17: **You can dissect each expression or component of a formula to see its cell reference, its formula, and its value.**

- Continue clicking **Evaluate** to return values for each of the cell references or expressions (again, underlined) to the right in the formula. Eventually, this will return the value for the cell.

- Click **Restart** to start the evaluation from the leftmost expression. (The Evaluate button changes to Restart after you have stepped through the formula.)

- Click **Step In** to view more data on the underlined cell reference.

- Click **Step Out** to return to the formula evaluation.

4. Click **Close** when finished.

Chapter 8
Creating the Presentation

This chapter describes how to create a presentation. You'll find that PowerPoint provides many methods for quickly and easily creating dramatic and effective presentations. Sometimes, you'll find what you need in the prepackaged themes and templates that are already designed with specific presentation types in mind (for instance, an academic or business presentation, or one for healthcare professionals). These may be available from the online gallery. Sometimes, you'll find what you need in previous presentations you've created, so you can simply borrow slides or design elements from past successful efforts. Sometimes, nothing you have in your presentation library or that is offered by PowerPoint can fill your particular requirements. In this case, you create your own template from scratch or with Office-wide themes and the styling assistance of PowerPoint. This chapter then looks

8

QUICKFACTS

DEFINING THEMES, LAYOUTS, AND MASTER SLIDES

Themes in PowerPoint lend presentations color and design coordination. Up to 20 theme templates are available in a ribbon gallery in PowerPoint, or you can download additional choices from Microsoft's online templates. Chapter 9 explains how themes can be changed and customized to give you almost unlimited variations in how your presentation looks.

Layouts define where the objects of a slide (such as the text, spreadsheets or diagrams, pictures, or headings and footers) will be placed and formatted. Objects are positioned on a slide using *placeholders* that identify the specific object being inserted (a text placeholder versus a chart placeholder, for instance). PowerPoint has defined several standard layout templates that you can choose when you insert a new slide. When you insert a new slide into a given theme, the slide takes on the colors and design elements of the theme, with the chosen layout attribute's placeholder positioning.

When you want to create your own themes and layouts to use in a future presentation, you create your own templates by saving them with a special file extension: .potx. Figure 8-1 explains some of the components of layouts and themes that you may have on a slide.

You can make your templates *master slides*—see Chapter 10 for additional information. Master slides, which are just another kind of template, define the parts of a slide that you want to be the same and in the background for a whole presentation or a group of contiguous slides. (You can have multiple master slides in a presentation.) In addition to any color and design elements (such as fonts) found in themes, master slides might include unique graphics (such as a logo), a specific header or footer, and options for inserting *placeholders* for text and other objects while you are creating a presentation.

at how to organize and manage your slides by creating and working with a presentation outline. Finally, you will see how to protect your presentations with passwords.

Create a Presentation

There are three ways to begin creating your presentation: using a theme and standard layouts that define the design and layout of a slide, using another existing presentation and then modifying it, and starting from scratch—creating your own template in the process.

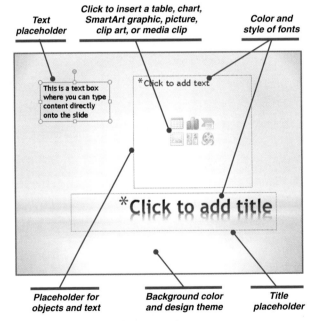

Figure 8-1: **These components make up the theme and layout of a slide and can be saved as a template.**

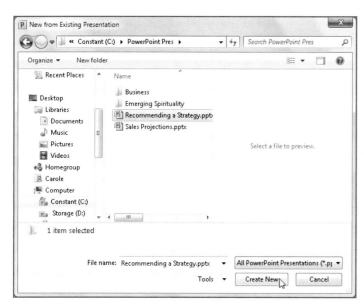

Figure 8-2: **In this window, you find the presentation you want to use as a model and create a new one.**

Create a Presentation from Another Presentation

The easiest and most direct way to create a new presentation is to start with an existing one. To copy a presentation, rename it, and then modify it according to your needs.

1. Click the **File** tab, and click **New**.
2. Under Available Templates And Themes, click **New From Existing**.
3. Find the presentation or template you want to use, and click **Create New**, as shown in Figure 8-2.
4. Modify the presentation by replacing the theme, highlighting text and replacing it with your own; deleting unnecessary slides; inserting new slides; inserting your own graphics, charts, and art; and rearranging the slides according to your needs (subsequent chapters in this book describe how to do these actions in detail).
5. Click the **File** tab, and click **Save As**. Enter a name for the presentation, choose the PowerPoint Presentation (.pptx) **Save As Type** option, and click **Save**.

Create a Presentation Using a Standard Theme

Themes are used to give your presentation a unified and professional look. They provide background color and design, predefined fonts, and other elements that hold a presentation together. Once you have defined the overall theme, it is a simple task to add slides with the appropriate layout for the data you wish to present. You select a theme from a predefined gallery available on the ribbon. (See the "Defining Themes, Layouts, and Master Slides" QuickFacts.) Follow these steps to find and use one of PowerPoint's standard themes:

1. Click the **File** tab, and select **New**.
2. Under Available Templates And Themes, double-click **Blank Presentation**, and a standard blank slide will open.
3. Click the **Design** tab, and in the Themes group, click the **Themes More** down arrow to see thumbnails of color and design themes listed. Hold your mouse pointer over individual thumbnails to see their effects on the slide beneath. When you find the theme you want to use, click its thumbnail.

NOTE

In order to see the file extensions in the Save As Type list, the reader must choose that option in Windows Explorer. In the Windows Explorer dialog box, click **Organize**, click **Folder And Search Options**, click the **View** tab, and click **Hide Extensions For Known File Types** to remove the check mark. By default, file extensions will not be displayed.

NOTE

Unless you change the folder location, the template will be saved in the default template folder where PowerPoint design templates are stored. If you do not change the folder location, the template will appear in the Themes menu under "Custom."

4. At this point you can either begin to add content to an actual presentation (see the "Adding Content to a Slide" QuickSteps) or you can create a template for a presentation (see "Create a Template").

Create a Template

A template contains one or more slides with attributes of the color themes and standard layouts you want to have available. First you create the slides with the desired themes and layouts (you may want to use a sample template to start with). Then you save your modified slides as a template so that they can be used to add formatting and your own color and design theme to new presentations. Template files have .potx extensions. When you create a new template, it will be displayed in the Available Templates And Themes view under My Templates. To create a new presentation:

1. Click the **File** tab, and click **New**. You can create a new template in two ways: you can open a sample template and modify it according to your needs, or you can create one from scratch. Under Available Templates And Themes:

   - Double-click **Blank Presentation** to see the basic slide layout and change it according to your needs.

   - Click **Sample Templates** and scroll through the samples available to find one you might use as a "starter set" of slides. If you find one you want, double-click it.

2. To prepare your slide:

   - Click the **Design** tab, and click the **Themes More** down arrow to select themes or design elements for the template. If you've used a sample template, you may not need to do this.

   - Click the **Home** tab, click the **New Slide** down arrow to list possible layouts, shown in Figure 8-3, and then click the layouts you want to use in the presentation.

3. When you have a template that carries the attributes you want the presentation to have, click the **File** tab, and click **Save As**.

4. In the File Name box, type a name for the new template.

5. In the Save As Type drop-down list box, click **PowerPoint Template (.potx)**.

6. Click **Save**. The templates are now available under My Templates in the File tab New view.

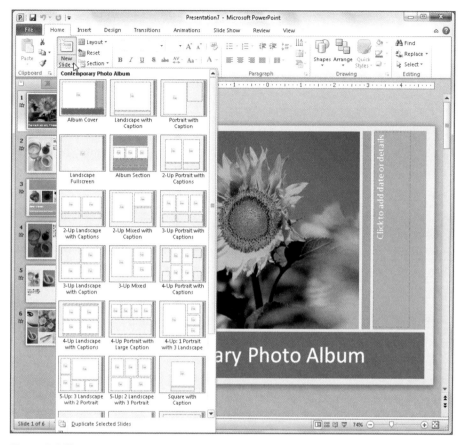

QUICKSTEPS

WORKING WITH THEMES

You can search Microsoft online resources to find other templates, apply a theme to selected or all slides in a presentation, or set a theme to be assigned to all future presentations by default, for a consistent business look, for example.

FIND OTHER MICROSOFT THEMES AND TEMPLATES

1. You can either search Office.com or update your themes gallery.

   • To search Office.com for new themes or templates, click the **File** tab, and click **New**. On the Office.com Templates title bar, click in the search text box (containing Search Office.com For Templates), and enter the type of template you want to find. Click the right arrow to start the search.

   Search Office.com for templates →

   • To update the Themes gallery content, click the **Design** tab, and click the **More** down arrow on the Themes group. Beneath the thumbnail gallery, click **Enable Content Updates From Office.com**.

   Enable Content Updates from Office.com...

2. On the Office.com window, click the thumbnail for the template or theme you want. Follow the download instructions to install the template. The new template will appear on a blank slide in PowerPoint.

   Continued . . .

Figure 8-3: **You want to prepare your template with the possible layouts you plan on using in your presentations.**

Create a Presentation from Scratch

When you create a presentation from scratch, you'll begin with blank slides and add layouts, color schemes, fonts, graphics and charts, other design elements, and text. You may also want to refer to "Understanding the Outlining Feature"

WORKING WITH THEMES (Continued)

APPLY A THEME TO ALL OR SELECTED SLIDES

Use the context menu for the theme thumbnail to select the option to apply the theme to all or selected slides. Then select the theme from the Themes group gallery.

1. If you want the theme to be applied to just some of the slides, select the slides by pressing **CTRL** while you click the thumbnails in the Slides tab or the Slide Sorter view. You don't have to select any of the slides if you want the theme to apply to all of the slides.

2. In the Design tab Themes group, right-click the theme thumbnail. From the context menu:

    ● Click **Apply To Selected Slides**.

    –Or–

    ● Click **Apply To All Slides**.

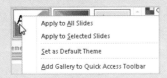

SET A DEFAULT THEME TO APPLY TO ALL FUTURE PRESENTATIONS

1. Under the Themes group in the Design tab, click the **More** down arrow, and right-click the thumbnail you want.

2. Click **Set As Default Theme**.

NOTE

A theme can be further modified by changing its components, color, font, and graphic effects. Chapter 9 describes how to work with themes in more detail.

QuickFacts in this chapter if you prefer to develop your presentation content with an outline.

1. Click the **File** tab, and click **New**. The Available Templates And Themes view will be displayed.

2. Double-click **Blank Presentation**. A blank title page slide will be displayed.

3. On the Design tab, select a theme for the background color and design for your presentation. If none of them are acceptable, click **More Themes On Microsoft Office Online** at the bottom of the list of thumbnails to search the themes available online.

4. Click and type over "Click To Add Title" to enter the title of your presentation. If you want to add a subtitle, click and type over "Click To Add Subtitle."

5. When you are satisfied with that slide, click **New Slide** on the Home tab to insert another blank slide with the layout you want.

    ● Click the **New Slide** button to see a slide with the last layout used.

    ● Click the **New Slide** down arrow to see a menu of layout choices.

6. Click the **Insert** tab, and click the relevant buttons to add text and other content to your slides. (See the "Adding Content to a Slide" QuickSteps.)

7. Repeat steps 5 through 6 for as many slides as you have in your presentation.

8. Save the presentation. Click the **File** tab, and click **Save As**. Enter a name and click **Save**.

Select a Layout

As mentioned earlier, you can add a slide and select a layout by accessing the New Slide button in the Home tab. Here is another way:

To add a slide and select a layout:

1. Right-click the slide immediately preceding the one you want to insert.

2. Click **New Slide** from the context menu.

3. Right-click the new slide, and on the context menu, click **Layout**. A submenu containing layout possibilities will be displayed.

4. Click the layout thumbnail you want.

TIP

For more typing room in the Outline tab, expand the tab by dragging its inside edge into the Presentation pane.

UICKSTEPS

ADDING CONTENT TO A SLIDE

The following elements are available to help you present the points you are making in the presentation. This is an overview of the procedures.

WORK WITH TEXT

Text can be added to placeholders, text boxes, and some shapes, or changed easily. Chapter 10 deals with text in detail. To add text, you click inside of a text box, some shapes, or a placeholder and begin to type.

1. To modify text attributes, highlight the text by dragging the pointer over it. A text toolbar will appear that you can use for simple changes.

2. Click the **Home** tab, and click any of the Font group buttons. On this same tab are the paragraph settings, which contain WordArt Styles options. (See Chapter 10 for additional information on using text.)

Continued . . .

Outline a Presentation

Outlining a presentation is easily done in PowerPoint. You simply display the Outline tab and begin typing. These sections explain how to create, manipulate, modify, and print an outline.

Create an Outline

The outline is created, modified, and viewed using the Outline tab, shown in Figure 8-4. An outline is created from scratch or by inserting text from other sources. You create an outline by indenting subtopics under topics. When you create a subtopic, or indent it under the one above it, you *demote* the point, or make it a lower level than the previous topic. It is contained within the higher level. When you remove an indent, you *promote* the point, making it a new topic. It becomes a higher level and may contain its own subtopics.

CREATE AN OUTLINE FROM SCRATCH

To create a fresh outline, type your text into the Outline tab.

1. To open a blank presentation, click the **File** tab, and click **New**. Click the type of presentation you want—for instance, **Blank Presentation**, **Recent Templates**, **My Templates**, **New From Existing**, or another choice.

2. On the View tab, click **Normal** in the Presentation Views group. (You can also click the **Normal** view button on the View toolbar.)

3. Click the **Outline** tab so that the outline view is available, as shown in Figure 8-4.

4. Click to the right of the Outline slide icon to place the insertion point.

5. Type the title (the title of your first slide is typically the title of your presentation). Press **ENTER** to insert a new slide.

6. Type your next title, typically the first topic or main point. Press **ENTER** when you are done. Another new slide will be inserted.

- To add points to the slide rather than to insert a new one, click **Increase List Level** on the Home tab Paragraph group to move the topic to the right. The new slide will become a subtopic under the previous slide.

8

ADDING CONTENT TO A SLIDE
(Continued)

ADD OR CHANGE COLOR SCHEMES

Ask yourself what color schemes you might want to use. Are there company colors that you want to use or colors you want to stay away from?

1. To see your standard options, click the **Design** tab, and click the **Themes More** down arrow to see a list of thumbnails of the standard choices. This establishes a design and color foundation for the presentation.

2. To change the color grouping for a theme, click the **Theme Colors** button in the Themes group and point to the various color combinations. When you find one you like, click the color group. (See Chapter 9 for more information.)

3. To change color for individual slides, you can add a colored background (see Chapter 9) by clicking **Background Styles** in the Design tab Background group.

SELECT AN ANIMATIONS OR TRANSITIONS SCHEME

- To display animated text on your slide, click the **Animations** tab. Highlight the text or graphic you want to be animated. Find the animation scheme you want in the Animations group, and click it.

- To control the transition of one slide to the next, click the **Transitions** tab. Click the slide and then the transition effect in the Transitions group you would like to see.

Continued . . .

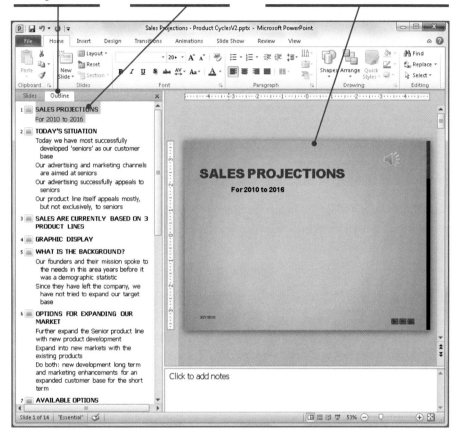

Outline tab, where you create, edit, and rearrange the slides

Selected slide is the "current slide" where the work is being done

Presentations pane, where you create the look and feel of your presentation with color, fonts, text, and design elements

Figure 8-4: The Outline tab is an alternative way that you can work with your slides to organize, create, and modify your presentations.

Click Decrease List Level to create a higher level topic (promote it)

- To move points to the left, making them a higher level, click **Decrease List Level** on the Home tab Paragraph group. The topic or subtopic will become either a higher level point or a new slide, depending on the original level.

Click Increase List Level to create a subtopic (demote it)

ADDING CONTENT TO A SLIDE

(Continued)

INSERT ART AND GRAPHICS

1. Click the **Insert** tab, and in the Illustrations group, click the button for the art or graphic object you want to insert.

2. Find the object and drag it where you want it, resizing as needed.

–Or–

Create and insert your own drawing using the Drawing group in the Home tab.

INSERT A TABLE

Insert a table to present more organized data. You can insert three types of tables: a PowerPoint-created table, one drawn by yourself, or one from Excel. On the Insert tab, click the **Table** down arrow, and select your choice. (See Chapter 14 for more information.)

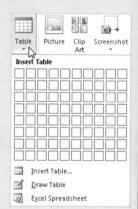

The names on the Outline and Slides tabs change to icons when the pane is too narrow for the words to appear.

---

7. Continue typing and pressing **ENTER** and clicking **Increase List Level** or **Decrease List Level** to move the text into headings and bulleted points until the presentation is outlined.

Instead of using the Increase List Level and Decrease List Level buttons, you can press **ENTER** to create a new bulleted line. Pressing **CTRL+ENTER** will create a new slide. Other options for working with outlines are specific keypresses (see the "Indenting with the Keyboard" QuickSteps) and the right-click context menu (see the "Using the Outlining Commands" QuickSteps).

Insert an Outline from Other Sources

You can create slides from an outline you have previously created in another document. Depending on the format of the text, the formatting retained and used by PowerPoint will differ.

- A **Microsoft Word (.doc)** outline will use paragraph breaks to mark the start of a new slide. Each paragraph will become a slide title. However, if the document is formatted with headings, Heading 1 will become the title of the slide, Heading 2 will be the second level, Heading 3 the third level, and so on. (See Figure 8-5.)

- An **HTML** outline will retain its formatting; however, the text will appear in a text box on the slide and can only be edited in the Presentation pane, not in the Outline tab. In addition, you must create a separate HTML file for each slide. (To see the HTML file in the Insert Outline dialog box, you may have to select .htm as the file type.)

- A **Rich Text Format (.rtf)** outline will adopt the styles of the current presentation. PowerPoint will use paragraph separations to start a new slide. The text cannot be edited in the Outline tab, only in the Presentation pane.

To insert an outline from another source:

1. On the Home tab Slides group, click the **New Slide** down arrow, and on the bottom of the menu, click **Slides From Outline**.

2. In the Insert Outline dialog box, find the location and name of the outline to be used, select it, and click **Insert**.

UNDERSTANDING THE OUTLINING FEATURE

PowerPoint's outlining feature is not only an organizational tool, but also is a quick way to create a cohesive and logical path for your presentation. As you type the outline, you are creating the actual slides in a presentation. This is an alternative way to create a presentation from scratch. If you like to outline your presentations prior to jumping in and typing your information, you'll like this way of building your presentation. The outline should contain:

- Main points you want to make that will become the titles of the slides

- Subsidiary points that support the main points and will become the bulleted content of each slide

Your main and subsidiary points are essential to the presentation. Although not essential at this point, certain secondary considerations are beneficial in flushing out your main points and the "feel" of your presentation. The more you think these through initially, the more smoothly your presentation will flow. What graphics will you want to use on each slide? Do you have charts or graphs that tell the story? Will photos take up part of the slide? Will you have a logo or other mandated identification on the chart?

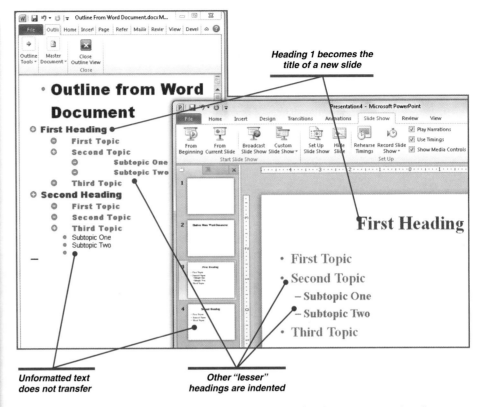

Heading 1 becomes the title of a new slide

Unformatted text does not transfer

Other "lesser" headings are indented

Figure 8-5: *Inserting an outline into a presentation from a Word document retains the heading-level formatting to separate slides and bulleted items.*

Preview and Print the Outline

To preview an outline and then print it:

1. Right-click the **Outline** tab, click **Expand**, and then click **Expand All** from the submenu to expand the entire outline so that all detail is showing.

2. Click the **File** tab, and click **Print**.

3. Under Settings, click the second drop-down list box, and click **Outline**, as seen in Figure 8-6.

4. Click **Print** to print the outline as it is previewed.

INDENTING WITH THE KEYBOARD

If you are interested in working with the keyboard rather than using the mouse, you can use these keypresses to work with the outlining feature, as shown in Table 8-1.

FUNCTION	KEYPRESS
Increase Indents (Demote)	Press **TAB** or
Increase Indents (Demote)	Press **ALT+SHIFT+RIGHT ARROW**
Decrease Indents (Promote)	Press **SHIFT+TAB** or
Decrease Indents (Promote)	Press **ALT+SHIFT+LEFT ARROW**
Move up a line	Press **ALT+SHIFT+UP ARROW**
Move down a line	Press **ALT+SHIFT+DOWN ARROW**

Table 8-1: **Indenting with the keyboard**

USING THE OUTLINING COMMANDS

Although some of the buttons available on the ribbon work well with the outlining function, you can display commands specifically for use with the Outline tab.

DISPLAY THE OUTLINING COMMANDS

1. Select the slide or line of text in the Outline tab.

2. Right-click and select one of the following commands described in the following sections.

Continued . . .

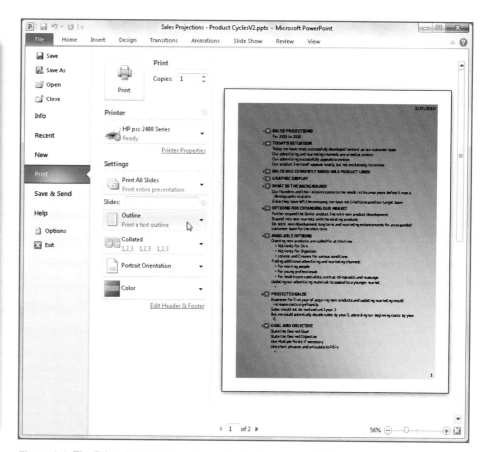

Figure 8-6: **The Print view previews the outline before you print it.**

PROMOTE OR DEMOTE OUTLINE TEXT

- Click **Promote** to move the selected text in a slide up one level.

- Click **Demote** to move the selected text in a slide down one level.

MOVE OUTLINE TEXT UP OR DOWN

- Click **Move Up** to move the selected text of a slide up one line or item.

- Click **Move Down** to move the selected text of a slide down one line or item.

COLLAPSE OR EXPAND A SLIDE

- Click **Collapse** and from the menu, click **Collapse** to hide the detail beneath the title of a selected slide; or click **Collapse All** to hide all the detail lines in the outline.

- Click **Expand** and from the menu, click **Expand** to show the detail beneath a title of a selected slide; or click **Expand All** to show all the detail lines in the outline.

— Collapse	▸	— Collapse
✦ Expand	▸	↑≡ Collapse All

SHOW FORMATTING

Click **Show Text Formatting** to toggle between showing and not showing the formatting in the outline text.

Protecting Your Presentation

You can set two levels of passwords restricting access to your presentation: You can deny access to even look at a presentation, and you can permit looking but deny modifying it. You can also strip personal information from the presentation—information that is automatically stored by PowerPoint, such as your name and certain file information.

Set Passwords for a Presentation

1. Open the presentation to be password-protected.

2. Click the **File** tab, and click **Save As**.

3. Click the **Tools** button to the left of Save, and click **General Options**. The General Options dialog box will appear.

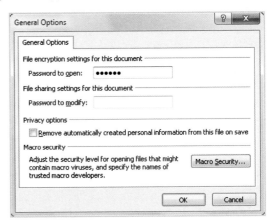

- To restrict anyone without a password from opening and looking at the presentation, type a password in the Password To Open text box.

- To restrict anyone from modifying the presentation, type a password in the Password To Modify text box.

4. Click **OK**.

5. You will have to confirm your intent and be warned that if you forget the password, the presentation cannot be recovered. In the Confirm Password dialog box, reenter the password and click **OK**.

6. Save the file by clicking **Save**.

When anyone tries to open or modify a protected file, they will see a message like this:

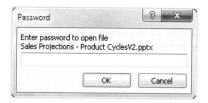

Remove Password Restrictions

1. Click the **File** tab, and click **Save As**.

2. Click **Tools** to the left of Save, and click **General Options**.

3. Clear any passwords in the Password To Open or Password To Modify text boxes.

4. Click **OK**.

5. Click **Save** and, if saving an existing file, confirm that you want to replace the existing file.

Strip File Information from the Presentation

When you set PowerPoint to strip personal information from a presentation, it is done when you save the file.

1. Click the **File** tab, and click **Save As**.

2. Click **Tools** to the left of Save, and click **General Options**.

3. Under Privacy Options, click the **Remove Automatically Created Personal Information From This File On Save** check mark.

4. Click **OK**.

5. Click **Save** and if saving an existing file, confirm that you want to replace it.

Chapter 9
Working with Slides

Getting around in a presentation and being able to manipulate slides easily is a critical skill in becoming a capable PowerPoint user. In this chapter you will find how to work with presentations at the slide level. In addition to navigating through the slides in various views of PowerPoint, you will learn to insert, delete, rearrange, and copy slides, as well as to change a presentation's basic components of themes, fonts, and colors. Finally, permissions are covered.

Navigate and Manipulate Slides

Working with slides enables you to find your way around PowerPoint and to manipulate the slides, both individually and globally. This section addresses how to insert and delete slides, display slides in a variety of ways, and move and duplicate slides.

QUICKSTEPS

NAVIGATING WITH THE KEYBOARD

If you are more comfortable working with the keyboard rather than the mouse pointer, you can work with slides using the keyboard.

ACCESS THE RIBBON AND RIBBON COMMANDS

- Press **ALT** to display the ribbon tags. To choose a specific tab, press the letter of the ribbon tag.

- To move among the ribbon commands, press **ALT** to turn off the ribbon tags, and then press **TAB** to move between commands within a group, or press **RIGHT ARROW** to move to the next tab in the ribbon. Then press **ENTER** to choose a command or menu.

MOVE TO THE NEXT OR PREVIOUS SLIDE

You have two ways on the keyboard to move to the next or previous slide on the Slides pane and the Slides tab.

- To move to the previous slide, press **PAGE UP** or press the **UP ARROW**.

- To move to the next slide, press **PAGE DOWN** or press the **DOWN ARROW**.

MOVE TO THE FIRST OR LAST SLIDE

- Press **CTRL+HOME** to move to the first slide.

- Press **CTRL+END** to move to the last slide.

MOVE TO THE NEXT PLACEHOLDER (DOTTED BOX) OR WINDOW AREA

- Press **CTRL+ENTER** to move to the next placeholder.

- Press **F6** to cycle between areas of a window: ribbon, Presentation pane, Slides/Outline panes, and Notes pane.

Continued . . .

Navigate from Slide to Slide

To move between the slides, you can use the Slides pane, the Outline tab, or the Slides tab to select and move to the slide you want.

- On the Slides tab, click the thumbnail of the slide you want.
- On the Outline tab, click the icon of the slide you want.
- On the Slides pane or either tab, click the vertical scroll bar to move to the next or previous slide.
- On the Slide Sorter view, click the vertical scroll bar to move to the next screen of thumbnails. Click the scroll bar's down arrow or up arrow to move more slowly. Click the up or down arrow on the scroll bar to move in increments. Click each slide to select it.

Insert a Slide

You can insert new slides in various ways in several places in PowerPoint. You can also insert slides from other presentations.

INSERT A NEW SLIDE

You can insert a new blank slide from several places in PowerPoint. The most common ways are:

- In the Home tab Slides group, click **New Slide**.

- In the Outline tab, when entering bulleted text, press **CTRL+ENTER**.

- In either the Slides or Outline tab, right-click the slide before the one you want to insert, and click **New Slide**.

  –Or–

  In either the Slides or Outline tab, click the slide or slide icon before the one you want to insert and press **ENTER**.

- In the Slide Sorter view, right-click the slide preceding the new one, and click **New Slide** or press **CTRL+M**.

NAVIGATING WITH THE KEYBOARD

(Continued)

OPEN AND CLOSE THE RIBBON

Press **CTRL+F1** to toggle the ribbon display.

START AND END SLIDE SHOWS

- To start a slide show on the current slide, press **SHIFT+F5**.

- To start a slide show beginning with the first slide, press **F5**.

- To close the slide show and return to Normal view, press **ESC**.

- To switch between the slide show and the Normal view, press **ALT+TAB**. (You must start with the slide show or else cycle through the thumbnails by clicking **TAB** until you can click the Normal view.)

Sales Projections - Product Cycles.pptx - Microsoft PowerP...

TIP

To delete a slide from the Slide Sorter view, the Outline tab, or the Slides tab: Click the thumbnail slide to select it, and press **DELETE**. You can also right-click the thumbnail slide, and click **Delete Slide** from the context menu.

INSERT A SLIDE FROM ANOTHER FILE

To insert a slide duplicated from another presentation, you must find and display the slides from the source presentation, and then select the slide or slides that you want to copy into your destination presentation.

1. In the Slides tab, click the slide positioned immediately before the one to be inserted.

2. Click the **Home** tab, and in the Slides group, click the **New Slide** down arrow. From the drop-down menu, click **Reuse Slides** (at the bottom of the menu). The Reuse Slides task pane will be displayed.

3. Click the **Browse** down arrow to find the source file containing the slide to be copied. Click **Browse Files**. When found, select the file and click **Open**. The Reuse Slides task pane, illustrated in Figure 9-1, will contain thumbnails of the presentation.

4. To insert the slides into the presentation, you must work back and forth between the Slides tab (destination) and the Reuse Slides (source) task pane.

   - Scroll to the thumbnail image in the source Reuse Slides task pane, and click the one to be inserted. It will be inserted when you click it.

   - To insert all the slides in the source Reuse Slides task pane, right-click a thumbnail and select **Insert All Slides** from the context menu.

   - To apply the formatting of the source slides to those in the destination Slides tab, right-click and choose **Apply Theme To All Slides** to copy the formatting to all of them, or select **Apply Theme To Selected Slides** to copy the format only to selected destination slides.

   - To retain the formatting of the source reuse slides as you copy them, click the **Keep Source Formatting** check box at the bottom of the task pane. ☑ Keep source formatting

Click the slide positioned immediately before the one to be inserted

Destination slides

Click a slide to copy it into the destination slides

Source slides

Click to locate the files with slides to be copied

Figure 9-1: *The Reuse Slides task pane allows you to find and copy one or more slides from another presentation into your current one.*

- To view a larger image of the Reuse Slides task pane, place the pointer over the slide thumbnail image, but do not click.

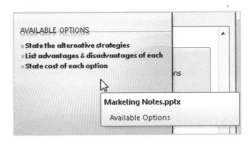

5. When you have inserted all the slides you want, click **Close** [x] to close the Reuse Slides task pane.

Display Multiple Presentations at Once

Opening and displaying two or more presentations opens many possibilities for dragging one slide from one presentation to another, copying color or formatting from one slide or presentation to another, and for comparing the presentations or slides side by side.

1. Open both presentations. Click the **File** tab, click **Open**, and complete the sequence of locating and opening the presentations.

2. Click the **View** tab, and from the Window group, choose one of the following views:

Tiles all open windows

Opens all windows in an "offset-stacked" view

Allows you to use arrow keys to move the split between the Slides pane and the Notes pane

Lists windows so you can switch between them

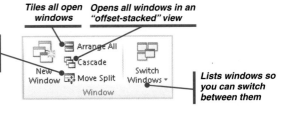

Figure 9-2: You can see each window separately by using the Arrange All command.

TIP

Another way to perform a move split action is to place the pointer over the border between the Slides pane and the Notes pane and drag the two-headed arrow icon up or down to increase or decrease a pane, respectively.

- Click the **Arrange All** button to display each presentation window side by side, as seen in Figure 9-2.

    –Or–

    Click **Cascade Windows** to see the windows cascading, as seen in Figure 9-3.

- Click **Move Split** and then press the **UP ARROW** and **DOWN ARROW** keys to move the split between the Slides pane and the Notes pane; press the **RIGHT ARROW** and **LEFT ARROW** keys to move the split between the Slides pane and the Outline/Slides tab. Press **ENTER** to exit the Move Split mode.

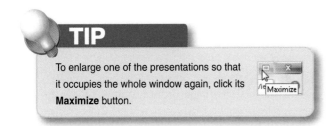

Figure 9-3: *Using the Cascade command, you can arrange the presentations in a cascading sequence.*

- Click **Switch Windows** to go back and forth between two or more presentations.

Duplicate a Slide

An alternate way to copy or duplicate a slide uses the Duplicate Slides command.

In the Slides tab, select the slide you want to copy. To copy multiple slides in the thumbnail views, press **CTRL** while you click the slides to select them. For contiguous slides, you can press **SHIFT** and click the first and last slide in the range. In Normal view, the active slide is the one that is selected.

- To duplicate a single slide or multiple selected slides, right-click the slide or slides, and click **Duplicate Slide** from the context menu.

- To duplicate multiple selected slides, click the **New Slide** down arrow (on the Home tab), and click **Duplicate Selected Slides** from the bottom of the menu. This also works for a single slide.

Copy a Design Using Browse

To copy just the design (and not the content) of a presentation, use the Browse feature of the Design Themes feature.

1. In Normal view, open the presentation to which you will apply the design of another presentation.

TIP

To enlarge one of the presentations so that it occupies the whole window again, click its **Maximize** button.

QUICKSTEPS

MOVING OR COPYING SLIDES

You can move or copy your slides most easily from the Outline tab, the Slides tab, or the Slides Sorter view.

- To copy a slide, right-click the slide to be copied, and click **Copy** on the context menu. Right-click the slide preceding where you want the new slide to go, and click **Paste** on the context menu.

- To move a slide, click the slide icon or thumbnail to be moved, and drag it to the new location. The insertion point will indicate where the slide will be inserted.

NOTE

To copy rather than move on the Slides tab and Slide Sorter view using the thumbnails, right-click and drag the selected slides to the new location. When you release the pointer, click **Copy** on the context menu that appears.

CAUTION

Where you place the insertion point will determine where the new slide will be positioned. It's possible to insert a slide into the middle of another one, splitting its contents unintentionally. Make certain you place the insertion point precisely where you want the new slide to go.

2. Click the **Design** tab, click the **Themes More** down arrow, and click **Browse For Themes**.

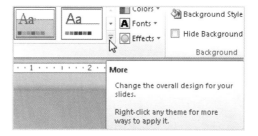

3. In the Choose Theme Or Themed Document dialog box, find the document or presentation containing the theme you want to copy and click it.

4. Click **Apply**, and the theme will be copied to the original presentation.

Use Zoom

You can zoom in or out of a slide, which enables you to work at a very detailed level or back off to see the total slide, respectively.

- To control the zoom with a specific percentage, click the **View** tab, and click the **Zoom** button in the Zoom group. When the Zoom dialog box appears, click the percentage you want displayed or use the **Percent** spinner. A smaller percentage will reduce the image; a larger percentage will increase it. Click **OK** when finished.

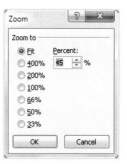

NOTE

If you have more than one design theme applied to a presentation, the first one will be copied; if you haven't opened the presentation recently, you will be asked if you want the remaining themes to be made available.

QUICKSTEPS

USING A KEYBOARD WITH SLIDES

If you are more comfortable using the keyboard than a mouse pointer, you have these commands and more. Some of the commands use a combination of pointer and keyboard commands, such as Copy.

START A NEW PRESENTATION

Press **CTRL+N**.

INSERT A NEW SLIDE

Press **ALT+H**, press **I**, and then use the arrow keys to select a layout from the menu. Press **ENTER** when finished.

REMOVE A SLIDE

Press **DELETE** or press **CTRL+X**.

COPY A SLIDE

- Move the arrow keys to the thumbnail you want (or click a thumbnail to select it), and press **CTRL+C**.

- Select the slide prior to the one you want to insert, and press **CTRL+V**.

COPY THE CONTENTS OF A SLIDE

- Move the arrow keys to the thumbnail you want (or click a thumbnail to select it), select the contents to be copied, and press **CTRL+C**.

- Move the insertion point to where you want the items copied, and press **CTRL+V**.

- To make the slide fit in the window, click the **View** tab, and then click the **Fit To Window** button in the Zoom group. The image will be reduced or increased in size to fit in the slide pane. If you are not in the View tab, a quicker way to do this is to click the **Fit Slide To Current Window** button ⊡ on the right of the status bar.

- To increase or decrease the zoom effect with a slider, drag the **Zoom** slider on the right of the status bar, or click the **Zoom In** or **Zoom Out** button on either side of the slider to zoom in or out in smaller increments. The percentage of the zoom will be shown to the left of the slider.   95% ⊖ ─🗆─ ⊕

Change the Look and Feel of Slides

At some point or another, you will want to change the look and feel of slides in a presentation. The slides may have been created from another presentation, and you want this one to be unique. You may need just to tweak a few components of the presentation. You can change the theme, color, fonts, and special effects of a presentation.

Change a Theme

As you have seen in Chapter 8, you can select a built-in (or PowerPoint standard) theme for your slides. These themes can be changed to fit your own presentation requirements. The theme can be changed for a single slide or the whole presentation by altering the fonts, color, and design elements.

CHANGE THE COLOR OF A THEME

Each theme consists of a set of four colors for text and background, six colors for accents, and two colors for hyperlinks. You can change any single color element or all of them. When you change the colors, the font styles and design elements remain the same.

1. With your presentation open, click the **Design** tab.

2. If you want to change the theme colors on only some of the slides, select those slides now. Use **CTRL**+click to select noncontiguous slides or use **SHIFT**+click to select contiguous slides.

3. Click **Theme Colors**. The menu of color combinations will be displayed, as seen in Figure 9-4. 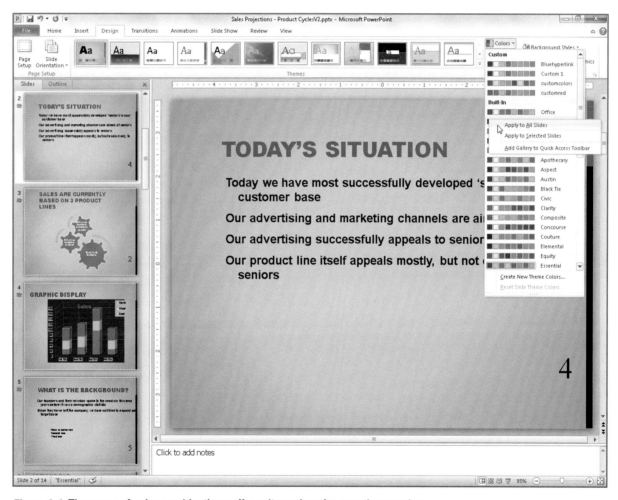 Colors ▾

4. Run the pointer over the rows of color combinations to see which appeals to you.

5. When you find the one you want, right-click the row and click **Apply To All Slides** to change the colors throughout the whole presentation, or click **Apply To Selected Slides** to change just the slides you have chosen.

*Figure 9-4: **The menu of color combinations offers alternatives for your theme colors.***

You may have to drag your text placeholder to the right or left to see the effects of the fonts as you pass your pointer over them.

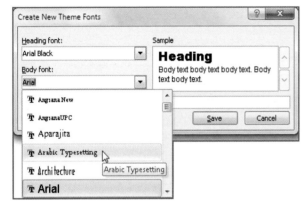

Figure 9-5: *You can choose a heading or body font from the fonts available in your Windows system.*

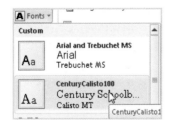

CHANGE THEME FONTS

Each theme includes two fonts. The *body* font is used for general text entry, and a *heading* font is used for headings. The default font used in PowerPoint for a new presentation without a theme is Calibri for headings and body text. Once a theme is assigned to slides, the fonts may be different, and they can be changed.

1. In the Design tab Themes group, click **Theme Fonts**. The drop-down list displays a list of theme fonts. The current theme font combination is highlighted in its place in the list.

2. Point to each font combination to see how the fonts appear on your presentation.

3. Click the font name combination you decide upon. If you click a font name combination, the font will replace both the body and heading fonts on all slides.

CREATE A NEW THEME FONT

You may also decide that you want a unique set of fonts for your presentation. You can create a custom font set that is available in the list of fonts for your current and future presentations.

1. In the Design tab Themes group, click **Theme Fonts**.

2. Click **Create New Theme Fonts** at the bottom of the drop-down list.

3. In the Create New Theme Fonts dialog box (see Figure 9-5), click either or both the **Heading Font** and **Body Font** down arrows to select a new fonts combination. View the new combination in the Sample area.

4. Type a new name for the font combination you've selected, and click **Save**. Custom fonts are available for selection at the top of the Theme Fonts drop-down list.

CHANGE THEMED GRAPHIC EFFECTS

Shapes, illustrations, pictures, and charts include graphic effects that are controlled by themes. Themed graphics are modulated in terms of their lines (borders), fills, and effects (such as shadowed, raised, and shaded). For example, some themes simply change an inserted rectangle's fill color, while other themes affect the color, the weight of its border, and whether it has a 3-D appearance.

1. In the Design tab Themes group, click **Theme Effects**. The drop-down list displays a gallery of effects combinations. The current effects combination is highlighted.

2. Point to each combination to see how the effects appear on your presentation, assuming you have a graphic or chart inserted on the slide (see Chapter 14 for information on inserting tables, charts, graphics, and drawings).

3. Click the effects combination you want.

Create a Custom Theme

You can create a new theme, save it, and use it in your presentations. You select a group of text, background, accent, and hyperlink colors and give them a name. To save changes to a theme, click the **More Themes** down arrow, and click **Save Current Theme** after having made any changes to the background, color, font, or effects in the current theme. Your altered theme is saved as a custom theme.

CHANGE THEME COLORS

To customize the color scheme:

1. Click the **Design** tab, and then in the Themes group, click **Themes Colors**.

2. At the bottom of the menu of colors, click **Create New Theme Colors**. The Create New Theme Colors dialog box will appear, as shown in Figure 9-6.

3. To select a color for one of the color groups, click the down arrow for the Text/Background/Accent/ and/or Hyperlink group, and click the color you want to test. It will be displayed in the Sample pane.

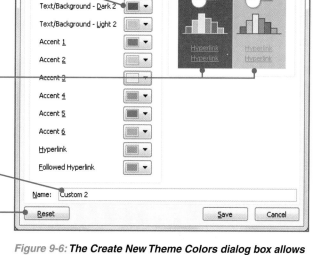

Displays a selection of colors for the named elements

Selected colors are reflected here

Type a name and click Save to create the custom theme

Click to reset the colors to the original selections

Figure 9-6: *The Create New Theme Colors dialog box allows you to create new themes to use in presentations.*

Colors ▾   Background Style
Custom
                 Bluehyperlin
                 Custom 1
Apply to All Slides
Apply to Selected Slides
Edit...
Delete...
Add Gallery to Quick Access Toolbar

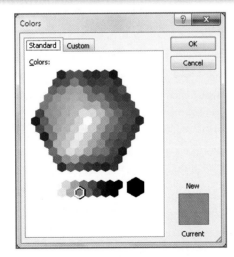

Figure 9-7: **You can change the color precisely by clicking the specific color shade you want.**

4. Go through each set of colors that you want to change.

5. When you find a group of colors that you like, type a name in the Name text box, and click **Save**.

USE CUSTOM COLORS

Using a similar technique to creating your own themes, you can create your own unique color mix for text, background, accents, and hyperlinks. Here is how you work with custom colors:

1. Select the slides to be affected with the new colors, whether all of them or a selected few.

2. Click the **Design** tab, and click **Theme Colors**. At the bottom of the rows of color combinations, click **Create New Theme Colors**. The Create New Theme Colors dialog box will appear.

3. Click the theme color group that you want to work with. The Theme Colors submenu will be displayed. Click **More Colors**.

    Standard Colors
    😊 More Colors...

4. In the Colors dialog box, you have two options.

    • Click the **Standard** tab to see the dialog box shown in Figure 9-7. Click the color unit you want and see it displayed in the New preview pane. When you want to see it in the Sample pane, click **OK**.

    • Click the **Custom** tab to see the dialog box shown in Figure 9-8. Click somewhere on the color rainbow to get the approximate color. Then drag the slider to get precisely the color you want. You will see it displayed in the New preview pane.

    –Or–

    • Click the **Red**, **Green**, or **Blue** up arrow or down arrow to get the precise color mix you want. Displayed is RGB (Red, Green, Blue color standard) color, but you can also select HSL (Hue, Saturation, and Luminosity color standard). When you are finished, click **OK**.

5. When you get the colors you want, type a name in the Name text box, and click **Save** to create a custom theme color.

CHANGE THE BACKGROUND STYLE

You can change the slide background on one or all slides in a presentation. When you change the background style when you have a theme already

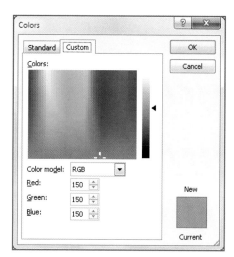

Figure 9-8: **You can create unique colors by "mixing" the combination of red, green, and blue.**

assigned to the slides in your presentation, the design elements from the theme will remain—only the background color or shading changes.

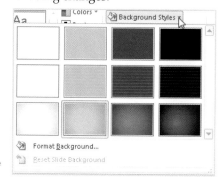

1. If you want only some of the slides changed, select those that are to be changed with a new background style.

2. Click the **Design** tab, and in the Background group, click **Background Styles**. A menu of styles will open.

3. Run your pointer over the thumbnails to see which appeals to you. As you do this, the slides in the Slides pane will reflect the selection.

4. When you find the style you want, click it to change all the slides. Or right-click the thumbnail and click **Apply To Selected Slides** to change only the selected slides. The menu will close and the slides in the presentation will be changed.

Copy Attributes with Format Painter

The Format Painter can be used to copy all attributes (such as fonts, alignment, bullet styles, and color) from one slide to another as well as from one presentation to another.

1. Display the source slides in the Slides tab or Slide Sorter view. Click the **Home** tab.

2. Find and click the source slide containing the color to be copied.

3. Click **Format Painter** in the Clipboard group once to copy the source format to one slide. If you want to use the source slide to reformat several slides, double-click **Format Painter** to turn it on until you click it again to turn it off (or press **ESC**).

4. Find the destination slide, and click it to receive the new attributes.

5. If you are copying the source attributes to multiple slides, continue to find the destination slides and click them.

6. When you are finished, click **Format Painter** to turn it off or press **ESC**.

USING FOOTERS ON SLIDES

To work with any aspect of footers, you need to display the Headers And Footers dialog box (shown in Figure 9-9). (Headers are available for notes and handouts only.) To display this dialog box, follow these three steps; then do the fourth one to complete the selection:

1. Select the slide or slides that need footers.

2. Click the **Insert** tab, and click **Header & Footer** in the Text group.

3. Click the **Slide** tab for footers for slides (see Chapter 10).

4. When you have finished making your selections, described next, click **Apply** to apply the choices to selected slides only, or click **Apply To All** for all slides.

DISPLAY TIME OR DATE

You must first display the Headers And Footers dialog box, as described previously, and then click the **Date And Time** check box.

- To apply a time or date that reflects the actual time or date, select **Update Automatically**. From the drop-down list box, click the date only, time only, or time and date format you prefer.

- To apply a fixed time or date, or other text, select **Fixed**. In the Fixed text box, type the text that will always appear in the footer.

Continued . . .

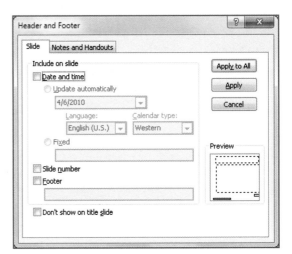

Figure 9-9: *You can add footers to selected slides or to the whole presentation.*

Work with Hyperlinks

Inserting hyperlinks in a presentation allows you to link to other files or presentations, to a website, to an e-mail address, or to another slide within the current presentation.

INSERT A HYPERLINK

To insert a hyperlink in the presentation:

1. On your slide, highlight the text by dragging the pointer over the characters that you want to contain the hyperlink.

2. Click the **Insert** tab, and in the Links group, click the **Hyperlink** button.

3. In the Insert Hyperlink dialog box, find the destination for the link.

   - If the destination is within the presentation outline itself, click **Place In This Document**, and click the slide, as seen in Figure 9-10.

QUICKSTEPS

USING FOOTERS ON SLIDES
(Continued)

ENTER A FOOTER

After displaying the Headers And Footers dialog box:

1. Select the **Footer** check box.

2. In the Footer text box, type the text for the footer.

HIDE FOOTERS ON THE TITLE PAGE

Once you have displayed the Headers And Footers dialog box, select the **Don't Show On Title Slide** check box if you don't want the footer displayed on the title page.

☑ Don't show on title slide

REMOVE HEADERS OR FOOTERS

Once you have displayed the Headers And Footers dialog box:

1. Clear the **Date And Time**, **Slide Number**, and **Footer** check boxes.

2. To remove the footer for selected slides, click **Apply**.

   –Or–

   To remove the footer for all slides, click **Apply To All**.

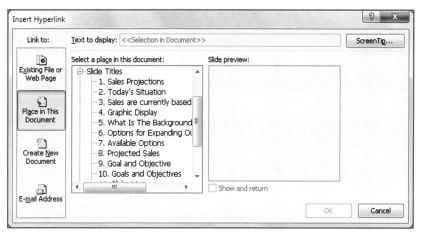

Figure 9-10: **Hyperlinks can provide a means to "jump" from one part of an outline to another.**

- If the destination is on an existing document or webpage, click **Existing File Or Web Page**, and follow the prompts to the destination.

- If you must create a new document for the hyperlink to point to, click **Create New Document**, and proceed as prompted.

- If you want to place a hyperlink to an e-mail address, click **E-mail Address**.

4. Click **OK**.

REMOVE A HYPERLINK

To remove a hyperlink from text or an object:

1. Right-click the text or object containing the hyperlink.

2. Select **Remove Hyperlink** from the context menu.

CHANGE A HYPERLINK COLOR

To change the color of hyperlinks in a presentation:

1. Highlight the link to be changed.

2. Click the **Design** tab, and click the **Theme Colors** button on the Themes group.

3. At the bottom of the list of color combinations, click **Create New Theme Colors**. The Create New Theme Colors dialog box will appear with your current theme's color selected in each of the sets.

4. Click the hyperlink color you want to change to open the colors gallery, and click the new color. As you click a color, you'll see it reflected in the Sample box.

5. Type a name in the Name text box, and click **Save** to make the change to the hyperlinks in the presentation. Your changed color will be applied to the links in your presentation and a custom theme color will be listed in the Theme Color list. By default, it will be named "Custom 1," unless you rename it.

Chapter 10

Working with Notes, Masters, and Slide Text

This chapter covers three important features that make a presentation more effective: notes, slide masters, and slide text. Using notes for preparing speaker and handout notes allows you to fully prepare a presentation so that you remember all you wanted to say and so that the audience remembers your important points as well. Slide masters allow you to make changes to your presentations that are reflected on each slide or on only some of them.

This chapter also addresses how to work with text, from selecting a layout or inserting a placeholder, to modifying text by editing, positioning, moving, copying, and deleting it. The Office Clipboard is covered, as is checking the spelling of standard and foreign languages. Special features, like AutoFit and AutoCorrect, are also discussed.

10

Work with Notes

Notes are used to create speaker notes that aid a speaker during a presentation and to create handouts given to the audience so that it can follow the presentation easily. The notes do not appear on the slides during a slide show presentation; they are only visible for the presenter's benefit.

Create a Note

To create speaker notes, which can also be used as handouts, you can either use the Notes pane in Normal view (as shown in Figure 10-1) or the Notes Page (shown in the upcoming Figures 10-2 and 10-3). In both views, you can see a thumbnail of the slide with your notes pertaining to it. Each slide has its own Notes Page. You can also add charts, graphs, or pictures to the notes. To add or change attributes or text to all notes in a presentation, make changes to the notes master.

CREATE A NOTE IN THE NOTES PAGE

1. To open the Notes Page, click the **View** tab, and in the Presentation Views group, click **Notes Page**. The Notes Page opens, as shown in Figure 10-2.

2. To increase the size of the notes area, click the **View** tab, and in the Zoom group, click **Zoom**.

3. Click the zoom magnification you want, and click **OK**.

4. To move to another slide, click the scroll bar.

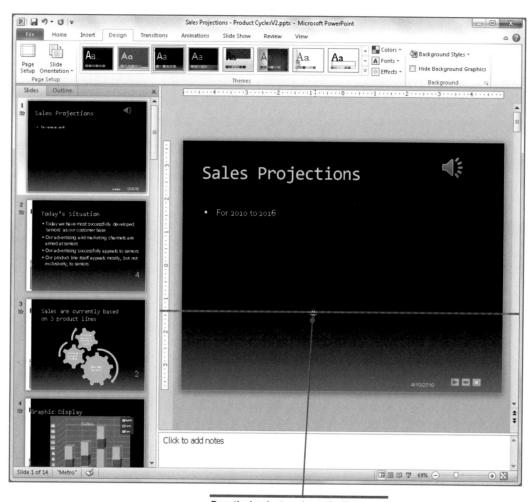

Figure 10-1: In the Notes pane of the Normal view, you can expand the area where you add your notes by dragging the border of the Notes pane upward to increase its size.

Drag the border to enlarge the Notes pane

Preview Speaker Notes

If you want to proof your notes before they are printed, you can preview them in the Print view. This allows you to see them as they will be printed.

1. Click the **File** tab File , and click **Print**. The Print view appears.

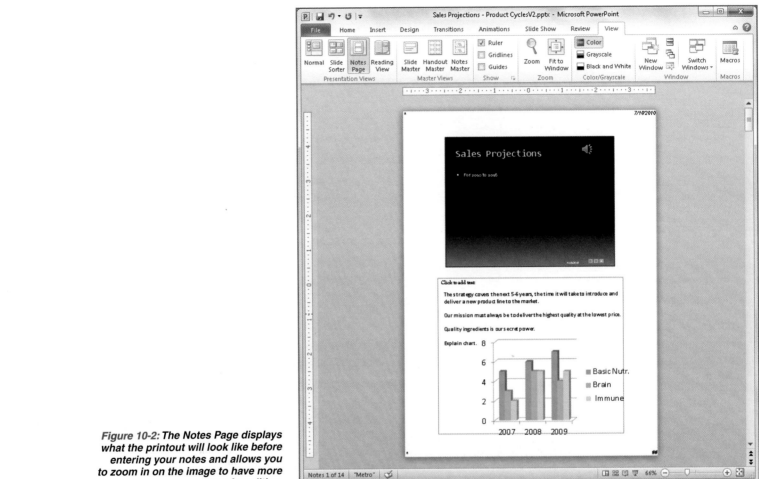

Figure 10-2: The Notes Page displays what the printout will look like before entering your notes and allows you to zoom in on the image to have more room for editing.

2. Under Settings, click the second drop-down menu, and click **Notes Pages**. You will see the preview of the Notes Page, as the notes will be printed, in the right pane, shown in Figure 10-3.

3. Click **Print** to print notes (see "Print Notes and Handouts"), or click the **File** tab again to toggle back to the Notes Page.

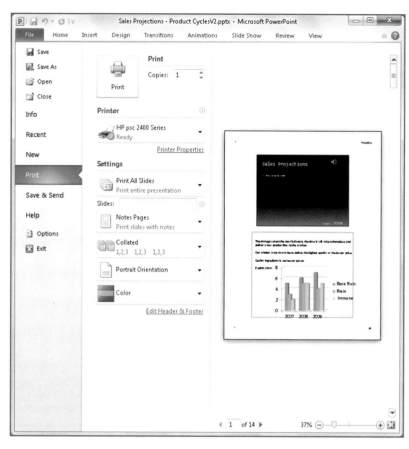

Figure 10-3: The Print Notes Page command displays a preview of the speaker notes with the accompanying slide.

Print Notes and Handouts

Speaker notes and handouts are printed in a similar way.

PRINT SPEAKER NOTES

To print your notes:

1. Click the **File** tab, and click **Print**. The Print view will appear, an example of which is displayed in Figure 10-3.

QUICKSTEPS

USING HEADERS AND FOOTERS ON NOTES AND HANDOUTS

To put headers and footers on notes and handouts:

1. Click the **View** tab, and in the Presentation Views group, click **Notes Page**.

2. Click the **Insert** tab, and then click **Header & Footer**.

3. Click the **Notes And Handouts** tab. The Header And Footer dialog box, shown in Figure 10-4, appears.

4. Choose the items you want by placing a check mark next to them.

   • To include a date or time in the header, click **Date And Time**, and choose between **Update Automatically**, for a time/date that updates according to the current date, or **Fixed**, for a time/date or other text that remains the same each time it is printed.

   • Click **Header**, click in the text box, and type the header text for notes and handouts.

   • Click **Page Number** to place a page number on the note or handout page. If a check mark is already in the check box, leave it to print a page number or clear it to suppress the page number.

   • Click **Footer**, click in the text box, and type footer text. If a check mark is already in the check box, leave it to print a footer or clear it to suppress the footer.

5. Click **Apply To All**.

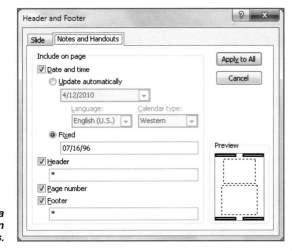

Figure 10-4: You can create a header and footer to display on note and handout pages.

2. Under Settings, click the second drop-down menu, and click **Notes Pages**. You have these options:

   • Under Settings, in the first drop-down menu, click **All**, **Current Slide**, or **Selection** to enter the slide numbers for specific slides or slide ranges in the Slide text box.

   • Click the **Portrait Orientation** drop-down menu (the fourth beneath Settings) to choose between Portrait (tall) or Landscape (wide).

   • Click the **Color** down arrow, and choose **Color**, **Grayscale**, or **Pure Black And White**.

   • Beside the Print button, enter the number of copies.

3. Click **Print** to print.

PRINT HANDOUTS

A printed handout contains a number of thumbnail slides, an example of which is shown in Figure 10-5.

1. Click the **File** tab, and click **Print**. The Print view appears.

2. Beneath Settings, click the second drop-down menu, and under the Handouts section, click the number of slides to be displayed in the handouts.

3. Set the number of copies, and make other adjustments as needed.

4. Click **Print** to print.

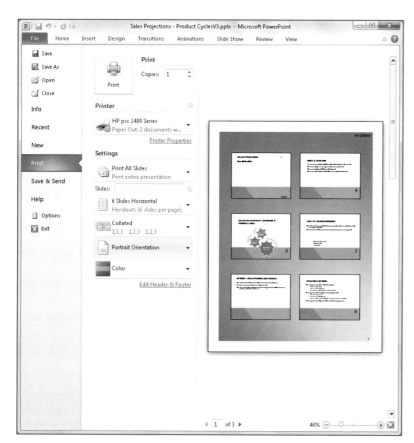

Figure 10-5: The Print view displays a preview of the printed handouts with thumbnails of slides and allows you to select the number of slides displayed on a page.

Work with Slide, Note, and Handout Masters

Working with masters gives you an opportunity to change a presentation globally. PowerPoint gives you a set of master slides for slides, notes, and handouts: The slide master controls the slides of a presentation; the notes master controls the global aspects of notes; and the handout master controls the handouts. Note and handout masters are not automatically created—they are only created if you want to use global attributes for them.

Manage Slide Appearance

A presentation has a *slide master* containing formatting and other design elements that apply to all slides in a presentation (or to a set of slides with the same "look"). Usually associated with that slide master are up to ten *layout masters* that apply to other slides in a presentation. The title slide, for example, has a layout master for unique positioning of page components, formatting, headings, and design elements. The slide master may get its specific formatting from a theme template that you used, and you can change the master without changing the original template. This is one way that you can customize your presentation even after using a suggested theme to get you going. The original theme is not changed—only the theme as it is in your presentation. You can save a presentation with its modified master slides as a custom template. In other words, themes are actually applied to masters, which are then applied to specific slides.

NOTE

To specify what will be included on the printed page, click the **Edit Header & Footer** link beneath the Settings options. Refer to the "Using Headers and Footers on Notes and Handouts" QuickSteps to modify the items on the Header And Footer dialog box that you want to add or remove from the page. Click **Apply To All**.

CHANGING FONT ATTRIBUTES

You can change font attributes either by changing the fonts or by applying WordArt styles to title text, for example.

MAKE FONT CHANGES

You can change the attributes of text on only one type of slide by changing a layout master, or you can change attributes throughout all slides by changing the font or character in the master slide. The following font commands are found in the Font group of the Home tab. (When you highlight text, a mini toolbar appears with additional commands available.) Figure 10-6 shows the possibilities for changing font attributes.

Use these commands to change text attributes:

- **Font** Changes the font face. Click the down arrow, and a list of font names is displayed.

- **Font Size** Changes the point size of fonts. Click the down arrow, and select a point size.

- **Increase Font Size** Increases the point size in increments. Click the button to increase it.

- **Decrease Font Size** Decreases the point size in increments. Click the button to decrease it.

- **Clear All Formatting** Removes all formatting from a selection and retains only plain text.

- **Bold** Applies boldface to selected text.

- **Italic** Applies italics to selected text.

- **Underline** Applies an underline to selected text.

- **Shadow** Applies a shadow effect to selected text.

- **Strikethrough** Applies a strikethrough to selected text.

Continued . . .

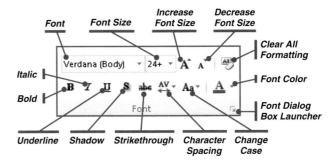

Figure 10-6: *This group of text-editing commands can be found on the Home tab.*

EDIT A SLIDE MASTER OR LAYOUT MASTER

In a set of slide masters is one slide master that sets the standards for all slides in the presentation. Editing a slide master changes all the slides to which it applies. The set of associated layout masters, about ten of them, will, by default, carry the slide master's theme and other formatting. The layout masters are specific to a type of layout that might be part of the presentation. For example, perhaps you will have one particular layout for all slides containing graphs. Another example for a specific type of layout is the title layout master. A layout master usually carries the same color, design elements, and formatting as the theme assigned to a master slide. You can change particular layouts to be different from the slide master, and then the overall theme will become a custom theme.

1. Click the **View** tab, and click **Slide Master**. The slide master is displayed (see Figure 10-7).

2. Add headings or subheadings and dates or slide numbers. Add graphics, themes, or background color. Add headers or footers or other elements of the master, just as you would a normal slide. Editing and formatting changes you can make include the following:

- To change the overall font style, click the first thumbnail to select the slide master. Either click the placeholder for the text you want to change or highlight the actual heading or body text. Click the button in the Font group for the attribute you want to modify—for example, Font for the font face. See the "Changing Font Attributes" QuickFacts.

CHANGING FONT ATTRIBUTES
(Continued)

- **Character Spacing** Increases or decreases the space between the characters of a word. Choose Very Tight, Tight, Normal, Loose, Very Loose, or More Spacing—where you can set specific points between characters and set *kerning*, a more sophisticated method of setting the space between characters.

- **Change Case** Changes the case of a word between several alternatives: Sentence Case, lowercase, UPPERCASE, Capitalize Each Word, and tOGGLE cASE.

- **Font Color** Changes the color of the font. Point at each of the colors to see the effect on the background slide.

- **Font Dialog Box Launcher** Opens a dialog box where character changes can be made.

CHANGE TO WORDART STYLES

You can also change the text to WordArt styles. When you double-click a text or title placeholder, the Drawing Tools Format tab becomes available, but not necessarily activated until you click the tab. So when you want to access a tool from the Tools Format tab, you'll need to click its tab. On it are the WordArt styles that can be applied to selected placeholders or text.

Click to add colored fill to characters *Click to change color of character outlines*

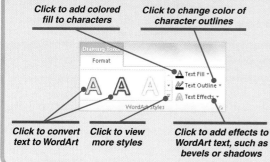

Click to convert text to WordArt *Click to view more styles* *Click to add effects to WordArt text, such as bevels or shadows*

Set the slide fonts for the presentation *The title layout master establishes the title, a logo (optional), and any other text you want on the title slide*

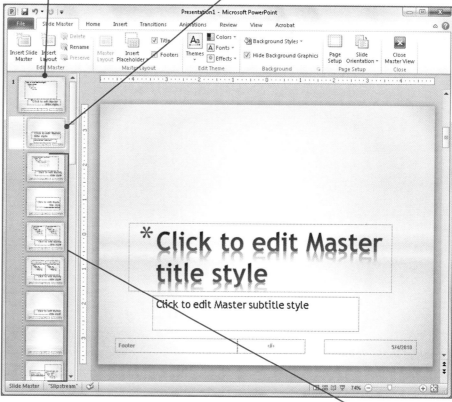

Figure 10-7: *The masters for a new presentation contain a slide master (no. 1) and several layout slides, here with the "Slipstream" theme.*

The layout masters give you standards for presentation or custom layouts

- To change the bullets for bulleted text, double-click the placeholder containing the bullets to change them all, or select just a specific level of bullet to change. Click the **Home** tab, and in the Paragraph group, click the **Bullets** down arrow, and click the style of bullets you like. You can point at each bullet type to see the results in the background master slide. To insert a picture that serves as a bullet, click **Bullets And Numbering** on the bottom of the list to display a dialog box. Click the **Bulleted** tab, click **Picture**, and click the bullet picture you want. To insert a new picture, click **Import** and then find the picture you want. Click **OK** on the Picture Bullet dialog box.

QUICKSTEPS

WORKING WITH SLIDE MASTERS

You can duplicate masters, create title masters that vary from the other masters, protect your masters from being accidentally or intentionally changed, or create multiple new title and slide masters.

DUPLICATE A SLIDE MASTER

To duplicate a slide master:

1. Click the **View** tab, and click **Slide Master**.

2. Right-click the master slide thumbnail to be duplicated. It may be a master slide or a layout master slide. The options on the context menu will vary, depending on the type of master you select.

Continued . . .

- To change the appearance of numbers for numbered lists, double-click the placeholder containing the numbered lists. Click the **Numbering** down arrow in the Paragraph group, and click the style of numbers you like. You can point at each item in the list to see the results in the background master slide. To get a size or color that isn't in the menu of choices, click **Bullets And Numbering** on the bottom of the list to display a dialog box. Click the **Numbered** tab, and click the **Size** spinner to increase or decrease the size. Click **Start At** to reset the beginning number. Click the **Color** down arrow to select a new color for the set of numbers. Click **OK** to close the Bullets And Numbering dialog box.

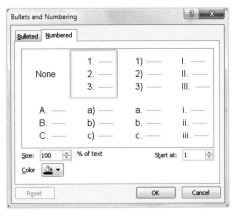

- By clicking the **Insert** tab and selecting **Header & Footer** in the Text group, you can include a footer, slide number, or time and date on the slide. Then, to change the format for the time or date, click a text placeholder to select it (you may have to click directly on the placeholder text to select it, such as on the Date Area placeholder). Then click the **Home** tab, and in the Font group, click the **Font** or **Font Size** down arrow, and select the font or size you want from the drop-down list.

CREATE MULTIPLE SLIDE AND TITLE MASTERS

Multiple slide masters and their associated sets of layout masters are used in a presentation to create different looks in layout or formatting for different sections of the presentation.

To create additional new slide masters:

1. Click the **View** tab, and click **Slide Master**.

2. Right-click the slide master, and click **Insert Slide Master**. A new slide master and its associated layout masters will be inserted.

3. Make any changes or incorporate different design templates to the new masters as needed.

4. Click the **Slide Master** tab, and then click **Close Master View** in the Close group to close the Slide Master view.

WORKING WITH SLIDE MASTERS

(Continued)

- For a slide master, click **Duplicate Slide Master**. The slide master and all the sets of layouts it carries will be duplicated.

- For a layout master, click **Duplicate Layout**, and just the layout master will be duplicated.

CREATE A TITLE MASTER

To make the format of your title page different from the rest of your slides, create a title master to contain its unique formatting or design elements.

1. Click the **View** tab, choose **Slide Master**, and click the layout thumbnail immediately beneath the slide master in the Slides tab. This is normally the title layout master.

2. Click in the title placeholder, and type your title. Enter a subtitle if necessary.

3. Format the text as needed.

4. Insert a logo or other graphic by clicking the **Insert** tab and clicking the type of graphic you want. Follow the prompts to find what you want.

RETAIN A SLIDE MASTER

To retain a slide master within the presentation, even if it is not being used, use the Preserve Master button. This option is unavailable for layout masters.

1. With the Slide Master tab active, right-click the slide master to be protected.

Continued . . .

Work with the Notes Master

To make global changes to all notes in a presentation, use the notes master. Here you can add a logo or other graphics, change the positioning of page components, change formats, and add headings and text design elements for all notes.

1. Click the **View** tab, and click **Notes Master**. The notes master will be displayed, as shown in Figure 10-8.

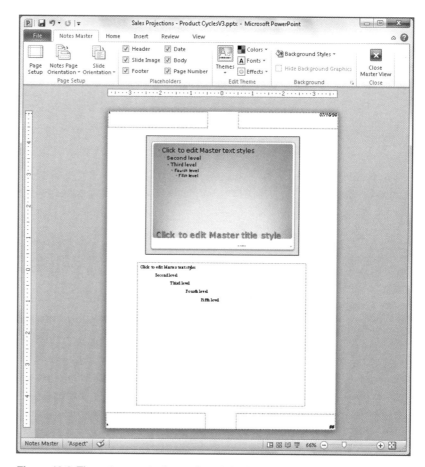

Figure 10-8: *The notes master is used to globally change such note features as headers, footers, logos, or graphics; note text formatting; and placement of note elements.*

10

QUICKSTEPS

WORKING WITH SLIDE MASTERS
(Continued)

2. From the context menu, click **Preserve Master** to protect the selected master. You will see a thumbtack or pushpin beside the master.

Thumbtack or pushpin indicates the selected master is protected

TIP

To add a text placeholder to the Notes pane, click the **Insert** tab, and click the **Text Box** button. Then drag the icon where you want the text box to be created, and type in the box. You can drag the text box to another location.

2. To adjust the zoom so that you can see the notes area better, click the **View** tab, and click **Zoom**. Choose the magnification and click **OK**.

3. You can change the notes master as follows:

- Change the formatting of the text elements, such as font size or style, or change the bullets or indents.

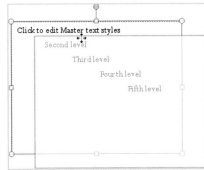

- Drag the position of the slide or note text placeholder (the dotted box) to a different location by placing the pointer over the border until you see a four-headed arrow and then dragging the border of the placeholder to resize it.

- Change the size of the slide or note text placeholder by placing the pointer over the border until you see a two-headed arrow and then dragging the border of the placeholder to resize it.

- Add a logo by clicking the **Insert** tab and clicking the **Picture**, **Shapes**, **Clip Art**, or other graphic button. Resize the graphic as needed, and drag it where you want it to appear on all notes.

- Add text that will appear on all notes, such as page number, date, or title.

4. Click the **Notes Master** tab, and then click **Close Master View** in the Close group to close the notes master.

Change the Handout Master

Handouts display thumbnails of the slides on a printed page. You can have one, two, three, four, six, or nine slides per page. To prepare your handouts for printing with titles and other formatting, use the handout master.

1. Click the **View** tab, and click **Handout Master**. The handout master will be displayed, as shown in Figure 10-9.

2. On the handout master ribbon in the Page Setup group, click **Slides Per Page** to set the number of slides to be displayed in the handout: one, two, three, four, six, or nine, or the slide outline.

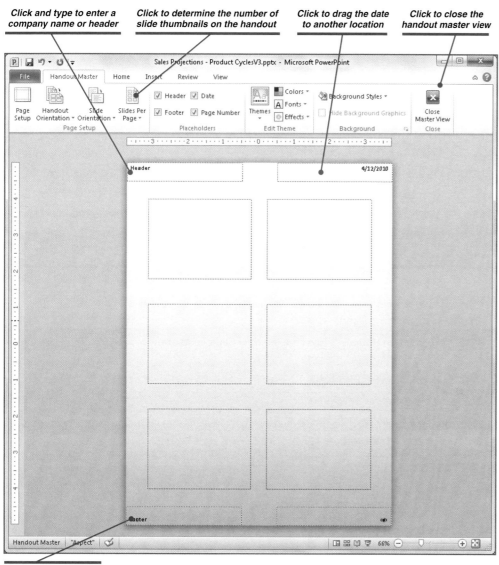

Click and type to enter a company name or header

Click to determine the number of slide thumbnails on the handout

Click to drag the date to another location

Click to close the handout master view

Click and type to enter footer information

Figure 10-9: The handout master allows you to add titles for handouts, vary the number of slides displayed in the handout, and add other text or objects as needed.

3. Make changes to the handout master as needed.

- Click **Page Setup** in the Page Setup group to set the slide size; initial numbering of slides; and orientation of slides and notes, handouts, and outline.

- Click **Handout Orientation** in the Page Setup group to give the handout a portrait or landscape orientation.

- Click **Slide Orientation** in the Page Setup group to give the slides on the handout a portrait or landscape orientation

- Click **Header**, **Date**, **Footer**, or **Page Number** in the Placeholders group to remove the check marks if you do not want them to appear on the handouts. They are selected by default. If you choose for headers and footers to be there, enter the text in the appropriate text boxes.

- To format the date, click in the date text box, click the **Insert** tab, and click **Date & Time**. Choose a format and click **OK**. Return to the Handout Master tab.

- To select a style for the background, click **Background Styles** in the Background group and choose one.

- If you want graphics to be hidden when printed, click the **Hide Background Graphics** check box in the Background group.

4. To close the handout master, click **Close Master View** in the Close group on the ribbon.

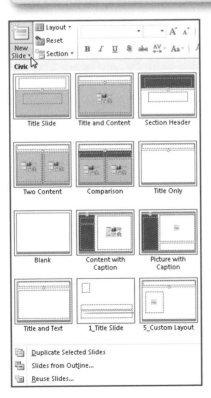

Figure 10-10: *You can choose among several standard layouts containing text boxes.*

Work with Text

Entering and manipulating text is a major part of building a presentation. Text is not only titles and bulleted lists. It is also captions on a picture or a legend or labels on a chart. Text can be inside a shape or curved around it on the outside. Text communicates in a thousand ways. Here is how you work with text in PowerPoint.

Use a Text Layout

To create the "look" of your presentation, you will want to insert text, columns, graphics, charts, logos, and other pictures in a consistent way. PowerPoint provides standard layouts that allow you to do this. Earlier chapters discussed layouts in more detail. In this chapter, we are concerned with text layouts.

When you create a new blank slide, you must choose whether to use an existing layout that Microsoft provides or to create your own layout (see Figure 10-10).

1. In Normal view, click the slide immediately preceding the one you want to insert.
2. Click the **Home** tab, and click the **New Slide** down arrow.
3. Look for the placement of text, titles, and content. Examples of text placeholders are shown in Figure 10-10.
4. Click the layout you want.
5. Click within the title or text placeholders to begin entering text.

Insert a New Text Box

Even when you use a predefined layout that Microsoft provides, you will find times when you want to insert a new text box.

1. Display the slide within which you will place the text box.
2. Click the **Insert** tab, and click **Text Box** in the Text group. The pointer first turns into a line pointer.

3. Place the pointer where you want to locate the text box, and drag it into a text-box shape. As you drag, the pointer will morph into a crosshair shape. Don't worry about where the box is located; you can drag it to a precise location later. When you release the pointer, the insertion point within the text box indicates that you can begin to type text.

4. Type the text you want.

5. When you are finished, click outside the text box.

Work with Text Boxes

You work with text and text boxes by typing text into a text box, moving or copying the text box, resizing the text box, positioning the text box, deleting it, rotating it, filling it with color, and more.

ENTER TEXT INTO A TEXT BOX

To enter text into a text box, simply click inside the text box; the insertion point will appear in the text box, indicating that you can now type text. Begin to type.

MOVE A TEXT BOX

To move a text box, you drag the border of the placeholder.

1. Click the text within a text box to display the text box outline.

2. Place the pointer over the border of the text box and between the handles. The pointer will be a four-headed arrow.

3. Drag the text box where you want.

RESIZE A PLACEHOLDER

To resize a placeholder, you drag the sizing handles of the text box.

1. Click the text to display the text box border.

2. Place the pointer on the border over the handles so that it becomes a two-headed arrow.

3. Drag the sizing handle in the direction you want the text box expanded or reduced. As you drag, the pointer will morph into a crosshair.

DELETE A TEXT BOX

To delete a text box:

1. Click the text within the text box to display the border.
2. Click the border of the text box again to select the text box, not the text (the insertion point will disappear and the border will be solid).
3. Press **DELETE**.

COPY A TEXT BOX

To copy a text box with its contents and drag it to another part of the slide:

1. Click the text within the text box.
2. Place the pointer on the border of the text box (not over the handles), where it becomes a four-headed arrow.
3. Drag the text box while pressing **CTRL**.

ROTATE A TEXT BOX

When you first insert a text box (or click it to select it), a rotate handle allows you to rotate the box in a circle.

1. Place the pointer over the rotate handle.
2. Drag it in the direction it is to be rotated.
3. Click outside the text box to "set" the rotation.

POSITION A TEXT BOX PRECISELY

To set the position of a text box precisely on a slide:

1. Click the text box to select it. A Drawing Tools Format tab will appear.
2. Click the **Format** tab, and in the Arrange group, click **Rotate**.
3. On the Rotate menu, click **More Rotation Options**. The Format Shape dialog box with the Size option selected will appear.
4. Click the **Position** option.

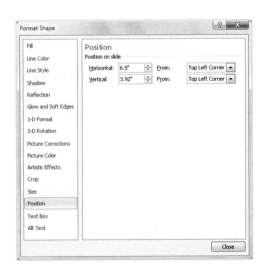

TIP

To rotate a text box or object that doesn't have a rotate handle, select the text box, and click the **Format** tab. Click the **Rotate** down arrow in the Arrange group. As you point at the various options in the context menu, you'll see the effects of the selected object. To see a dialog box so you can enter more precise measurements, click **More Rotation Options**.

5. Click the **Horizontal** or **Vertical** spinner to enter the exact measurements in inches of the text box. Click the drop-down list boxes to select the originating location of the text box between the upper-left corner and center.

6. Click **Close**.

CHANGE THE FILL COLOR IN A TEXT BOX

To change the background color of a text box, you use the Drawing Tools Format Shape dialog box.

1. Right-click the text box, and click **Format Shape** from the context menu. The Format Shape dialog box appears.

2. Click **Fill** and then select the type of fill you want to see. A group of options will appear, depending on your choice.

3. Click the **Preset Colors**, **Color**, or other drop-down list box to select a color. Set other attributes as you wish. Drag the dialog box to one side so that you can see the changes in the text box as you try out different shades or types of fill, as illustrated in Figure 10-11.

4. When finished, click **Close**.

SET PARAGRAPH AND TAB SETTINGS

To change the default paragraph spacing and tab settings, you can use the Paragraph dialog box, as seen in Figure 10-12.

1. Click the paragraph text in a placeholder or text box to be changed. Click the **Home** tab, and click the **Paragraph Dialog Box Launcher** on the lower-right area of the Paragraph group.

–Or–

Right-click the paragraph text in a placeholder or text box to be changed, and click **Paragraph**. The Paragraph dialog box appears.

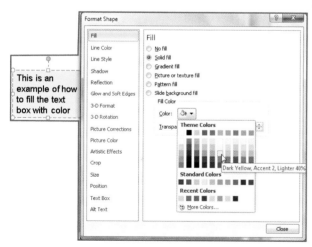

Figure 10-11: You can drag the dialog box (or sometimes the text box) to the side so that you can see the effects of settings as you work with the options.

QUICKSTEPS

SETTING MARGINS, WORD WRAP, AUTOFIT, AND COLUMNS

All of the procedures in this section make use of the Drawing Tools Format Shape dialog box. To display it, right-click the text box and select **Format Shape**. Select **Text Box** from the menu on the left, as shown in Figure 10-13.

SET MARGINS IN A TEXT BOX

To change the margins in a text box, change the Internal Margin setting to **Left**, **Right**, **Top**, or **Bottom**.

DISABLE WORD WRAP FOR TEXT

To disable (or enable) the word-wrap feature for text in a text box, click **Wrap Text In Shape**. A check mark in the check box indicates that word wrap is turned on.

☑ Wrap text in shape

ANCHOR TEXT IN A TEXT BOX

To anchor the text layout within a text box, select the position where the text will start, click the **Vertical Alignment** down arrow, and click the position to which you want the text anchored. Your choices are Top, Middle, Bottom, Top Centered, Middle Centered, and Bottom Centered.

ROTATE TEXT WITHIN A TEXT BOX

To rotate text within a text box, click the **Text Direction** down arrow, and choose an option: Horizontal, Rotate All Text 90°, Rotate All Text 270°, or Stacked.

SET UP COLUMNS WITHIN A TEXT BOX

To set up columns within a text box, click the **Columns** button. The Columns dialog box appears. Click the **Number** spinner and the **Spacing** spinner to set your column attributes, and click **OK**.

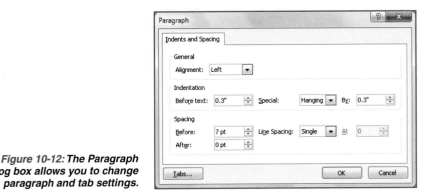

Figure 10-12: *The Paragraph dialog box allows you to change paragraph and tab settings.*

2. Configure the settings as required.

- Set the general positioning by clicking the **Alignment** down arrow, and then click **Left**, **Centered**, **Right**, **Justified**, or **Distributed** (which forces even short lines to be justified to the end of the line), depending on how you want the text aligned.

Figure 10-13: *A text box can have its own margins and alignment. You can set defaults for AutoFit and automatic word-wrap features, and establish columns.*

USING LISTS

Lists are either numbered or bulleted. You can choose the shapes of bullets, change the style of numbering, and use SmartArt for your lists.

CHOOSE BULLET SHAPES

1. Select the text to be bulleted.

2. Right-click the text and point to **Bullets**. The context menu opens.

   –Or–

   On the Home tab, click the **Bullets** down arrow. A context menu will open.

3. Use the options presented, or, to display more options, click **Bullets And Numbering** at the bottom of the menu. The Bullets And Numbering dialog box appears, as shown in Figure 10-14.

4. To select the bullet appearance, click one of the seven options:

   - To change the size, adjust the **Size** spinner to the percentage of text you want the bullet to be.

   - To change the color, click the **Color** down arrow, and click a color.

   - To select or import a picture to use as a bullet shape, click **Picture** and select one of the menu images; or click **Import** to find your own. Then click **OK**.

   - To select a character from a variety of symbol fonts, click **Customize**. Make your selection, and then click **OK**.

5. Click **OK** to close the dialog box.

Continued ...

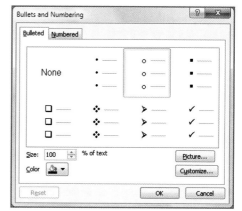

Figure 10-14: **The Bullets And Numbering dialog box offers ways to** *change the appearance, size, and color of bullets or numbers in a list.*

- Set the indentation. Click the **Before Text** spinner to set the spacing before the text begins on a first line; click the **Special** down arrow to allow for hanging indents, an indented first line, or no indents.

- Set the spacing. Click the **Before** spinner to set spacing before the line starts (in points); click the **Line Spacing** down arrow, and click **Single**, **Double**, **1.5**, **Exactly** (where you set the exact spacing in points in the At box), or **Multiple** (where you enter the number of lines to space in the At box).

- Click the **Tabs** button to set tabs precisely in the Tabs dialog box. Click **OK**.

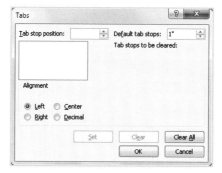

3. Click **OK**.

Use the Font Dialog Box

To set multiple font and character attributes at once or to set the standard for a slide, it is easier to use the Font dialog box than individual buttons. (See the "Changing Font Attributes" QuickFacts earlier in this chapter.)

1. Select the text to be changed.

2. Click the **Home** tab, and click the **Font Dialog Box Launcher** in the lower-right area of the Font group. The Font dialog box will appear, as shown in Figure 10-15.

3. Click the **Latin Text Font** down arrow, and select the type of theme text (Heading or Body) or font name. This establishes what will be changed in the selected text.

4. Choose the options you want, and click **OK**.

CHANGE CAPITALIZATION

To set your capitalization standard or to correct text typed in the wrong case:

1. Select the text on which you want to change the case.

2. Click the **Home** tab, and click the **Change Case** Aa▾ button in the Font group.

3. Select one of the following options:

   • **Sentence case** capitalizes the first word in a sentence.

   • **lowercase** makes all text lowercase.

   • **UPPERCASE** makes all text uppercase.

   • **Capitalize Each Word** capitalizes all words.

   • **tOGGLE cASE** switches between uppercase and lowercase letters, for instance, when you have accidentally typed text in the wrong case.

Align Text

You have several ways to align text: horizontally on a line, vertically on a page, or distributed horizontally or vertically. This section describes how to use these aligning techniques.

ALIGN TEXT ON A LINE

You align text by centering (placing text in the center of the horizontal margins), left-justifying, right-justifying, or justifying it (where the left

USING LISTS *(Continued)*

–Or–

Right-click the list or place on the slide where you want special effects applied, and in the context menu, point to **Convert To SmartArt**. A gallery of styles is displayed.

3. Point to the options to see the effects on the selected list. When you want to try one, click an option, and you will see the SmartArt effect on the slide plus a text box enabling you to enter the text into the list, as displayed in Figure 10-16. Type your text into the text box, and it will appear in the SmartArt object. Drag the shape to resize it.

4. To change shapes, right-click the SmartArt icon, and point to **Change Shape**. A gallery of shapes will be displayed. Click the one you want.

5. When you are finished, click outside the text box.

EDITING WITH THE KEYBOARD

Working with text in PowerPoint is similar to working with text in Microsoft Word. This section presents familiar ways to move the pointer and to select, delete, and insert text.

MOVE THE POINTER WITHIN YOUR TEXT

- To move to the beginning of the line, press **HOME**.

- To move to the end of a line, press **END**.

- To skip to the next word, press **CTRL+RIGHT ARROW**.

- To skip to the previous word, press **CTRL+LEFT ARROW**.

Continued . . .

Figure 10-15: Using the Font dialog box, you can change all occurrences of certain fonts within selected text.

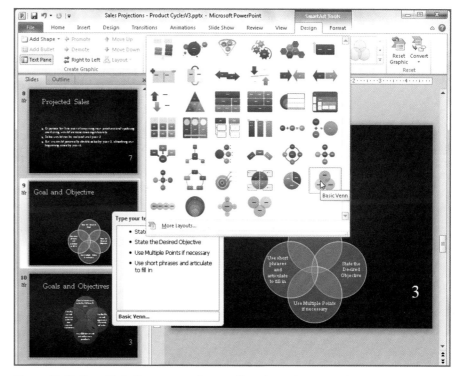

Figure 10-16: SmartArt effects can make your lists dramatic and professional-looking.

EDITING WITH THE KEYBOARD

(Continued)

SELECT TEXT

- To select all text contained within a text box, press **CTRL+A**.
- To select a word, double-click it.
- To select a paragraph, click within the paragraph three times.
- To select all text from where your cursor is to the end of the line, press **SHIFT+END**.
- To select all text from where your cursor is to the beginning of the line, press **SHIFT+HOME**.
- To select multiple lines, press **SHIFT+UP ARROW** or **DOWN ARROW**.
- To select one character at a time, press **SHIFT+LEFT ARROW** or **RIGHT ARROW**.

DELETE TEXT

- To delete the character to the right, press **DELETE**.
- To delete the character to the left, press **BACKSPACE**.
- To delete other text as needed, select text using the keyboard, highlighting it, and press **DELETE**.

INSERT TEXT

To insert one or more characters within a text box, click within the text box, place the pointer where you want to type, and then type.

and right edges are equal). All four options are available on the Home tab Paragraph group.

1. Select the text to be aligned, and click the **Home** tab.
2. From the Paragraph group, choose one of these options:

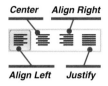

- To center text, click the **Center** button.
- To left-align text, click the **Align Left** button.
- To right-align text, click the **Align Right** button.
- To justify text, click the **Justify** button.

ALIGN TEXT IN A PLACEHOLDER

To align text with the top, middle, or bottom of a text box or placeholder, click the **Align Text** button (Home tab Paragraph group), and click your choices from the menu. Click **More Options** to precisely specify measurements.

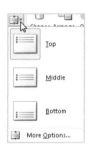

ALIGN TEXT TO THE SLIDE

You can align a placeholder or text box horizontally or vertically on a slide—that is, the spacing on the top and bottom will be equal or the spacing from the left and right edges of the slide will be distributed evenly.

1. Click the placeholder or text box to select it.
2. On the Drawing Tools Format tab, click the **Align** button in the Arrange group. A menu will appear.

NOTE

All the cut-and-paste techniques can also be used to copy information. Just select **Copy** instead of Cut from the context or ribbon menus, or press **CTRL+C**. To copy using the drag-and-drop technique, right-drag the text (drag with the right mouse button depressed), and click **Copy Here**.

QUICKSTEPS

MOVING OR COPYING TEXT

There are at least four ways you can move text. You can use the cut-and-paste technique, use the ribbon, right-click from a context menu, or use the drag-and-drop technique.

CUT AND PASTE TEXT WITH THE KEYBOARD

1. Select the text to be moved, and press **CTRL+X** to cut the text.

2. Click the pointer to place the insertion point, and press **CTRL+V** to paste the text in the new location.

CUT AND PASTE WITH THE RIBBON

1. Select the text to be moved.

2. Click the **Home** tab, and click Cut ✂ in the Clipboard group.

3. Click where you want the text inserted, and click **Paste** 📋 in the Clipboard group.

Continued . . .

3. Click one of these options:
   - Click **Distribute Horizontally** to align the object horizontally to the slide.
   - Click **Distribute Vertically** to align the object vertically on the slide.

Copy Formatting with Format Painter

To copy all formatting attributes from one placeholder to another, you use Format Painter. With it, you can copy fonts, font size and style, line and paragraph spacing, color, alignment, bullet selection, and character effects.

1. Select the text containing the formatting attributes to be copied.

2. On the Home tab, click **Format Painter** 🖌 in the Clipboard group.

3. Find the destination text to contain the copied attributes, and drag the paintbrush pointer over the text to be changed.

If you want to copy more than one text selection, double-click the Format Painter to turn it on. You can copy multiple text selections, one after the other. To turn it off, click Format Painter again or press ESC.

Use AutoCorrect

AutoCorrect is a feature that helps you type information correctly. For example, it corrects simple typing errors and makes certain assumptions about what you want to type. You can turn it off or change its rules.

TURN AUTOCORRECT OPTIONS ON OR OFF

The AutoCorrect feature assumes that you will want certain corrections always to be made while you type. Among these corrections are change two initial capital letters to the first one only, capitalize the first letter of each sentence, capitalize the first letter of table cells and names of days, correct accidental use of the **CAPS LOCK** key, and replace misspelled words with the results it assumes you want. (See "Change AutoCorrect Spelling Corrections" to retain

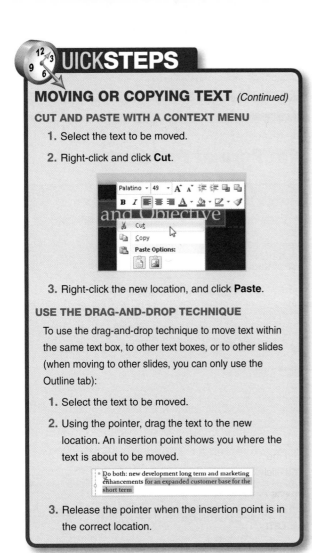

UICKSTEPS

MOVING OR COPYING TEXT *(Continued)*

CUT AND PASTE WITH A CONTEXT MENU

1. Select the text to be moved.

2. Right-click and click **Cut**.

3. Right-click the new location, and click **Paste**.

USE THE DRAG-AND-DROP TECHNIQUE

To use the drag-and-drop technique to move text within the same text box, to other text boxes, or to other slides (when moving to other slides, you can only use the Outline tab):

1. Select the text to be moved.

2. Using the pointer, drag the text to the new location. An insertion point shows you where the text is about to be moved.

3. Release the pointer when the insertion point is in the correct location.

the correction of misspelled words but to change the correction made.) To turn off the automatic spelling corrections that PowerPoint makes:

1. Click the **File** tab, and click **Options**.

2. Click **Proofing**, and the dialog box shown in Figure 10-17 will appear.

3. Find the option you want to turn off or on, and click the relevant check box. If a check mark is in the box, the option is enabled. If it is not, the option is turned off.

USE AUTOFIT

AutoFit is used to make text fit within a text box or AutoShape. It often resizes text to make it fit. You can turn it on or off.

1. Click the **File** tab, click **Options**, and then click **Proofing**.

2. Under AutoCorrect Options, click **AutoCorrect Options**. The AutoCorrect dialog box appears.

3. Click the **AutoFormat As You Type** tab.

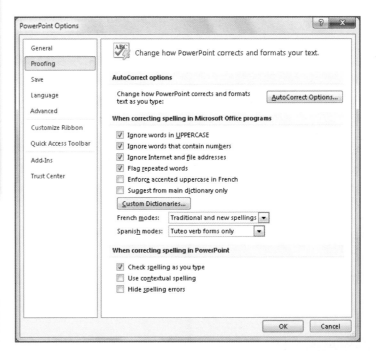

Figure 10-17: The AutoCorrect dialog box is where you change the automatic corrections made to text and spelling.

![QUICKSTEPS](clock icon with 12 9 6 3)

USING THE OFFICE CLIPBOARD

The Office Clipboard is shared by all Microsoft Office products. You can copy objects and text from any Office application and paste them into another. The Clipboard contains up to 24 items. The 25th item will overwrite the first one.

OPEN THE CLIPBOARD

To display the Office Clipboard, click the **Home** tab, and then click the **Clipboard Dialog Box Launcher** in the Clipboard group. The Clipboard task pane will open. Clipboard 🔲

ADD TO THE CLIPBOARD

When you cut or copy text, it is automatically added to the Office Clipboard.

COPY CLIPBOARD ITEMS TO A PLACEHOLDER

To paste one item:

1. Click to place the insertion point in the text box or placeholder where you want the item on the Office Clipboard inserted.

2. Click the item on the Clipboard to be inserted.

   –Or–

   With the Clipboard item selected but no insertion point placed, right-click where you want the item.

3. Select **Paste** from the context menu.

To paste all items:

1. Click to place the insertion point in the text box or placeholder where you want the items on the Office Clipboard inserted.

2. Click **Paste All** on the Clipboard. 🔲 Paste All

Continued . . .

---

4 of 24 - Clipboard ▼ ✕

🔲 Paste All   🗶 Clear All

Click an item to paste:

🔲

🔲 Expanding Our Market

🔲 years before it was a demographic statistic Since they have left the...

🔲 Graphic Display

Options ▼

---

4. Under the Apply As You Type section, choose these options:

   ● To remove the AutoFit feature for titles, clear the **AutoFit Title Text To Placeholder** check box.

   ● To remove the AutoFit feature for body text, clear the **AutoFit Body Text To Placeholder** check box.

5. Click **OK** twice.

Apply as you type
☑ Automatic bulleted and numbered lists
☑ AutoFit title text to placeholder
☑ AutoFit body text to placeholder

CHANGE AUTOCORRECT SPELLING CORRECTIONS

PowerPoint may automatically correct spellings that are not really incorrect. You can add a new spelling correction, replace a current spelling correction with a new one, or replace the result that is now used. You do this by replacing one word with another in the AutoCorrect dialog box. When you first open the dialog box, both the Replace and With boxes are blank. In this case, you simply add what you want. To replace an entry, you first delete an entry—one that is not a mistake you typically make—and then you replace it with a typing error you commonly make. To replace a current spelling result, you type over the current result with the correction you want.

1. Click the **File** tab, and click the **Options** button. Then click **Proofing**.

2. Click the **AutoCorrect Options** button, and the AutoCorrect dialog box appears. If it is not already selected, click the **AutoCorrect** tab. Figure 10-18 shows this dialog box.

   ● To add new entries when both the Replace and With boxes are blank, fill in the **Replace** and **With** boxes, and click **Add**.

   ● To replace entries in the Replace and With boxes, click the text in either box, and replace it with your new entries. Click **Add**. The "old" text will not be deleted; it is still in the list. You must use the **DELETE** button to actually get rid of an entry in the list.

   ● To delete and replace an entry, click the entry to be replaced, and press **DELETE**. Then type the new spelling option. Click **Add**.

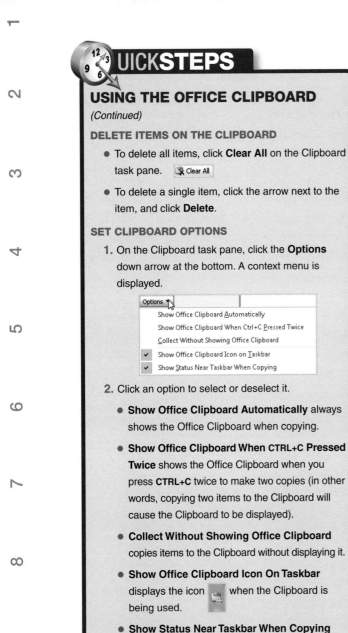

USING THE OFFICE CLIPBOARD

(Continued)

DELETE ITEMS ON THE CLIPBOARD

- To delete all items, click **Clear All** on the Clipboard task pane. [🗙 Clear All]

- To delete a single item, click the arrow next to the item, and click **Delete**.

SET CLIPBOARD OPTIONS

1. On the Clipboard task pane, click the **Options** down arrow at the bottom. A context menu is displayed.

Options ▼	
Show Office Clipboard <u>A</u>utomatically	
Show Office Clipboard When Ctrl+C <u>P</u>ressed Twice	
<u>C</u>ollect Without Showing Office Clipboard	
✓ Show Office Clipboard Icon on <u>T</u>askbar	
✓ Show <u>S</u>tatus Near Taskbar When Copying	

2. Click an option to select or deselect it.

- **Show Office Clipboard Automatically** always shows the Office Clipboard when copying.

- **Show Office Clipboard When CTRL+C Pressed Twice** shows the Office Clipboard when you press **CTRL+C** twice to make two copies (in other words, copying two items to the Clipboard will cause the Clipboard to be displayed).

- **Collect Without Showing Office Clipboard** copies items to the Clipboard without displaying it.

- **Show Office Clipboard Icon On Taskbar** displays the icon when the Clipboard is being used.

- **Show Status Near Taskbar When Copying** displays a message about the items being added to the Clipboard as copies are made.

Use the Spelling Checker

One form of the spelling checker automatically flags words that it cannot find in the dictionary as potential misspellings. It identifies these words with a red underline. However, even when the automatic function is turned off, you can still use the spelling checker by manually opening it.

CHECK THE SPELLING IN A PRESENTATION

The spelling checker goes through all text in all placeholders on a slide, looking for words that are not in the spelling dictionary. When it finds one, it displays the Spelling dialog box, seen in Figure 10-19.

1. Click in the presentation where the spelling checker should begin.

2. To display the spelling checker, click **Spelling** in the Review tab Proofing group. The Spelling dialog box will appear when the spelling checker finds a word that is not in the dictionary.

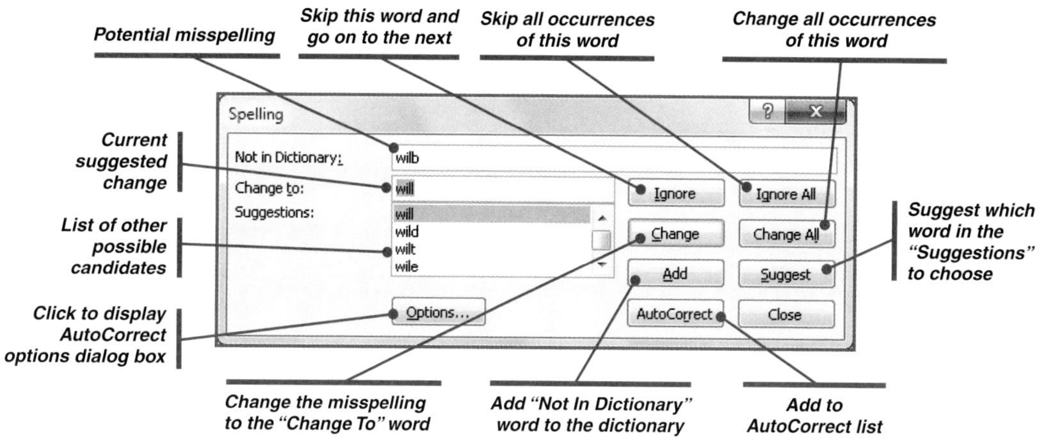

Potential misspelling   Skip this word and   Skip all occurrences   Change all occurrences
                         go on to the next   of this word   of this word

Current
suggested
change

List of other
possible
candidates

Click to display
AutoCorrect
options dialog box

Suggest which
word in the
"Suggestions"
to choose

Change the misspelling   Add "Not In Dictionary"   Add to
to the "Change To" word   word to the dictionary   AutoCorrect list

Figure 10-19: Use the Spelling dialog box to look for misspellings, correct them with suggested words or your own, and add words to the dictionary.

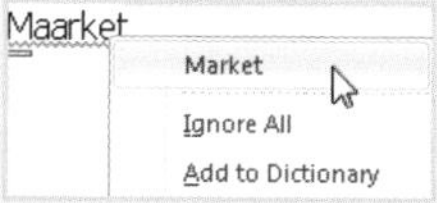

3. Choose any of these options to use the spelling checker:

- If the word is incorrect, look at the Suggestions list, and click the one you want to use. It will appear in the Change To box. Click **Change** to change the one occurrence of the word, or click **Change All** to change all occurrences of that same word.

- If the identified word is correct but not in the dictionary, you can add the word to a custom dictionary by clicking **Add**, or you can skip the word by clicking **Ignore** or **Ignore All** (to skip all occurrences of the same word). The spelling checker will continue to the next misspelled word.

- Click **AutoCorrect** to add the word to the AutoCorrect list of automatic spelling changes that will be made as you type. Immediately the word will be placed in the AutoCorrect list.

- Click **Suggest** if you are unsure of the correct spelling and want PowerPoint to suggest the most likely spelling.

- Click **Options** to open the AutoCorrect Options dialog box.

4. Click **Close** to end the search for spelling errors. When the spelling checker is finished, a message will be displayed to that effect. Click **OK**.

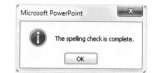

How to...

Chapter 11
Using Outlook and Receiving E-mail

When someone mentions Outlook, the first thought is generally the sending and receiving of e-mail. Outlook does handle e-mail quite competently, but it also does a lot more, including managing contacts, scheduling activities, tracking tasks, keeping a journal, and using notes. This chapter covers how to work with the Outlook windows, create e-mail accounts, receive e-mail, and deal with the messages that come in. You'll also learn how to manage the Calendar.

Explore Outlook

The Outlook 2010 window, in keeping with the upgrades to Office 2010, uses a wide assortment of windows, toolbars, menus, the ribbon, and special features to accomplish its functions. Much of this chapter and the next couple of chapters explore how to find and use the most common of these items. In this section you'll explore the primary Outlook window, including the parts of the window, the ribbon, buttons on the principal toolbars, and the major menus. Also, you'll see how to use the navigation pane and Outlook Today.

Explore the Outlook Window

The initial view when you first start Outlook is for handling mail, as shown in Figure 11-1. It contains the primary tools for navigating and performing tasks within Outlook.

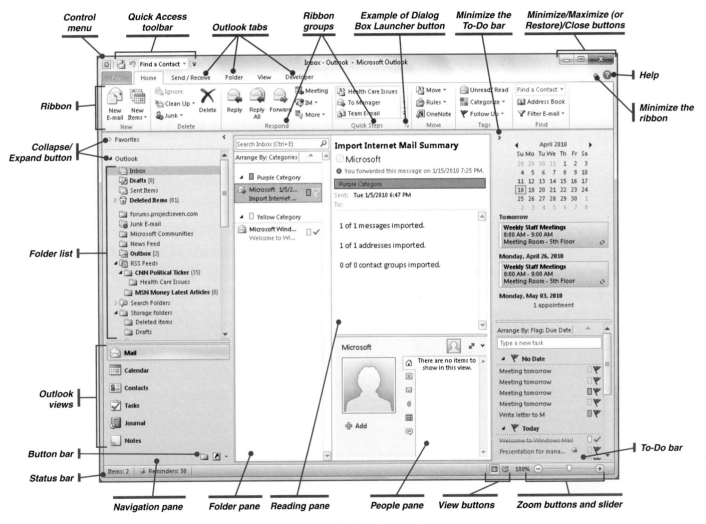

Figure 11-1: The default Outlook window is used for handling mail.

Here is a quick overview of how you use these features—most will be more fully explained in this chapter and the next two chapters:

- **Control menu**   Contains controls for the window itself
- **Quick Access toolbar**   Contains the most common commands you use. You can customize this toolbar so that it contains exactly the tools and commands you need all the time.
- **Outlook tabs**   Contain commands organized for a specific function. For example, the Send/Receive folder contains the commands you need to send and receive e-mail.
- **Ribbon groups**   Contain groups of commands needed for a specific task. For example, in the Send/Receive tab, you have a group of commands for Send & Receive tasks, and a Download group of commands for dealing with downloaded information.
- **Dialog Box Launcher button**   Opens a dialog box containing additional options for the group of commands. Not all groups have Dialog Box Launcher buttons.
- **Minimize/Maximize (or Restore)/Close buttons**   Allow you to maximize, minimize, or close the Outlook window. You can place an icon on the taskbar by minimizing it, vary the size of the window with the Maximize/Restore button, or exit Outlook altogether.
- **Help**   Opens the Help system for Outlook.
- **Minimize the ribbon**   Allows you to remove the ribbon from the window except for the tabs. You restore the ribbon by clicking the Minimize button again or clicking a tab.
- **Minimize the To-Do bar**   Hides the To-Do bar and then redisplays it as you wish.
- **To-Do bar**   Contains today's appointments plus a calendar with upcoming appointments and a list of meaningful dates. You can click a date on the calendar to see what is up for another day, or double-click an appointment to view it or to change it.
- **Zoom buttons and slider**   Contain tools for controlling the magnification of the window. You can either click the buttons on either end of the slider to vary the view by increments, or you can drag the slider to vary the size. You can also type the percentage you want instead.
- **View buttons**   Contain a quick way to vary your views of the window. The Normal view contains the various panes as displayed in Figure 11-1. The Reading pane replaces the Folder pane and the To-Do bar with an enlarged Reading pane.
- **People pane**   Contains information about the person sending you the currently selected message.

- **Reading pane**   Contains the content for the selected message.
- **Folder pane**   Contains a list of the messages that are in the currently selected folder in the Folder List on the navigation pane.
- **Navigation pane**   Contains the Folder List, with all the folders that you have within Outlook and, it displays the Outlook views, such as Mail or Calendar.
- **Status bar**   Contains information about the items being viewed, such as how many items are in the selected folder. The information displayed will vary, depending on the Outlook view. For example, the Mail view displays different information than the Contacts view.
- **Button bar**   Contains a Folder List button to display folders, a Shortcut button to display an alternative selection to the folders, and a Configuration button that allows you to customize the Outlook view and navigation pane elements.
- **Outlook views**   Lists the Outlook views available with a simple click. This list can be tailored to display the views you are working with. By default, it does not list Tasks, Journal, and Notes, but you can add them, as was done in Figure 11-1.
- **Folder list**   Displays the list of folders available to you in Outlook. Outlook contains standard folders, such as Inbox and Sent Items, as well as custom folders you may wish to insert to organize your e-mail in the way that suits you.
- **Collapse/Expand** button—Displays or hides the information within a particular folder.

Change Views

The view you will have on the main Outlook window can be changed, depending on what you want to see. Typically, as shown earlier in Figure 11-1, you will see the navigation pane, Folder pane, Reading pane, and To-Do bar, with the middle two related to the mail component. You may change these by clicking another Outlook view. For example, clicking Calendar view in the lower part of the navigation pane will replace the Folder pane, Reading pane, and To-Do bar with the current day's calendar. Alternatively, in Mail view, clicking the Reading view button on the right of the status bar closes the navigation pane and the To-Do bar to provide a lot more room to read an e-mail message.

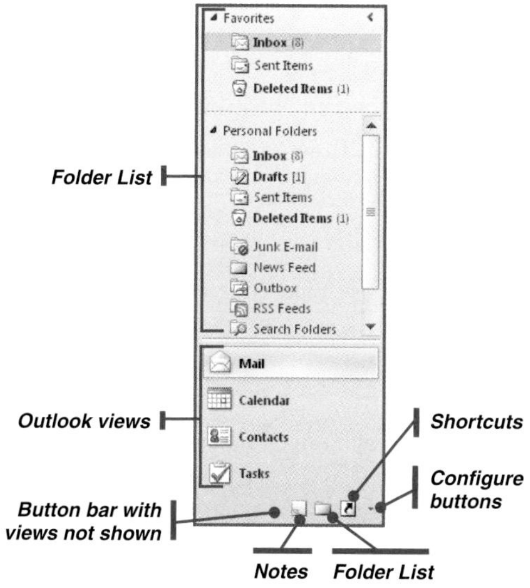

Folder List

Outlook views

Button bar with
views not shown

Shortcuts

Configure
buttons

Notes   Folder List

*Figure 11-2: **The navigation pane provides the primary control over which area and which folder you are working with.***

Use the Navigation Pane

There are three main areas of the navigation pane, as shown in Figure 11-2.

- **Folder List**, at the top, is where you can select the folder you want to open.
- **Outlook views**, in the middle, are where you can select the view in which to work.
- **Button bar**, at the bottom, lets you access views not available in the Outlook views.

SELECT A VIEW

The Outlook view determines which area of Outlook you will work in—for example, Mail, Calendar, or Contacts. To select a view:

- Click the appropriate Outlook view.

  –Or–

- Click the appropriate button in the button bar (see Figure 11-2).

OPEN A FOLDER

The folder that is open determines which specific documents you will work on, for example, incoming messages in the Inbox folder or notes in the Notes folder. To open a folder:

- Click the appropriate folder in the Folder List.

  –Or–

- Click the related Outlook view or button in the button bar.

DISPLAY OUTLOOK VIEWS

The number of Outlook views displayed depends on the size of the Outlook window and the size of the pane dedicated to these views. To change the number of views displayed:

- Drag the bottom window border up or down.

  –Or–

- Drag the handle between the top view and the bottom of the Folder List.

DISPLAY BUTTONS

The buttons in the button bar are just an extension of Outlook views. When you reduce the number of view bars, the options become buttons on the button bar. To change the buttons on the button bar, in addition to changing the number of Outlook views that are displayed:

1. Click the **Configure** button on the right of the button bar.

2. Click **Add Or Remove Buttons**, and then click the button you want to add or remove.

REORDER NAVIGATION PANE BUTTONS

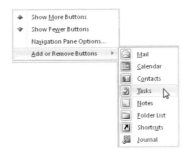

To change the buttons or the order of the buttons in the navigation pane:

1. From the View tab Layout group, click **Navigation Pane**, and click **Options**. The Navigation Pane Options dialog box will appear.

2. Check the buttons you want on the navigation pane.

3. Highlight a button, and click **Move Up** or **Move Down** to reorder the list. Click **OK** twice.

MINIMIZE THE NAVIGATION PANE

If you need more room to display a folder and its contents, you can close the navigation pane.

- Click the **Minimize** button at the top of the navigation pane to reduce its size. Click it again (now the Expand button) to restore the navigation pane to its regular size.

  –Or–

- Click the **View** tab, click **Navigation Pane**, and click **Minimized**. To restore the navigation pane, repeat the process, clicking **Normal** so that a check mark is in the check box.

Use Outlook Today

Outlook Today gives you a summary of the information in Outlook for the current day. You can see a summary of your messages, your appointments and meetings, and the tasks you are slated to do, as shown in Figure 11-3.

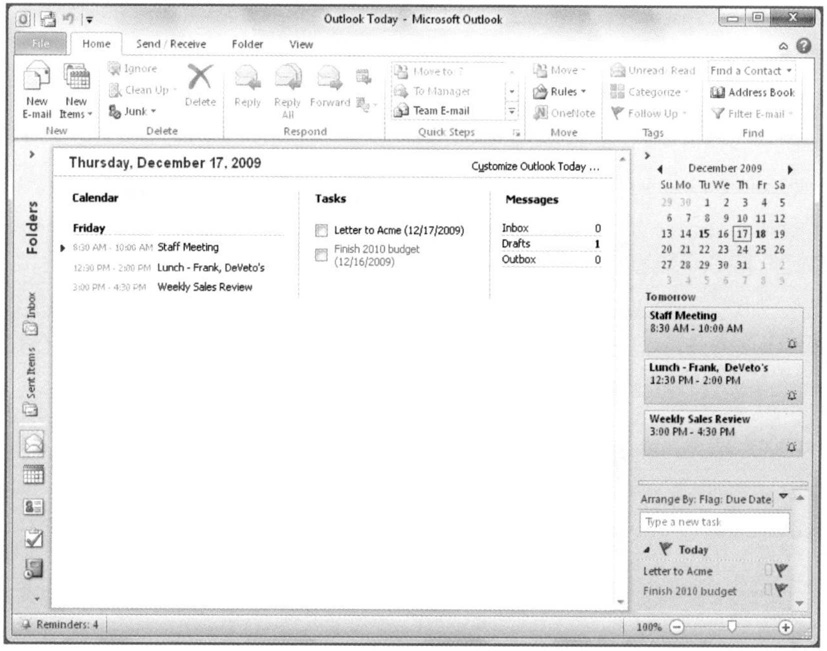

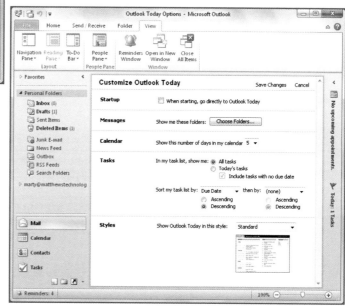

Figure 11-3: *Outlook Today provides a summary of information for the current day, such as appointments and tasks.*

OPEN OUTLOOK TODAY

If the navigation pane is open, click **Personal Folders** at the top of the Folder List ("Personal Folders" is called "Outlook Data File" by default). (If the navigation pane is not open, click the **View** tab, click **Navigation Pane**, and click **Normal**.)

CHANGE OUTLOOK TODAY

Click **Customize Outlook Today** in the upper-right corner of the Outlook Today folder. Customize Outlook Today will open, as shown in Figure 11-4. Customize Outlook Today ...

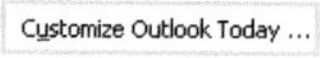

Figure 11-4: *You can tailor Outlook Today to contain only the information you want.*

MAKE OUTLOOK TODAY YOUR DEFAULT PAGE

To display Outlook Today by default when you open Outlook:

1. In the Customize Outlook Today pane, opposite Startup, click **When Starting, Go Directly To Outlook Today**.

2. Click **Save Changes**.

Customize the To-Do Bar

You can only access the To-Do Bar options if the To-Do bar is visible in either a Normal or Minimized state. It's off by default. You turn it on by clicking **To-Do Bar** in the View tab Layout group and selecting **Normal** or **Minimized**.

To customize the To-Do bar and determine what is displayed in it:

1. Click the **View** tab, click **To-Do Bar**, and click **Options**.

   –Or–

   Right-click the To-Do bar, and click **Options** in the context menu.

2. Click the check boxes next to the options you want, and click **OK**.

MINIMIZE THE TO-DO BAR

If you need additional room for the Reading pane, you can minimize the To-Do bar.

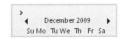

● Click the **Minimize** button at the top-left corner of the To-Do bar. Click it again (now the Expand button) to restore the To-Do bar to its regular size.

   –Or–

● Click the **View** tab, click **To-Do Bar**, and click **Minimized**. To restore the navigation pane, repeat the process, clicking **Normal** so that a check mark is in the check box.

Find a Message

No matter how many messages your e-mail folders contain, Outlook can help you find a specific one. You can perform instant searches for large files, related messages, or messages from a particular sender. You can further qualify the search by having Outlook search only certain folders, or by specifying content for which you're searching. (See "Set Up E-mail" if your account is not yet established.)

Search text

Arrange by

Search results

Clear search

Toggle oldest/ newest on top

Search all Outlook folders

*Figure 11-5: **An instant search is immediate and highly versatile for finding specific e-mail.***

PERFORM INSTANT SEARCHES

Click in the search text box in the Inbox Folder pane (or whichever folder you want to search in), and type the text for which you want to search. The search will immediately display the found messages beneath the search text box (see Figure 11-5).

You have these options:

- Click **Clear Search** to clear the text box and restore the previous contents. You can enter a new search.
- Click **Arrange By** to change the order for search results from the context menu.
- Click **Oldest/Newest On Top** to toggle the date ascending/descending sequence.
- Click **Try Searching Again In All Mail Items** to expand the search to additional folders.

REFINE SEARCHES

In addition to the instant search found on the Folder pane, you can use the Search Tools Search contextual tab to refine your searches.

1. Perform an instant search as described previously. When you complete the search, the Search Tools Search contextual tab will open with the following tab groups that can be used to refine a search:

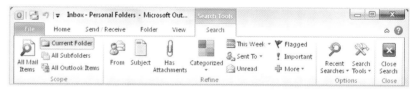

- **Scope** lets you choose the folders you want to include in the search.
- **Refine** lets you choose the elements you want to search on. The More drop-down list provides many more elements you can search on.
- **Options** lets you repeat previous searches and open one of the following dialog boxes for more sophisticated searching:

  - **Indexing Status** displays a message box telling you the extent to which Outlook messages have been indexed.

  - **Locations To Search** lets you choose which of your accounts you want to search.

11

12

13

14

- **Advanced Find** displays the Advanced Find dialog box, where you define a search on multiple criteria with considerable detail.

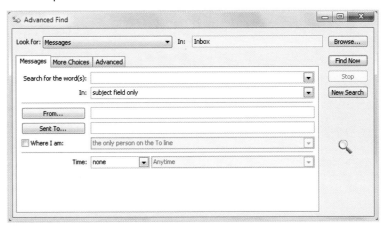

- **Search Options** opens Outlook Options with the Search option selected. See the following section.

2. Click your choice and type the information needed. Click **OK** if needed. (If your choice of option does not require a dialog box, you will not need to click OK.)

CHANGE SEARCH OPTIONS

You can change some of the search defaults used with instant search in the Outlook Options Search options shown in Figure 11-6.

1. Display the Search options, either as described in the previous section or by clicking the **File** tab, clicking **Options**, and clicking **Search**.

2. Click **Indexing Options** and then click **Modify** to select the drives and folders to be indexed so that searches can be faster. Click **OK** and then click **Close** to close both Indexing dialog boxes.

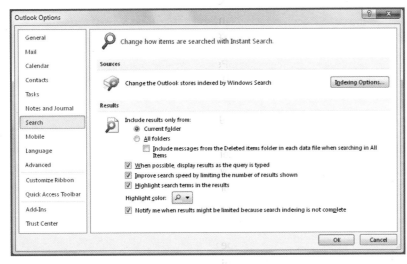

Figure 11-6: In Search options, you can change the search defaults that are used in an instant search.

3. Choose, as a default, whether to search just the currently selected folder or all folders.

4. Determine whether you want to change the defaults to display results as you type the search text, to limit the number of results so that the searches are faster, or to highlight the search text in results and change the highlight color.

5. If you choose, deselect the default to display a message if the indexing is incomplete for a selected file. If this message is displayed, it tells you that the indexing is still in process and that results will be incomplete.

6. Click **OK**.

Set Up E-mail

The Internet provides a global pipeline through which e-mail flows; therefore, you need a connection that lets you tap into that pipeline. Both local and national Internet service providers (ISPs) offer e-mail with their Internet connections. At your work or business, you may have an e-mail account over a local area network (LAN) that also connects to the Internet. You can also obtain e-mail accounts on the Internet that are independent of the connection. You can access these Internet accounts (Gmail by Google, for example) from anywhere in the world. These three ways of accessing Internet e-mail—ISPs, corporate connections, and Internet e-mail—use different types of e-mail systems.

- **POP3** (Post Office Protocol 3), used by ISPs, retrieves e-mail from a dedicated mail server, and is usually combined with SMTP (Simple Mail Transfer Protocol) to send e-mail from a separate server.

- **MAPI** (Messaging Application Programming Interface) lets businesses handle e-mail on Microsoft Exchange Servers and LANs.

- **HTTP** (HyperText Transfer Protocol) transfers information from servers on the World Wide Web to browsers (that's why your browser's address line starts with "http://") and is used with Hotmail and other Internet mail accounts.

Get Online

Whether you choose dial-up or a high-speed service like DSL (digital subscriber line) or cable Internet, getting online requires hardware, software, and some system configuration. It's possible that everything you need is already installed or that your computer came with extra disks for getting online. First, find an ISP.

- **Get a recommendation** from satisfied friends.

- **Look in the yellow pages** under "Internet Service Providers" or "Internet Access Providers."

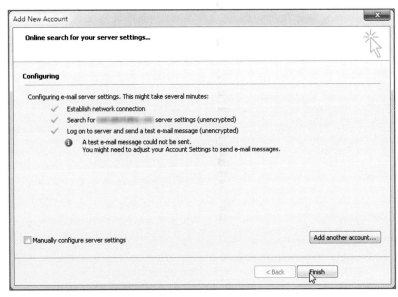

NOTE

If you have been running another e-mail program, such as Outlook Express, Windows Mail, or Windows Live Mail, and then install Outlook, you may see a message when you run the Outlook 2010 Startup Wizard asking if you want to upgrade from your other e-mail program and if you want to import your messages and addresses. See "Upgrade to Outlook."

- **Look on your computer.** Many computer manufacturers include software from nationwide Internet providers, such as AOL, EarthLink, and others.

If you find what you want in an Internet provider already on your computer, double-click the provider's icon, or click the link and follow the instructions. If you have a disk that came with your computer or from an ISP, pop it in and follow the instructions. If you use a local provider, their tech support people will usually walk you through the entire setup process on the phone.

Use the Startup Wizard

The first time you start Outlook on either a new computer with Office 2010 or a new installation of Office 2010, the Outlook 2010 Startup Wizard will open with the Outlook 2010 Startup screen.

1. Click **Next**. Accept the default response of Yes to configure an e-mail account, and click **Next**.

2. Type your name, e-mail address, and password. Then retype the password. Click **Next**.

3. E-mail configuring will take several minutes. Click **Next** for both an encrypted account and one that is unencrypted. If necessary, click **Manually Configure Server Settings**, click **Next**, click **Internet E-mail**, click **Next**, enter the information provided by your Internet mail provider, and click **Next**.

4. When the configuration has finished, you will see a dialog box showing the steps that were taken and the results, as shown in Figure 11-7. Click **Finish**. The wizard will close and Outlook will open. See "Explore Outlook" earlier in this chapter.

5. If you have been using another e-mail program, you'll be asked if you want to make Outlook 2010 your default e-mail program. If you do (this is recommended), click **Yes**.

6. If you are asked if you want to add an Outlook Connector account and you have a Web-based e-mail account on Google mail, Hotmail, or Yahoo!, click **Next**; enter your e-mail address, password, and name you want to use; and click **OK**.

Figure 11-7: You will see this message when your e-mail setup has successfully completed.

TIP

You can save the Import Summary report by clicking **Save In Inbox**.

NOTE

If you want to import Outlook Express, Windows Mail, or Windows Live Mail files from another computer, locate the files by starting the program on the other computer, click the **Tools** menu (if you don't see the Tools menu, press **ALT**), choose **Options**, click the **Advanced** tab (the Maintenance tab in Outlook Express), click the **Maintenance** button (skip this in Outlook Express), and click **Store Folder**. Drag across the entire address line, press **CTRL+C**, and click **OK** to close the Store Location dialog box. Then click **Start**, click **Computer**, click the computer icon at the left end of the address bar, press **CTRL+V** to copy the contents into the address bar, and click the **Go To** button or press **ENTER**. This will show you the e-mail files. Copy these e-mail files to the new computer, import them into your previous e-mail program on that computer, and then use the instructions under "Upgrade to Outlook" to import the files into Outlook.

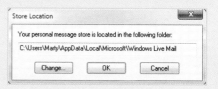

Upgrade to Outlook

If you have been using Outlook 2003 or 2007, Outlook 2010 should automatically locate your previous message and contact files and move them over to it. You cannot have two versions of Outlook on your computer, so Outlook 2010 will uninstall your previous version and pick up your old files.

If you have been using Outlook Express, Windows Mail, or Windows Live Mail and you install Office 2010, you may be asked if you want to upgrade from your previous program. If you choose to upgrade, you will be asked if you want to import your e-mail messages and addresses. Click **Yes**, and you will see the progress as the files are being imported and will see a summary upon completion.

If you have been using one of these programs and were not asked by the Outlook 2010 Startup Wizard if you want to upgrade, you can still import your e-mail files into Outlook.

1. Start Outlook in one of the ways described earlier in this chapter.

2. Click the **File** tab, click **Open**, and click **Import**. The Import And Export Wizard will open.

3. Click **Import Internet Mail And Addresses**, and click **Next**.

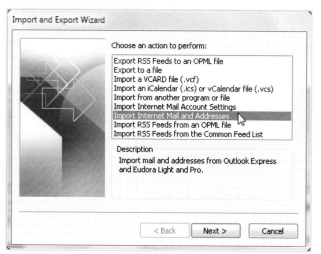

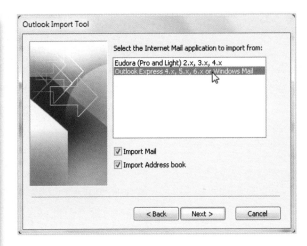

UICKSTEPS

GETTING A GMAIL ACCOUNT

Gmail by Google, one of many Internet-based HTTP services, is free, and you can access it from any Internet connection in the world, so you don't even need to own a computer. You can see the Gmail opening window in Figure 11-8. To set up a Gmail account:

1. In Windows XP and Vista, click **Start** and click **Internet**. In Windows 7, click the **Internet Explorer** icon on the taskbar.

2. In your browser's address bar, type www.gmail.com, and press **ENTER**.

3. Click C**reate An Account**.

4. Fill in all the applicable fields on the registration form. Enter the login name you want for the account, leaving out the "@gmail.com" part, and then click **Check Availability** to check whether the login name you want is available. Read the Google Terms of Service agreement, and click **I Accept**.

5. Read the introductory information, and click **Show Me My Account** to look at your Gmail account on a browser, as shown in Figure 11-9.

6. When you are ready, reopen Outlook, click the **File** tab, and in Info view, click **Add Account**. Enter your name, your new Gmail e-mail address (someone@gmail.com), and your Gmail password (twice); and click **Next**.

7. When you are told that your new account has been found and set up, click **Finish**. Back in Outlook, your Gmail messages will appear, as shown in Figure 11-10.

Figure 11-8: A Google Gmail account gives you a large amount of free storage and allows the sending and receiving of large files.

4. Click **Outlook Express** (which includes Windows Mail), and make sure that the **Import Mail** and **Import Address Book** check boxes are selected.

5. Click **Next**, choose how you want to handle duplicates, and then click **Finish**.

You will be told the progress as the files are being imported and will see a summary upon completion.

Figure 11-9: *Gmail's browser mail application allows you to send and receive mail from any location with a computer.*

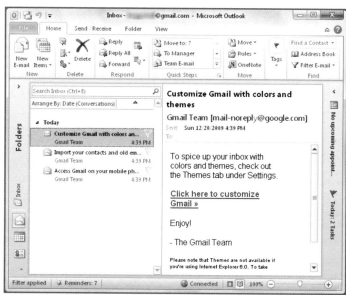

Figure 11-10: *In addition to seeing your Gmail in a browser window, you can see it in Outlook.*

NOTE

To get a Gmail account, you must already have an Internet browser and a connection to the Internet. The instructions here assume you do.

TIP

To remove an e-mail account, click the **File** tab, in Info view click the **Account Settings** down arrow, and then click **Account Settings** again to open the Account Settings dialog box. Click the account to select it, and then click **Remove**. Click **Yes** to confirm the removal of the account, and click **Close**.

Receive E-mail

With at least one e-mail account installed in Outlook, you're ready to receive mail. Everything is done in Outlook's Mail view, shown in Figure 11-11, which is opened by clicking **Mail** in Outlook views in the lower-left area of the Outlook window.

Check for E-mail

Once you are set up, it's easy to download mail.

1. Make sure you're connected to the Internet or can be automatically connected and that **Mail** is selected in the Outlook views of the navigation pane.

2. Click **Send/Receive** 🖃 on the Quick Access toolbar.

   –Or–

   Press **F9**.

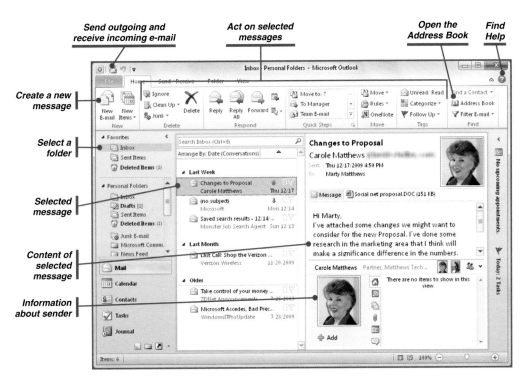

Send outgoing and receive incoming e-mail

Act on selected messages

Open the Address Book

Find Help

Create a new message

Select a folder

Selected message

Content of selected message

Information about sender

Figure 11-11: *The Mail view provides one-click access to the most common operations.*

3. If it is not already open, click the **Inbox** icon in the navigation pane, and watch the mail come in. If you have several e-mail accounts, you can select the Inbox icon from among the several that you have. You may need to scroll through the Folder List and first click the account to see the Inbox.

RECEIVE E-MAIL AUTOMATICALLY

Not only can Outlook periodically check your e-mail provider for you, but it can also do it automatically. Desktop alerts are subtle, given the way they quietly fade in and out.

1. Click the **File** tab, click **Options**, and click **Advanced**.

2. Under Send And Receive, click **Send/ Receive**. The Send/Receive Groups dialog box appears, as you can see in Figure 11-12.

3. Under the Setting For Group "All Accounts" section, click **Schedule An Automatic Send/Receive Every**, type or click the spinner to enter the number of minutes to elapse between checking, and click **Close**.

Read E-mail

Besides being easy to obtain, e-mail messages are effortless to open and read. There are two ways to view the body of the message:

● Double-click the message and read it in the window that opens, as shown in Figure 11-13.

–Or–

● Click the message and read it in the Reading pane, scrolling as needed.

TIP

Be sure to share your e-mail address with the friends you'd like to hear from.

TIP

If you like where the old Preview pane was located in earlier versions of Outlook, you can place the Reading pane beneath the Folder pane: Click the **View** tab, click **Reading Pane**, and click **Bottom**. (You can also turn it off and open its Options dialog box.)

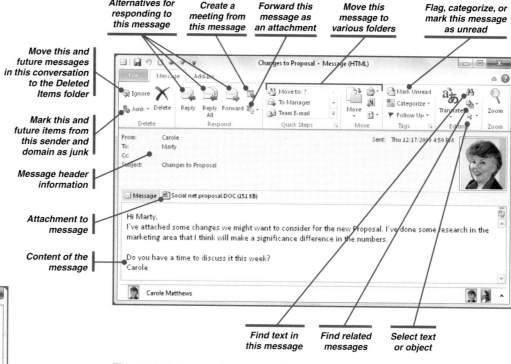

Alternatives for responding to this message

Create a meeting from this message

Forward this message as an attachment

Move this message to various folders

Flag, categorize, or mark this message as unread

Move this and future messages in this conversation to the Deleted Items folder

Mark this and future items from this sender and domain as junk

Message header information

Attachment to message

Content of the message

Find text in this message

Find related messages

Select text or object

Figure 11-13: *An e-mail message window contains all the information and tools you need to respond to the message.*

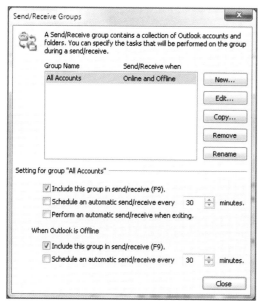

Figure 11-12: *The Options dialog box is where you can customize many Outlook processes.*

Of course, you can also control which accounts you check, what kinds of e-mail you let in, and how it is presented to you.

Download Sender and Subject Information Only

If you are inundated with e-mail, or if messages contain really large files (like lots of photos), you might want to choose among your messages for specific ones to download to Outlook. You can save time downloading e-mail, especially with large files—which you may want to download at a later time. This only works on your POP server e-mail, not on HTTP server e-mail, such as Gmail. First, you instruct Outlook to download only the headers, and then you mark the headers for which you want to download the messages.

RECEIVE HEADERS MANUALLY

1. Click **Inbox** (or whatever folder you want to download).

2. Click the **Send/Receive** tab, and click **Download Headers** in the Server group.

   The headers, assuming you have e-mail waiting to be downloaded, will be downloaded to your selected folder. There will be an identifying icon like this:

MARK HEADERS TO DOWNLOAD, COPY, OR DELETE

1. Double-click a header-only message in the Inbox folder to open the Remote Item Header dialog box, which allows you to unmark the header or mark its message to be downloaded, copied on the server, or deleted.

   –Or–

   Right-click a header-only message in the folder to open the context menu, which also allows you to mark the header message to be downloaded or deleted, as well as many of the moving and categorizing actions on a message's Home tab.

2. Repeat the process for all headers, and then click **Send/Receive** to perform the actions selected.

RECEIVE HEADERS AUTOMATICALLY

If you want to download only headers from your POP server accounts every time, you can set up Outlook to do so.

1. Click the **File** tab, click **Options**, and click **Advanced**.

2. Under Send And Receive, click **Send/Receive**. The Send/Receive Groups dialog box will appear.

3. Make sure **All Accounts** is selected, and click **Edit**. All your e-mail accounts are listed on the left.

4. Click the desired POP account.

5. Under Folder Options, click **Download Headers Only**, as shown in Figure 11-14, click **OK**, click **Close**, and click **OK** once more to return to Outlook.

PROCESS HEADERS

When your headers have been marked, you can download them.

1. Click the **Send/Receive** tab.

2. Click **Process Marked Headers** in the Server group.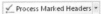

NOTE

The *domain* in a person's e-mail address is the part of the address after "@." In an Internet address (URL, or uniform resource locator), the domain is the part after the "http://www"—for example, "whidbey.net" (a local ISP) or "loc.gov" (the Library of Congress website).

NOTE

One easy way to reduce the junk e-mail you get is to *avoid* replying to any suspicious message. If you reply and tell them to go away, they learn that they reached a valid address, which they will hit again and again.

11   12   13   14

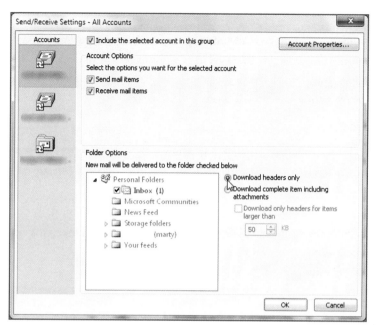

Figure 11-14: *Outlook can be set up to download only headers for all messages.*

Filter Junk Mail

Outlook can automatically filter out a lot of annoying spam before you ever see it, and it can set aside suspicious-looking messages in a Junk E-mail folder. It does this in two ways: by analyzing message content based on a protection level you choose, and by having you identify good and bad senders.

Outlook also prevents pictures and sounds from being downloaded into messages that contain HTML formatting. Up to now, savvy spammers have been able to design messages that only download images when you open or preview the message. They plant *Web beacons* in the messages, which tell their server that they have reached a valid address so that they can send you even more junk. Outlook blocks both the external content, as shown in Figure 11-15, and the beacon, unless you tell it to unblock it.

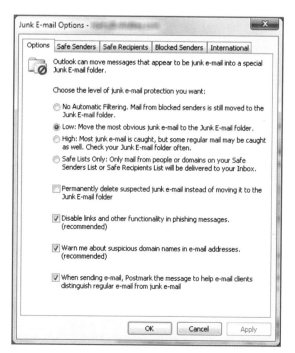

Figure 11-15: *The Junk E-Mail Options dialog box is where you can block image and sound files, as well as specific senders.*

CHOOSE A PROTECTION LEVEL

The amount of junk e-mail you receive suggests the level of protection you need. By default, Outlook sets the level at Low, but you might decide that another option would work better for you. Table 11-1 shows some considerations in choosing a level.

To set the protection level:

1. In the Home tab Delete group, click the **Junk** down arrow, and click **Junk E-mail Options**.
2. Beneath Choose The Level Of Junk E-mail Protection You Want, click the desired protection level. See Table 11-1 for explanations.

ADD ADDRESSES TO FILTER LISTS

The four other tabs in the Junk E-mail Options window provide a means for you to specifically identify good and bad e-mailers.

OPTION	RESULT	PROS	CONS
No Automatic Filtering	Only mail from blocked senders goes to the Junk E-mail folder.	You have total control.	Your Inbox could be stuffed; you or others might see unsolicited pornography.
Low (default)	Outlook scans messages for offensive language and indications of unsolicited commercial mailings.	The worst of the junk gets caught.	Some canny spammers will still find ways around the protections.
High	Pretty much all the junk e-mail gets caught.	Considerably fewer rude shocks in the Inbox.	Some regular mail will inadvertently get sent to the Junk E-mail folder.
Safe Lists Only	Only mail from Safe Senders and Safe Recipients lists goes to the Inbox.	Complete protection.	Lots of friendly mail will be junked.
Permanently Delete Suspected Junk E-Mail Instead Of Moving It To The Junk E-Mail Folder	Filtered junk mail never gets onto your computer.	You never have to inspect the Junk E-Mail folder.	Unless you chose the No Automatic Filtering option, you are sure to lose some friendly mail.
Disable Links And Other Functionality	Phishing mail is less dangerous.	You don't have to worry as much about phishing mail.	None.
Warn Me About Suspicious Domain Names	Warning message is produced with suspicious names.	Added level of protection.	May get an occasional unwanted warning.
When Sending E-Mail, Postmark The Message	Sent messages are not held up.	Your messages get to the addressee.	None.

Table 11-1: Junk E-mail Protection Levels

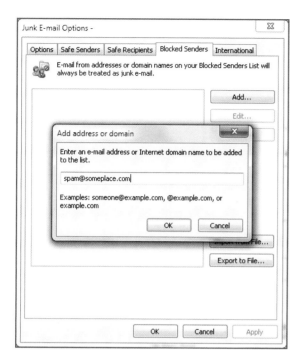

Figure 11-16: *It is worth entering the addresses of senders you want to block if you think you'll otherwise see more of their mail.*

- **Safe Senders** specifies e-mail senders from whom you always want to receive messages. This list automatically contains your contacts, so Outlook never identifies their messages as junk, no matter how silly their jokes are. If you subscribe to a newsgroup or some other mass mailing, you might need to specifically add it to the list.

- **Safe Recipients** ensures that mailing lists you subscribe to treat you as a safe sender when you contribute messages to the list.

- **Blocked Senders** sends messages from specified senders straight to the Junk E-mail folder. It's especially useful to add obnoxious domains to this list so that no address from that source makes it to your Inbox (see Figure 11-16).

- **International** allows you to block international e-mails by foreign domain codes or by language.

UPDATE LISTS QUICKLY

1. Sender and recipient addresses can be added quickly to the Safe Senders, Blocked Senders, and Safe Recipients lists from an Outlook folder. Right-click a message whose sender you want to put on a list.

2. Point at **Junk**, and click the appropriate option.

UNBLOCK PICTURE DOWNLOADS

By default, picture downloads are blocked to speed up the downloading of e-mail. To change that for specific items:

- For a **single opened message**, click **Click Here To Download Pictures** in the information bar at the top of the message, or right-click an individual picture.

☒	Right-click here to download pictures. To help protect your privacy, Outlook prevented automatic download of this picture from the Internet

- For all mail from the source of the open message, right-click a blocked item, point at **Junk**, and click **Never Block Sender's Domain (@example.com)**.

- For all HTML mail (not recommended), click **File**, click **Options**, click **Trust Center**, and clear the **Don't Download Pictures Automatically In HTML E-mail Messages Or RSS Items** check box. Click **OK**.

Handle E-mail Messages

E-mail has a way of building up fast. Outlook lets you sort your messages just about any way you want. Here, we'll consider ways to sort and mark messages so that they don't get lost in the crowd.

TIP

You can scroll through a selected message by pressing
SPACEBAR. To disable this feature, click the **View** tab, and
click **Reading Pane** in the Layout group. Click **Options**,
and in the Reading Pane dialog box, clear the **Single
Key Reading Using Space Bar** check box.

NOTE

You can also insert a Today red flag beside a selected
message by pressing **INSERT** on the keyboard. (Press
again to toggle between the Follow-Up red flag and
a Complete check mark.)

TIP

To group all of your flagged messages in a minimized
window, in the View tab Arrangement group, click
Arrange By, and click **Flag: Start
Date** or **Flag: Due Date**. If you are
viewing a maximized window or
larger window size versus a smaller
one, click the **Arrangement More**
button instead to see the menu of
options with Flag: Start Date or Flag:
Due Date.

Mark Messages as Read or Unread

A message is marked as "read" after you have selected it so that its contents
display in the Reading pane for a designated time (see "Change the Time for
Being Read"). The header in the Folder List changes from boldface to plain
type. A message can get lost in the pile if it's accidentally selected and you don't
notice or forget about it. You can easily mark it as unread again by right-clicking
the message and clicking **Mark As Unread**.

Change the Time for Being Read

To change the time that a message must be selected before it is marked as read:

1. Click the **File** tab, click **Options**, and click **Advanced**.

2. In the Outlook Panes area at the top, click the **Reading Pane** button. The Reading
   Pane dialog box will appear.

3. Click one of these options:

   - **Mark Items As Read When Viewed In The Reading Pane** allows you to set the
     number of seconds that a message must be selected before being marked as read.
     You can set the number of seconds to zero if you want an item to be marked as
     read as soon as you select it.

   - **Mark Item As Read When Selection Changes** marks the message as read as
     soon as the pointer selects another message in the Folder pane. This is the default
     setting.

4. Click **OK** to close the dialog box.

Flag Your Messages for Follow-up

You can place colored flags beside messages you want to do something with
later. The flag will appear in the flag column of the Folder pane.

- Click the flag outline in the flag column of the message
  header in the Folder pane to add the default red flag for
  a task that is due today. This is a toggle between the
  Follow-Up red flag and the Complete check mark.

  –Or–

- Select the message you want to flag, in the Home tab Tag group, click the **Follow Up** down arrow to open its context menu, and click the type of flag you want to insert.

  –Or–

- Right-click the flag column of the selected message, and on the context menu, click the type of flag you want to insert.

FINE-TUNE YOUR FLAGS

You can fine-tune the follow-up actions of the flags and specify that a reminder appear so that an e-mail message can be responded to in a timely manner.

1. In the Folder pane, right-click the flag column, and click **Custom**.

   –Or–

   For a message open in the Reading pane, click **Follow Up** in the Tags group of the Home tab, and click **Custom**.

   –Or–

   For a message open in a message window, click **Follow Up** in the Tags group of the Message tab, and click **Custom**.

2. In the Custom dialog box, click the **Flag To** down arrow, and click an action.

3. Click the **Start Date** down arrow, and click a date to indicate when the message is to be flagged.

4. Click the **Due Date** down arrow, and click a date that indicates when the response to the e-mail is to be completed.

5. Click **Reminder** to place a check mark in the check box and to display the date when the reminder is to begin. Click the date down arrow, and click a date. Click the time down arrow, and click a time for the reminders to begin.

6. Click the **Sound** icon to remove the default setting in which a sound file is played when the reminder displays on the screen.

7. Click **OK**.

8. At the designated time, a reminder will be displayed, as shown in Figure 11-17. To repeat the reminder, click the **Snooze** down arrow, click an interval until the next sound, and then click **Snooze**.

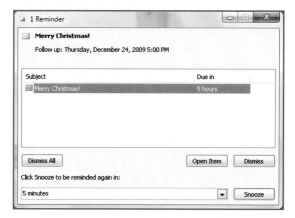

Figure 11-17: *You can set a flag to display a reminder with a sound that alerts you that an important e-mail has not been handled.*

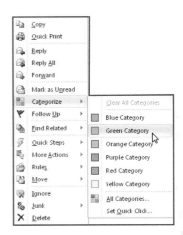

Figure 11-18: The Categorize menu shows colors, which you can define as categories according to your needs.

Arrange Messages in a Folder

Outlook contains 13 types of Inbox arrangements. You can have Outlook organize messages by the date they were sent, which Outlook uses by default; alphabetically by who sent them or by first word in the subject line; or by clustering those with attachments, colored flags you give them, or categories you created for your own use. Outlook can even group *conversations*, e-mail exchanges in which senders clicked Reply, thus preserving the subject line. To arrange messages:

1. Click **Inbox** or another specific mail folder in the navigation bar on the left side.

2. Click the **View** tab, in the Arrangement group, click **Arrange By** (or click the **More** button in an expanded window), and click one of the arrangements listed.

ADD COLORED CATEGORIES

Assigning categories to mail is one way of separating your messages by a colored code that you determine. You might categorize by project, priority, sender, etc. You determine what a color will mean when it is assigned to a message. Once your e-mail contains categories, it can be sorted and arranged so that you can find or track it more efficiently. The colors make the categories highly visible in lists. Mail is only one kind of item that you can categorize. You can assign categories to whatever you create in Outlook—tasks, appointments, contacts, notes, journal entries, and documents. You can also create new categories in the list.

1. Right-click a message header in the Folder pane, and click **Categorize**. The Categorize menu opens, as shown in Figure 11-18. (You can also click **Categorize** in the Tag group of the Home tab.)

2. Do one of the following:

   - Click a color category for the item.

   - Click **All Categories** to assign more than one category to a message (or to edit a category—see "Edit a Category" later in this chapter). Click a color to select it (place a check mark in the check box), and then click **OK**.

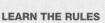

UICKSTEPS

MANIPULATING THE RULES

To get to the Rules And Alerts dialog box, in the Home tab Move group, click the **Rules** button, and then click **Manage Rules & Alerts**. The Rules And Alerts dialog box appears and lists any current rules under the names you gave them.

LEARN THE RULES

Select a rule in the list, and review it in the description pane below it.

CHANGE THE RULES

1. Click a rule in the list, click **Change Rule**, and click an action from the drop-down list.

   –Or–

   Double-click the rule to open the Rules Wizard.

2. If you opened the wizard, change the contents as needed, click **Next**, click **Finish**, and click **OK**.

3. If you selected an option under Change Rules with an icon beside it, add any requested information or fill in any new underlined variable in the description, and click **OK** until the window is closed.

Continued . . .

---

3. View items sorted into categories by clicking the **View** tab, selecting **Arrange By** (or the **More** button), and clicking **Categories**.

EDIT A CATEGORY

You can edit a category to change its name, color, or assigned shortcut.

1. Right-click a message to be categorized, click **Categorize** from the context menu, and click **All Categories**.

2. Select from among these options:

   ● To create a new category, click **New**. In the Add New Category dialog box, type a name; click the **Color** down arrow, and click a color; click the **Shortcut** key down arrow, and click a shortcut key if you want one. Click **OK**.

   ● To rename a category, click a category, click **Rename**, and type the new name in the category name text box.

   ● To delete a category, click the category and click **Delete**.

     ● To change the color, click the **Color** down arrow, and click a replacement color.

     ● To assign a shortcut key, click the **Shortcut Key** down arrow, and click a shortcut key combination.

3. Click **OK** to close the Color Categories dialog box.

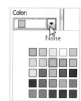

Make Up Your Own Rules

When it comes to sorting e-mail, you can make up the rules as you go along, and Outlook will follow them. Or you can pick from a list of predefined rules for common situations, like having Outlook send a message to your cell phone if you win an eBay auction or flagging all messages from your son at college for follow-up. (This only works for POP3 server accounts.)

1. With Mail selected, click the **File** tab, and in the default Info view, click **Manage Rules & Alerts**. The Rules And Alerts dialog box appears, as shown in the background of Figure 11-19.

2. Click **New Rule** (shown in the upper-left area of Figure 11-19) to open the Rules Wizard, and click one of the options in the list under step 1 in one the following categories.

QUICKSTEPS

MANIPULATING THE RULES *(Continued)*

MAKE A SIMILAR RULE

1. Click a rule in the list, click **Copy**, accept the default folder or type a folder name to copy the rule to, and click **OK**. ☑ Copy of Micoa

2. Double-click the copy.

3. Step through the wizard, changing settings as necessary and clicking **Next** as you go.

4. Give the rule a new name, and click **Finish**.

CANCEL A RULE

1. Select a rule in the list, and click **Delete**.

2. Click **Yes**.

REARRANGE THE RULES

You might want rules to be applied in a certain order.

1. Select a rule in the list that you want to move.

2. Click the **Move Up** or **Move Down** arrow until the rule resides where you want it in the sequence.

BASE A RULE ON A MESSAGE

1. In the Mail Folder pane, right-click the message, click **Rules**, and click **Create Rule**.

2. Select the desired options in the Create Rule dialog box.

3. To use the more detailed specifications in the Rules Wizard, click **Advanced Options**, step through the wizard (with information from the dialog box supplying some of the underlined values), click **Next** as needed, and then click **Finish**.

4. If using the Create Rule dialog box, click **OK**.

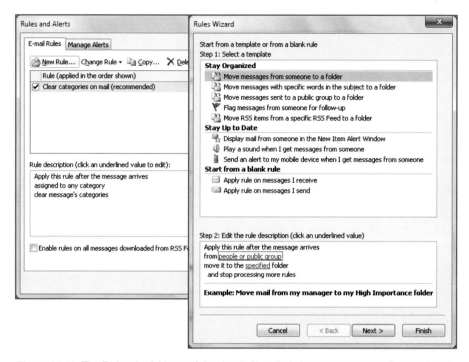

Figure 11-19: The Rules And Alerts dialog box's New Rule button opens the Rules Wizard, which is where you establish rules for handling e-mail, including alerts for the arrival of e-mail.

In step 2, if desired, click the option link and complete the dialog box as follows:

- **Stay Organized** lets you move and flag messages in a variety of ways.

- **Stay Up To Date** alerts you when new mail arrives by displaying it in a special window, playing a sound, or alerting your mobile device.

- **Start From A Blank Rule** lets you build a custom rule for receiving or sending messages.

3. Click **Next**. Click all conditions under which you want the rule applied in step 1, clicking any underlined value in step 2 and changing it as needed. The information is added to the scenario. Click **Next**.

TIP

When reading your mail, it's easiest to expand the ribbon (**CTRL+F1** or click the small arrow on the right side of the screen) so you don't have to continually re-open the Home tab to delete, reply, forward, or otherwise respond to your e-mail.

4. Step through the wizard, selecting circumstances and actions, changing values as needed in step 2, and clicking **Next**.

5. Type a name for the rule where requested, click an option specifying when the rule goes into effect, click **Finish**, and click **OK**.

Delete Messages

Outlook creates two stages for deleting messages by providing a Deleted Items folder, which holds all the items you deleted from other folders. In the first stage, you remove deleted items to a separate folder, and in the second you remove the messages from your computer.

DELETE MESSAGES FROM THE INBOX

Delete messages by opening a folder in the navigation pane and performing one of the following actions:

- **Delete one message** by clicking a message in the Folder pane and in the Home tab Delete group, clicking **Delete**. ✗

 –Or–

 Right-clicking a message in the Folder pane and clicking **Delete**.

- **Delete a block of messages** by clicking the first message, holding down **SHIFT**, clicking the last message (all of the messages in between are selected as well), and in the Home tab Delete group, clicking **Delete**.

- **Delete multiple noncontiguous messages** by pressing **CTRL** while clicking the messages you want to remove, and then in the Home tab Delete group, clicking **Delete**.

EMPTY THE DELETED ITEMS FOLDER

1. Click the **Deleted Items** folder. 🗑 **Deleted Items** (1)

2. Choose one:

   - Right-click the **Deleted Items** folder, and click **Empty "Deleted Items" Folder**.

   - Press **CTRL+A** to select all items in the folder, click **Delete**, and click **Yes**.

   - Select files to be permanently deleted as you did earlier, click **Delete**, and click **Yes**.

11

12

13

14

ARCHIVING MESSAGES

Archiving is for people who have a hard time throwing things away. Outlook is set up on a schedule, which you can see by clicking the **File** tab, clicking **Options**, clicking **Advanced**, and under AutoArchive, clicking **AutoArchive Settings**.

The AutoArchive dialog box that appears allows you to turn on AutoArchive, set the time interval between archive functions, determine when to delete old messages, specify the path to the archived file, and other settings. Click **OK** when you are finished.

If you selected Apply These Settings To All Folders Now, a dialog box appears, asking if you are ready to archive files; you can click **Yes** and be assured of finding the messages later. They are saved in a file structure that mirrors your Personal folders yet compresses the files and cleans up the Inbox. To open archived files:

- Click **Expand** ▷ beside Archive Folders in the navigation pane, and click a folder.

NOTE

Remember to review the contents of the Sent Items folder on a regular basis and delete what you can, as it can get huge.

Manage Attachments

Messages that contain files, such as pictures and documents, display a paper clip icon in the second message line within the Folder pane to show that there's more to see. Attachments are listed in the message itself in the Reading pane, as shown in Figure 11-20. Since computer vandals like to broadcast debilitating viruses by way of attachments, you should be sure that you are dealing with a trusted source before you open any attachments. Also, it's important to have an up-to-date antivirus program running on your system, as well as any protection provided by your ISP. Make sure you have it, and keep your virus definitions up-to-date. If you are running Windows Vista or Windows 7, several Internet and e-mail protections are built into them.

When a message comes in with an attachment, you can preview the attachment, open it, or save it first.

*Figure 11-20: **A single message can contain one or many attachments, consisting of all kinds of files, which may be previewed before opening.***

If you preview an attachment, it will open in the Reading pane, where you can scroll through the document. To return to the message body, click the **Message** icon next to the attachment at the top of the message (see Figure 11-20).

TIP

To select multiple attachments in an e-mail at one time—for example, to copy or save them—right-click one attachment and click **Select All**. Then right-click one of the selected attachments, and choose the activity.

OPEN ATTACHMENTS

The attachment can only be opened or viewed in the Reading pane.

- Double-click the attachment.

  –Or–

- Right-click the attachment and click either **Preview** or **Open**.

SAVE ATTACHMENTS

If you have My Computer or Windows Explorer open to the folder where you want to save the attachment, you can drag the attachment there. Otherwise:

1. Right-click the attachment icon, and click **Save As**.
2. Use the Save Attachment dialog box to navigate to the desired folder.
3. Type a name in the File Name text box, and click **Save**.

OPEN SAVED ATTACHMENTS

1. Navigate to the folder where you saved the file.
2. Double-click the file.

Print Messages

Occasionally, you might receive something that you want to print and pass around or save as a hard copy. Outlook lets you print in a hurry with the default print settings, or you can control certain parts of the process.

PRINT QUICKLY

Right-click the message or an attachment, and click **Quick Print**. The message will be printed on your default printer.

CHOOSE PRINT SETTINGS

1. Select or open the message.
2. Click the **File** tab, and click **Print**. The Print window appears with a preview of what you will print and settings you can configure, as shown in Figure 11-21.

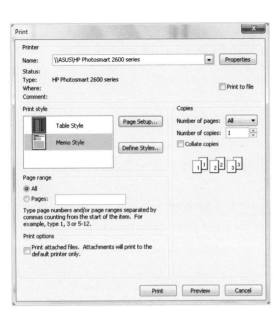

3. Open the **Printer** drop-down list, and choose the printer you want to use.

4. Click **Print Options** to open the Print dialog box.

5. Click **Properties**, select the layout or quality, and click **OK**.

6. Click **Page Setup** to open the Page Setup dialog box. Review the **Format**, **Paper**, and **Header/Footer** tabs for settings you may want to make, and click **OK**.

7. Click **Print** to begin printing.

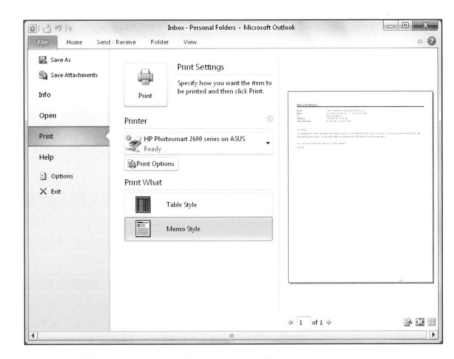

Figure 11-21: You can customize how a message is printed.

How to...

Chapter 12

Creating and Sending E-mail

As the saying goes, you have to send mail to get mail. The beauty of Outlook e-mail is that the messages are so easy to send and respond to that you can essentially carry on conversations. Outlook also makes it just as easy to send a message to 1 person or to 50, bedeck messages with fancy backgrounds known as *stationery*, insert links to Internet sites, include pictures—even add a distinctive signature. In this chapter you will learn how to create and enhance messages, as well as how to send copies, respond to others, and control how and when e-mail is sent.

Write Messages

Creating an e-mail message can be as simple as dispatching a note or as elaborate as designing a marketing poster. It's wise to get used to creating simple messages before making an art project of one. Without your having to impose any guidelines, however, Outlook is set to create an attractive basic e-mail message.

NOTE

The Outlook 2010 new Message window has many of the features of the Microsoft Word 2010 window and provides many of the tools available in Word.

TIP

To gain more working space, you can minimize the size of the ribbon. To do this, click the **Minimize Ribbon** button on the right, next to the Help icon, or double-click the active tab name. Either click **Minimize Ribbon** or double-click the active tab again to restore the size of the ribbon. You can also press **CTRL+F1** to toggle the size of the ribbon. ⌂ ⊘

Create a Message

One click starts a message, and the only field you have to complete is the address of the recipient. Normally, at least three fields are filled in before you send the message:

- **Recipient** One or more e-mail addresses or names in your Address Book
- **Subject** Words indicating the contents of the message (used by the Find tool in a search)
- **Message body** Whatever you want to say to the recipient

To start a message:

With Outlook open and Mail selected in the navigation pane, click the **New E-Mail** button on the Home tab New group. A new Message window opens, as shown in Figure 12-1.

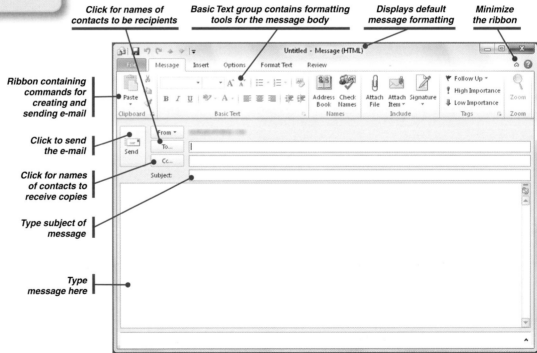

Figure 12-1: *The window for creating a message contains important differences from the one in which you read them.*

Address a Message

Outlook is the lazy person's dream for addressing messages. Of course, the address itself is simple: *username@domain.extension* (such as "mary@someisp .com"). Once you have entered names in the Contacts workspace, however, you can address your messages with almost no typing. In this chapter we will focus on what happens to the e-mail itself. The following alternatives come into play as soon as you create a new message by clicking **New** on the toolbar.

TYPE THE ADDRESS

This is the most basic addressing technique. As soon as you click **New**, the cursor blinks in the To field on the message.

- For a **single recipient**, type the address.
- For **multiple recipients**, type each address, separating them with semicolons (;) and a space. (You can also separate with commas and a space. Outlook will automatically replace them with semicolons once it recognizes the entries as e-mail addresses.)

SELECT A NAME FROM THE ADDRESS BOOK

1. Click **To**. The Select Names dialog box displays your Address Book, shown in Figure 12-2.
2. Scroll through the list, and double-click the name you want.
3. For multiple names, if a comma or semicolon wasn't automatically added after a name you selected or entered, type one of those characters between names or e-mail addresses.
4. Repeat steps 2 and 3 as needed until all desired names are listed in the To text box. An alternate way is to hold down **CTRL** while you scroll manually and click all desired names. Then click **To**.
5. Click **OK**.

COMPLETE ADDRESSES AUTOMATICALLY

Outlook runs AutoComplete by default. As soon as you type the first letter of an address, Outlook begins searching for matches among names and addresses you've typed in the past.

1. Begin typing a name or address in the To field in the Message window. The closest names to what you have typed will be displayed in the Name list.

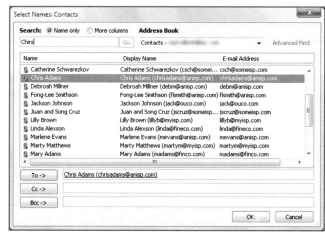

Figure 12-2: *Your Outlook Address Book can become a valuable repository.*

NOTE

You can turn off AutoComplete if you wish: Click the **File** tab, click **Options**, and click **Mail** in the left pane. Under Send Messages, clear the **Use Auto-Complete List To Suggest Names When Typing In The To, Cc, And Bcc Lines** check box. Click **OK** to close.

☐ Use Auto-Complete List to suggest names when typing in the To, Cc, and Bcc lines

2. If the name you want appears in the list, click it, or press **DOWN ARROW** (if necessary) until the name is highlighted, and then click it or press **ENTER** to accept the address. The name displays, a semicolon follows it, and the cursor blinks where the next name would appear.

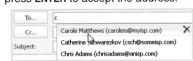

3. If you wish to add another recipient, begin typing another name, and repeat the process as needed.

4. Press **TAB** to go to the next desired field.

Use a Contact Group

You can group your contacts into *contact groups* or distribution lists, giving you an even quicker way to add multiple addresses to messages. Use any of the preceding procedures to enter individuals in the Address Book, and enter or select the name of the contact group as it appears in the Address Book. After selecting the contact list, its name will have a plus sign next to it, which you can click to expand the contact list name and see the individuals in the list (you will be warned that once expanded, you can't contract it. When you send it), the message will go to everyone on the list.

To... ⊞ **Fineco;** |

Add Carbon and Blind Copies

You may never have seen a real carbon copy, but Outlook keeps the concept alive by way of this feature located just below the To field in the new Message window. Persons who receive a message with their e-mail address in the *Cc* (carbon copy) line understand that they are not the primary recipients—they got the message as an FYI (for your information), and all other recipients can see that they got it (see Figure 12-3). A *Bcc* (blind carbon copy) hides addresses entered in that line from anyone else who receives the message.

INCLUDE OR REMOVE BCC ON NEW MESSAGES

1. In the Message window, click the **Options** tab.

2. In the Show Fields group, click **Bcc** to toggle the Bcc field on and off.

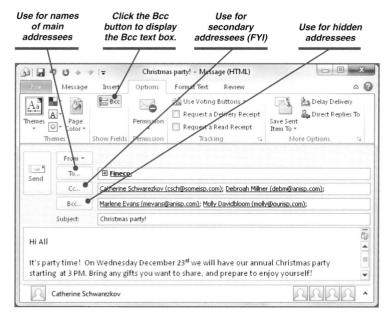

Use for names of main addressees · **Click the Bcc button to display the Bcc text box.** · **Use for secondary addressees (FYI)** · **Use for hidden addressees**

Figure 12-3: The way a message is delivered suggests different roles for the various recipients.

ADDRESS THE COPIES

Type addresses in the Cc and Bcc fields completely or with the aid of AutoComplete. You can also use the Address Book: Click **Cc** or **Bcc** in the Message window, begin typing a name to scroll through the names, and double-click the name(s) in the Address Book you want to be copied.

Edit a Message

E-mail can be created in any of three formats and has the additional option of using the powerful formatting capability of Microsoft Word for composing messages. Outlook handles all three formats quite easily, but sometimes you need to consider your recipients' computer resources and Internet connections.

- **HTML** (HyperText Markup Language), the default format, lets you freely use design elements, such as colors, pictures, links, animations, sound, and movies (though good taste and the need to control the size of the message file might suggest a little discretion!).

- **Plain Text** format lies at the other extreme, eliminating embellishments so that any computer can manage the message.

- **Rich Text Format** (RTF) takes the middle ground, providing font choices—including color, boldface, italics, and underlining—basic paragraph layouts, and bullets.

With Outlook, you can edit messages you create as well as those you receive. Regardless which of the three formats you choose, some editing processes are always available, as shown in Table 12-1.

Using HTML or Rich Text Format provides a wide range of options for enhancing the appearance of a message. See the "Formatting Messages" QuickSteps for a rundown of additional formatting selections. Finally, you can also create the message in another program and copy and paste it into a message body. HTML will preserve the formatting exactly, and Rich Text Format will come close.

TO		DO THIS	
Insert new text in the message body		Click where new text belongs, and type new text.	
Indent the start of a paragraph		Click before the first letter of the paragraph, and press **TAB**.	
Replace a	Word	Double-click the word.	Type new text.
	Line	Click to the left of the line.	
	Paragraph	Double-clicking to the left selects a paragraph. Triple-clicking to the left selects all the text in the message.	
Move a	Word	Double-click the word.	Drag to a new location in the message.
	Line	Click to the left of the line.	
	Paragraph	Double-click to the left of the paragraph.	
Delete a	Word	Double-click the word.	Press **DELETE**.
	Line	Click to the left of the line.	
	Paragraph	Double-click to left of the paragraph.	

Table 12-1: Standard Editing Operations

SELECT A MESSAGE FORMAT

The type of message format being used is displayed in the title bar of the new Message window. You either can set a format for an individual message, or you can set a default for all message formats. Christmas party! - Message (HTML)

To set a default format for all e-mail:

1. In either the Outlook window or a Message window, click the **File** tab, click **Options**, and click Mail in the left pane to open the Mail options, some of which are shown in Figure 12-4.

2. Click the **Compose Messages In This Format** down arrow, and select one of the choices.

3. Click **OK** to close the Options dialog box.

To set formatting for an individual message:

1. In the Message window, click the **Format Text** tab.

2. In the Format group, click the formatting button you want.

**Click to select the
default message format**

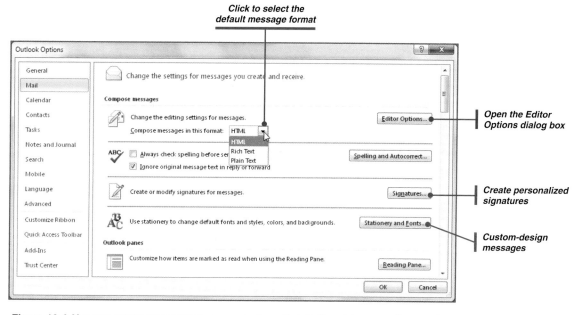

Figure 12-4: You can create personal message designs that distinguish you as the sender.

Use Stationery

It's easy to choose stationery for a message. You can pick a different type of
stationery for every new message or set a default style for all messages (until
you change it).

SET A DEFAULT STATIONERY THEME

You can set a default for your stationery that will be used each time you write a
new e-mail. You can also select a theme for your stationery and still have your
own unique fonts. You can vary fonts as well, either for new e-mails or for those
you reply or forward. To set a default stationery:

1. Click the **File** tab, click **Options**, and click **Mail** in the left pane.

2. Make sure that **HTML** has been selected as the message format.

NOTE

If your Message window is not maximized, you
may not see all available formatting buttons. In
some cases, the commands will be available
in menus. You can click the group down arrow
to see the menu of commands, or click the
Maximize button on the title bar to increase the
size of the window.

QUICKSTEPS

FORMATTING MESSAGES

To format text in the Message window, use the Format Text tab or the Message tab to access formatting commands. You can format text before you start typing, or you can select text and then format it after composing the message. See Table 12-1 for a list of selection methods.

CHOOSE A FONT AND ITS SIZE

A font can immediately set the tone of your message.

- Select your text or paragraph.

- In either the Format Text tab Font group or the Message tab Basic Text group, click the Font down arrow, and move the pointer over several fonts and see how they affect your selected text. Select a font you want to use.

- Click the **Font Size** down arrow next to the font, and again move the pointer over several sizes and notice the effects. The default size is 11. Select a type size you want.

CREATE BOLD, ITALIC, UNDERLINED, AND STRIKETHROUGH

Select the text, and click the **Bold**, **Italic**, **Underline**, or **Strikethrough** effect in the Font group.

Continued . . .

3. Click the **Stationery And Fonts** button. Click the **Personal Stationery** tab to open the dialog box shown in Figure 12-5. Select from these choices:

- Click the **Theme** button, and under Choose A Theme, click the theme you want, and click **OK**. When you choose a theme, the fonts will be automatically defined for you, and those buttons will become unavailable or grayed.

- If, after choosing a theme, you want to use another font, click the **Font** down arrow, and click either **Always Use My Fonts** or **Use My Font When Replying Or Forwarding Messages**. This will enable you to select a font for all new messages or for replying and forwarding to e-mails.

- If you want to use your fonts, click the appropriate **Font** button, and select the font, font style, size, and color you want.

- If you want to insert your name, click the **Mark My Comments With** check box. Type over the default text, if desired.

- If you want your replies or forwards to be in a different color, click **Pick A New Color When Replying Or Forwarding**.

4. Click **OK** twice to close the Options dialog box.

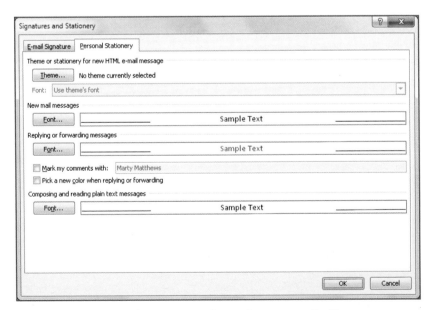

Figure 12-5: You can design custom stationery for your e-mail with your own theme, fonts, and colored replies and forwards.

QUICKSTEPS

FORMATTING MESSAGES *(Continued)*

CHOOSE A FONT COLOR

Select the text, click the **Font Color** down arrow, and select a color. A⁻

ALIGN PARAGRAPHS

Select the text and click an alignment, which, from left to right, provides a left-aligned margin, centered text, a right-aligned margin, or justified margins (where both the left and right margins end evenly).

CREATE NUMBERED, BULLETED, OR MULTILEVEL LISTS

Select the text to be affected, and click the **Bullets**, **Numbering**, or **Multilevel List** button (the latter is only in the Format Text tab Paragraph group).

SHIFT THE PARAGRAPH

The Decrease Indent and Increase Indent buttons move the selected paragraph in fixed increments. You can alternate clicking them until you are satisfied with the location. However, because they will not move the paragraph beyond the message margins, they have limited effect on centered paragraphs.

Click within a paragraph to be shifted, and click the appropriate button.

INSERT LINES OR BORDERS

Set off paragraphs with lines or borders.

1. Click where a line is desired (usually at the end of a paragraph), or select the paragraph(s) around which you want a border.

2. In the Format Text tab Paragraph group, click the **Borders** down arrow, and click the type of line or border that you want.

APPLY STATIONERY TO A SINGLE MESSAGE

1. Click the **Insert** tab in the Outlook Message window, and click the **Signature** button in the Include group. Click **Signatures** on the menu. The Signature And Stationery dialog box appears.

2. Click the **Personal Stationery** tab.

3. Change the theme and fonts, as described in "Set a Default Stationery Theme."

4. Click **OK**.

USE A STANDARD MICROSOFT OFFICE THEME

You can use a standard Microsoft Office theme in your e-mail that differs from the Outlook themes used for stationery. You might use these to coordinate your regular Word correspondence with your e-mail, thus creating a consistent and professional look. These themes are easy to use and available in your new Message window.

1. In the new Message window, click the **Options** tab if it is not already selected.

2. In the Themes group, if you can't see Colors, Fonts, and Effects, click **Themes**. Then, in any case, click the **Themes** down arrow, and click the standard theme you'd like to use for your e-mail, as shown in Figure 12-6.

   - Click **Colors** and click a combination of colors to change the color scheme.

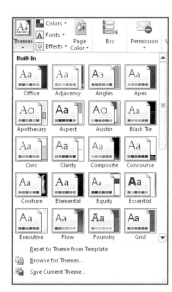

Figure 12-6: Using a standard Office theme allows you to coordinate your e-mail and regular Word correspondence.

NOTE

Be aware that the Stationery feature can increase the size of messages, making it take longer for recipients to download the message, especially those on dial-up connections.

NOTE

In the Message window, when you click the **Themes** button in the Themes group on the Options tab, you will see additional options at the bottom of the gallery of theme thumbnails. You can search for additional themes online by clicking **Browse For Themes**. If you alter a standard theme with new colors, fonts, or effects, you can save these changes as a custom theme to use again later by clicking **Save Current Theme**.

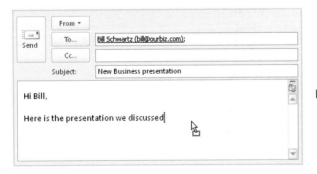

- Click **Fonts** and click a font style to change the fonts used.
- Click **Effect** and click an effect to change the special effects of the graphics.

3. Type your new message and send it.

CHOOSE TO NOT USE STATIONERY

If you don't want to use your selected stationery for a single new message:

- In the Outlook window Home tab New group, click **New Items**, click **E-Mail Message Using**, and select **HTML**. A new message will appear without your stationery.

To stop using stationery as a default:

1. In the Outlook window, click the **File** tab, click **Options**, and click **Mail** in the left pane.

2. Click the **Stationery And Fonts** button.

3. On the Personal Stationery tab, click **Theme** and click (**No Theme**) at the top of the theme list.

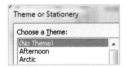

4. Click **OK** three times.

Attach Files

Sometimes you will want to send or receive a message that is accompanied by other files: pictures, word-processed documents, sound, or movie files. Creating attachments is like clipping newspaper stories and baby pictures to a letter. If you are editing or otherwise working on the item you want to attach, make sure that you save the latest version before you proceed. After that, click **New** to open the new Message window, and use one of the following attachment procedures.

DRAG A FILE TO A MESSAGE

Find the file to be attached by using My Computer or Windows Explorer, and drag it to the message.

INCLUDING HYPERLINKS

You can add hyperlinks (whether to an Internet site, to other locations in the current document, or to other documents) to your e-mail by typing them into the message body or by copying and pasting them. Outlook creates a live link, which it turns to a blue, underlined font when you type or paste any kind of Internet protocol (such as http://, mailto:, or www.something.com), regardless of what mail format you use.

DEFINE A HYPERLINK

In addition to typing the hyperlink address, you can use a dialog box to select the location of the link—on your computer, the Web, a new document, or an e-mail address.

1. In the Insert tab Links group, click **Hyperlink**.
2. In the dialog box that appears, find and select the location of the link—in an existing file, a place in a document, a webpage, a new document, or an e-mail address.
3. Click **OK**.

TYPE OVER HYPERLINKS

In HTML and Rich Text Format, you can substitute different text for the actual Uniform Resource Locator (URL) or e-mail address and still retain the link. An example might be displaying a link entitled, "Click here to view the photo gallery" with an actual link of "www.someorg.com/mygallery.html."

1. Establish the link as a hyperlink by clicking **Hyperlink** in the Insert tab Links group. Click **OK** on the dialog box, regardless of the selected location.
2. Drag the URL hyperlink to select it.
3. Type something different.

INSERT A FILE

When you attach a file to an e-mail message, it can either be attached as a file or entered as text into the body of the message. In some cases, it may be attached as a hyperlink. The attached file and its commands are identified with a paper clip icon.

1. To display the Insert File dialog box:
   - Click the **Insert** tab, and then click **Attach File** in the Include group.
   –Or–
   - In the Message tab, click the **Attach File** icon in the Include group.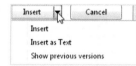

2. The Insert File dialog box appears. Find and select the file to be attached. Then:
   - Click **Insert** to insert the file as an attachment. If the e-mail format is HTML or plain text, it will be attached in a field labeled "Attached" beneath the Subject field. If the format is Rich Text Format, the file attachment will be in the body of the message.

Attachment identified for HTML or plain text format

Attachment identified for Rich Text Format

   - Click the **Insert** down arrow, and choose between inserting the file as an attachment and inserting it as text in the body of the message. If you choose **Insert As Text**, the file is entered as text in the message. The file content of certain file types, such as .txt, .doc, and .eml, and the source code of others, such as HTML or HTA (HTML Application), will become part of the message. Everything else—pictures, sound, and movies—will generate nonsense characters in the message body.
   - Click **Insert As Hyperlink** to insert the selected file as a hyperlink. (This option is often not available from the Attach File command.)
   - Click **Show Previous Versions** to list the previous versions of the files so that you can select the version you want to attach.

3. Complete and send the e-mail message.

Figure 12-7: You can insert a picture or a link to it using the Insert Picture dialog box.

NOTE

If you link a picture to your message rather than embed it, you will need to either send the picture with the document or store the picture in a shared network folder available to the message recipient. Otherwise, your e-mail will be seen with a red X where the photo should be.

EMBED A PICTURE INTO A MESSAGE

Though any kind of file you save on your computer or on a disk can be sent by following the previous steps, you have the added option of placing pictures (.gif, .jpg, .bmp, .tif, and so on) right into the message body.

1. Click in the message body to set the insertion point.

2. Click the **Insert** tab, and click **Picture** in the Illustrations group. The Insert Picture dialog box appears, as shown in Figure 12-7.

3. Select the picture file you want, and click the **Insert** down arrow. From the submenu:

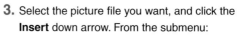

- Click **Insert** to embed the picture in the message. You can then drag it to size it correctly for your message or right-click to display the Format Picture dialog box and edit the photo.

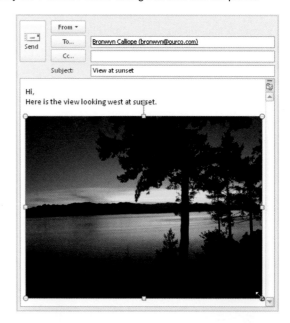

- Click **Link To File** to send a link to where the file is stored. This reduces the size of the message, but requires that the recipient have access to where the file is stored.

- Click **Insert And Link** to both embed the photo and send a link to its location.
- Click **Show Previous Versions** to list the previous versions of the files so that you can select the version you want to attach.

4. Complete and send the e-mail message.

Sign Messages

You can create closings, or signatures, for your e-mail messages. Outlook signatures can contain pictures and text along with your name. You can create signatures in different styles for the different kinds of messages you write: friendly, formal, or business.

CREATE A SIGNATURE

With Outlook open:

1. Click the **File** tab, and click **Options**. The Outlook Options window opens. Click **Mail** in the left pane.

2. Click **Signatures** in the right pane, and then click **New**.

3. Type a name for your signature, and click **OK**. This identifies the signature group that the signature serves. It will not be displayed on the message. The Signatures And Stationery dialog box appears with the E-mail Signature tab selected.

4. In the Edit Signature text box, type (or paste from another document) any text you want to include in your closing, including your name, as shown in Figure 12-8.

5. To apply formatting, select the text and click any of the formatting buttons in the toolbar. You can even insert a business card, picture, or hyperlink. Use the tips found earlier in the "Formatting Messages" QuickSteps. Plain text messages, by definition, cannot be formatted.

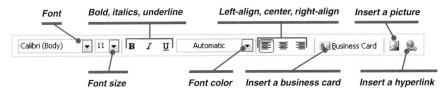

6. Click **OK** twice to close the dialog boxes.

USING SIGNATURES

You can use certain signatures for certain accounts, and you can still pick a different one for a particular message.

Click the **File** tab, click **Options**, and in the Outlook Options window, click **Mail** in the left pane.

ASSIGN SIGNATURES TO ACCOUNTS

1. Click the **Signatures** button, and then click the **E-mail Signature** tab.

2. Click the **E-mail Account** down arrow, and select an account.

3. Click the **New Messages** down arrow, and click the signature name to be used.

4. Click the **Replies/Forwards** down arrow, and click the signature name to be used.

5. Repeat steps 2–4 for each of your accounts, and then click **OK** twice.

INSERT A SIGNATURE IN A MESSAGE

Sometimes, you will want to replace a defined signature with another one or define a signature when you create a message.

1. Create an e-mail message.

2. Click in the body of the message where you want the special closing. Click the **Insert** tab, and click **Signature** in the Include group. Choose one of the following options:

   • Click the name of an existing signature, and it will be inserted in the message. If you already have a message that was inserted automatically, it will be replaced by the one you select.

Continued . . .

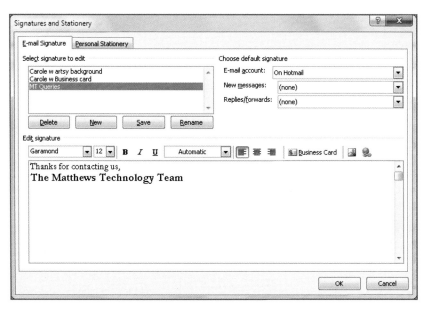

Figure 12-8: You can create one or more signatures with custom-designed characteristics that will be included in the bottom of your e-mail.

Use Digital Signatures

A *digital signature* certifies that everything contained in the message—documents, forms, computer code, training modules, whatever—originated with the sender. Computer programmers and people engaged in e-commerce use them a lot. To embed a formal digital signature, you need to acquire a *digital certificate*, which is like a license, from a certificate authority, such as VeriSign, GeoTrust, or GlobalSign.

Alternatively, you can create your own digital signature, although it is not administered by a certificate authority. A self-signed certificate is considered unauthenticated and will generate a security warning if the recipient has his or her security set at a high level.

QUICKSTEPS

USING SIGNATURES (Continued)

- Click **Signatures**, and the Signatures And Stationery dialog box will appear. Create a new signature, as described in "Sign Messages." For the current message, once again click **Signature** in the Insert tab, and click the name of your new signature.

TIP

You can also do an Internet search on "Get a digital ID" and find other sources of digital IDs, some of which are free for an initial period.

Encrypted e-mail

- ☐ Encrypt contents and attachments for outgoing messages
- ☑ Add digital signature to outgoing messages
- ☑ Send clear text signed message when sending signed messages
- ☐ Request S/MIME receipt for all S/MIME signed messages

ACQUIRE A DIGITAL CERTIFICATE

If you do not already have a digital certificate, Outlook can lead you to a website where you can find a commercial certification authority to issue one. Make sure you are online before you begin.

1. Click the **File** tab, click **Options**, click **Trust Center**, and click **Trust Center Settings**. The Trust Center window opens. Click **E-mail Security** in the left pane.

2. Under Digital IDs (Certificates), click **Get A Digital ID**. A Microsoft webpage on digital IDs will open.

3. Follow the instructions on the page to select a vendor and obtain a certificate.

IMPORT OR EXPORT A DIGITAL ID

If you already have a digital ID in another application, you can import into Outlook, or you can export your digital ID in Outlook so you can use it in another application.

1. Click the **File** tab, click **Options**, click **Trust Center**, and click **Trust Center Settings**. The Trust Center window opens. Click **E-mail Security** in the left pane.

2. Under Digital IDs (Certificates), click **Import/Export**. The Import/Export Digital ID dialog box appears.

3. Click **Import Existing Digital ID From A File** to import a digital ID, or click **Export Your Digital ID To A File** to export your own digital ID.

4. Fill in the requested information, and click **OK** three times.

ADD A DIGITAL SIGNATURE TO MESSAGES

1. Click the **File** tab, click **Options**, click **Trust Center**, and click **Trust Center Settings**. The Trust Center window opens.

2. Click the **E-mail Security** option.

3. Under Encrypted E-mail, click the **Add Digital Signature To Outgoing Messages** check box.

4. To make sure that recipients can read the message if they don't have Secure/Multipurpose Internet Mail Extensions (S/MIME) security, click the **Send Clear Text Signed Message When Sending Signed Messages** check box.

5. To receive a message confirming that your message got to the recipient, click the **Request S/MIME Receipt For All S/MIME Signed Messages** check box.

6. Click **OK** twice.

For exploring misspelled words, you will find a reference source by clicking **Research** in the Proofing group on the Review tab of the Message window.

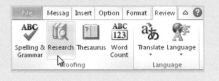

The personal, or custom, dictionary can get long, and misspellings can be added accidentally. To edit the dictionary from Outlook, click the **File** tab, click **Options**, and click **Mail** in the left pane. Click **Spelling And AutoCorrection**. In the Editor Options window, click **Custom Dictionaries**. In the Custom Dictionaries dialog box, click **Edit Word List**. Remove a word by clicking it, pressing **DELETE** (to fix it, type the correct spelling instead), and then clicking **OK** four times.

Check Spelling

Even though many abbreviations have emerged with e-mail, instant messaging, and texting, unintentional spelling errors still can be a problem. You can have Outlook check the spelling of your message when you finish, or you can have it automatically check messages as you are writing them.

CHECK A MESSAGE

Create a message and as you type, spelling errors will be automatically flagged for you with a red wavy line as you type. You will have these options:

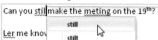

- Right-click the flagged word, and if a correct spelling is suggested, click it.

- If you do not see the correct spelling, then the flagged word cannot be found in the dictionary. Either look it up in a reference source and type it in, or type another spelling to see if it is correct.

- If you know the flagged word is correct and you want to add it to the dictionary, right-click the word and click **Add To Dictionary**. Also, see "Add a Word to the Dictionary," next.

ADD A WORD TO THE DICTIONARY

To add a flagged word to the dictionary so that it will not continue to be flagged as a potential misspelling:

1. Highlight the flagged word, and click **Spelling & Grammar** in the Proofing group of the Review tab. The Spelling And Grammar dialog box will appear, as seen in Figure 12-9.

2. Click **Add To Dictionary**.

3. Click **Close**.

CHECK MESSAGES BEFORE SENDING

To automatically check spelling in messages before sending them:

1. Click the **File** tab, and click **Options**. The Outlook Options window opens. Click **Mail** in the left pane.

2. Click **Always Check Spelling Before Sending**, and click **OK**.

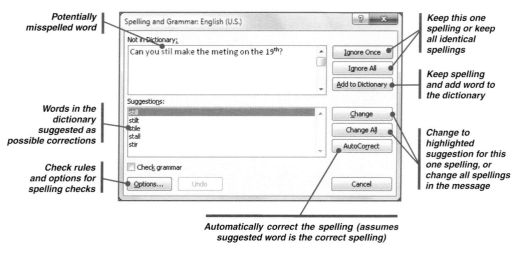

Potentially misspelled word

Words in the dictionary suggested as possible corrections

Check rules and options for spelling checks

Keep this one spelling or keep all identical spellings

Keep spelling and add word to the dictionary

Change to highlighted suggestion for this one spelling, or change all spellings in the message

Automatically correct the spelling (assumes suggested word is the correct spelling)

Figure 12-9: *The default spelling dictionary contains everyday words rather than technical or scientific terms. You can add special words to it.*

Send Messages

No extra postage, no trip to the post office, no running out of envelopes. What could be better? Once a message is ready to go, you can just click a button. Outlook provides features that let you exercise more control over the process than you could ever get from the postal service, or "snail" mail.

Make sure that your message is complete and ready to send, and then click **Send** on the upper-left area of the message.

Change the From Address

When you have more than one account, your Message window contains a From button that is not available otherwise. This can be helpful if you want to send a message that appears as though it's from an account that you haven't set up in Outlook (such as if you usually read your Gmail online, but want to send this particular message as if it were from your Gmail account). It's just a header spoof, of course, but most recipients wouldn't notice. To send a message from a particular account, choose one of these options:

- Click From above the To button in the Message window, select an account, and click **Send**.

- Click **From** and click **Other E-mail Address**. The Send To Other E-mail Address dialog box appears. If your name account is already set up, click **Send Using** and select the account you want. If you need to open a new account, click **From** and choose a name from the contact list. Click **OK** twice.

Reply to Messages

When you receive a message that you want to answer, you have three ways to initiate a reply:

- Open the message and click **Reply** in the Respond group on the Message tab.

  –Or–

- Right-click the message in the Folder pane, and select **Reply** from the context menu.

  –Or–

- Click the message in the Folder pane, and click **Reply** in the Home tab Respond group.

Whichever way you choose, a reply Message window opens, as shown in Figure 12-10. The message will be formatted using the same format the sender used, and the subject will be "RE:" plus the original subject in the Subject line. By default, the pointer blinks in the message body above the original message and sender's address (see also "Change the Reply Layout"). Treat it like a new Message window: Type a message, add attachments or links, and click **Send**.

REPLY TO ALL RECIPIENTS

If the To field in the message contains several recipients, all of whom should read your reply, Outlook makes this simple. Using any of the three ways just listed, click **Reply All**. The reply Message window will list all original recipients in the To and Cc fields. Send the message as usual.

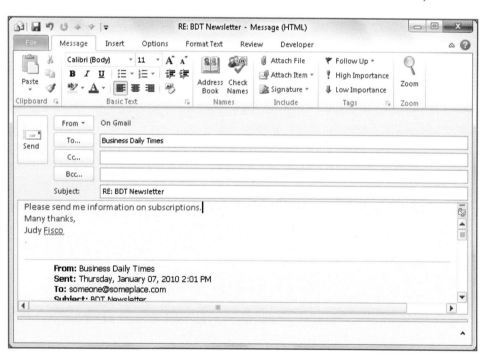

Figure 12-10: The Reply window uses the sender's message format and subject to make the e-mail conversation easy to track and respond to.

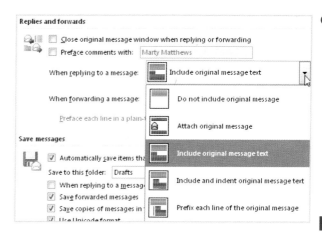

CHANGE THE REPLY LAYOUT

You can select from five different ways to incorporate the original message. Also, if you'd rather just insert your responses into the original text, Outlook lets you decide how to identify your remarks.

1. Click the **File** tab, click **Options**, and click **Mail** in the left pane.

2. Beneath Replies And Forwards, click the **When Replying To A Message** down arrow, and select how you want the original message included.

3. Click the **Preface Comments With** check box, and type the label you want.

4. Click **OK**.

Forward Messages

When you forward a message, you send an incoming message to someone else. You can send messages to new recipients, using the same techniques as with the Reply feature.

When you receive a message that you want to forward to someone else, use one of these techniques:

- Open the message and click **Forward** in the Respond group on the Message tab.

  –Or–

- Right-click the message in the Folder pane, and select **Forward** from the context menu.

  –Or–

- Click the message in the Folder pane, and click **Forward** on the Home group.

A Forward Message window opens, with the cursor blinking in the To field and a space above the original message for you to type your own. Once the Forward Message window opens, the simplest action is to enter the recipient's (or recipients') address(es), insert attachments as needed, and send as usual.

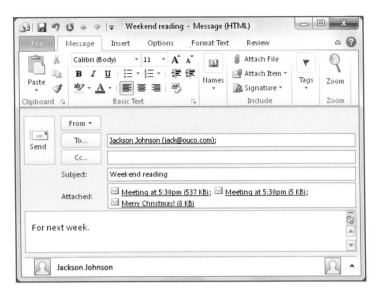

Figure 12-11: You can group and forward e-mails as attachments.

QUICKSTEPS

SENDING MESSAGES

You can fire off your messages now or later, or on a schedule.

SEND MESSAGES MANUALLY

By default, as long as you are connected to the Internet, clicking **Send** in the Message window sends the completed message. You can turn this off so that clicking Send in the Message window only puts the message in the Outbox folder. You must then click **Send/Receive** in the Outlook standard toolbar to send all the messages in the Outbox folder.

Continued . . .

FORWARD MULTIPLE MESSAGES

Rather than forward a bunch of messages one by one, you can bundle them and forward them in one message.

1. Press **CTRL** while you click each message that you want to forward.

2. Right-click one of the messages in the group, and click **Forward**. A new mail message opens with the messages included as attachments, as seen in Figure 12-11. You may also see the attachments in the Attached box rather than in the message area.

3. Complete the message and send as usual.

Set Message Priority

If your recipient gets a lot of messages, you might want to identify your message as important so that it will stand out in his or her Inbox. Outlook includes a red exclamation point in the message list to call attention to messages set with high importance and a blue down arrow to indicate messages with low importance. In the Message window, you flag your e-mail messages with the appropriate flag.

1. Create a message. In the Options group on the Message tab, select one of these options:
   - Click **High Importance** to insert a red exclamation point to indicate high importance.
   - Click **Low Importance** to insert a blue down arrow to indicate low importance.

2. Send the message as usual.

Request Receipts

Anyone who has sent an important message and has not heard a peep from the recipient can appreciate receipts. When the addressee receives or reads the message, you are notified. You can request receipts for all your messages or on a message-by-message basis.

QUICKSTEPS

SENDING MESSAGES (Continued)

TURN OFF AUTOSEND

To prevent a message from being automatically sent unless you click Send in the Message window:

1. Click the **File** tab, click **Options**, and click **Advanced** in the left pane.

2. Under Send And Receive, clear the **Send Immediately When Connected** check box.

3. Click **Send/Receive**. Under Settings For Group "All Accounts," clear the **Schedule An Automatic Send/Receive Every** check box. Also clear the **Perform An Automatic Send/Receive When Exiting** check box.

4. Click **Close** and then click **OK**.

SEND MESSAGES AT A CERTAIN TIME

1. Create the message and click the **Options** tab.

2. Click the **Delay Delivery** button in the More Options group. The Message Options dialog box appears.

Delay
Delivery

3. Under Delivery Options, click **Do Not Deliver Before**.

4. Click the date and time down arrows, and select a day and time.

5. Click **Expires After** and click the date and time down arrows to set the end time.

Delivery options

- [ ] Have replies sent to:
- [✓] Do not deliver before: 1/3/2010   5:00 PM
- [ ] Expires after: None   12:00 AM

6. Click **Close**.

Continued . . .

OBTAIN RECEIPTS FOR ALL MESSAGES

1. Click the **File** tab, click **Options**, and click **Mail** in the left pane.

2. In the Outlook Options window, scroll down to **Tracking**.

3. To request a receipt, click **Read Receipt Confirming The Recipient Viewed The Message, Delivery Receipt Confirming The Message Was Delivered To The Recipient's E-mail Server**, or both.

4. If you like, choose an option for responding to other senders' requests for a receipt—**Always Send A Read Receipt, Never Send A Read Receipt**, or **Ask Me Each Time** (the default).

5. Click OK three times.

OBTAIN A SINGLE RECEIPT

1. Create a message and click the **Options** tab in the Message window.

2. In the Tracking group, click **Request A Delivery Receipt, Request A Read Receipt**, or both. (If you have set these options for all mail, this message will reflect those settings.)

Delay Delivery with a Rule

You can create a rule to control when messages leave your system after you click Send.

1. In the Outlook window Home tab Move group, click **Rules**, and click **Manage Rules & Alerts**.

2. If you are told that messages sent and received with HTTP (such as Hotmail, Gmail, and Yahoo!) cannot be filtered using rules and alerts, click **OK**.

QUICKSTEPS

SENDING MESSAGES *(Continued)*

SAVE A SENT MESSAGE

You can select the folder within which a sent message will be saved.

1. On the Message window, on the Options tab in the More Options group, click **Save Sent Item To**.

2. In the submenu, select whether you want to save the message to the default folder, to another folder (which you find and select in the Select Folder dialog box), or to not save the message at all.

3. In the Rules And Alerts dialog box, click **New Rule**.

4. In the Rules Wizard, under Start From A Blank Rule, click **Apply Rule On Messages I Send**, and click **Next**.

5. Click to select any desired conditions that limit which messages the rule applies to, and then click the link in the description pane (shown in Figure 12-12), which may display a dialog box to specify the exact criteria. Complete the dialog box, click **OK**, and click **Next**.

6. Under Select Action(s), click **Defer Delivery By A *number* Of Minutes**.

7. In the description pane, click the link for *a number of* minutes, and in the Deferred Delivery dialog box, type the total minutes (up to 120) that you want messages delayed, click **OK**, and click **Next**.

8. Click any exceptions, specify them in the description pane, click **OK** if necessary, and click **Next**.

9. Type a name for the rule, and click **Finish**. You are returned to the Rules And Alerts dialog box, which will now show your new rule, as you can see in Figure 12-13.

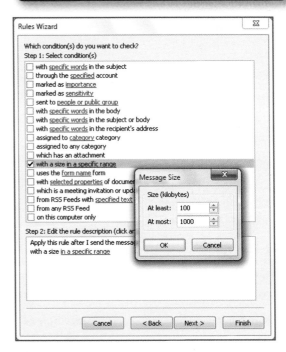

Figure 12-12: Outlook's rule-making feature has a large number of conditions that you can organize into rules.

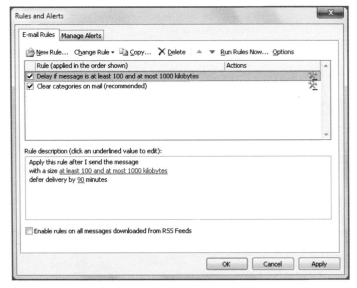

Figure 12-13: The Rules And Alerts dialog box, opened from the Home tab Move group, provides for the creation and management of rules.

Chapter 13

Scheduling and the Calendar

The Calendar is second only to mail in its importance in Outlook. The Calendar works closely with Contacts and Tasks to coordinate the use of your time and your interactions with others. It lets you schedule appointments and meetings; establish recurring activities; and tailor the Calendar to your area, region, and workdays.

In this chapter, you will see how to use and customize the Calendar, schedule and manage appointments, and schedule and track meetings and resources.

Explore the Calendar

The Calendar has a number of unique items in its Outlook window, as seen in Figure 13-1.

- Buttons allow you to quickly switch the view of your calendar between daily, weekly, and monthly views, as well as to show or hide details of your activities.

Ribbon tabs   Calendar grid   Current date   Recurring appointments

Ribbon

Date
navigator

Time bar

Event
banner

Total
reminders

Task pane   Appointment indicators   View buttons

Sizing
slider

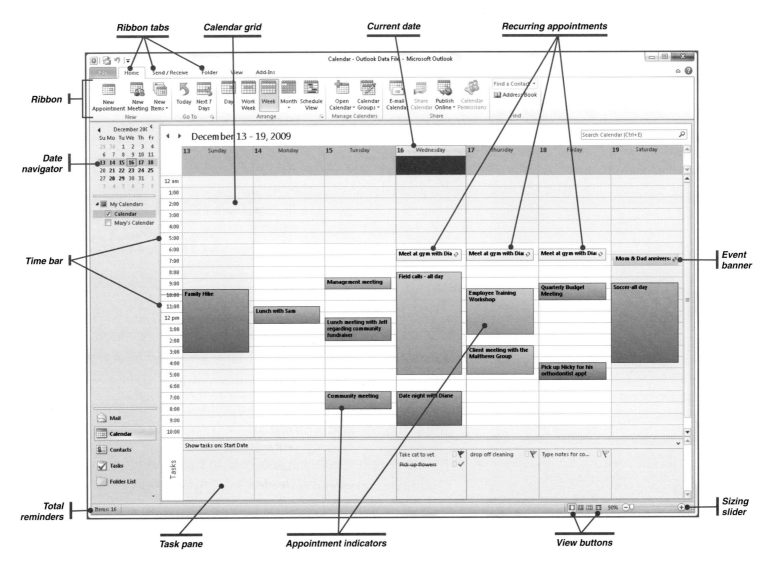

Figure 13-1: The Outlook Calendar displays your day, week, work week, month, or schedule at a glance.

Appointments	Appointments only involve you. They take time on your calendar, are less than 24 hours long, and do not require inviting others within Outlook to attend. Examples include a sales call, lunch with a buyer, or time you want to set aside to write a report.	appointment icon
Meetings	Meetings are appointments that require that others be invited and/or that resources be reserved. Meetings are set up using e-mail. They happen at a scheduled time, just like an appointment. You invite others via e-mail, and the meeting displays in your calendar with the location and organizer's name.	meetings icon
Events	All-day events are 24 hours or longer, do not occupy time on your calendar, and appear as a banner on each day's calendar. Examples are conferences, birthdays, or your vacation. Since events that you put on your calendar do not block out time like a meeting or an appointment, you can have other entries for that day display on your calendar.	
Tasks	Tasks are activities that do not need specific time scheduled for them and are your own personal tasks, even if they are part of a larger project of which you are a team member. Your tasks will display in the Day and Week views of your calendar, as well as on your To-Do bar.	task icon

Table 13-1: Common Calendar Activities

- The current date and each appointment are displayed on the calendar in Normal view.
- Your tasks appear at the bottom of each day in the Day, Work Week, and Week views.

Create Calendar Appointments and Tasks

The Calendar is designed for you to easily keep track of appointments, meetings, events, due dates, anniversaries, birthdays, and any other date-related happening. You can schedule several different types of activities, as shown in Table 13-1.

CREATE AN APPOINTMENT

These steps offer a quick overview of how you set up an appointment. Refer to "Use the Calendar" in this chapter to learn more about how to create appointments, events, recurring appointments, and reminders.

1. Click **Calendar** in Outlook Views (the lower pane in the navigation pane).
   –Or–
   Press **CTRL+2** on the keyboard.
2. Click a date on the Calendar Navigator, and that day displays in Day view. If the calendar shows in Work Week, Week, or Month view, double-click any date on the calendar.
3. A new Appointment window opens, as shown in Figure 13-2. See "Create Appointments" elsewhere in this chapter for more information.
4. After you have entered your information, click **Save & Close** to close the Appointment window.

CREATE A NEW TASK

1. In the Home tab New group, click **New Items** and then click **Task** to open a Task window. In Outlook, a task is an item you track until it is completed. It may not have a specific timetable, but it is something you want to monitor.
2. After you have created the task, click the appropriate choice in the Task's Follow-Up group. Click **Save & Close** to close the Task window.

13

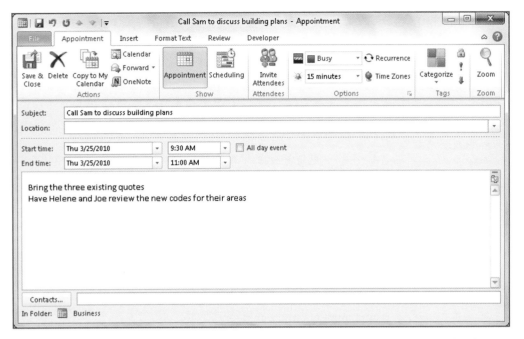

Figure 13-2: *An appointment or an all-day event can be any date-related activity, such as due dates or birthdays.*

Customize the Calendar

As you have seen with the rest of Outlook, there are many ways you can customize the calendar to meet your needs. You can change the way the calendar displays time intervals, the font size and face, the background color, and any additional options as you require.

CHANGE THE TIME SCALES

The default display of time intervals, or *scales*, on your Calendar grid is 30 minutes. If you want to change these scales to reflect another time interval:

1. In the Calendar grid, right-click any blank area.

2. In the View tab Arrangement group, click **View Settings** to open a menu of options.

3. Click the time scale setting you want to show in the calendar.

CHANGE THE FONT FACE AND SIZE

You can change the font in both your calendar and your Task list.

1. Right-click any blank area in the Calendar grid.

2. Click **View Settings** to open the Advanced View Settings Calendar dialog box.

3. Click **Other Settings** to open the Format Day/Week/Month View dialog box.

QUICKSTEPS

NAVIGATING THE CALENDAR

The Date Navigator, which by default is in the upper-left corner of the Outlook View, allows you to pick any date from April 1, 1601, to September 30, 4500. To cover this almost 2,900-year span, Outlook provides several efficient tools.

December 2009

Su	Mo	Tu	We	Th	Fr	Sa
29	30	1	2	3	4	5
6	7	8	9	10	11	12
13	14	15	16	17	18	19
20	21	22	23	24	25	26
27	28	29	30	31	1	2
3	4	5	6	7	8	9

- **Display a day** by clicking it in the Date Navigator. Or, from anywhere in Outlook, click **Calendar** on the Outlook View.

- **Display a day with appointments** by clicking a boldface day in the Date Navigator.

- **Display a week** by clicking to the left of the first day of the week.

- **Display several weeks** by clicking to the left of the weeks and dragging the pointer over multiple weeks.

- **Display a month** by dragging across the weeks of the month.

- **Change the month from one to the next** by clicking the left or right arrow in the month bar.

- **Scroll through a list of months** by clicking the month name in the Calendar Navigator to display a month list, and moving the pointer up or down to select an individual month.

- **Directly display any date** by clicking the **Go To Date Dialog Box Launcher** at the right of the Go To group in the Home tab. This opens the Go To Date dialog box. Type in the date, and click **OK**. You can also open the Go To Date dialog box by pressing **CTRL+G**.

Go To Date

Date: Tue 4/20/2010   ▼
Show in: Week Calendar   ▼

            OK   Cancel

–Or–

In the View tab Current View group, click **View Settings** to open the Advanced View Settings Calendar dialog box, and click **Other Settings**.

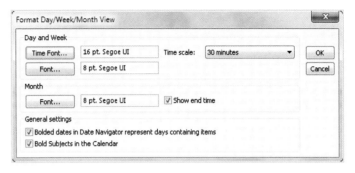

Format Day/Week/Month View

Day and Week

| Time Font... | 16 pt. Segoe UI | Time scale: | 30 minutes ▼ | OK |
| Font... | 8 pt. Segoe UI | | | Cancel |

Month

Font...   8 pt. Segoe UI   ☑ Show end time

General settings

☑ Bolded dates in Date Navigator represent days containing items
☑ Bold Subjects in the Calendar

4. Click **Time Font** to open the Font dialog box to change the font face and size for times in the Day, Work Week, and Week views.

- Click **Font** to change the font face.

- Click **Font Style** to choose from the various font styles, such as Regular, Italic, Bold, and so on. The styles available will vary, depending on which font face you have chosen in the previous step.

- Click **Size** to set the size of the font that will show the times on your calendar in Day, Work Week, and Week views.

- Click **OK** to close the Font dialog box and save your choices.

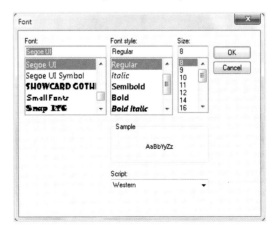

Font

Font:	Font style:	Size:	
Segoe UI	Regular	8	OK
Segoe UI	Regular	8	Cancel
Segoe UI Symbol	Italic	9	
SHOWCARD GOTHI	Semibold	10	
Small Fonts	Bold	11	
Snap ITC	Bold Italic	12	
		14	
		16	

Sample

AaBbYyZz

Script:
Western ▼

NOTE

You can also access the time scale using the Advanced View Settings. Right-click the **Calendar** grid, click **View Settings**, click **Other Settings**, click the **Time Scale** down arrow, and choose the time scale you want. Then click **OK** twice to close the dialog boxes.

TIP

To quickly change your Calendar display from Day view to Work Week, Week, or Month view, click the appropriate button in the View tab Arrangement group.

5. Click **Font** to open the Font dialog box to change how information other than the time displays in Day, Work Week, and Week views.

6. Click **OK** to close the Font dialog box and save your choices.

7. Click **Font** under Month, and follow steps 5–7.

8. Click **OK** to close the Format Day/Week/Month View dialog box. Click **OK** once more to close the Advanced View Settings Calendar dialog box.

CONFIGURE ADDITIONAL SETTINGS

You can open the Advanced View Settings dialog box in two different ways:

● From the View tab Current View group, click **View Settings** in the Current View group.

–Or–

● Right-click any blank section of the Calendar grid, and click **View Settings** at the bottom of the context menu.

From the Advanced View Settings dialog box, you can tell Calendar how to display the items in your Calendar and Date Navigators.

1. In the Format Day/Week/Month View dialog box, under General Settings, Bolded Dates In Date Navigator is set by default. If you do not want these dates to appear in bold text, clear this check box.

2. Clear the **Bold Subjects In The Calendar** check box to have the headings or subjects of your activities appear in regular font in your Calendar grid.

3. Click **OK** to close the dialog box.

UNDERSTAND THE VIEW TAB

The View tab includes several options, some of which are also available when you display a menu by right-clicking in a blank area of the Calendar grid.

1. Open the Outlook Calendar, and click the **View** tab.

2. In the Arrangement group, you see several options, including:

● **Day** displays detailed information about each appointment in Day view.

● **Work Week** displays all the appointments you have set on this calendar for the days you have set in your work week, normally Monday through Friday.

QUICKSTEPS

USING THE NAVIGATION AND READING PANES

While the default views in Outlook Calendar are designed to display your information in the way many users need to see it, you can change how the navigation and Reading panes display information.

CUSTOMIZE THE OUTLOOK VIEW IN THE NAVIGATION PANE

By default, the Outlook View appears at the left of the Calendar grid on the navigation pane. However, you can choose to minimize it, turn it off entirely, or change the buttons that display on it. To make these changes:

1. On the View tab Layout group, click **Navigation Pane** to open a drop-down menu.

   - Click **Minimized** to minimize the navigation pane's display.

   - Click **Off** to turn it off entirely.

2. Click **Options** to open the Navigation Pane Options dialog box from which you can choose which buttons appear on the Outlook View and the order in which they appear.

3. Click **OK** when you are finished making changes.

USE THE READING PANE

In Outlook Calendar, the Reading pane is available when you want to see the contents of the appointments, meetings, and tasks displayed on your Calendar. By default, it is turned off, but you can change this. From the View tab Layout group, click **Reading Pane** to open a drop-down menu.

1. Choose **Right** to display the Reading pane at the right side of the Calendar grid.

2. Select **Bottom** to display it at the bottom of the grid.

Continued . . .

- **Week** displays a seven-day work week, including Sunday, shown on the left of the week's Calendar grid, and Saturday, shown on the right.

- **Month** shows an entire month on the Calendar grid. If you click the down arrow, a menu opens with options for displaying appointments in various degrees of details—from low detail to high detail.

- **Schedule** displays your appointments, meetings, and other commitments in a timeline format.

- **Time Scale** opens a menu on which you can change how time intervals in the time bar display on your Calendar grid, as well as a link to change the time zone.

3. Click **Color** in the Color group to change the default grid colors.

4. The Layout group lets you tell Outlook how to display the information you have entered.

   - Click **Daily Task List** to tell Outlook how to display your tasks in the Day, Work Week, and Week views.

   - Click **Outlook View** and **Reading Pane** to choose which buttons are displayed and in which order. See the "Using the Navigation and Reading Panes" QuickSteps for more information.

   - Click **To-Do Bar** to tell Outlook how to display the To-Do bar.

5. The People Pane group connects Outlook to online social networks such as LinkedIn and Facebook. You can connect with both your business and personal contacts without leaving Outlook. Click the down arrow to set your options.

   - Click **Normal** to display the People pane at the bottom of the Calendar grid.

   - Click the **Minimized** setting to shrink the People pane.

   - Click **Off** to turn off the Internet connection.

   - Click **Account Settings** to add new settings or modify your current settings.

6. The Window group has several buttons.

   - Click **Reminders Window** to see a list of open reminders.

   - Click **Open In New Window** to open your calendar in a new window.

   - Click **Close All Items** to open the Close Meeting dialog box.

USING THE NAVIGATION AND READING PANES *(Continued)*

3. Click **Off** to turn off the Reading pane entirely.

4. If the Options button is grayed out (unavailable), click **Right** or **Bottom** again to make the Options choice available. Click **Options** to open the Reading Pane dialog box to make the following choices:

   • Click **Mark Items As Read When Viewed In the Reading Pane** to have each item marked as being read.

   • Type the number of seconds you want Outlook to wait before marking the item.

   • Click **Mark Item As Read When Selection Changes** to show items as having been read without any time delay.

   • Clear the **Single Key Reading Using Space Bar** to turn off the ability to read through items one key at a time by pressing the **SPACEBAR** on your keyboard.

5. Click **OK** to close the Reading Pane dialog box.

Customize Calendar Views

As with Mail and Contacts, you can create customized calendar views, either by modifying an existing view or by creating a new one. You create or modify a view from the View tab Current View group.

MODIFY A DAY, WORK WEEK, WEEK, OR MONTH VIEW

1. Click **Calendar** in Outlook View to open the Calendar.

2. From the View tab Current View group, click **Change View**.

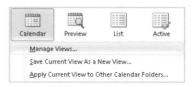

3. From the drop-down menu, click **Manage Views** to open the Manage All Views dialog box.

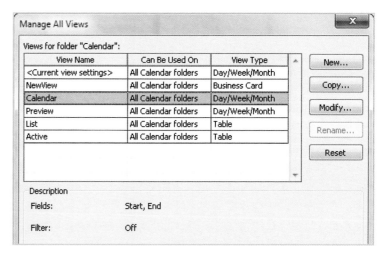

4. Select the view name you want to modify. Click **Modify** to open the Advanced View Settings dialog box for your selection, as seen in Figure 13-3. To simplify your choices, click **Only Show Views Created For This Folder**.

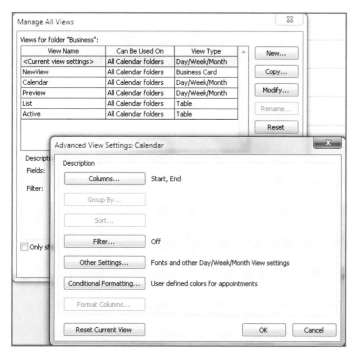

Figure 13-3: You can modify existing views as well as create new views to suit your needs.

5. Click the **Columns** button to open the Date/Time Fields dialog box. Select a field from the Available Date/Time Fields list. The Start and End fields set how each date and time item is displayed within the current view. Choose from the following:

   ● Click **Created** if you want the start or end time to be the time and date the item was created.

   ● Click **Due By** to have either the start or end time be the date and time at which the item must be completed.

   ● Click **End** to display the ending time or date in either the Start or End field.

   ● Click **Recurrence Range End** or **Recurrence Range Start** to show when a recurring appointment starts or ends.

   ● Click **Start** to show when an appointment begins.

   ● Click the **End** button if the new field is to replace the End field.

   ● Click **OK** to close the dialog box.

6. After you have made your selection from the Available Date/Time Fields list, click **Start** to have your choice appear in the Start field.

7. Click **End** to have it appear in the End field.

8. Click the **Select Available Fields From** down arrow to open a list of other field lists from which you can choose.

9. Click **OK** when you have completed your choices. You are returned to the Advanced View Settings dialog box.

10. Click **Filter** to open the Filter dialog box. You can use filters to create a customized view that shows only specific types of appointments. For example, you can create a view that shows only management meetings or family events.

   ● In the Appointments And Meetings tab, enter any words by which you want to filter your calendar entries for this view.

   ● In the More Choices tab, click **Categories** to select the category or multiple categories that you want to display.

   ● Select what types of items you want to include in this view, as well as the size of the items to display.

   ● In the Advanced tab, you can enter specific criteria to display in your view, as well as set conditions.

You can also open the Advanced View Settings dialog box from a Day, Work Week, Week, or Month view by right-clicking an empty part of your Calendar grid and clicking **View Settings**.

- After you have finished making your choices, click **OK** to save your view and return to the Advanced View Settings dialog box.
- Click **OK** one more time to return to the Manage All Views dialog box.
- Click **Apply View** to set your new view.
- Click **OK** to apply the view and exit the dialog box, or click **Close** to close the dialog box and cancel any changes.

11. Reopen the Manage All Views dialog box, and click **Modify** as described earlier. Click **Other Settings** to open the Format Day/Week/Month View Settings dialog box as described in "Customize the Calendar" earlier in this chapter.

12. Again, reopen the Manage All Views dialog box and click **Modify** as described earlier. Click **Conditional Formatting** to open the Conditional Formatting dialog box.
    - Click **Add** to create a new rule.
    - Click in the **Name** text box, and type a name for this rule.
    - Click the **Color** down arrow to choose a color for this rule.
    - Click **Condition** to open the Filter dialog box. Type the word or words to create this filter.
    - Click **In** to choose where Outlook is to find the words you are searching for.
    - Enter any additional filter information you require.
    - Click **OK** to close the Filter dialog box.
    - Click **OK** to close the Customize View dialog box.

13. Click **OK** to save your changes.

14. If you want to undo a change you made to the current view, click **Reset Current View** in the Advanced View Settings dialog box.

MODIFY A LIST VIEW

1. In Outlook, click **Calendar** on Outlook View to open the calendar.

2. Click **Change View** in the Current View group to view your choices.

3. Select **Manage Views** to open the Manage All Views dialog box, and then click **List** in the Views For Folder Calendar.

4. Click **Modify** to open the Advanced View Settings: List dialog box, as seen in Figure 13-4.

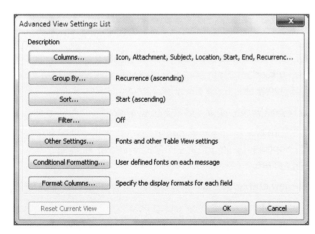

Figure 13-4: The Advanced View Settings: List dialog box offers more choices than the Calendar view.

5. Click **Columns** to set the columns that will display in this modified view. Choose from the Available Columns list, and click **Add** to add them to your list.

   - Select an item in the Show These Columns In This Order list, and click **Move Up** or **Move Down** to change its position in your modified list.

   - Select an item in the Show These Columns In This Order list, and click **Remove** to delete the item from the list.

6. Click **Group By** to set how items are grouped.

7. Click **Sort** to determine how the items are sorted. You can select up to four fields, and each field can be sorted either A–Z (ascending) or Z–A (descending).

8. Click **Filter** to set filters for this view.

9. Follow the same steps as described in "Modify a Day, Work Week, Week, or Month View" earlier in this chapter for the Other Settings, Conditional Formatting, and Format Columns fields.

10. Click **OK** to close the Advanced View Settings: List dialog box.

CREATE A NEW VIEW

1. In Outlook, click **Calendar** on Outlook View to open the calendar.

2. On the View tab, click **Change View** in the Current View group to view your choices.

3. Select **Manage Views** to open the Manage All Views dialog box, and click **New**.

4. The Create A New View dialog box appears.

   - Type a name for this new view.

   - Click the type of view this will be from the six options displayed.

   - Click **This Folder, Visible To Everyone** if you want to make your new view available in this folder to everyone. Choose one of the other two options, if required.

   - Click **OK** to open the Advanced View Settings dialog box for your new view.

   - Depending on the view you are creating, options in the Advanced View Settings dialog box vary. Not all the options described in the "Modify a Day, Work Week, Week, or Month View" section are available for every type of view.

   - Click **OK** to save the new view and close the dialog box.

5. Your new view will appear on the Manage All Views dialog box.

6. Click **Apply View** to immediately see the new view, or click **Close** to close the dialog box and stay in the current view. The next time you click Change View, the new view is included on the list.

Set Up the Calendar

Calendar allows you to define your normal work week in terms of the days it contains and when it starts, the normal start and end of your working day, the holidays you observe, and what you consider the first week of the year. To set up your calendar:

1. Click **Calendar** in the Outlook View. From the View tab Arrangement group, click the **Calendar Options Dialog Box Launcher** at the bottom-right area to open the Outlook Options dialog box.

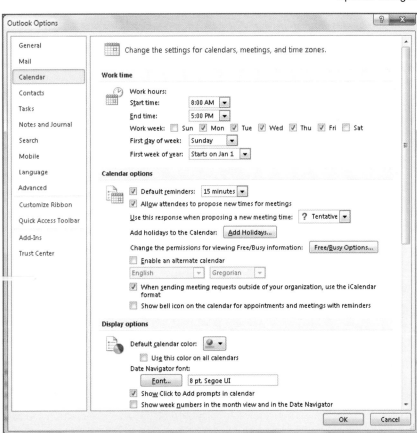

2. In the Outlook Options dialog box, click **Calendar** to display the Calendar Options view, if it does not already appear, as shown in Figure 13-5.

3. Click the **Start Time** down arrow to choose the normal start time for your working day if it is other than 8:00 A.M. Click the **End Time** down arrow to change the end of your working day if it is other than 5:00 P.M.

4. Click the days of the week you consider workdays if they are different from the default of Monday through Friday.

5. Click the **First Day Of Week** down arrow to select the day of the week you want considered the first day of the week if it is a day other than Sunday. The weeks in the Date Navigator will begin with this day.

6. Click the **First Week Of Year** down arrow to choose a definition for the first week of the year if it does not begin January 1. If you turn on week numbering, week number 1 is defined in this manner.

7. Under Calendar Options, change the **Default Reminder** times to other than the 15 minutes that shows, if necessary.

8. Click **Allow Attendees To Propose New Times For Meetings** if you choose to allow this.

9. Click the **Use This Response When You Propose New Meeting Times** down arrow to change the automatic response to new meetings.

Figure 13-5: You can set Calendar options, such as defining your work week and displaying week numbers, the time zone, and holidays.

10. Click **Add Holidays** to open the Add Holidays To Calendar dialog box.

   a. Click the check box for the country and/or religious holidays you want added.

   b. Click **OK** to close the dialog box.

11. Click the **Free/Busy Options** button if you want to make changes to how your time is displayed to others. See "Set Free/Busy Options" next.

12. Click **Enable Alternate Calendar**, if desired, and use the drop-down lists to choose them.

13. Under most circumstances, it is best to leave the **When Sending Meeting Requests** check box selected.

14. Clear the **Show Bell Icon** check box if you do not want this reminder icon to display.

15. Clear **Show "Click To Add" Prompts On The Calendar** if you do not want this default prompt to display.

16. Under Display Options, click the **Default Color** down arrow to choose from a list of colors other than the default blue for the background on your Calendar grid.

17. Click **Use This Color On All Calendars** if you want this new color to be used on all calendars you create.

18. Click the **Font** button to change the Date Navigator font.

19. Click **Show Week Numbers In The Month View And Date Navigator** to display week numbers.

20. Make any necessary changes to remaining options, including when you want to show your free time in Schedule View and to vary views when more than one calendar is displayed.

21. Under Time Zones, make any changes necessary. You can choose up to two time zones to display. You can define and name your current time zone, as well as an additional one, if you choose.

   ● If you are going to use two time zones, click in the **Label** text box, and type a name that will identify the current time zone appearing in the Time Zone drop-down list.

   ● Click **Show A Second Time Zone** to add a second time zone.

   ● Click in the **Label** text box, and type a name identifying this second time zone.

   ● Click the **Time Zone** down arrow to display a list of time zones from which you can choose.

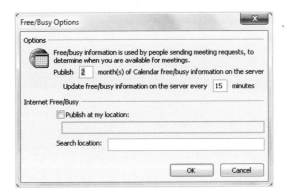

- Click **Adjust For Daylight Saving Time** if it applies to either time zone you've selected.
- Click **Swap Time Zones** to swap which time zone displays on the left of the time bar.

22. Make any necessary adjustments in the Scheduling Assistant and Resource Scheduling sections to display calendar details or to manage resources, such as conference room or automobile availability.

23. Click **OK** to save your changes.

SET FREE/BUSY OPTIONS

If you and your coworkers are part of a Microsoft Exchange network, are willing to share your schedules over the Internet, or can all access a common server, you can store your free/busy times and make them available to each other to schedule meetings and other times together. In this case, requests for meetings are handled automatically. The request will be matched against the group's free/busy schedule, and meetings will be scheduled at available times. For an individual to set up his or her free/busy options:

1. From the File tab, click **Options** and click **Calendar**.

2. In the Calendar Options section, click **Free/Busy Options**. The Free/Busy Options dialog box appears.

3. Click in the **Publish** box to type the number of months of free/busy information you want to store on the server.

4. Click the **Update Free/Busy Information** text box to enter how often you want the server to update your information.

5. In the Internet Free/Busy section, click **Publish At My Location**, and enter the URL (Uniform Resource Locator, or Web address) of your Internet calendar if that applies to your situation. See the "Understanding Internet Calendars" QuickFacts later in this chapter.

6. Click **Search Location** and type the URL of servers you want Outlook to search for the free/busy information of others.

7. Click **OK** to return to the Outlook Options dialog box.

Maintain Multiple Calendars

If your calendar is becoming cluttered and hard to use, you might try separating it into two side-by-side calendars. For example, create one for business appointments and one for family appointments.

1. Click **Calendar** in the Outlook View.

2. On the Folder tab, click **New Calendar** in the New group.

3. Click **Name** and type a name for your new calendar.

4. Click the **Folder Contains** down arrow, and select the type of information the calendar will contain.

5. In the Select Where To Place The Folder area, determine where the calendar will be created.

6. Click **OK** to close the Create New Folder dialog box. Your new calendar displays in the navigation pane, above the Outlook Views.

7. Click the check box to the left of your new calendar to display it side by side with your original calendar, as seen in Figure 13-6.

VIEW MULTIPLE CALENDARS

You can view a calendar in a new window, side by side with other calendars, or stack transparent calendars over each other to find a common free time slot on several different calendars.

To view a second calendar in a new window:

1. Click **Calendar** in the Outlook View, and right-click the name of the second calendar in the Folder list under My Calendars.

2. In the resulting menu, click **Open In New Window**.

To open several calendars side by side:

1. In the Calendar Outlook View, click the check box for each calendar you want to view.

2. All the calendars will be displayed next to each other in your Calendar grid.

To overlay your calendars:

1. In the Calendar, from the Folder List, click the check box for each calendar you want to stack. The calendars display next to each other in your Calendar grid.

CAUTION

At least one calendar must always be displayed, but you can create up to 30 calendars if you choose.

13

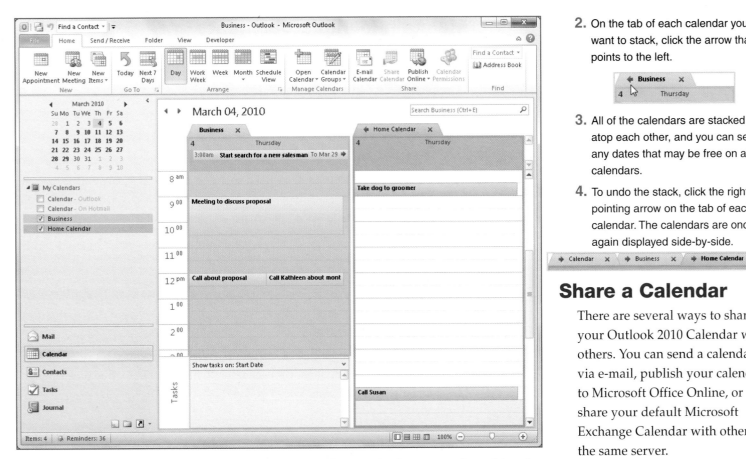

Figure 13-6: By displaying two calendars side-by-side, you can, for example, show personal appointments that have no effect on your work calendar.

2. On the tab of each calendar you want to stack, click the arrow that points to the left.

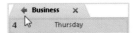

3. All of the calendars are stacked atop each other, and you can see any dates that may be free on all calendars.

4. To undo the stack, click the right-pointing arrow on the tab of each calendar. The calendars are once again displayed side-by-side.

| Calendar X | Business X | Home Calendar X |

Share a Calendar

There are several ways to share your Outlook 2010 Calendar with others. You can send a calendar via e-mail, publish your calendar to Microsoft Office Online, or share your default Microsoft Exchange Calendar with others on the same server.

SEND A CALENDAR IN E-MAIL

You can send any calendar you own to another in the body of an e-mail message. The person receiving the calendar will see a snapshot of it at a given moment in time. If the recipient uses Outlook 2010, he or she can open the calendar snapshot as an Outlook Calendar and display it either side by side or as an overlay with any other calendars. The downside of using a calendar snapshot is that the calendar you send is not automatically updated when

you make changes. If the e-mail recipient needs a regularly updated calendar, consider publishing your calendar to Microsoft Office Online, using a calendar-publishing Web service, or, if your office has it, sharing your calendars via an Exchange server.

To send a calendar snapshot:

1. In Calendar's Outlook View, select the calendar you want to share.

2. On the Home tab Share group, click **E-mail Calendar**.

   –Or–

   In the Outlook View, right-click the calendar you want to share. From the context menu, click **Share** and click **E-mail Calendar**.

   In either case, an e-mail message box opens with the Send A Calendar Via E-Mail dialog box in the message portion of the e-mail window.

3. Click the **Calendar** down arrow, and click the calendar you want to e-mail.

4. Click the **Date Range** down arrow, and click the time period of the calendar that you want to send.

5. Click the **Detail** icon, and select the type of calendar information you want to send.

6. If you chose Availability Only in step 5, click **Show Time Within My Working Hours Only** if that is what you want.

7. Click **Advanced** and, if desired, click **Include Details Of Items Marked Private** and/or click **Include Attachments**.

8. Click **E-mail Layout** and click either the **Daily Schedule** or **List Of Events** format.

9. Click **OK** to close the dialog box.

10. Click **To** and type the recipient's e-mail address.

11. Click **Send** to send the e-mail.

PUBLISH A CALENDAR TO MICROSOFT OFFICE ONLINE

Microsoft offers a publishing service for your calendars. This method does not require Microsoft Exchange for either the user or the owner of the calendar. The first time you use the service, you must register using your Microsoft

CAUTION

Be careful when you set the date range of a calendar snapshot. If you set it for a long period, the e-mail file might be too big for the recipient's e-mail Inbox.

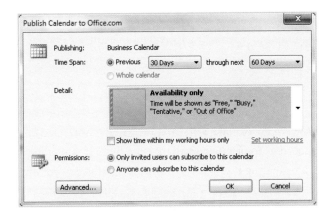

Windows Live ID account. If you don't yet have an account, you may follow the instructions on the screen to obtain one for free.

1. In Calendar's Outlook View, right-click the calendar you want to share.

2. Click **Share** and click **Publish To Office.com**. Go through the registration procedure, if needed. The Publish Calendar To Office.com dialog box appears.

3. Click a **Time Span** button to choose whether you want to send a section of the calendar (recommended) or all of it. If selecting a time range, click the **Previous** and **Through Next** down arrows to set the time span for the calendar.

4. Click **Only Invited Users Can Subscribe To This Calendar** if you want to restrict access to your calendar.

5. Click **Anyone Can Subscribe To This Calendar** if you want to share your Calendar with anyone.

6. Click **Advanced** to open the Published Calendar Settings dialog box.

7. Click **Automatic Uploads** if you want Outlook 2010 to periodically update your published calendar automatically.

8. Click **Single Upload** if you do not want to have your calendar updated.

9. Click **OK** to publish your calendar.

10. After your calendar has been successfully published, you are prompted to create an e-mail announcing this fact. Click **Yes** to create the e-mail, or click **No** to close the dialog box.

Use the Calendar

Within the calendar, you can enter appointments, meetings, events, and tasks. These can be entered in several ways and with a number of options, as you'll see in this section.

Create Appointments

Appointments can be entered in any view and in several different ways. Independent of the view you are using, the different ways can be grouped into direct entry and window entry. *Direct entry* means simply typing directly on the calendar, while *window entry* uses a window to gather the information, which is

TIP

Try using text dates, as described in the "Entering Dates and Times" QuickSteps, and you'll be amazed at how Outlook can interpret what you enter.

13

QUICKFACTS

UNDERSTANDING INTERNET CALENDARS

There are several types of Internet calendars. We've discussed sharing the calendar via e-mail and publishing it to Microsoft Office Online. There is another type of Internet calendar that is downloaded from calendar-publishing services or special websites that host calendars. This downloaded calendar is created and saved in Outlook. Most Internet calendar companies charge a subscription fee for this service. While calendar snapshots are not updated with any regularity, a subscription to an Internet calendar means that your calendar is synchronized on a regular basis with a calendar saved on a web server. The updates that result from the synchronization are downloaded to your Internet calendar.

TIP

Combine direct entry and window entry to get the benefits of both.

NOTE

You can move an appointment without changing the duration by dragging it in any direction. This will change your start and end times but leave the duration constant.

---

then displayed on the calendar. Direct entry is fast if you want to make a quick notation. Window entry allows you to select and set a number of options.

ENTER APPOINTMENTS DIRECTLY

You can directly enter an appointment on the calendar in any view by clicking a date or time and typing the description. If you want the entry longer or shorter than the default half-hour (or whatever standard duration you have selected), just drag the top or bottom border up or down to change the time. If you want to move the appointment, simply drag it to where you want it in the current day or to another day in either the calendar itself or the Date Navigator. To change the properties of an appointment, double-click the appointment, which opens the context menu, where a number of properties can be set.

To directly enter appointments:

1. Click any date and time in the Calendar grid in the Day, Work Week, Week, Month, or Schedule view. Type a short description of the appointment, and press **ENTER**.

2. Place the mouse pointer on the sizing handle at the bottom border of the appointment. Drag the border down until the end of the appointment time.

3. If you need to change the beginning time of your appointment, drag the top border up or down until the proper time is reflected in the calendar.

ENTER ALL-DAY EVENTS DIRECTLY

An all-day event is an activity that normally lasts at least 24 hours, although you can designate something as an event that lasts less than 24 hours but takes most of your time that day, such as a company picnic. Examples of events are conferences, seminars, and holidays. If events are tied to specific dates, they are considered annual events, such as a birthday or holiday. When you enter an event, it is considered free time, not busy. You create events differently than appointments. All events appear in the banner at the top of the daily schedule, while all appointments are on the calendar itself. To directly enter an event:

1. With the Outlook Calendar open in Day, Work Week, or Week view, select a day in the Calendar grid when the event will take place.

2. Click in the colored area at the top of the daily schedule, just under the date header, type the event name, and press **ENTER**.

QUICKSTEPS

ENTERING DATES AND TIMES

The Outlook Calendar allows you to enter dates and times as text and convert that text to numeric dates and times. For example, you can type "<u>next tue</u>" and be given next Tuesday's date, or you can type "<u>sep ninth</u>" and see that date. You can type this way in any date or time field in Outlook, such as the Go To Date dialog box, reached by pressing **CTRL+G**, or right-clicking any empty spot on the Calendar grid while in Day, Work Week, Week, or Month view. Likewise, you can type in the start and end date and time fields in the appointment and event views or the Meeting dialog box. Some of the things you can do include:

- Abbreviate months and days (for example, *Dec* or *fri*).

- Ignore capitalization and other punctuation (for example, *wednesday, april,* and *lincolns birthday*).

- Use words that indicate dates and times (for example, *noon, midnight, tomorrow, yesterday, today, now, next week, last month, five days ago, in three months, this Saturday,* and *two weeks from now*). Words you can use include *after, ago, before, beforehand, beginning, end, ending, following, for, from, last, next, now, previous, start, that, this, through, till, tomorrow, yesterday, today,* and *until.*

- Spell out specific dates and times (for example, *August ninth, first of December, April 19th, midnight, noon, two twenty p.m.,* and *five o'clock a.m.*).

- Indicate holidays that fall on the same date every year (for example, *New Year's Eve, New Year's Day, Lincoln's Birthday, Valentine's Day, Washington's Birthday, St. Patrick's Day, Cinco de Mayo, Independence Day, Halloween, Veterans' Day, Christmas Eve, Christmas Day,* and *Boxing Day*).

ENTER APPOINTMENTS IN A WINDOW

As an alternative to directly entering appointments and events, you can use a New Appointment window, seen in Figure 13-7, to accomplish the same objective and immediately be able to enter a lot more information. To open a New Appointment window:

1. In the Outlook Calendar, in the Home tab New group, click **New Appointment**.

2. Click **Subject** and type the subject of the appointment. This text becomes the description in the calendar, with the location added parenthetically and the date and time determining where the appointment goes on the calendar.

3. Press **TAB**. Type the location, if relevant, in the Location text box.

4. Click the **Start Time** down arrow on the left to display a small calendar in which you can choose a date.

5. Click the down arrow on the right, and select a start time.

6. Click the **End Time** down arrows, and select the end date and time. By default, the end date for an appointment is the same date as the start date unless you have selected All Day Event.

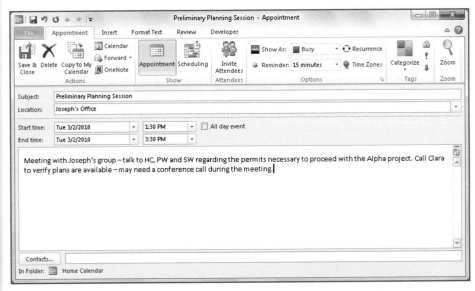

Figure 13-7: The Appointment window is used to set up or change an appointment.

Depending on where you click in the Calendar grid,
the window that opens may be either an Appointment
window or an Event window. The only difference, other
than the title, is that All Day Event is selected and the
free/busy indicator is set to Free for an event. If you
get an Event window when you want an Appointment
window, simply clear the All Day Event check box.

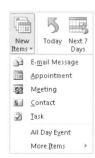

7. If you have selected more than one time zone, select the appropriate time zone for this appointment.

8. Type any notes or other information necessary in the message section of the Appointment dialog box.

9. In the Appointment tab Options group, click the **Show As** down arrow, and tell Outlook how to display this time slot on your calendar.

   • **Free** This time is available to be scheduled for an appointment.

   • **Tentative** This time is potentially scheduled, but is currently not finalized.

   • **Busy** This time is now unavailable to be scheduled for anything else.

   • **Out Of Office** This time is unavailable and cannot be scheduled.

10. In the Appointment tab Options group, click the **Reminder** down arrow, and set the reminder time. See "Use Reminders" later in this chapter for more information.

11. In the Appointment tab Actions group, click **Save & Close** to save your appointment.

ENTER AN EVENT IN A WINDOW

To enter an all-day event:

1. In the Outlook Calendar, from the Home tab New group, click **New Items**.

2. Click **All Day Event**. The New Event window opens.

3. Click **Subject** to enter text describing the event as it will appear on your calendar.

4. Click **Location** to type information about the location. By default, All Day Event is selected.

5. Repeat steps 8–11 from "Enter Appointments in a Window." The start and end times become unavailable; the reminder, by default, goes to 18 hours; and Show Time As changes to Free, as seen in Figure 13-8.

Enter Recurring Appointments

Often, you'll have appointments and events that recur predictably, for example, a weekly staff meeting, a monthly planning meeting, a monthly lunch with a friend, and birthdays. You obviously do not want to re-enter these every week, month, or year. Outlook has a feature that allows you to enter these activities

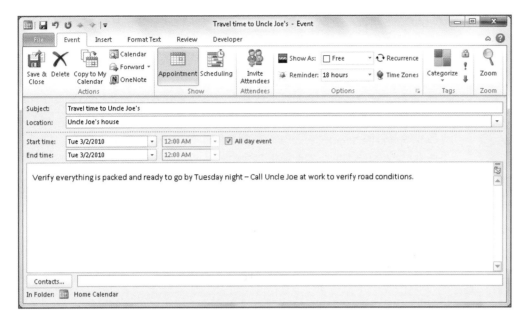

Figure 13-8: An Event window looks much like the Appointment window, except All Day Event is selected.

Recurring appointments and events can save you a lot of time re-entering activities, but they can also generate a lot of entries, which may unnecessarily fill your calendar. Enter only the recurring appointments that you want to remember.

once and have them reappear on a given frequency for as long as you want.

1. Create a new appointment as described in "Enter Appointments in a Window."

2. In the Appointments tab Options group, click **Recurrence**. The Appointment Recurrence dialog box appears, as shown in Figure 13-9.

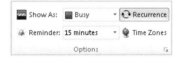

3. Click the **Start** down arrow, and select the start time of this recurring appointment.

4. Click the **End** down arrow, and select the end time.

5. Click the **Duration** down arrow, and select the length of time this appointment lasts.

6. Click **Recurrence Pattern** and choose how often this appointment occurs. The specific fields you enter to complete the pattern will differ, depending on the appointment interval you choose.

7. Under Range Of Recurrence, click the **Start** down arrow, select the date this appointment starts, the number of times it occurs, and its ending date.

8. Click **OK** to close the Appointment Recurrence dialog box.

9. Click **Save & Close**.

EDIT RECURRING APPOINTMENTS

To change one instance of a recurring appointment:

1. In the Outlook Calendar, locate and double-click a recurring appointment in any calendar view. The Open Recurring Item dialog box appears.

2. Click **Open This Occurrence** if you want to make a change to only this instance of the appointment.

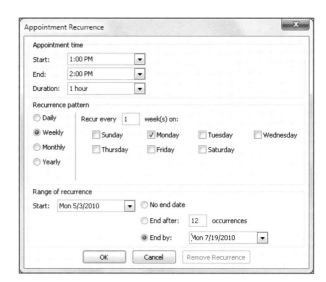

Figure 13-9: *Use the Appointment Recurrence dialog box to schedule recurring appointments automatically.*

3. Click **OK** to open the Appointment window and make the necessary changes to this occurrence of the appointment.

4. In the Appointment Occurrence tab Actions group, click **Save & Close**.

To change all instances of a recurring appointment:

1. In the calendar, locate and double-click the recurring appointment in any calendar view. The Open Recurring Item dialog box appears.

2. Click **Open The Series** if you want to make a change to the recurring appointment itself.

3. Click **OK** to open the Appointment window.

4. In the Appointment Occurrence tab Options group, click **Recurrence** (if you forgot to click Open The Series in step 2, you will see "Edit Series" in place of "Recurrence"). The Appointment Recurrence dialog box appears.

5. Make the necessary changes to this appointment, and click **OK**.

6. In the Appointment Occurrence tab Actions group, click **Save & Close**.

Move Appointments

If an appointment changes times within a day, you can move it to its new time by simply dragging it to that new time, as you saw earlier. If you entered an event on the wrong day, or if an appointment changes days, you can drag it to the correct day in the Work Week, Week, or Month view or in the Date Navigator. You cannot drag a recurring appointment to a date that skips over another occurrence of the same appointment. You can, however, change a recurring appointment to another date before the next one occurs. The different ways to move appointments or events are:

- Drag the appointment to the day you want in a Work Week, Week, or Month view; Calendar Navigator; or Date Navigator. You can drag an appointment anywhere in the Calendar grid by dragging from anywhere in the appointment, except at the expansion points on the middle of the sides.

- When you drag an appointment to a new day, it will be placed in the same time slot. You can change the time by dragging it to the new time, either before or after you move it to the new day.

TIP

You can delete a single instance of a recurring activity without affecting the rest of the series. If you choose to delete a recurring activity, the dialog box asks if you want to delete the current instance of the activity or the entire series.

TIP

You can copy an activity by right-dragging it (use the right mouse button) to where you want the copy and selecting **Copy** from the context menu that appears when you release the right mouse button.

NOTE

Reminders are wonderful if they are used sparingly. If they are constantly going off and you dismiss them, then they are of little value. The default is for a reminder to be automatically turned on, so you must turn it off in a new appointment if you don't want it.

Use Reminders

When you have set a reminder for an appointment, the Reminder dialog box appears at the time you have set before the appointment. You have several choices in the dialog box.

- Click **Dismiss All** to close the reminder and tell it not to appear again.
- Click **Snooze** to tell the dialog box when to remind you again but close the reminder for now.
- Click **Open Item** to open the Appointment window so that you can make changes to the appointment, the reminder, or both.
- Click **Dismiss** to close only the highlighted reminder.

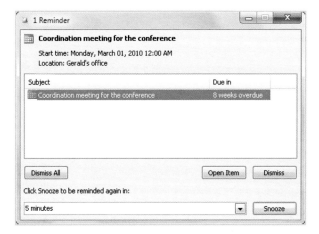

Print Calendars

When you have completed making entries on your calendar, you may want to take it with you, away from your computer, for reference and to jot new appointments on. For this reason, Outlook includes a number of printed formats to fit your needs.

To print your calendar:

1. In any view in Outlook Calendar, click the **File** tab.
2. Click **Print** to open the Print Setting dialog box, as seen in Figure 13-10.

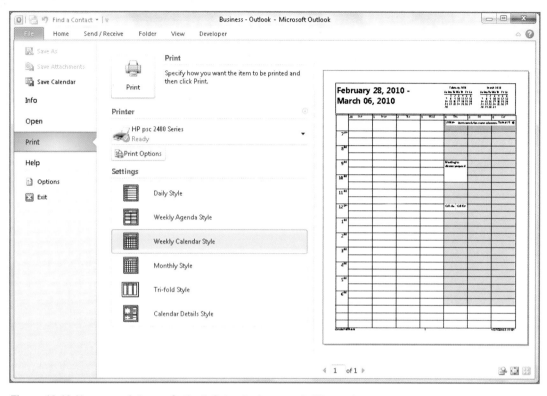

Figure 13-10: You can print your Outlook Calendar in several different formats.

3. In the Settings area, select the format for your printed calendar. There are several from which to choose, and each style will display in the Preview area.

4. Click **Print Options** and click the print style you want to print. Your choices are determined by the Calendar view you have chosen.

5. Click **Page Setup** to open the Page Setup dialog box shown in Figure 13-11.

   a. Click the **Format** tab, and make any changes in the Options and Fonts sections.

   b. Click the **Shading** check box if you want gray shading to be used in your printed calendar.

   c. Click the **Paper** tab to choose the paper specifications.

13

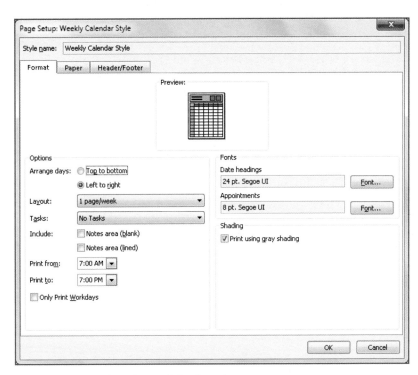

Figure 13-11: The Page Setup dialog box gives you considerable flexibility with regard to the print style, the format, paper specifications, and header/footer information.

d. Click the **Header/Footer** tab to add the professional touch of a header and/or a footer.

e. When you are ready, click **Preview** to see how your printed calendar will look.

f. Click **Print** to print your calendar.

Plan Meetings and Request Attendance

In addition to using Outlook 2010 for scheduling appointments and events, you can use Outlook to plan and schedule meetings. In Outlook, a meeting is an appointment to which others are invited.

Schedule a Meeting

You create a meeting by identifying the people you want to invite and picking a meeting time. You e-mail a meeting request to people in your Outlook Contacts who you want to attend.

1. Open the calendar.

2. From the Home tab New group, click **New Meeting**.

   –Or–

   Press **CTRL+SHIFT+Q**.

   In either event, the New Meeting window opens, as seen in Figure 13-12.

3. Click **To**, double-click your attendees from your Contacts list, and click **OK**.

4. Click in the **Subject** text box, and type a description for your meeting. This description will appear on all calendars.

5. If you do not see additional text fields, such as the Location field, enlarge the dialog box by dragging the bottom border. Then you'll be able to complete the following steps.

6. Click in the **Location** text box, and type the location information, if necessary.

7. Click the **Start Time** down arrow, and select the date and time the meeting is to start.

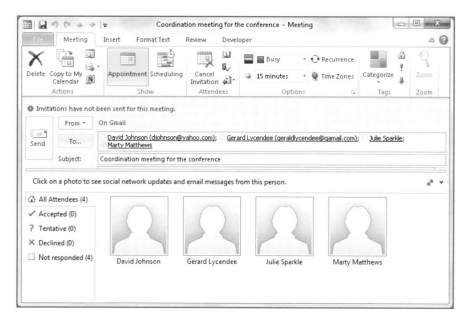

Figure 13-12: *The Meeting window allows you to send out invitations, track who can attend, and schedule resources for the meeting.*

8. Click the **End Time** down arrow, and select the date and time the meeting is scheduled to end.

9. Click **All Day Event**, if necessary.

10. Enter any additional information in the Notes section of the Meeting window that may be needed by the attendees.

11. In the Meeting tab Show group, click **Scheduling**. In the All Attendees column, click **Click Here To Add A Name** to include others in the meeting. (If you don't see it, enlarge the window.) If necessary, click **Add Others** to add names.

12. If you want to change the meeting times, you can enter the start and ending times, or you can drag the edges of the vertical meeting line, as shown in Figure 13-13.

13. Click **Close** to open the Close Meeting dialog box. Choose to save your changes and either send or not send the meeting announcement or not to save changes.

Respond to an Invitation

When you receive a meeting request, a message appears in your Inbox with an icon that is different from the normal e-mail icon.

1. In Outlook, open the meeting notification or request.

2. On the Message tab Respond group, click one of the following:

- Accept
- Tentative
- Decline

3. To send your response with no comments, click **Send The Response Now**. Click **OK**.

4. To include comments with your response, click **Edit The Response Before Sending**.

5. Type your comments and click **Send**.

6. To send no response, click **Don't Send A Response**, and click **OK**. The meeting is added to your calendar.

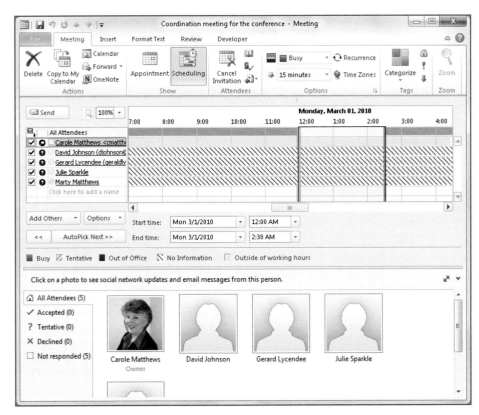

Figure 13-13: *The Scheduling dialog box allows you to send out invitations, track who can attend, and schedule resources for the meeting.*

Chapter 14
Printing, Using Mail Merge, and Graphics

The printing capabilities provided by Office 2010 go beyond just printing a document. In this chapter you will learn how to set specific parameters with regard to what is printed. Office also includes a convenient feature called Mail Merge within Word that you can use to merge mailing lists into documents, including letters or envelopes.

Graphics is a term used to describe several forms of visual enhancements that can be added to a document. In this chapter you will learn how to insert, format, and manage graphic files (*pictures*), such as digital photos and clip art images. In addition, you will see how to embed products of other programs (*objects*) alongside your text and how to produce organizational charts and other business-oriented *diagrams*.

NOTE

Due to the wide variety of printers available, this chapter cannot cover them all. The examples and figures in this chapter use an HP Photosmart 2600 printer. Depending on your printer model and how it's configured, you may see differences between your screen and what is shown in the figures and illustrations here.

HP Ph
2600 s
A

| Open |
| Open in new window |
| See what's printing |
| Set as default printer |
| Printing preferences |
| Printer properties |
| Create shortcut |
| Troubleshoot |
| Remove device |
| Properties |

Sna

NOTE

If there is a check mark next to the Printer icon, that printer is already set as the default printer.

NOTE

You can also "print" to a fax and OneNote by selecting them as your printer.

Print Documents

While printing documents may seem like a fairly basic function, there are several tasks associated with it that deserve attention, including setting up the default printer and printing envelopes and labels.

Set a Default Printer

1. From Windows Vista or Windows 7, click **Start**, click **Control Panel**, and then, under Hardware And Sound (or Devices And Printers for Windows 7), click **Printer**.

2. Right-click the icon for the printer you want to use as the default printer, and then click **Set As Default Printer** from the context menu that appears. A check mark is displayed next to the icon you have selected.

Define How a Document Is Printed

Your printer options, such as number of copies, printer, pages to print, and so on, are set in the Print view. The options for printing will vary by application and also by printer.

CUSTOMIZE A PRINT JOB

Customizing the print settings is done in the Print view, shown in Figure 14-1.

1. Click the **File tab**, and click **Print**. The Print dialog box appears. The options available will differ, depending on the printer you have and the Office application. Those displayed in Figure 14-1 are for Word and the HP Photosmart 2400 series.

2. Click the **Printer** down arrow if more than one printer is available to you, and select the printer you want to use. Usually, the default printer is displayed automatically in the Printer list box.

3. Click the **Copies** spinner to set the number of copies to be printed.

4. Under **Settings**, select any of these options:

   - Select an option in the first drop-down list in Figure 14-1 (normally entitled Print All Pages), choosing between All, Current Page, Selection (for the text you've selected), and Pages for a range of pages. To print contiguous pages, use a hyphen (for example, 1-4); to print noncontiguous pages, use commas (for example, 1, 3, 5).

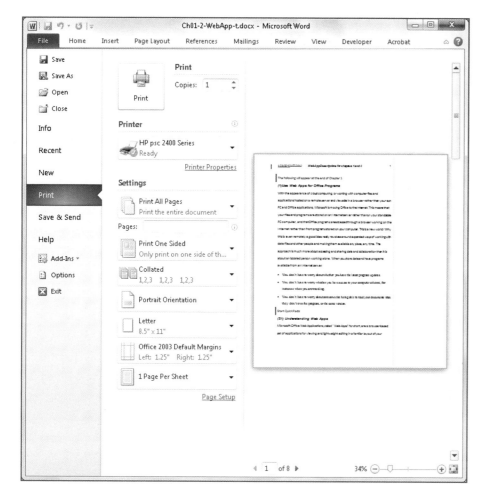

Figure 14-1: The Word Print view provides a preview of your document and many options for printing it.

- Click the **Print One Sided** drop-down list to choose between printing on only one side of the paper and printing on two sides. If you choose Manually Print On Both Sides, the printer will print every other page. When it finishes the first run, you'll need to take the paper out of the printer and reload it so that it is printed on the back of the printed page, and right-side up (so that the back page is not upside down.)

- If you are printing multiple copies and do not want the copies collated, click the **Collated** drop-down list and click **Uncollated**. By default, multiple copies will print collated.

- Click the **Portrait Orientation** drop-down list, and choose between Portrait Orientation and Landscape Orientation (tall vs. wide, respectively). By default, your document is printed in Portrait Orientation.

- Click the **Letter** drop-down list to select the paper size. Here is where you choose between an 8-½–size letter, labels, an envelope, or a legal or tabloid-size document, if your printer handles those sizes.

- Click the **Margins** drop-down list to choose the document margins you want to use. For instance, if you want to print fewer pages, you can create narrower margins; to print with more white space, create wider margins.

- Click **1 Page Per Sheet** if you can print more than one page on a sheet of paper. This only makes sense for small-page documents. The other options can be used for proofreading or approving the layout of documents when you want to save paper.

5. Click the **Page Setup** link beneath the Settings options to set more precise margins, page size, or layout settings.

6. Click the **Printer Properties** link beneath the Print button to set other properties for your printer. These options will differ for each printer, and will duplicate many of the options set in the main Print view.

7. When you have selected all the options you want and are ready to print your document, click **Print**. Your document is printed.

VIEW YOUR DOCUMENT IN FULL-SCREEN MODE

In Excel and Word you can view a document in full-screen mode without the ribbon, status bar, or scroll bars present, as shown in Figure 14-2. This view is available in Office 2010 from the View tab Document Views group. Click **Full Screen Reading**. As shown in the figure, you can set certain options to vary the appearance of the page. When you are finished, click **Close** on the far right of the title bar to return to the regular window.

Print a Document

If you're in a hurry, or if you don't care about changing margins, then printing a document can be as easy as clicking a **Print** icon on the Quick Access toolbar. By default, that icon isn't on that toolbar, but you can add it. To set specific options before printing your document, you need to use the Print dialog box.

Print an Envelope in Word

You can print a mailing address on an envelope to give your correspondence a more professional look. If you have a business letter with an address in the normal location, Word will pick up that address and suggest it for the envelope. If you don't have a letter, you can still create and print an envelope.

1. In the Mailings tab Create group, click **Envelopes**. The Envelopes And Labels dialog box appears with the Envelope tab selected, as shown in Figure 14-3.

2. In the Delivery Address box, if an address wasn't picked up from a letter, enter the mailing address.

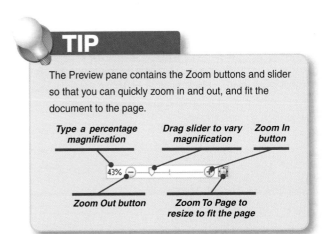

TIP

The Preview pane contains the Zoom buttons and slider so that you can quickly zoom in and out, and fit the document to the page.

Type a percentage magnification   *Drag slider to vary magnification*   *Zoom In button*

43%

Zoom Out button   *Zoom To Page to resize to fit the page*

Declaration of Independence

IN CONGRESS, JULY 4, 1776

The unanimous Declaration of the thirteen united States of America

When in the Course of human events it becomes necessary for one people to dissolve the political bands which have connected them with another and to assume among the powers of the earth, the separate and equal station to which the Laws of Nature and of Nature's God entitle them, a decent respect to the opinions of mankind requires that they should declare the causes which impel them to the separation.

We hold these truths to be self-evident, that all men are created equal, that they are endowed by their Creator with certain unalienable Rights, that among these are Life, Liberty and the pursuit of Happiness. — That to secure these rights, Governments are instituted among Men, deriving their just powers from the consent of the governed, — That whenever any Form of Government becomes destructive of these ends, it is the Right of the People to alter or to abolish it, and to institute new Government, laying its foundation on such principles and organizing its powers in such form, as to them shall seem most likely to effect their Safety and Happiness. Prudence, indeed, will dictate that Governments long established should not be changed for light and transient causes; and accordingly all experience hath shewn that mankind are more disposed to suffer, while evils are sufferable than to right themselves by abolishing the forms to which they are accustomed. But when a long train of abuses and usurpations, pursuing invariably the same Object evinces a design to reduce them under absolute Despotism, it is their right, it is their duty, to throw off such Government, and to provide new Guards for their future security. — Such has been the patient sufferance of these Colonies; and such is now the necessity which constrains them to alter their former Systems of Government. The history of the present King of Great Britain is a history of repeated injuries and usurpations, all having in direct object the establishment of an absolute Tyranny over these States. To prove this, let Facts be submitted to a candid world.

He has refused his Assent to Laws, the most wholesome and necessary for the public good.

He has forbidden his Governors to pass Laws of immediate and pressing importance, unless suspended in their operation till his Assent should be obtained; and when so suspended, he has utterly neglected to attend to them.

He has refused to pass other Laws for the accommodation of large districts of people, unless those people would relinquish the right of Representation in the Legislature, a right inestimable to them and formidable to tyrants only.

He has called together legislative bodies at places unusual, uncomfortable, and distant from the depository of their Public Records, for the sole purpose of fatiguing them into compliance with his measures.

He has dissolved Representative Houses repeatedly, for opposing with manly firmness his invasions on the rights of the people.

He has refused for a long time, after such dissolutions, to cause others to be elected, whereby the Legislative Powers, incapable of Annihilation, have returned to the People at large for their exercise; the State remaining in the mean time exposed to all the dangers of invasion from without, and convulsions within.

He has endeavoured to prevent the population of these States; for that purpose obstructing the Laws for Naturalization of Foreigners; refusing to pass others to encourage their migrations hither, and raising the conditions of new Appropriations of Lands.

He has obstructed the Administration of Justice by refusing his Assent to Laws for establishing Judiciary Powers.

He has made Judges dependent on his Will alone for the tenure of their offices, and the amount and payment of their salaries.

He has erected a multitude of New Offices, and sent hither swarms of Officers to harass our people and eat out their substance.

He has kept among us, in times of peace, Standing Armies without the Consent of our legislatures.

He has affected to render the Military independent of and superior to the Civil Power.

He has combined with others to subject us to a jurisdiction foreign to our constitution, and unacknowledged by our laws; giving his Assent to their Acts of pretended Legislation:

For quartering large bodies of armed troops among us:

For protecting them, by a mock Trial from punishment for any Murders which they should commit on the Inhabitants of these States:

For cutting off our Trade with all parts of the world:

For imposing Taxes on us without our Consent:

For depriving us in many cases, of the benefit of Trial by Jury:

For transporting us beyond Seas to be tried for pretended offences:

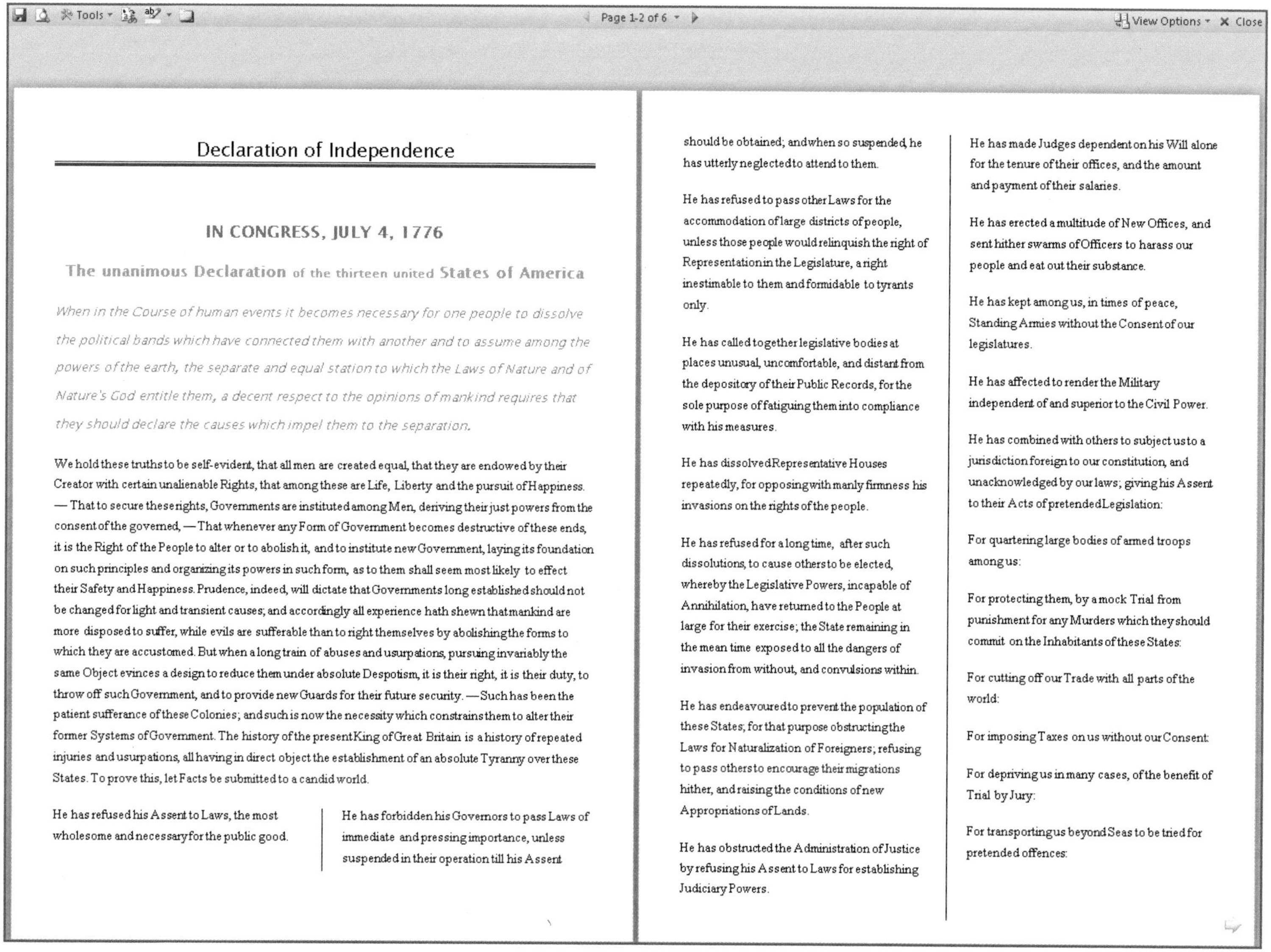

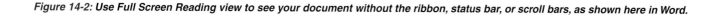

***Figure 14-2:** Use Full Screen Reading view to see your document without the ribbon, status bar, or scroll bars, as shown here in Word.*

Figure 14-3: Printed envelopes give your correspondence a professional look.

NOTE

The Feed box shows a default view that may be totally wrong for your printer. You need to use trial and error (which you can do on plain paper to save envelopes) to find the correct way to feed envelopes. When you find the correct pattern, click the feed image, select the correct image, and click **OK**.

TIP

For many HP inkjet printers, the envelopes are fed with the flap facing up on the left of the envelope and positioned on the far right of the feed tray, like this:

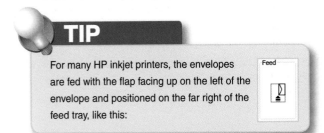

3. In the Return Address box, accept the default return address, or enter or edit the return address. (If you are using preprinted envelopes, you can omit a return address by clicking the **Omit** check box.)

4. Click the **Add Electronic Postage** check box if you have separately installed electronic postage software and want to add it to your envelope.

5. To set options for the electronic postage programs that are installed on your computer, click **E-Postage Properties**.

6. To select an envelope size, the type of paper feed, and other options, click **Options**, select the options you want, and then click **OK**.

7. To print the envelope now from the Envelopes And Labels dialog box, insert an envelope in the printer, as shown in the Feed box (see the accompanying Note), and then click **Print**.

8. To attach the envelope to a document you are currently working on and print it later, click **Add To Document**. The envelope is added to the document in a separate section.

Print Labels in Word

You can print labels for a single letter or for a mass mailing, such as holiday cards, invitations, or for marketing purposes. You can also create labels for a mass mailing using the techniques described later in the chapter in the section "Merge Lists with Letters and Envelopes."

To print a single label:

1. In the Mailings tab Create group, click **Labels**. The Envelopes And Labels dialog box appears with the Labels tab displayed, as shown in Figure 14-4.

2. In the Address box, do one of the following:
   - If you have a business letter open in Word with an address in the normal location, that address will appear in the Address box and can be edited.
   - If you are creating a mailing label, enter or edit the address.

Figure 14-4: *You can print a sheet of labels one at a time by specifying the row and column to be printed.*

- If you want to use a return address, click the **Use Return Address** check box, and then edit the address if necessary.
- If you are creating another type of label, type the text you want.

3. In the Print area, do one of the following:

- Click the **Single Label** option to print a single label. Then type or select the row and column number on the label sheet for the label you want to print.
- Click **Full Page Of The Same Label** to print the same information on a sheet of labels.

4. To select the label type, the type of paper feed, and other options, click **Options**, select the options you want, and then click **OK**. If the type of label you want to use is not listed in the Product Number box, you might be able to use one of the listed labels, or you can click **New Label** to create your own custom label.

5. To print one or more labels, insert a sheet of labels into the printer, and then click **Print**.

6. To save a sheet of labels for later editing or printing, click **New Document** and save the labels document. You can also use the New Document option to quickly set up a document in Word to create multiple labels on a sheet. Use the Labels dialog box to tell Word which brand/type of labels you're using, and then click **New Document**. You're presented with a blank document with a table set for the proper number of columns and rows for that label type. You can use this to quickly create file folder labels, etc., where the information is different for each one.

QUICKSTEPS

E-MAILING

You can e-mail documents that you create in Word, Excel, or PowerPoint as attachments to e-mail messages. To attach and send a document in an e-mail:

1. Click the **File** tab, and then click **Send & Save**.

2. Click **Send Using E-mail**, and choose one of the following options in the right pane:

   - **Send As Attachment** to attach a copy of the document to the e-mail

   - **Send A Link** to insert a link to the document on a network or server

   - **Send As PDF** to attach the PDF document to the e-mail. This requires Adobe Acrobat Reader, which can be downloaded for free.

   - **Send As XPS** to send as an alternative to PDF files. This requires Windows, but since it is a Microsoft file extension, it requires no other software.

   - **Send As Internet Fax** to send the document as a fax over the Internet without a fax machine.

     A new message is opened with your document title automatically filled in the Subject line and the document automatically attached or inserted to the e-mail as specified.

3. Fill in the **To** and **Cc** fields (if you are sending the document to multiple recipients), and add anything you want to the body of the message.

4. When you're ready, click **Send**.

Merge Lists with Letters and Envelopes

The *Mail Merge* feature allows you to combine a mailing list with a document to send the same thing to a number of people. You can merge a mailing list to letters, e-mail messages, envelopes, and labels. A mail merge combines two kinds of documents: the *main document*, which is the text of the document—for example, the body of a letter—and the *data source*, which is the information that changes with each copy of the document—for example, the individual names and addresses of the people who will be receiving the letter.

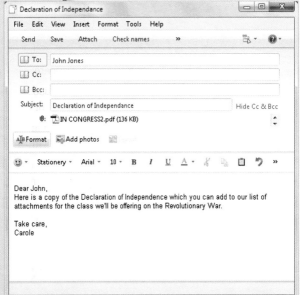

The main document has two parts: static text and merge fields. *Static text* is text that does not change—for example, the body of a letter. *Merge fields* are placeholders that indicate where information from the list or data source goes. For example, in a form letter, "Dear" would be static text, while <<First Name>> <<Last Name>> are merge fields. When the main document and the data source are combined, the result is "Dear John Doe," "Dear Jane Smith," and so on.

The following sections will show you how to create a data source, create a main document, and then merge them together.

Begin a Mail Merge

You can compose the static text in a document first and then insert the merge fields, or you can compose the static text and insert the merge fields as you go. You cannot insert merge fields into a main document until you have created the data source and associated it with your main document.

14

You cannot use the Mail Merge feature unless a document is open, although this can be a blank document.

NOTE

Word also allows you to take a list other than a mailing list—a parts list, for example—and merge it with a document to create a catalog or directory.

Figure 14-5: The Mail Merge task pane is where you begin the merge process.

To create a merge document:

1. In Word, open the document you want to use as your primary document, or open a new document.

2. Click the **Mailings** tab, click **Start Mail Merge** in the Start Mail Merge group, and click **Step By Step Mail Merge Wizard**. The Mail Merge task pane is displayed, as shown in Figure 14-5.

3. In the Select Document Type area, select one of the following options:

   ● **Letters** are form letters designed to be sent to multiple people.

   ● **E-mail Messages** are form letters designed to be sent to multiple people via e-mail.

   ● **Envelopes** are envelopes addressed to multiple people.

   ● **Labels** are labels addressed to multiple people.

   ● **Directory** is a collection of information regarding multiple items, such as a mailing list or phone directory.

4. Click **Next: Starting Document** at the bottom of the task pane.

5. In the Select Starting Document area, select one of the following options:

   ● **Use The Current Document** uses the currently opened document as the main document for the mail merge.

   ● **Start From A Template** uses a template you designate as the main document for the mail merge.

   ● **Start From Existing Document** uses an existing document you designate as the main document for the mail merge.

6. See the following section, "Set Up a Name and Address List," to create a data source.

Set Up a Name and Address List

A name and address list is a data source. A data source has two parts: fields and records. A *field* is a category of information. For example, in a mailing list, First Name, Last Name, and Street Address are examples of fields. A *record* is a set of fields for an individual. For example, in a mailing list, the record for John Doe would include all the relevant fields for this individual—his first and last name, street address, city, state, and ZIP code.

Figure 14-6: Use the New Address List dialog box to create your mailing list.

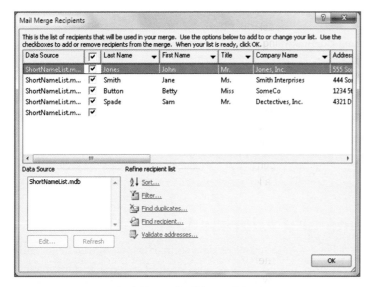

Figure 14-7: Use the Mail Merge Recipients dialog box to manage your mailing list prior to completing the merge.

To set up a name and address list:

1. Follow steps 1–6 in the previous section, "Begin a Mail Merge."

2. Click **Next: Select Recipients** at the bottom of the task pane. In the Select Recipients area, click **Type A New List**. (If your Contacts are already set up, you can also choose **Select From Outlook Contacts**, in which case you'll be given an opportunity to choose the Contact folder you want to use and then to edit the recipient list.)

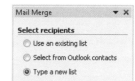

3. Click **Create** in the middle of the pane in the Type A New List area. The New Address List dialog box appears, as shown in Figure 14-6.

4. Enter the information for the first record in the fields you want to use. You may want to delete some of the columns or reorder them to facilitate entering data. Click **Customize Columns** to do that. Press TAB to move to the next field, or press SHIFT + TAB to move back to the previous field.

5. When you have completed all the fields you want for the first record, click **New Entry** and provide information for the second record.

6. Repeat steps 4 and 5 until you have added all the records you want to your list. When you are done, click **OK**.

7. A Save Address List dialog box appears. Type a file name for the list, select the folder on your computer where you want to save it, and click **Save**.

8. The Mail Merge Recipients dialog box appears, as shown in Figure 14-7. Clear the check boxes next to the recipients you do not want to include in the list. To make further changes to the name list, select the file name in the Data Source list box, and click **Edit**.

9. Click **OK** when finished. See the following section, "Create a Merge Document."

Create a Merge Document

After creating the data source, you need to write the letter and insert the merge fields. This section will tell you how, after creating the main document, to insert merge fields in general. The example uses a letter;

Sort the merge recipients by clicking the field name at the top of the list that will provide the sort order. For example, if you want the list ordered alphabetically by last name, click **Last Name**.

additional sections will show you how to use merge fields when creating envelopes and labels.

1. Follow the steps in the previous two sections, "Begin a Mail Merge" and "Set Up a Name and Address List."

2. Click **Next: Write Your Letter** at the bottom of the Mail Merge task pane. In the document pane, write the body of the letter—don't worry about the addressee and the greeting.

3. Place the cursor in the document where you want to insert a merge field, such as the addressee. Do one of the following:

- Select one of the three items in the top of the Mail Merge task pane if you want to insert a predefined block of merge fields, such as an address or a greeting. If you select anything other than More Items, a dialog box will appear and ask you to select options and formatting for that item (see Figure 14-8).

- Click **More Items** (the fourth item in the list) to insert an individual merge field. The Insert Merge Field dialog box appears. Verify that **Database Fields** is selected, and then select the field that you want to insert (for example, First Name and Last Name). Click **Insert** to insert the merge field into your document. Click **Close** when you are done inserting all the fields you need.

4. Add commas, spaces, and other punctuation marks to the address as needed. Figure 14-9 shows an example of a letter with merge fields inserted. See the following section, "Preview a Merge."

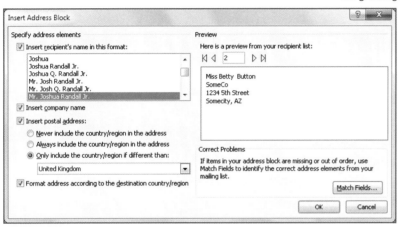

Figure 14-8: You can customize the predefined field blocks to meet your mail-merge needs.

Figure 14-9: Merge fields are a convenient way to create a form letter for multiple recipients.

Preview a Merge

Prior to actually completing the merge, the Mail Merge task pane presents you with an opportunity to review what the merged document will look like. This way, you can go back and make any last-minute changes to fine-tune your merge.

USING RULES

Rules (also called *Word Fields*) apply merge fields or static text if certain conditions are met. One of the most common variable fields is the If…Then…Else rule. The If rule performs one of two alternative actions, depending on a condition you specify. For example, the statement, "If the weather is sunny, we'll go to the beach; if not, we'll go to the museum," specifies a condition that *must* be met (sunny weather) for a certain action to take place (going to the beach). If the condition is not met, an alternative action occurs (going to the museum).

This is how an example of using an If rule in Word looks with the field codes turned on:

{IF { MERGEFIELD City } = "Seattle" "Please call our office." "Please call our distributor." }

This works as follows: If the current data record contains "Seattle" in the City field, then the first text ("Please call our office.") is printed in the merged document that results from that data record. If "Seattle" is not in the City field, then the second set of text ("Please call our distributor.") is printed. Using a rule is easy and doesn't require writing such a complex statement at all.

To insert a variable field into a merge document:

1. Position the insertion point where you want the rule.

2. In the Mailings tab Write & Insert Fields group, click **Rules** . A drop-down list appears.

3. Select the rule you want, for example, If…Then… Else.

4. The Insert Word: If dialog box appears, as in Figure 14-10. Fill in the text boxes with your criteria, and click **OK** when finished.

To preview a merge:

1. Follow the steps in the previous three sections, "Begin a Mail Merge," "Set Up a Name and Address List," and "Create a Merge Document."

2. Click **Next: Preview Your Letters** at the bottom of the Mail Merge task pane.

3. In the Mail Merge task pane, use the right and left arrow buttons under Preview Your Letters to scroll through the recipient list.

4. If you want to exclude a particular recipient from the merge, click **Exclude This Recipient**.

   –Or–

   In the Make Changes area in the task pane, click **Edit Recipient List** to edit a particular recipient's information. If you click this link, the Mail Merge Recipients dialog box appears again (see Figure 14-7). Click the file name under Data Source, click **Edit**, modify the information, and click **OK**. Click **OK** again to close the Mail Merge Recipients dialog box.

Complete a Merge

The last step in performing a mail merge is to complete the merge—that is, to accept the preview of how the merge will look and direct Word to perform the merge.

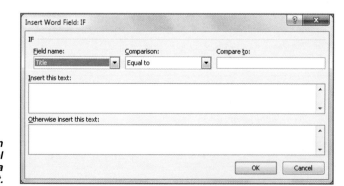

Figure 14-10: You can define rules to control what text appears in a merge document.

14

LINKING PICTURE FILES

Pictures are *embedded* by default when inserted in a document. Embedding means that the picture files become part of the Office file and their file size is added to the size of the saved document. In a document with several high-resolution pictures, the document's size can quickly rise into several megabytes (the greater the number of pixels in a picture, the higher the resolution and the larger the file size). To dramatically reduce the size of a document that contains pictures, you can *link* to the picture files instead. In this case, the addresses of picture files are retained in the document file, not the pictures themselves. Alternatively, you can reduce the resolution and compress embedded pictures, although the reduction in file size won't be as large as with linked files. Another characteristic of linked picture files is that any changes made and saved in the source file will be updated in the Office document. Linking does have the downside of requiring the picture files to remain in the same folder location they were in when the link was created. In addition, documents with linked files are not suitable for sharing outside your local network. The *Insert And Link* option allows you to both embed the picture and to retain a link to it. This contains both the upside and the downside of both options.

To link a picture to a file:

1. To link a picture file when you are inserting a picture into a document, click the **Insert** tab, and click **Picture** in the Illustrations group to open the Insert Picture dialog box.

2. Click the **Insert** down arrow in the lower-right corner, and click **Link To File**.

To complete a merge:

1. Follow the steps in the previous four sections, "Begin a Mail Merge," "Set Up a Name and Address List," "Create a Merge Document," and "Preview a Merge."

2. Click **Next: Complete The Merge** at the bottom of the Mail Merge task pane.

3. Click **Print** in the Merge area. The Merge To Printer dialog box appears.

4. Select one of the following options:

   - **All** prints all records in the data source that have been included in the merge.

   - **Current Record** prints only the record that is displayed in the document window.

   - **From/To** prints a range of records you specify. Enter the starting and ending numbers in the text boxes.

5. Click **OK** when finished. The Print dialog box appears.

6. Select the print options you want, and click **OK**. Your merged document is printed.

7. If you wish, save your merge document.

Work with Pictures

Pictures can be manipulated in a number of ways once you have them within Word. You can organize your clip art collections, resize images, and move them into the exact positions that you want.

Add Pictures

You can browse for picture files, use the Clip Art task pane to assist you, drag them from other locations, or import them directly from a scanner or digital camera.

BROWSE FOR PICTURES

1. Place your insertion point in the paragraph, slide, cell, or table where you want to insert the picture.

14

NOTE

Pictures are files that are produced by a device, such as a digital camera or scanner, or that are created in a painting or drawing program, such as Microsoft Paint or Adobe Illustrator. In either case, the files are saved in a graphic format, such as JPEG or GIF (popular formats used on the Internet) or TIF (used in higher-end printing applications).

NOTE

Often, when you insert a picture, it is not the size that you want it to be or placed where you want it to be. You can easily make a picture the size you want by dragging the corners of the picture to resize it. You can drag the picture itself to other locations.

TIP

Besides using the Insert Pictures command in Word to add pictures, you can drag picture files from the desktop or Windows Explorer into an open document. To best use Windows Explorer, close or minimize all windows other than your Office document and Windows Explorer. Right-click a blank area of the Windows taskbar, and click either **Show Windows Stacked** or **Show Windows Side By Side** on the context menu. Locate the picture file you want in the right pane of Windows Explorer, and drag it to the location in the document where you want it.

2. In the Insert tab Illustrations group, click **Picture**. The Insert Picture dialog box appears.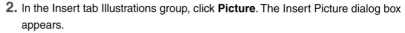

3. Browse to the picture you want, and select it. (If you do not see your pictures, click the **Views** down arrow on the dialog box toolbar, and click **Medium Icons** or a larger size.)

4. Click **Insert**. The picture is displayed in the document.

ADD CLIP ART

1. Place your insertion point in the paragraph, slide, cell, or table where you want to insert the clip art.

2. In the Insert tab Illustrations group, click **Clip Art**. The Clip Art task pane opens.

3. In the Search For text box, type a keyword.

4. Click the **Results Should Be** down arrow, and refine your search to specific collections. (The Web Collections category includes thousands of clips maintained at Office Online; therefore, it can take considerable time to find what you're looking for.)

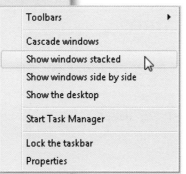

5. Click the **Results Should Be** down arrow, and clear all file types other than clip art.

6. Click **Go**. In a few moments, thumbnails of the search results will appear, as shown in Figure 14-11.

7. Click the thumbnail to insert it in your document.

QUICKFACTS

USING THE PICTURE TOOLS FORMAT TAB

Pictures are manipulated primarily by using the Picture Tools Format tab, shown in Figure 14-12. This tab on the ribbon differs slightly in PowerPoint and Excel. The Format tab automatically appears when a graphic image is selected in a document. The tab has four groups that allow you to adjust the characteristics of an image, determine its style, arrange an image on a page or in relation to other images or to text, and size an image. In addition, the two Dialog Box Launchers in the Picture Styles and Size groups provide a number of other settings.

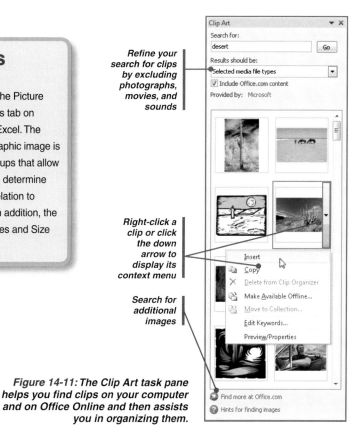

Refine your search for clips by excluding photographs, movies, and sounds

Right-click a clip or click the down arrow to display its context menu

Search for additional images

Figure 14-11: The Clip Art task pane helps you find clips on your computer and on Office Online and then assists you in organizing them.

Remove Unwanted Areas

You can remove areas from a picture that you do not want by using the Crop tool on the Picture toolbar.

1. Open and select the picture you want to crop. See "Add Pictures" earlier in this chapter.

2. On the Picture Tools Format tab, click **Crop** in the Size group (not the down arrow). The picture redisplays with eight sizing handles on the corners and sides, and the mouse pointer becomes a cropping icon when outside the picture, as shown in Figure 14-13.

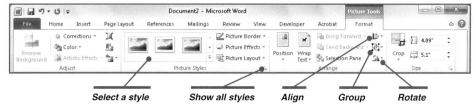

Select a style   Show all styles   Align   Group   Rotate

Figure 14-12: The Picture Tools Format tab, from Word in this case, is your one-stop shopping venue for accessing picture-related options.

Figure 14-13: Cropping removes the area of a picture outside the dashed area.

TIP

In Word, you can add a caption to inserted pictures to give a uniform appearance to your picture identifiers. Right-click a picture and click **Insert Caption**. In the Caption dialog box, choose a label (create your own labels by clicking **New Label**), where you want the caption, and a numbering format. You can also have Word use AutoCaption to automatically add a caption based on the type of picture or object inserted.

TIP

You can make pictures be inline with text, or, in a sense, be treated like a big character and have paragraph-formatting characteristics. To do this, right-click the picture and click **Size And Position**. Then click the **Text Wrapping** tab. Click a thumbnail that will allow you to position the picture independently of text, similar to drawings.

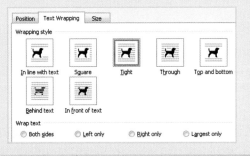

3. Place the cropping tool over one of the eight sizing handles (it will morph into an angle or T icon), and drag the tool so that the area of the picture is cut away or cropped by what you have dragged over.

4. Release the mouse button. The area of the picture shows what will be cropped when you press **ESC** or click outside of the image to turn off the Crop tool. You can adjust this area as needed.

Add Shapes

Shapes are small, prebuilt drawings that you can select, or you can create your own by modifying existing shapes or drawing your own freeform shapes. The prebuilt shapes and tools for creating your own are added either from the Insert tab Illustrations group or from the Drawing tools Format tab Insert Shapes group.

1. In the Insert tab Illustrations group, click **Shapes** to open the Shapes drop-down menu.

2. Choose a shape by doing one of the following:

   Click a shape from one of the several categories.

   –Or–

   Click one of the lines or basic shapes to begin your own shape.

3. Drag the mouse crosshair pointer in the approximate location and size you want.

Create a Diagram

You can quickly create and modify several different types of diagrams, some of which are easily interchangeable. One type, an organization or hierarchy chart, provides special tools and features that streamline the structuring of this popular form of charting.

1. In the Insert tab Illustrations group, click **SmartArt**. The Choose A SmartArt Graphic dialog box appears, as shown in Figure 14-14. ⊞ SmartArt

2. Click **Hierarchy** in the left column, and then double-click the upper-leftmost diagram to display the start of an organization chart and the SmartArt Tools Design tab, shown in Figure 14-15. Then personalize your chart by doing one or more of the following:

TIP

Several other shapes are available from clip art collections. Type <u>autoshapes</u> in the Search For text box in the Clip Art task pane. Choose to search in all collections, and click **Go** (see "Add Clip Art" earlier in the chapter).

NOTE

You can fill a drawing or shape with a picture. First select the shape. Then click **Picture** on the Shape Fill drop-down menu. The Select Picture dialog box appears. Browse for the picture you want, select it, and click **Insert**. The picture will be inserted into the background of the drawing shape.

14

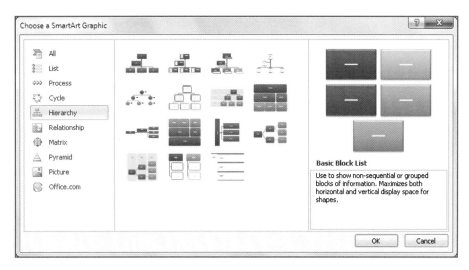

Figure 14-14: SmartArt allows you to easily create a number of diagram types, such as organizational charts.

- Click the highest level, or manager position, and in the SmartArt Tools Design tab, click **Layout** in the Create Graphic group to open a menu of hierarchical options. Click the structure that best matches your organization.

- Click a current box on the chart. On the Design tab Create Graphic group, click **Add Shape**, and select the type of new position you want to add to the current structure. For a higher level, click **Add Shape Above**; for a subordinate level, click **Add Shape Below**; for a co-worker level, click either **Add Shape Before** or **Add Shape After**.

- To place text in a shape after adding a new shape, simply start typing. You can also click the insertion point in either the text pane ("Type Your Text Here" or "Text") or the organization chart shape, and then add new text or edit existing text. Type the name, title, or other identifier for the position. The font size will change to fit the text box. Press **SHIFT+ENTER** after each line for a subordinate line (like a name after a position), or press **ENTER** for a second but equal line. Format text in the shapes as you would standard text, using the Home tab and its associated options.

- Click **Right To Left** to flip the names and shapes on the right with the ones on the left.

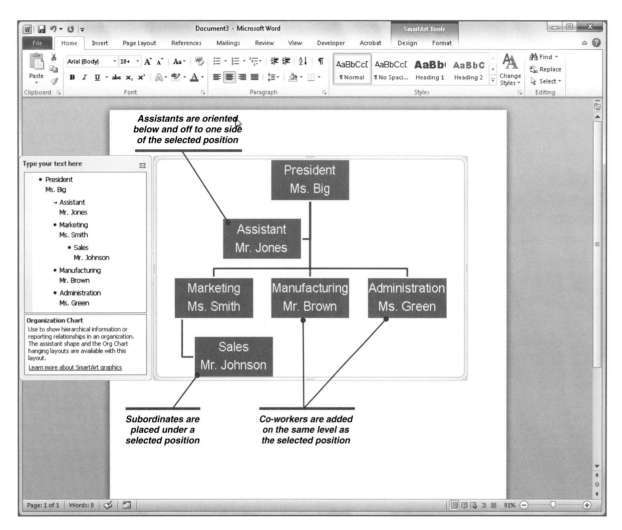

Assistants are oriented below and off to one side of the selected position

Subordinates are placed under a selected position

Co-workers are added on the same level as the selected position

Figure 14-15: Organization charts are easily laid out and formatted using SmartArt in Word.

- Click **Promote** or **Demote** in the Create Graphic group to move a shape and its text up or down in the organization chart.

- Click **Text Pane** in the Create Graphic group to turn the text pane on or off.

- Point at any of the layouts, colors, or SmartArt styles to see how your chart would look with that change. Click the layout, color, or style to make the change permanent.

- If you make a "permanent" change, as just described, you can return to the previous layout, color, or style by clicking **Reset Graphic** in the Reset Graphic group.

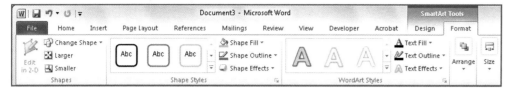

Figure 14-16: Quickly redesign the overall appearance of your organization chart.

- To select a group of shapes and their text so that they can be acted upon all at once, hold down **CTRL** while clicking each shape (including the connecting lines). Or draw a selection area around the group of shapes by moving the mouse pointer to just outside the upper-left shape and then dragging the mouse to just outside the lower-right shape.

- Click the **SmartArt Tools Format** tab to display several options for changing the shape and its text, as shown in Figure 14-16.

Modify Graphics

Pictures (those that use an absolute positioning layout) and shapes or drawings share a common Format dialog box, although many of the features and options are not available for every type of graphic you can add to an Office document. This section describes formatting and other modifications you can apply to graphics.

Resize and Rotate Graphics Precisely

You can change the size of graphics by setting exact dimensions and rotating them. (You can also drag handles to change them interactively. See "Use Handles and Borders to Position Graphics" later in this chapter for ways to resize and rotate graphics with a mouse.) The dialog boxes for size differ slightly between Word, PowerPoint, and Excel.

1. Click the graphic you want to resize to select it. In the Picture (or other graphic type) Tools Format tab, click the **Size Dialog Box Launcher** in the Size group. (For some graphics, such as an organization chart, the Size Dialog Box Launcher will not exist. You can resize organization charts and similar graphics manually.)

2. Click the **Size** tab, and, if it isn't already selected, click the **Lock Aspect Ratio** check box to size the graphic proportionally when entering either width or height values.

3. Under **Size And Rotate** (depending on the graphic, the option may be Height And Width), enter either the height or the width dimension, or use the spinners to increase or decrease one of the dimensions from its original size.

NOTE

Diagrams are really just combinations of shapes that fit a specific need. As such, you can, for example, delete an element of a diagram by selecting it and pressing **DELETE**. Or you can delete the entire diagram by selecting its border and pressing **DELETE**. See "Modify Graphics" to learn how to format the overall diagram, as well as how to change various components of shapes.

TIP

Right-click a graphic (on the handle), and click **Format Shape** (or AutoShape or Object, depending on the graphic) to open a dialog box that makes available only the options that pertain to that type of graphic. For example, if you right-click a rectangle shape you inserted, the Arrows area of the Line Style option is unavailable because this is not an action you can do with this type of graphic.

CAUTION

Enlarging an image beyond the ability of the pixels to span it can cause unwanted effects.

QUICKFACTS

UNDERSTANDING GRAPHIC POSITIONING IN WORD

When you position a graphic (picture, clip art, drawing, or shape) on the page, the position can be *inline*, or *relative*, to the text and other objects on the page, where the graphic moves as the text moves, like a character in a word. The alternative is *absolute* positioning, where the graphic stays anchored in one place, regardless of what the text does. If the graphic uses absolute positioning, you can then specify how text will wrap around the graphic, which can be on either or both sides, or along the top and bottom of the graphic. Also, for special effects, the text can be either on top of the graphic or underneath it. See "Position a Graphic Relative to Areas in a Document."

–Or–

1. Under Scale, enter a percentage for either the height or the width to increase or decrease it, or use the spinners to increase or decrease the percentage of the original picture size.

2. To rotate the graphic, under Size And Rotate (or Rotation), enter a positive (rotate clockwise) or negative (rotate counterclockwise) number of degrees of rotation you want.

3. Click **OK**. The picture will resize and/or rotate according to your values.

Position Graphics

Graphics (including pictures that use absolute positioning) can be positioned anywhere in the document by dragging or setting values. In either case, the graphic retains its relative position within the document as text and other objects are added or removed. You can override this behavior by anchoring the graphic to a fixed location. You can also change how text and other objects "wrap" around the graphic. Figure 14-17 shows several of these features.

POSITION A GRAPHIC RELATIVE TO AREAS IN A DOCUMENT

Besides dragging a graphic into position, you can select or enter values that determine where the graphic is placed in relation to document areas.

1. Click the graphic that you want to position to select it. In the Drawing or Picture Tools Format tab, click **Text Wrapping** in the Arrange group. A menu is displayed.

2. Click **More Layout Options** to open the Layout dialog box.

3. Click the **Position** tab. Select or enter the horizontal- and vertical-positioning entries by selecting them from the drop-down menus, entering the values, or using the spinners to increase or decrease distances, as shown in Figure 14-18.

4. To anchor a graphic in place, regardless of whether other content is added or removed—for example, a graphic you want in the upper-left corner of a specific page—click the **Lock Anchor** check box and clear all other options.

5. Click **OK** to close the Advanced Layout dialog box.

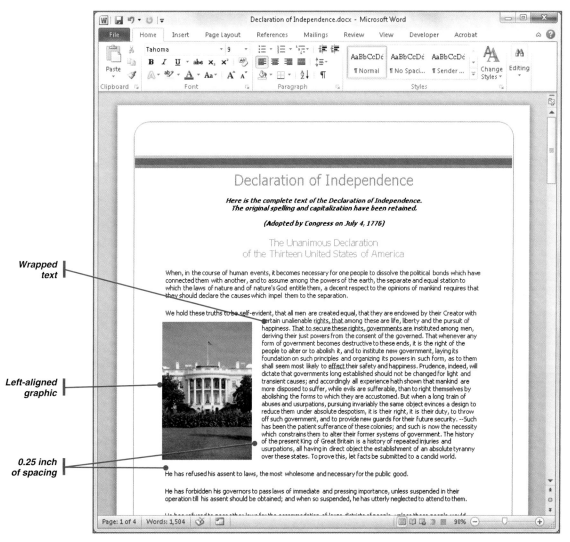

Wrapped text

Left-aligned graphic

0.25 inch of spacing

Figure 14-17: You can easily arrange text and graphics in several configurations using dialog box options.

14

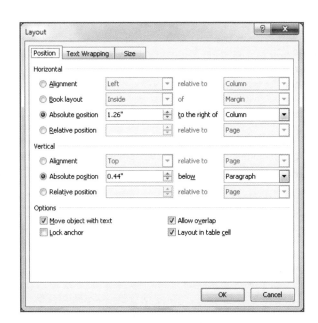

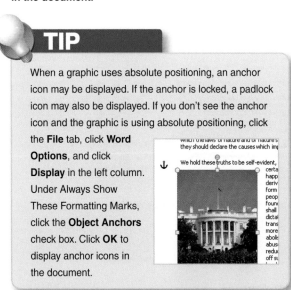

Figure 14-18: Using absolute positioning, you can choose where to place a graphic relative to other objects in the document.

TIP

When a graphic uses absolute positioning, an anchor icon may be displayed. If the anchor is locked, a padlock icon may also be displayed. If you don't see the anchor icon and the graphic is using absolute positioning, click the **File** tab, click **Word Options**, and click **Display** in the left column. Under Always Show These Formatting Marks, click the **Object Anchors** check box. Click **OK** to display anchor icons in the document.

Use Handles and Borders to Position Graphics

Graphics are easily manipulated using their sizing handles and borders.

- **Select a graphic**   You select a graphic by clicking it. Handles appear around the graphic and allow you to perform interactive changes. Two exceptions include text boxes and text in text boxes.

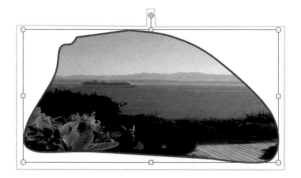

- Click in a text box. A dotted border appears around the perimeter of the text box. (In Excel and PowerPoint, the border itself becomes dotted.)

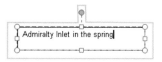

- Place the mouse pointer in the text in a text box; it will become an I-beam pointer. Click it to place an insertion point, or drag across the text to select it. The mini toolbar will dimly appear. Move the mouse pointer over the toolbar for it to fully appear, and then make a selection to change the formatting.

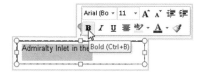

NOTE

You can also right-click the graphic you want to change and click **Bring To Front** or **Send To Back** in the context menu. If you don't see the stacking options on the context menu when you right-click one of the graphics in a stack, click outside all the graphics, and then click one of the other graphics.

QUICKSTEPS

WORKING WITH GRAPHICS

While graphics can be positioned absolutely by simply dragging them or choosing placement relative to other objects in a document, Office also provides a number of other techniques that help you adjust where a graphic is in relation to other graphics.

MOVE GRAPHICS INCREMENTALLY

Select the graphic or group of graphics (see "Combine Graphics by Grouping"), and press one of the arrow keys in the direction you want to move the graphic by very small increments (approximately .01 inch).

REPOSITION THE ORDER OF STACKED GRAPHICS

You can stack graphics by simply dragging one on top of another. Figure 14-19 shows an example of a three-graphic stack. To reposition the order of the stack in Word, Excel, or PowerPoint, click **Bring To Front** or **Send To Back** (see the following for a description) in the Format tab Arrange group. You'll see a menu. Then click one of the following:

- **Bring To Front** moves the graphic to the top of the stack.

- **Send To Back** moves the graphic to the bottom of the stack.

Continued . . .

- **Resize a graphic** Drag one of the square or round (if using absolute positioning) sizing handles surrounding the graphic—or at either end of it, in the case of a line—in the direction you want to enlarge or reduce the graphic. Hold SHIFT when dragging a corner sizing handle to change the height AND length proportionately. (You can proportionally resize a graphic without pressing SHIFT. In the Picture or Drawing Tools Format tab, open the **Size group Dialog Box Launcher dialog box** and click the **Size** tab. Then select the **Lock Aspect Ratio** checkbox.)

- **Rotate a graphic** Drag the green dot in the direction you want to rotate the graphic. Hold SHIFT when dragging to rotate in 15-degree increments.

- **Change a graphic's perspective** If the graphic supports interactive adjustment, a yellow diamond adjustment handle is displayed. Drag the yellow diamond toward or away from the graphic to get the look you want.

Figure 14-19: You can change the order of stacked graphics to achieve the look you want.

WORKING WITH GRAPHICS *(Continued)*

- **Bring Forward** moves the graphic up one level (same as Bring To Front if there are only two graphics in the stack).

- **Send Backward** moves the graphic down one level (same as Send To Back if there are only two graphics in the stack).

- **Bring In Front Of Text** moves the graphic on top of overlapping text.

- **Send Behind Text** moves the graphic behind overlapping text.

ALIGN GRAPHICS

To align two or more graphics relative to one another, select the graphics by holding down **SHIFT**. Then click the **Align** command in the Format tab Arrange group, and click an option.

EVENLY SPACE GRAPHICS

Select the graphics by holding down **SHIFT**. In the Tools Format tab Arrange group, click **Align** and then click **Distribute Horizontally** or **Distribute Vertically**, depending on their orientation.

Combine Graphics by Grouping

You can combine graphics for any number of reasons, but you typically work with multiple graphics to build a more complex rendering. To prevent losing the positioning, sizing, and other characteristics of the individual components, you can group them so that they are treated as one object.

- To group graphics, select the graphics to be grouped by clicking the first graphic and then holding down **SHIFT** while selecting other drawings and pictures. In the Tools Format tab Arrange group, click **Group** and then click **Group** again; or right-click one of the selected graphics, click **Group** and click **Group** again. A single set of selection handles surrounds the perimeter of the graphics. Coloring, positioning, sizing, and other actions now affect the graphics as a group instead of individually.

- To separate a group into individual graphics, select the group. In the Tools Format tab Arrange group, click **Group** and click **Ungroup**; or right-click the group, click **Group**, and then click **Ungroup**.

- To recombine a group after ungrouping it, in the Tools Format tab Arrange group, click **Group** and then click **Regroup**; or right-click a member graphic, and click **Group** and then click **Regroup**.

Symbols

' (apostrophe), using with numbers in
Excel, 113
* (asterisk) wildcard, using in Find, 42
@ (at sign) wildcard, using in Find, 42
• (bullet) symbol, entering, 30
[cc] wildcard, using in Find, 42
[c-c] wildcard, using in Find, 42
[!c-c] wildcard, using in Find, 42
¢ (cent) symbol, entering, 30
: (colon), using to reference cell range, 162
, (comma)
using to reference unions, 162
using with shortcut keys, 31
© (copyright) symbol, entering, 30
— (em dash) symbol, entering, 30
– (en dash) symbol, entering, 30
= (equal sign), using with formulas,
165–166
€ (Euro) symbol, entering, 30
< (left angle bracket) wildcard, using in
Find, 42
– (minus), using in navigation, 38
{n,} wildcard, using in Find, 42
{n,m} wildcard, using in Find, 42
{n} wildcard, using in Find, 42
+ (plus), using in navigation, 38
£ (pound) symbol, entering, 30
? (question mark) wildcard, using in Find, 42
® (registered) symbol, entering, 30
> (right angle bracket) wildcard, using
in Find, 42
™ (trademark) symbol, entering, 30

A

A1 cell referencing scheme, changing, 161
absolute positioning, using with graphics,
340, 342
absolute references, explained, 160–161
Activate Microsoft Office feature,
accessing, 15
active cell. See also cells
changing direction of, 114
filling data into, 121
identifying in Excel, 110–111
moving to cells, 114
moving to next row, 114

moving to right, 113
staying in, 113
address and name list. See name and
address list
Address Book, selecting names for
e-mail, 273
addresses. See e-mail addresses
aligning, paragraphs, 58–61
aligning text, keyboard shortcut, 51
alignment
changing in worksheets, 149–151
vertical, 73
animations, displaying on slides, 190
apostrophe ('), using with numbers in
Excel, 113
appointments in Calendar
creating, 295–296
editing recurring, 314–315
entering all-day events directly, 311
entering directly, 311
entering in windows, 312–313
explained, 295
moving, 311, 315
using reminders for, 316
art, inserting in slides, 191
asterisk (*) wildcard, using in Find, 42
at sign (@) wildcard, using in Find, 42
attachments. See e-mail attachments
AutoArchive dialog box, using with
e-mail, 267
AutoComplete
turning off for e-mail, 274
using in Excel, 119
AutoCorrect. See also Math AutoCorrect
text; Word writing aids
adding or deleting entries, 98–99
configuring in Word, 98
using to create numbered lists, 65
using with Excel, 129–130
using with PowerPoint, 235–238
using with spelling checker, 239
AutoFill, disabling in Excel, 121
AutoFit, using with PowerPoint, 236–237
AutoFormat, using in Word, 99–100. See
also formatting
AutoRecover, using, 45
AutoSend, turning off for e-mail, 291
AutoSum technique, using with functions,
178–179

B

backgrounds, adding to worksheets,
151–152
bar tab, setting, 87
Bcc (blind carbon copy), including and
removing, 274
binding, adding space for, 72
blind carbon copy (Bcc), including and
removing, 274
body style
applying, 53
choosing, 81
bold text keyboard shortcut, 51
border lines, autoformatting, 100
borders. See also cell borders
adding to text, 69
using to position graphics, 342–343
browse buttons, using, 37
Browse feature, using to copy presentation
design, 202–203
building blocks. See also text
creating, 100–101
defined, 100
deleting, 102
inserting, 101–102
Quick Parts feature, 100–101
bullet (•) symbol, entering, 30
bulleted lists
autoformatting, 99
changing in slide masters, 221
changing to numbered lists, 68
creating, 66
customizing, 66–67
keyboard shortcut, 51
bullets
applying to lists, 66
removing from lists, 68

C

Calendar
Advanced View Settings dialog box,
298, 302
changing font face and size, 296–298
changing time scales, 296, 298
copying activities, 315
creating appointments, 310–313

entering dates and times, 312
features of, 293–294
free/busy options, 306
navigating, 297
Navigation pane, 299
Reading pane, 299–300
setting up, 304–306
using text dates, 310
View tab options, 298–299
Calendar activities
appointments, 295
events, 295
meetings, 295
tasks, 295
Calendar Date Navigator
displaying days, 297
displaying months, 297
displaying weeks, 297
Calendar views
Active view, 303
changing quickly, 298
creating, 303
modifying, 300–302
modifying list views, 302–303
calendars
Internet, 311
maximum number available, 307
printing, 316–318
publishing to Microsoft Office
Online, 309–310
sending in e-mail, 308–309
setting date range of snapshots, 309
sharing, 308–310
viewing multiple, 307–308
capitalization, changing, 57
caps keyboard shortcut, 51
captions, adding to pictures, 336
carbon copy (Cc), addressing, 275
case of text, toggling, 57
Categorize menu, using with e-mail, 264
Cc (carbon copy), addressing, 275
cell borders. See also borders
drawing in worksheets, 137
picking in worksheets, 136
previewing in worksheets, 136
cell contents
editing in Excel, 119
removing in Excel, 120–121
replacing in Excel, 119

left tab, setting, 87
license terms, getting information about, 15
line breaks
    inserting, 31–32, 64
    showing marks for, 70
line spacing
    keyboard shortcut, 52
    reducing, 63
    setting, 62
lines. *See also* horizontal lines
    counting, 104
    navigating, 37
    selecting, 33
    specifying space between, 63
links. *See* external links; hyperlinks
lists
    applying bullets to, 66
    applying numbering to, 66
    creating multilevel, 66
    removing bullets from, 68
    removing numbering from, 68
Live Preview, using to compare cells, 174
locking
    columns in worksheets, 154
    rows and columns together, 154
    rows in worksheets, 153–154
lowercase, toggling, 57

M

Mail Merge feature, overview of, 328.
    See also merge document
Mail view, displaying in Outlook, 255–256
MAPI (Message Application Programming
    Interface), 251
margins
    mirror margins option, 72
    setting, 70–71
master slides, using in PowerPoint, 184.
    See also slides in PowerPoint
Math AutoCorrect text, displaying, 104.
    See also AutoCorrect
mathematical equations. *See* equations
mathematical operations, standard order
    of, 165
Maximize/Restore window, location of, 4
meetings in Calendar
    explained, 295

responding to invitations, 319–320
    scheduling, 318–319
menus
    opening, 6–7
    opening submenus of, 7
merge document. *See also* documents; Mail
    Merge feature
    completing, 332–333
    creating, 329–331
    inserting variable fields in, 332
    previewing, 331–332
    using rules with, 332
merge recipients, sorting, 331
message headers
    marking, 258
    receiving, 258
Message window in Outlook 2010
    components of, 272
    maximizing, 277
messages. *See* e-mail messages;
    Outlook 2010
.mht file extension, file type associated
    with, 29
.mhtml file extension, file type associated
    with, 29
Microsoft Office, activating, 15
mini toolbar
    hiding, 6
    making clearer, 7
    using, 6, 52
Minimize window, location of, 4
minus (−), using in navigation, 38
mirror margins, using, 72
mixed references, explained, 160–161
Month view
    displaying in View tab, 298
    modifying in Calendar, 300–302
months, displaying in Date Navigator, 297
mouse. *See also* I-beam mouse pointer
    opening tabs and menus with, 5–6
    selecting text with, 33
    using, 5–6
    using to move insertion point, 30
    using to navigate documents, 36
moved text, undoing, 35
multilevel lists
    creating, 66
    customizing, 66–67

N

name and address list
    data sources, 330
    fields and records, 330
    setting up, 331
Name Manager, using in Excel, 163–164
named cells. *See also* cells
    deleting, 163
    sorting and filtering, 164
New Document dialog box, options in, 23
Next Page, beginning section break on, 85
Normal style, keyboard shortcut, 52
Normal template
    changes applied to, 84
    changing default, 82–83
    explained, 23
notes for presentations
    adding objects to, 214
    changing background of, 214
    creating, 214
    expanding area for, 214–215
    previewing, 215–216
    printing, 216–218
    using headers and footers on, 218–219
notes master, using, 223–224
Notes pane, adding text placeholder, 224
Number tab, displaying in Excel, 117
numbered lists
    autoformatting, 99
    changing in slide masters, 222
    changing to bulleted lists, 68
    creating using AutoCorrect, 65
    customizing, 66–67
numbering
    applying to lists, 66
    removing from lists, 68
numbers
    converting to percentages, 118
    converting to scientific notation, 113
    entering in Excel, 112–113
    interpreting as text in Excel, 113
    using apostrophe (') with in Excel, 113

O

objects
    defined, 321
    manipulating with mouse, 6

Odd Page, beginning section break on, 85
.odt file extension, file type associated
    with, 29
Office Clipboard. *See also* Clipboard
    adding to, 237
    capacity of, 237
    deleting items on, 238
    opening, 237
    setting options for, 238
Office programs
    creating desktop shortcuts for, 3
    Getting Started option, 15
    leaving, 3
    pinning to top of Start menu, 3
    starting from Start menu, 2
    starting from taskbar, 3
    verifying version of, 15
OneNote, "printing" to, 322
online access, getting, 251–252
online templates, using, 25
OpenDocument Text files, importing in
    Word, 28
organization charts, creating with
    SmartArt, 336, 338
orientation
    changing in worksheets, 149–150
    choosing for printer, 323
    determining, 72
    landscape, 71–72
    orientation, choosing, 71–72
    portrait, 71–72, 323
Outline tab, using with presentations,
    189–190
Outline view
    explained, 97
    using in Word, 8
outlines. *See also* PowerPoint outlines
    assigning heading levels, 97
    creating and using, 96–97
    defined, 96
    moving headings, 97
outlines for presentations
    creating from scratch, 189–191
    inserting from other sources,
    191–192
Outlining tab
    inserting subdocuments, 95
    manipulating subdocuments, 95
    using for table of contents, 94–95

View buttons, 4
view ruler, 4
Zoom buttons and slider, 4
PowerPoint outlines. *See also* outlines
    collapsing slides, 194
    creating from scratch, 189–191
    demoting text, 194
    expanding slides, 194
    indenting with keyboard, 193
    inserting, 191–192
    moving text up or down, 194
    outlining commands, 193
    previewing, 192–193
    printing, 192–193
    promoting text, 194
    Show Text Formatting, 194
PowerPoint presentations
    Cascade Windows, 200, 202
    changing background style, 208–209
    changing hyperlink color, 211–212
    changing numbering styles for
      lists, 232
    changing theme colors, 207–208
    checking spelling in, 238–239
    choosing bullet shapes for lists, 231
    copying attributes with Format
      Painter, 209
    copying design with Browse feature,
      202–203
    creating from presentations, 185
    creating from scratch, 187–189
    creating notes in Notes pane, 214
    creating templates, 186–187
    creating using standard themes,
      185–186
    customizing colors, 208–209
    customizing themes, 207–209
    displaying multiple, 200–202
    enlarging, 202
    extensions in Save As Type list, 186
    inserting hyperlinks, 210–211
    inserting outlines, 191–192
    modifying themes, 188
    move split action, 201
    previewing outlines, 192–193
    printing outlines, 192–193
    removing hyperlinks, 211–212
    removing passwords, 195
    retrieving templates, 186

    selecting layouts, 189–191
    setting passwords, 194–195
    starting, 204
    stripping file information from, 195
    Switch Windows, 201
    themes, 187–188
    typing in Outline tab, 189
    using custom colors, 208
    using lists, 231–233
    using SmartArt for lists, 232–233
preference settings
    display elements to show, 11
    formatting marks, 11
    General options, 12
    user name, 12
presentations. *See* PowerPoint
    presentations
Preview pane, Zoom buttons in, 324
print jobs, customizing, 322–324
Print Layout view, 97
printer, setting default for, 322
printing
    calendars, 316–318
    documents, 324
    e-mail messages, 269
    to fax, 322
    handouts, 218
    labels in Word, 326–327
    notes for presentations, 216–218
    to OneNote, 322
    outlines for presentations, 192–193

Q

question mark (?) wildcard, using in
    Find, 42
Quick Access toolbar
    adding commands to, 9
    location of, 4
    moving, 9
    in Outlook window, 242–243
    in ribbon, 5
Quick Parts feature, using with building
    blocks, 100–101
Quick Styles, creating and saving, 77.
    See also styles
Quick Styles gallery
    deleting styles from, 78

    displaying, 76–77
    restoring styles to, 78
quotation characters, replacing, 99

R

R1C1 references, changing to, 161
range name, displaying in Name box, 161
ranges. *See also* cells
    defined, 162
    referencing, 162
receipts, requesting for e-mail, 290–291
recent documents, opening, 27
recipients, using Reply All feature with, 288
recovering work, 45
recurring appointments
    deleting in Calendar, 315
    editing in Calendar, 314–315
Redo icon, identifying, 37
referencing types
    absolute, 160–161
    external (3D), 160
    mixed, 160–161
    relative, 160–161
registered (®) symbol, entering, 30
relative positioning, using with graphics, 340
relative references, explained, 160–161
reminders, using with appointments, 316
Repeat option, change from Redo, 37
Replace option, using with text, 41–42
replacing data in Excel, 126
reply layout, changing for e-mail, 289
Reply window, using with e-mail, 288
Research command, using, 13–14
reset character formatting keyboard
    shortcut, 52
reset paragraph formatting keyboard
    shortcut, 52
resource center, accessing, 15
Reuse Slides task pane, opening, 199–200
ribbon
    closing for slides, 199
    commands and tools on, 5
    contextual tab, 5
    Dialog Box Launcher, 5
    features of, 5
    File tab, 5
    groups in, 5
    labeled buttons in, 5

    location of, 4
    menu options, 5
    minimizing in Outlook, 242–243
    minimizing size of, 6
    opening for slides, 199
    Quick Access toolbar, 5
    using with slides, 198
rich text files, importing in Word, 28
right alignment, applying to text, 58
right angle bracket (>) wildcard, using in
    Find, 42
right indent, changing, 60–61
right side indent, setting, 62
right tab, setting, 87
right-clicking objects with mouse, 6
row height, adjusting in worksheets, 132–134
rows
    adding to worksheets, 132
    hiding in worksheets, 135
    locking in worksheets, 153
    maximum number in Excel, 124, 136
    removing from worksheets, 134
    selecting in Excel, 123–124
    unhiding in worksheets, 135
rows and columns
    locking together, 154
    unlocking, 155
RTF (Rich Text Format), using in e-mail, 275
.rtf file extension, file type associated with, 29
ruler
    displaying, 62, 87
    using for indents, 62–63
    using to set tabs, 87–88
rules
    applying to e-mail, 292–293
    using with merge documents, 332
Rules And Alerts dialog box, accessing in
    Outlook, 265–266

S

Save Workspace option, using with Excel
    windows, 154
saving
    copies of documents, 45–46
    documents, 45–46
    documents as templates, 46
    documents automatically, 48
    documents for first time, 45–46

V

versions of programs, verifying, 15
vertical alignment, setting, 73
View buttons
    location of, 4
    using, 97
"view buttons" in status bar, effect of, 37
view ruler, location of, 4
views
    displaying in Excel, 8
    displaying in PowerPoint, 8
    displaying in Word, 7–8
    switching to, 97
voting options, inserting e-mail, 283

W

Watch Window, using with cells, 180–181
Web Apps, features of, 16–17. *See also* Excel
    Web App
Web beacon, explained, 259
Web Layout view, explained, 97
Web page files, importing in Word, 28
Week view
    displaying in View tab, 298
    modifying in Calendar, 300–302
weeks, displaying in Date Navigator, 297
Widow/Orphan control, using, 64
wildcards, using in searches, 41–42. *See also*
    characters in words; search

windows
    defaults for, 4
    navigating, 37
Windows Explorer, dragging pictures
    from, 334
Windows Live ID, establishing, 17
Word 2010
    Close window, 4
    commands in tabs on ribbon, 4
    default windows for, 4
    Document Views group, 7
    Draft view, 8
    File tab, 4
    finding and opening documents, 26
    Full Screen Reading view, 7
    Help icon, 4
    Help window, 12
    importing documents in, 28–29
    Maximize/Restore window, 4
    Minimize window, 4
    online templates, 25
    Outline view, 8
    overtype mode, 31
    positioning graphics in, 340–341
    positioning text in, 340–341
    Print Layout view, 7
    printing envelopes in, 324, 326
    printing labels in, 326–327
    Quick Access toolbar, 4
    ribbon, 4
    scroll arrow, 4
    scroll bar, 4

scroll button, 4
searching for documents in, 27
status bar, 4
templates, 23–24
title bar, 4
View buttons, 4
view ruler, 4
views in, 7–8
Web Layout view, 7
Zoom buttons and slider, 4
Word Count icon, identifying, 104
Word Web App, editing documents in,
    46–48
Word writing aids. *See also* spelling checker
    AutoCorrect, 98
    AutoFormat, 99–100
WordArt styles, applying, 221
WordLingo translator, accessing, 14–15
WordPerfect files, importing in
    Word, 28
words
    adding to dictionary, 45
    counting, 104
    searching, 39
    selecting, 33
    translating, 14
Work Week view
    displaying in View tab, 298
    modifying in Calendar, 300–302
workbooks. *See also* Excel worksheets
    adding cells styles from
        workbooks, 148

changing automatic updating,
    172–173
changing side-by-side display, 155
comparing, 158
editing in Excel Web App, 128–130
ensuring common look and feel, 146
saving as templates, 146
Works files, importing in Word, 28
worksheets. *See* Excel worksheets
.wpd file extension, file type associated
    with, 29
.wps file extension, file type associated
    with, 29
writing aids. *See also* spelling checker
    AutoCorrect, 98
    AutoFormat, 99–100

X

XE (Index Entry) fields, visibility of, 94
.xml file extension, file type associated
    with, 29
XML files, importing in Word, 28

Z

zip codes, formatting in Excel, 118
Zoom buttons
    displaying in Preview pane, 324
    using with slides, 203–204
Zoom buttons and slider, location of, 4